TRYON COUNTY, NORTH CAROLINA

MINUTES OF THE COURT OF PLEAS AND QUARTER SESSIONS

1769–1779

BY

BRENT H. HOLCOMB

HERITAGE BOOKS
2018

HERITAGE BOOKS

AN IMPRINT OF HERITAGE BOOKS, INC.

Books, CDs, and more—Worldwide

For our listing of thousands of titles see our website
at
www.HeritageBooks.com

Published 2018 by
HERITAGE BOOKS, INC.
Publishing Division
5810 Ruatan Street
Berwyn Heights, Md. 20740

International Standard Book Numbers
Paperbound: 978-0-7884-5833-0

APPROXIMATE BOUNDARIES

OF TRYON COUNTY

AT ITS FORMATION

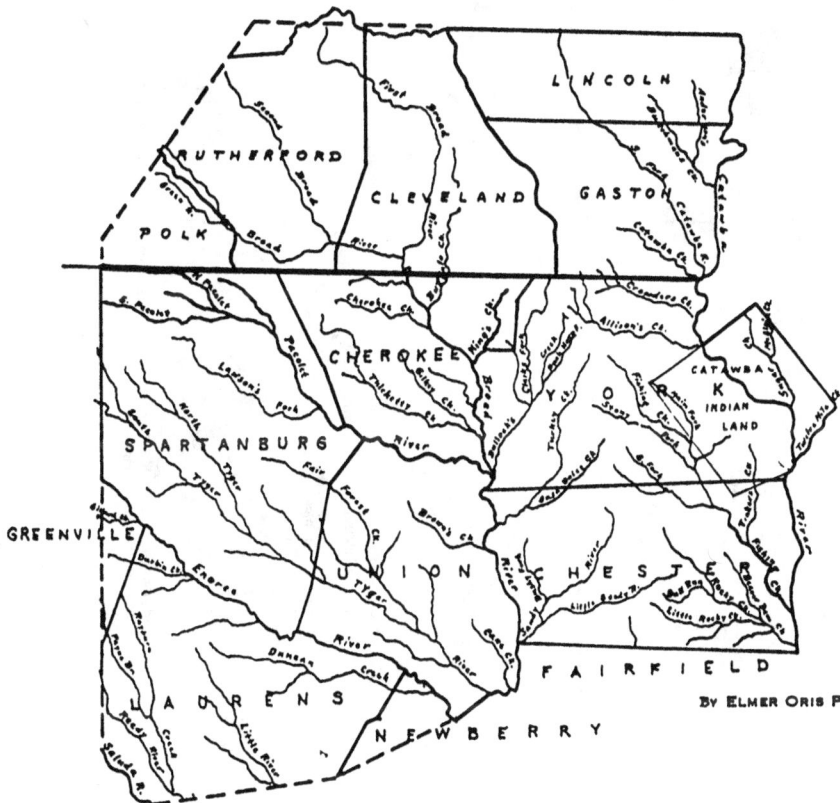

By Elmer Oris Parker

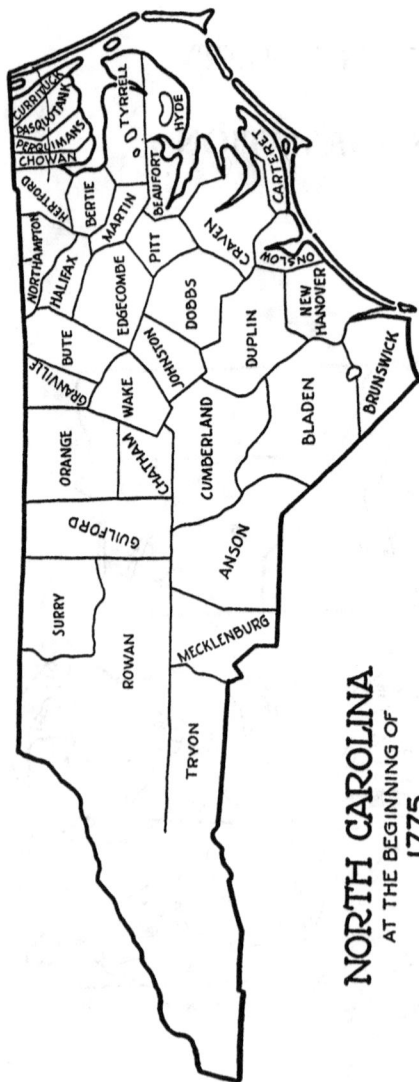

NORTH CAROLINA
AT THE BEGINNING OF
1775

Showing Approximate County Divisions
within Present State Boundaries

Map by
L. Polk Denmark

Reprinted from David L. Corbitt, *The Formation of the North Carolina Counties, 1663–1943*, State Department of Archives and History (Raleigh, 1950).

INTRODUCTION

The single most important record for any North Carolina county is the minutes of the Court of Pleas and Quarter Sessions. The court of Pleas and Quarter Sessions is the lowest court of record for the county. It was where the business of the county was carried on. As the title of the court suggests, the court met four time a year, or quarterly. From a genealogical point of view, the names of more people will appear in this court record than in any other body of county records. In fact, the only place where some names will be found is within such court minutes. Lists of deeds proved and recorded are found in the court minutes, as well as lists of wills proved or administrations on intestate estates taken out. The construction of roads and the road juries (sometimes called road gangs) who were to lay out and maintain the roads are spelled out in these records. Civil suits involving less than $150 (usually over debt), minor criminal cases, depositions, jury lists, tax officials' names with their districts, tavern licenses and tavern rates, and care of the poor of the county are among the many kinds of records included in the court minutes. The records in this volume were extracted from the microfilm copy (produced by the North Carolina Department of Archives and History) of the Tryon County Court Minutes (C.094.30001). The original volumes from which the microfilm was made are housed in that Archives in Raleigh.

Tryon County was in the southwesternmost part of North Carolina. It was formed in 1769 from the western part of Mecklenburg County, and it was bound on the north by Rowan County. Its western boundary was the Indian line run in 1767, and its southern boundary (the South Carolina line) was not surveyed west of the Catawba River until 1772. The first court for Tryon County was held at the plantation of Charles McLean, a location which is in present-day York County, South Carolina. The border survey of 1772 reduced the size of Tryon County by approximately one-half. The map included in this work indicates the approximate area covered by Tryon County at its largest. Tryon County was abolished in 1779 to form Lincoln and Rutherford counties. Of the four counties involved in the North Carolina-South Carolina border problem in the colonial period (Tryon, Mecklenburg, Anson, and Bladen), Tryon County is the only one which has extant court minutes for the period prior to the border surveys. The deeds, wills, and estates were abstracted and published by the author in 1977. Many of the Tryon County grants and plats are included in *North Carolina Land Grants in South Carolina* also by the author.

My thanks to Mr. James D. McKain for preparing the indices.

Brent H. Holcomb
September 13, 1993

TRYON COUNTY, NORTH CAROLINA
MINUTES OF THE COURT OF PLEAS AND QUARTER SESSIONS
1769-1779

[April term 1769]

Pursuant to an Act of Assembly of the Province aforesaid, bearing date of the fifth of December, One thousand seven hundred and sixty-eight, and, in the ninth year of his Majesty's reign, for dividing Mecklenburg County into two distinct counties by the Name of Mecklenburg county and Tryon County, and other purposes in the said Act mentioned.

His Majesty's commission under the Great Seale of the Province aforesaid, appointing Thomas Neil Ju'r, William Moore, William Watson, William Twitty, John Retzhoupt, James Mcilwean, Henry Clark, Jonas Bedford, John Gordon, John Walker, Henry Holman, Robert Harris Jr, and David Anderson, Esqrs., Justices, assigned to keep the peace for the county of Tryon aforesaid was read in open court, and also a Commission and Dedimus Potestatum empowering the said justices to administer all oaths, appointed by Act of Parliament for the qualifications of all public officers, and also such other oaths as are appointed by the Act of Assembly for the qualification of all officers, according to their several commissions.

Agreeable to the above Commissioners, Thomas Neil Jr., William Moore, William Watson, and John Retzhoupt, came into open Court and took the oaths appointed by Law for the qualification of Public Officers and also the Oath of Justices of the Peace for the County of Tryon afsd., made and subscribed the declaration and took their seats on the bench accordingly.

Ezekial Polk came into court and produced his commissions [page torn] and took the oath....

At the same time came Alexander Martin into court and produced a license appointed him Attorney for the Crown in said county, who took the oaths by Law appointed for the qualification of public officers, subscribed the test, took the oath of an Attorney and took his place accordingly.

At the same time came Waightstill Avery produced a license appointed him Attorney for the Crown in said county, who took the oaths by Law appointed for the qualification of public officers, subscribed the test, took the oath of an Attorney and took his place accordingly.

At the same time John Dunn, Samuel Spencer, and James Forsyth appeared in court and took the oaths by Law appointed for the qualification of public officers, subscribed the test, took the oath of an Attorney and took their places accordingly.

Ordered by the Court that David Byers & John Brandon serve as Constables in room of John Black and he [sic] swear in before William Watson.

Court adjourned for One Hour. Met according to adjournment. Present: Thomas Neil Jr., William Moore, William Watson, and John Retzhoupt, Esquires.

John Walker and David Anderson came into court and took the oaths by Law appointed for the qualification of public officers, subscribed the test, took the oath ... [torn] their place accordingly.

Aaron Lockart petitioned the Court that a Tub grist mill built and erected by Thomas Mitchel on Broad River and now in the possession of the petitioner, may be recorded as

1

<u>April term 1769</u>

a publick mill, agreeable to Act of Assembly of this Province and under the same Rules, restrictions and regulations as other mills. Granted.

A Deed of Sale from Andrew Armour to Andrew Patrick dated 5th of February 1769 for 145 acres of land Proved by Andrew Goforth Evidence thereto Ordered to be Registered.

A Deed of Sale from John Rigs to Thomas Brandon dated 3rd of February 1769 for 300 acres of land. Proved by Francis Travers Evidence thereto Ordered to be Registered.

A Deed of Sale from Patrick Laverty & Prudence his [wife] to John Fulton dated the 18th day of April 1769 for 100 acres of land Proved by Robert McCurdy Evidence thereto Ordered to be Registered.

A Deed of Sale from John Bennet and Agnes his wife to William Anderson dated 17th day of January 1769 for 100 acres of land Proved by Frederick Hambright Evidence thereto Ordered to be Registered.

A Deed of Lease and Release from Thomas Mitchell and Agnes his wife to Aaron Lockard dated 20th day of April 1769 for 100 acres of land Proved by John Miles Evidence thereto Ordered to be Registered.

A Deed of Sale from Patrick Lafferty and Prudence his wife to Robert McCurdy dated 24th day of April 1769 for 150 acres of land Proved by John Fulton Evidence thereto Ordered to be Registered.

Court adjourned til to morrow 8 o'clock. Met according to adjournment. Present: John Retzhoupt, William Moore and David Anderson, Esqr.

Ordered by the Court that James Alcorn & William Henry serve as Constables in the room of John Crage and that they swear in before Thomas Neel, Esqr.

Ordered by the Court that George Rutledge serve as Constable in the room of James Adear & that he swear in before William Moore, Esqr.

Ordered by the Court that Lewis Lineberger serve as Constable in the room of John Mires and that he swear in before John Retzhoupt, Esqr.

On motion of John Dunn, it was ordered that Nathaniel Clark have license to keep ordinary at his dwelling house in the County of Tryon, he complying with the Act of Assembly in that case made, and, provided he proposes for security, Matthew Floyd and John Nuckles. Granted.

John Tagert came into court and produced a Commission from His Excellency appointing him Sherriff of the County of Tryon and took the oaths by Law appointed for the qualification of public officers, subscribed the test, took the oaths of a Sherriff and took his place accordingly.

At the same time came John Knuckles into court and took the oaths by Law appointed for the qualification of publick officers, subscribed the test, took the oath of a Deputy Sherriff and entered in the duty of his office.

April term 1769

The Grand Jury: James Lewis, foreman

2	James McKnabb	10	William McMullin
3	John Reed	11	Robert Wilson
4	Abel Beaty	12	Thomas Moore
5	Wm. Adams	13	John Woods
6	Jacob Randal	14	John Carrol
7	John Robinson	15	John Laughlin
8	Frederick Hambright	16	Andrew Armour
9	Joseph Harden	17	David Byers
		18	William McMurry

Sworn and charged.

On motion of James Forsyth Letters of Administration were granted to Margaret Shaw & Samuel Watson for the Goods Chattels and Effects of Robert [Shaw], deceased Who took the Oaths Administrators and proposed for Security John Jarvin & John Hall. Bound in the sum of 150 pounds. Granted.

Ordered by the Court that Eleanor Caldwell an orphan girl at the age of two year & eight months be bound to David Watson till she arrives at the age of Eighteen and by him to be Taught to read under a proper teacher agreeable to law and also that he give her the said Apprentice a suit of clothes when free & in other things to comply with the Act of Assembly in that made & provided.

Henry Clark and John Gordon came into Court took the oaths by Law appointed for the qualification of publicks officers, subscribed the test, and took the oath of Justices of the Peace and took his seat accordingly.

Court adjourned for one hour, and met according to adjournment.

Present: John Retzhoupt, John Gordon, Jacob Costner, Esqr.

Ordered by the Court that Letters Testamentary issue to Comford Langham of all and singular, the goods and chattels of John Langham, deceased, who took the oath of Executor.... [check]

Ordered by the Court that Peter Aker serve as Constable in the district of Jacob Cosner, and that he swear in before said Jacob Cosner.

Ordered by the court that Isaac Wilson & Joseph Jones serve as Constables for the district of David Anderson, Esqr., and they swear in before the said David Anderson, Esqr.

Ordered by the Court that Michael Proctor serve as Constable in the district of John Walker, and that he swear in before said John Walker.

Ordered by the Court that William Patrick serve as Overseer for the Road leading from Crowders Creek to Allisons Creek, and that he enter on this charge accordingly.

After proclamation the court proceeded to the election of a Sheriff accordingly. There being eight magistrates on the bench to wit, Thomas Neal, William Moore, John Gordon, John Walker, Henry Clark, Jacob Cosnear, John Ritzhoupt, and David Anderson Who did Elect & Choose John Taggert, James Hannah & William Henry being freeholders to be Recommended to the Governor to be Commissioned to Execute the office of Sheriff for

<u>April term 1769</u>

the County of Tryon for the ens'g year it appearing by the pole that John Tagert had eight Votes, James Hannah six and William Henry five. Ordered to be Recommended accordingly.

Ordered by the Court that William Hanna serve as Constable for the district of John Gordon Esqr., and that he swear in before said John Gordon accordingly.

Ordered by the court that Henry Smith & Simcock Cannon serve as Constables for the district of Henry Clark, Esqr., and they swear in before the said Henry Clark accordingly.

John Gillispy of Tryon Co'ty & Province of North Carolina for divers Goods Causes and for £5 currt. money of Virg'a by Jno Long of Augusta co'ty in the Province of Virg'a hat sold one grey mare, flea bitten about the head and neck, seven years old, branded on the off side thus WE... 24th day of December 1766. John Gillaspy (LS), Wit: John Mackleroy, George King, Robt. Hambleton.

A Deed of Sale from Francis Beaty to John Beeman dated 18th of April 1769 for 350 acres of land proved by Christopher Carpenter Evidence thereto Ordered to be Registered.

A Deed of Sale from Ephraim McClean & Elizabeth his wife to Richard Venables dated 16th of Dec'r 1768 for 220 acres of land proved by John Venables Evidence thereto Ordered to be Registered.

A Deed of Sale from James Walker & Elizabeth his wife to James Campbel dated 2d day of March 1768 for 155 acres of land Proved by Joseph Brown Evidence thereto Ordered to be Registered.

A Deed of Sale from John Sloan Jr. to John Huggins dated 21st of April 1769 for 150 acres of land Acknowledged by John Sloan ordered to be Registered.

A Deed of Sale from John Miller & William Neely to John Young dated 20th day of April 1769 for 350 acres of land Proved by James Young Evidence thereto Ordered to be Registered.

A Deed of Sale from William McDowell & Eleanor his wife to William Stevenson dated 18th day of February 1769 for 150 acres of land Proved by Alexander Stephenson Evidence thereto Ordered to be Registered.

A Deed of Sale from James Watson & Jean Watson dated 26th day of April 176[9] for 350 acres of land Proved by James Hanna Evidence thereto Ordered to be Registered.

A Deed of Sale from John Sertain to Thomas Wade dated the 26th day of April 1769 for 100 acres of land Acknowled[ged] in Open Court Ordered to be Registered.

A Deed of Sale from Abraham Kuykendal to Peter Kuykendal dated the 6th day of June 1768 for 63 acres of land Proved by James Young Evidence thereto Ordered to be Registered.

A Deed of Sale from William Glover Bishop to William Barron dated the 25th day of January 1768 for 100 acres of land Proved by James Barron Evidence thereto Ordered to be Registered.

<u>April term 1769</u>

A Deed of Sale from John Miller & Margaret his wife to John Otts dated the 5th day of April 1769 for 100 acres of land Proved by Charles Moore Evidence thereto Ordered to be Registered.

A Deed of Sale from James Miller to William Sharp dated 5th day of January 1769 for 250 acres of land Proved by Charles Moore Evidence thereto Ordered to be Registered.

A Deed of Sale from Benejah Penniton to Thomas Baron dated the 7th day of February 1769 for 300 acres of land Proved by Alex'r Stephenson Evidence thereto Ordered to be Registered.

A Deed of Sale from John McKinny to John Thompson dated 23rd day of March 1769 for 440 acres of land Acknowledged in Open Court Ordered to be Registered.

A Deed of Sale from David Watson to John Watson dated the 26th day of April 1769 for 200 acres of land Acknowledged in Open Court Ordered to be Registered.

A Deed of Sale from Peter Kuykendal & Abraham Kuykendal to James Young dated the 6th day of June 1768 for 80 acres of land Proved by John Risk Evidence thereto Ordered to be Registered.

A Deed of Sale from Andrew Sprot & Mary his wife to Joseph Bigger dated the 19th day of April 1769 for 230 acres of land Proved by Thomas Polk Evidence thereto Ordered to be Registered.

A Deed of Sale from Casper Sheagler and Elizabeth his wife to Archibald Elliot dated the 1st day of Sep'r 1768 for 768 acres of land Proved by Casper Club Evidence thereto Ordered to be Registered.

A Deed of Sale from Peter Culp to Henry Culp dated the 7th day of January 1769 for 190 acres of land Proved by Archibald Elliot Evidence thereto Ordered to be Registered.

A Deed of Sale from John Thomas to William Barron dated the 15th day of September 1768 for 767 acres of land Proved by James Miskelly Evidence thereto Ordered to be Registered.

A Deed of Sale from John Garvin & Martha his wife to Thomas Garvin dated the 20th day of October 1768 for 150 acres of land Proved by James Miskelly Evidence thereto Ordered to be Registered.

A Deed of Sale from David Vance & Ruth his wife to Thomas Garvin dated the 20th day of October 1768 for 100 acres of land Proved by John Garvin Evidence thereto Ordered to be Registered.

A Deed of Sale from James McAfee & Margaret his wife to Thomas Polk dated the 25 day of November 1768 for Three hundred acres of land Proved by John Tagert Evidence thereto Ordered to be Registered.

A Deed of Sale from Christian Carpenter to Joseph Goode dated the 13th day of January 1769 for 300 acres of land Acknowledged in Open Court Ordered to be Registered.

North Carolina. James Daniel of Province of North Carolina and County of Tryon, planter, for divers good causes have appointed James Wammack, Esqr., of Tryon County, my true

<u>April term 1769</u>

& Lawful attorney, 4 April 1769. James Daniel (LS), Wit: James Attwood, James Capshaw (jurate), William Capshaw.

North Carolina, Tryon County. Teter Havener of aforesaid county do sell unto Derrick Ramsour, one negro boy caled Tonday, for £18 s18 d 10, 3rd February 1769. Teter Heavenor (LS), Wit: John Fondron, James Maxwell, Jacob Rinehart (ER).

Court adjourned till Tomorrow 8 o'clock. Met according to Adjournment. Present Thomas Neel, William Watson, Henry Clark, Esquires.

Ordered by this Court that James Miskelly serve as Overseer of the Road leading from the mouth of the south fork of Catawba to Charles Town from John Gordons to the South Line & that he Enter upon his Charge accordingly.

A Deed of Sale from Jacob Cobron to Charles McClean dated 27th day of August 1768 for 240 acres of land formerly in Mecklenburg County now Tryon proved by James Templeton Evidence thereto Ordered to be Registered.

A Deed of Sale from Jacob Cobron to Charles McClean dated 27th day of August 1768 for 300 acres of land formerly in Mecklenburg County now Tryon proved by James Templeton Evidence thereto Ordered to be Registered.

A Deed of Sale from John Hartness to William McCulloh dated 27th day of April 1768 for 200 acres of land Acknowledged in Open Court Ordered to be Registered.

A Deed of Sale from Charles McKnight & Jennet his wife dated 22d day of July 1768 for _____ proved by Charles McClean Evidence thereto Ordered to be Registered.

William Reid came into Court and took the oaths by law appointed for the qualification of publick Officers subscribed the Test took the oath of a Sub Sheriff & Took his place accordingly.

Court Adjourned for half an hour and the Orphans Court Met. Present Thomas Neel, William Watson, Henry Clark, Esquires.

On motion of Alexander Martin, Johnathan Kuykendal being an Orphan son of James Kuykendal deceased & of the full age of Fourteen years to Choose his Guardian came into Court & Made Choice of John Carrol Jun'r for his Guardian Who Offered Joseph Carrol & Abel Beaty securitys to be Bound in the sum of five Hundred pounds proc. approved of by the court Gave Bond and Entered on his Charge Accordingly.

Orphans Court Adjourned. Inferior Court Met according to adjournment. Present Thomas Neel, Wm. Watson, Henry Clark, Wm. Moore, Esqr. Court adjourned to the court in Course.

North Carolina, Tryon County. At an Inferior Court of Pleas & Quarter Sessions Begun & Held for the County of Tryon on the Fourth Tuesday in July AD 1769. Present the worshipful Thomas Neel, John Ritzhoupt, John Walker, Esqrs.

A Deed of Sale from Christopher Guice & Margaret his wife dated the 6th day of December 1768 for 200 acres of land Proved by Jacob Forney Evidence thereto Ordered to be registr'd.

Court adjourned till tomorrow & OClock. Met according to adjournment. Present William Moore, John Ritzhoupt, David Anderson, Esquires.

Ordered by the Court that Letters of Administration be granted to Katharine Sailor of the Goods & Chattles of Joseph Sailor Deceased Who took the oath of an administrator and proposed for Security Leonard Sailor and Welrich Crowder Bound in the sum of two hundred pounds. Granted.

The Grand Jury: Moses Moore, Foreman

2 Saml Richardson	9 John Earls
3 John Jordan	10 Benjn. Thompson
4 John Barber	11 William Marchbanks
5 John Venable	12 Zachariah Gibbs
6 David Porter	13 Thos Collins
7 William Burris	14 John Alexander
8 James Bridges	15 Joseph Clark
Sworn and charged.	

Ordered by the Court that Waighstill Avery act as attorney for the Crown During this Term in the Absence of Alex'r Martin.

On Motion of Jno Dunn, Letters of Testamentary was Granted to Nicholas Welsh of the Goods & Chattels of john Welsh Deceased who took the oath of an Executor and proposed for Security Alexander Lockhart and William Ramsey Bound in the sum of 300 pounds. Granted.

Court adjournd for One hour. Met according to adjournment. Present Wm. Moore, Henry Clark, Wm Watson, Esq'rs.

Ordered by the Court that Nicholas Leaper Serve as Overseer of the Road Leading from Armours Ford on the Cataba River to Crowders Creek and that he enter on his Charge accordingly.

Ordered by this Court that James Faires shall serve as Overseer of that part of the Road Leading from Armour Ford to Charlestown Lying between Crowders Creek & The Indian Line and that he enter on his Charge accordingly.

Ordered by this Court that William Bratton serve as Overseer of the Road Leading from Armours Ford on Cataba to Charles Town Lying between Jno Gordons & the South Line and that he enter on his Charge accordingly.

Ordered by this Court that Wm Murphy, Geo. Davis, Geo. Freeland, John Reynolds, Henry Willis, Edward Ison, James Neaton, Jno Alex'r, Solomon Beson, Joseph England, John Hardin & Benjamin Hardin act as Jurors to law out a Road the nearest and best way from Little Broad River to Benjamin Hardin's Mill and from thence to the gap of Kings Mountain and from Kings Mountain to William Brattons.

July term 1769

A Deed of Lease & Release from Wm Adair & Mary his wife to David Sturat [Starret] dated the 25th day of July 1769 for 285 acres of land Proved by Saml. Niesbet Evidence thereto Ordered to be Registered.

A Deed of Sale from John Stanford to Esix Capshaw dated 13th day of December 1769 [sic] for 150 acres of land Proved by Hugh Quin Evidence thereto Ordered to be Registered.

A Deed of Sale from Henry Ferguson to Adam Keruth dated 24 day of Jan'y 1769 for 200 acres of land Proved by Frederick Hambright Evidence thereto Ordered to be Registered.

A Deed of Sale from John Mayers & Sarah his wife to Andrew Hayell dated 14th day of June 1769 for 270 acres of land Proved by John Retzhoupt Evidence thereto Ordered to be Registered.

A Deed of Sale from John Jarrot to Wm McKown Dated the ___ day of February 1769 for 200 acres of land Proved by Nath'l Clark Evidence thereto Ordered to be Registered.

A Deed of Sale from John Steen to Robert Bishop Dated the 29th day of July 1768 for 100 acres of land Proved by Zachariah Bullock Evidence thereto Ordered to be Registered.

A Deed of Sale from Wm. Barnet to William Cromikel Dated the 16 February 1769 for 450 acres of Land Acknowledged in Open Court Ordered to be Registered.

A Deed of Sale from David McCarty to Garrat Vanzant Dated the 24 day of Octo'r 1768 for 400 acres of Land Proved by Frederick Hambright Evidence thereto Ordered to be Registered.

A Deed of Sale from Thomas Johnston to Thomas McFaddon Dated the 12th day of July 1769 for 300 acres of Land Proved by John Walker Evidence thereto Ordered to be Registered.

A Deed of Sale from Jeremiah Routh to Joseph Clark Dated the 31st day of August 1768 for 200 acres of Land Proved by Richard Powel Evidence Ordered to be Registered.

A Deed of Sale from Wm. Armstrong &C to Jacob Sides Dated the 27th day of March 1769 for 200 acres of Land Proved by Leonard Sailor. Ordered to be Registered.

A Deed of Sale from Hardy Glover to Joab Mitchel Dated the 24 of July 1769 for 600 acres of Land Proved by John Head. Ordered to be Registered.

A Deed of Sale from Hugh Moore to Joseph Collins Dated the 30th of August 1769 for 400 acres of Land Proved by Zachariah Bullock. Ordered to be Registered.

A Deed of Sale from Thos & Benjamin Rainy to Thos Brown Dated the 8th of July 1768 for 500 acres of Land proved by James Moore. Ordered to be Registered.

A Bill of Sale from Daniel Higdon for all his Indian Corn and Potatos & Flax now Growing also 22 head of Cattle Some marked & Branded with a Swallow fork & half moon under the Right Ear Swallow fork & hole in the Left Ear & Branded with W the Rest of the Brand not known also 34 hogs marked as follows fore old sows marked with a Crop & half Crop in Each Ear & Slit in the Left the thirty young hogs Marked the same with the Cattle dated the 22d day of July 1769. Proved by John Hail Evidence thereto.

July term 1769

A Deed of Sale from John Webb to Hugh Quin Dated the 20 September 1768 for 300 acres of Land Proved by Peter Quin. Ordered to be Registered.

A Deed of Sale from Saml Johnston to James Cook Dated the 25 of July 1769 for 300 acres of Land proved by Jno Grindal. Ordered to be Registered.

A Deed of Sale from Robt Blackburn to Thos Welsh Dated 20 of July 1769 for 150 acres of Land proved by Alexr Lockart. Ordered to be Registered.

A Deed of Sale from George Heatherly to Wm. Young Dated 1st of June 1768 for 100 acres of Land proved by Austin Yancy. Ordered to be Registered.

A Deed of Sale from Joab Mitchell to Robt. Wilkins Dated 29 May 1769 for 300 acres of Land Acknowledged in Open Court. Ordered to be Registered.

A Deed of Sale from Zachariah Bullock & Jno Fondron Dated 27 of April 1769 for 300 acres proved by Jno Nuckols. Ordered to be Registered.

A Deed of Sale from John & Elizabeth Walker to Wm. Barr Dated 1st of July 1769 for 300 acres of land Acknowledged in Open Court. Ordered to be Registered.

A Deed of Sale from Micajah & Rachel Peninton to Wm. Cole Dated 15 of June 1768 for 152 acres of land Wm Muckmurry Evidence thereto. Ordered to be Registered.

A Deed of Sale from Wm. Sims to Perregreen Magnes 23 of January 1769 for 300 acres of Land Ack'd in Open Court. Ordered to be Registered.

A Deed of Sale from Jas Watson & Jane to Robert Faries Dated 1st of April 1769 for 200 acres of land Wm Watson Evidence thereto. Ordered to be Registered.

A Deed of Sale from Joel Blackwell &C to Hugh Quinn Dated 2d day of September 1768 for 300 acres of land Joseph Green Evidence. Ordered to be Registered.

A Deed of Sale from Jas Watson & Jane to Robert Faries Dated 1st of April 1769 for 200 acres of land Wm Watson Evidence thereto. Ordered to be Registered.

A Deed of Sale from Joseph Harden to John Mulinax Dated 22d of July 1769 for 200 acres of land Ack'd in Open Court. Ordered to be Registered.

A Deed of Sale from Wm. McKown to Thomas Wade Dated 26 of July 1769 for 194 acres of land Benjamin Thompson Evidence thereto. Ordered to be Registered.

A Deed of Sale from Joab Mitchell to David Robinson Dated 22 of July 1769 for 250 acres of land Acknowledged in Open Court. Ordered to be Registered.

A Deed of Sale from Hugh & Margaret Quin to Hugh Custion 21 July 1769 for 400 acres of land Ack'd in Open Court. Ordered to be Registered.

A Deed of Sale from Joab Mitchell to John Beckham Dated 24 of July 1769 for 478 acres of land ack'd in Open Court. Ordered to be Registered.

A Deed of Sale from John & Catharine Biger to Archibald McNeal 1st of June 1769 for 400 acres of land. Peter Jonston Evidence. Ordered to be Registered.

July term 1769

A Deed of Sale from Peter Duncan to Thos Jeans Dated 3d of April 1769 for 300 acres of Land. John Walker Evidence. Ordered to be Registered.

A Deed of Sale from John Williams Ju'r to John Walker Dated 7 of June 1769 for 300 acres of Land. Wm Sims Evidence. Ordered to be Registered.

A Deed of Sale from Robert & Mary Gordon to John Woods Dated 7 of June 1769 for 250 acres of Land. James Davies Evidence. Ordered to be Registered.

A Deed of Sale from Ab'm Kuykendal to James Armstrong Dated the 11 of March 1769 for 333 acres of Land. John Gordon Evidence. Ordered to be Registered.

A Deed of Sale from Christopher & Margaret Guice to Welrick Crowder Dated 6th day of September 1768 for 200 acres of Land. Jacob Forney Evidence. Ordered to be Registered.

A Deed of Sale from Wm. Sims & Wm. Marchbanks to Rob't Moore Dated 28 March 1769 for 400. Ackn'd in Open Court. Ordered to be Registered.

A Deed of Sale from Owen & Mary Carter to John Steen Dated 19 of June 1769 for 300 acres of Land. Ephraim Ledbetter Evidence. Ordered to be Registered.

A Deed of Sale from John Ankram to Jno Lusk Dated 20 of Decem'r 1768 for 300 acres of Land. Rob't Haris Jr. Evidence. Ordered to be Registered.

A Deed of Sale from John Sanford & Sary his wife to George Tub Dated the 26 July 1769 for 150 acres of Land. James Forsyth Evidence. Ordered to be Registered.

A Deed of Sale from Hugh Quinn & Margaret his wife to Menarter Saunders Dated 19 of May 1769 for 200 acres of Land. Ack'd in Open Court. Ordered to be Registered.

A Bill of Sale from Charles Robinson to John Parks for Twelve head of Cattle, two Cows marked a Crop in the Right Ear & Slit in the Let & One Do. Crop in the Right Ear & Swallow fork in Left to one Do Crop & Slit in Each Ear three Ditto heifers half year Old not marked, One heifer two year Old not marked One two year old Bull not marked, One Stear two year Marked Crop & Slit in Each Ear Dated 3d of May 1769. Proved by Robert Coleman Evidence thereto. Ordered to be Registered.

A Deed of Gift from Wm. Mills to Jesse Mills for Twenty head of Cattle marked with an under keel in each ear Likewise three breeding mares branded LM and One Feather Bed & Three dishes 2 Basons & Eight Plates & five pounds proc. money. Ack'd in Open Court. Ordered to be Registered.

A Deed of Gift from John Lindsey to Ezekiel Lindsey One Light Gray mare Branded with 3 BBB on the mounting shoulder & Buttock one Bright Bay mare & Cole neither Branded Dock nor Ear marked One Red pided Cow dimly branded with TE on the Right Side & Sundry Other goods & Chattels prov'd by Benjamin Thompson Evidence thereto. Ordered to be Registered.

A deposition of John Clark taken before John Ritzhoupt proved by Phillip Rudisale Evidence thereto.

July term 1769

Court adjourned till tomorrow 8 OClock. Met according to adjournment. Present Thomas Neel, Wm. Moore, Wm Watson, Esq'rs.

A Deed of Mortgage from James Collins to John McKnitt Alexander dated the 27th July 1769 for 200 acres Acknowledged by the Parties.

Thomas Clark came into court & Took the Oaths by Law appointed for Qualification of Publick Officers, Subscribed the Test took the Oath of a Deputy Sheriff & Entered on the Duty of his office.

On Motion of John Dunn it was ordered by the Court that Letters of administration Be granted to Phillip Henson of the Goods & Chattles of Nicholas Henson deceased as Being Father and highest Creditor of the said deceased. Who took the Oath of an Administrator and proposed for Security Wm. Sims & Zachariah Bullock in the Sum of One hundred & Twenty pounds.

And in Consequence of the above order of Administration Diana Henson Widow & Relick of the said Nicholas Henson deceased by Saml Spencer her atty; Enters a Caveat in the Secretarys office according to the act of the assembly in that case made & provided as the said Philip Henson having administration pursuant to the above order till the Controversy Be heard & determined by his Excellency the Governor and Council....

On motion of W. Avery attorney for the Crown Jno Tevonhill was Brought to the Barr and fined the sum of ten shillings or sit in the stocks two hours for profane swearing in Open Court.

The King vs Wm. Armstrong. Petty Larceny. The Petty Jury. David Watson, Foreman.

2 John Laughlin	Rideras Clark 7
3 John Fondron	Wy Byars[?] 8
4 John Buchanan	Joseph Carrol 9
5 Wm. McMurry	Marshall Lovelath 10
6 Phillip Henson	Jno Steen[?] 11
	Nathaniel Clark 12

Being a Jury empanneled Tryed & Sworn find: y'e defendant Guilty of the Charge aledged against him in the indictment.

Judgment by the Court that the defendant be detained in the Sheriffs custody till the Costs on this prosection be paid and that at the hour of Four OClock this day the said Defendant on his Bear Back at the publick whipping post received Thirty nine Lashes well laid on.

Ordered by the Court that Robert Lepar, Wm. Howe, Robert Patric, Joseph Howe, John Faires, David Garrison, Thomas Patrick, John Hall, Wm. Hagerty, Robert Harris, Robert johnston and Andrew Patrick act as Commissioners to Lay Out a Road the nighest & Best way from Robt. Leepars mill to Lands Ford on the Cataba River.

A Deed of Sale from Thomas Rainy & Benjamin Phillips to John Fondron Dated the 7th of May 1769 for 150 acres of Land Proved by John Gordon Evidence. Ordered to be Registered.

A Deed of Sale from Jno Miller & Marget his wife to Moses Cotter dated the __ day of February 1768 for 400 acres of Land. Thomas Collins Evidence. Ordered to be Registered.

TRYON COUNTY NC COURT MINUTES 1769-1779

July term 1769

A Deed of Sale from Moses Ferguson to James Ferguson Dated the 26th of September 1768 for 200 acres of Land. Robert Ferguson Evidence. Ordered to be Registered.

A Deed of Sale from Jno McCulloh to George Patterson Dated 25 of May 1769 for 375 acres of Land proved by Ezekiel Polk Evidence thereto. Ordered to be registered.

Court adjourned till Tomorrow 8 OClock. Met according to adjournment. Present Thomas Neel, Wm. Watson, Jacob Cosnear, Esq'rs.

Ordered by the Court that Henry Clark, John Patton, Joseph Harden, Charles McClain, James Henry, & John Robinson Serve as Venire men to attend at Salsbury on the 4 day of September 1769.

North Carolina, Tryon County to wit. July Court 1769. Present his Majestys Justices. Then were the Ordinary keepers Prices rated as Follows. That is to say.

Lodging in a Good feather Bed & Clean Sheets P'r Night	£0	0	4
Breakfast & Supper Each	0	0	8
Every dinner not Less than 2 dishes of Good Meat	0	1	0
Madeira & Port win P'r Quart	0	3	0
Claret wine P'r Quart	0	4	0
Punch with Loaf Sugar & West India Rum Pr Qu't	0	1	6
Tody with Loaf Sugar & West India Rum P'r Quart	0	1	4
Tody with Loaf Sugar & New Engl'd Rum P'r Quart	0	0	6
Brandy Tody P'r Quart	0	0	8
Grog of West India Rum			
Grog of New Engl'd Rum			
Bear P'r Quart	0	0	6
Cider P'r Quarter	0	0	6
W. India Rum P'r half pint	0	0	10
New England Ditto	0	0	6
Brandy or Whisky P'r half pint	0	0	6
Pasturage for every horse or mare for 24 hours	0	0	4
Stab'g w't hay or foder for Every 24 hours	0	1	0
Indian Corn, Oats, Barley, Rye &C.			

Court adjourned till Court in Course. Thomas Neel, Wm. Watson, Jacob Cosnear.

North Carolina, Tryon County. Tryon Inferior Court of Pleas & Quarter Sessions Begun & held the Fourth Tuesday in October AD 1769. Present William Watson, John Retzhopt, James McIlwean, Esq'rs.

Ordered that Hugh Quinn, Wm. Yancey, Jas. McIntire, Joseph Green, Geo. Blanton, James Collins, William Watson, Geo. Julian, Geo. Gibson, John McKinny, Wm. Hillis & John Brandon serve as Jurors Lat out a Road from Richardsons Shoals on Second Broad River Leading by Capt. Kuykendals to Cross first Broads River at Sheltons ford thence by Hugh Quins & Julians Mill on Kings Creek thence by Geo: Gibsons on Bullocks Creek & Thence into Charlestown Trading Road by Wm. Hillises.

Ordered by the Court that Aaron Burleston Serve as Overseer of the Road Leading from Richardsons Shoals on Second Broad River to Charlestown (that part Between first & Second Broad River) & that he Enter on his Charge accordingly.

12

October term 1769

Ordered that Jno Standford serve as Overseer of said Road between first Broad River & Buffalo Creek & That he Enter on his Charge accordingly.

Ordered that Geo. Dulan Serve as Overseer of said Road that part Between Buffalo & Kings Creek & that he Enter on his Charge accordingly.

Ordered that Geo. Gibson Serve as Overseer of said Road from Kings Creek to Bullocks Creek & that he Enter on his Charge accordingly.

Ordered that Charles Stice Serve as Overseer of said Road between from Eullock Creek to the South Line & That he Enter on his Charge accordingly.

On Motion of Samuel Spencer it was Ordered by the court that Charity Karr have Letters of Administration of the Goods & Chattels of William Karr De'd as wife & Relick of the said Deceased. She proposes for Security George Gibson & Henry Smith Bound in the sum of Three hundred pounds.

Ordered that William Wilson Serve as Overseer of the Road Leading from the So fork to Charles town (that part Between Kings Mountain & Ezekiel Polks) & that he Enter on his Charge accordingly.

Ordered that Charles McClean Serve as Overseer of said Road that part Between Ez'l Polks & the head of Fishing Creek & that he Enter on his Charge accordingly.

Ordered that David Byars Serve as Overseer of said Road from the head of Fishing Creek to Michael Megaritys & that he Enter on his Charge accordingly.

Ordered that William Braton Serve as Overseer of the aforesaid Road from Mic'l Megaritys to the s'd Brattons house & that he Enter on his Charge accordingly.

Charity Karr Returns an Inventory of the Goods & Chattles of Wm. Karr Dec'd prays an order of Sale which was Granted accordingly.

A Deed of Gift from Jno Stanford to Esix Capshaw Dated the 23 Oc'r 1769 for 75 acres acknowledged in Open Court. Ordered·to be Registered.

A Deed of Sale from Lewis Henry Derossett to Hugh Pollock Dated 23d December 1769 [sic] for __ acres proved by Will Red [Reed] Evidence thereto. Ordered to be Registered.

A Deed of Sale from Hugh Pollock to Jas Foster Dated 7th August 1769 for 450 acres proved by Jno Tagert Evidence thereto. Ordered to be Registered.

A Deed of Sale from Nicholas Fisher to Jno Stanford Dated 13th December 1768 for 200 acres proved by Hugh Quin Evidence thereto. Ordered to be Registered.

A Deed of Sale from Peter Kuykendal to John Duncan Dated 1st April 1769 for 300 acres proved by Jas Young Evidence thereto. Ordered to be Registered.

A Deed of Sale from William Coal to Mesheck Stalin [Michael Staten] Dated the 25 March 1769 for 152 acres proved by Jno Duncan Evidence thereto. Ordered to be Registered.

A Deed of Sale from Nicholas Grindstorff to Frederick Wirtenberg Dated the 7th August 1769 for 400 acres proved by Jno Retzhoupt Evidence thereto. Ordered to be Registered.

<u>October term 1769</u>

A Deed of Lease & Release from Richard Love to Sam'l Barnet dated 18th & 19th days of August 1769 for 400 acres of land proved by Thos Gilham Evidence thereto. Ordered to be Registered.

Court adjourned till tomorrow 8 OClock. Met according to adjournment. Present Wm Watson, Jno Gordon, Jas McElwean, Esquires.

Margaret Shaw returns an Inventory of the Goods & Chattles of Robert Shaw deceased prays an Order of Sale which was accordingly granted.

In pursuance of an Order of July Court, it is ordered that Letters Testamentary issue of Phillip Henson of the Goods & Chattels of Nicholas Henson Deceased.

A Deed of Sale from Thomas Black to Richard Ward Dated the 8th March 1769 for 251 acres proved by William Sims Evidence thereto. Ordered to be Registered.

The Grand Jury. James Lewis, Foreman

2	John Crage	9	Thomas Morgan
3	John Anderson	10	Matthew Porter
4	Jno Robinson	11	Christopher Coleman
5	Solom'n Beson	12	____ Ford
6	Joseph Clark	13	Wm Yancey
7	Tho's Price	14	James Henry
8	Jno Potts	15	Peter Kuykendal

A Deed of Sale from Peter Limeberger to Peter Limeberger dated the 5th of November 1768 acknowledged in Open Court. Ordered to be Registered.

A Deed of Sale from Ubey Crowder & Charity his wife to Jno Limeberger dated the 6th Sep'r for 200 acres proved by Jno Ritzhoupt Evidence thereto. Ordered to be Reg'd.

A Deed of Sale from James Weyat & Behethelum his wife to Daniel Wyatt Dated the 24th of April 1768 for 100 acres proved by Geo Lamkin Evidence thereto. Ordered to be Reg'd.

A Deed of Sale from John Russel Jr to Tho's Wade dated the 28th of July 1767 for 100 acres proved by Henry Smith Evidence thereto. Ordered to be Registered.

A Deed of Sale from Edward Lacey to Joshua Lacey & Ruben Lacey dated the 13th Day of June 1769 for 3OO acres Proved by Oliver Walace Evidence thereto. Ordered to be Registered.

Court adjourned till tomorrow 8 OClock. Met According to adjournment. Present William Watson, Jno Gordon, Jon Ritzhoupt, David Anderson, Esq'rs.

Ordered by the Court that John McFaddon Serve as Constable under Jonas Bedford that he swear in before said Jonas Bedford, Esquire.

Hugh Quinn vs Jno McFaddon. Case

The Petty Jury

1 William Laughlin   7 John Pearson

October term 1769

2	William Morrison	8	Nathl Clark
3	Andrew McNabb	9	Ja's Hanna
4	Wm Hagerty	10	Ja's Smith
5	Thomas Brattin	11	John Venable
6	James Steen	12	Thomas Bullion

Jury Impannelled Tryed & Sworn find that the Def't did assume and assess the platfs Damages to £6 14 10-d & /6 Cost.

On motion of Alex'r Martin it was ordered by the court that John Potts have Letters of Administration of all & singular the Goods Chattels Rights & Credits of Jeremiah Potts Deceased, who took the oath of an Administrator & proposed for security Hugh Quinn, Solomon Beson, John Stevenson & Sam'l Davison Bound in the sum of One thousand pounds. accepted.

John Case vs Wm. Anderson. T A B

The Petty Jury

1	Wm. Laughlin	7	James Smith
2	Wm. Morrison	8	Jno Venable
3	And'w Patrick	9	Hugh Quinn
4	Wm. Henry	10	Jno Gordon
5	Jno Pearson	11	David Watson
6	Nath'l Clark	12	James Price

Jury Impanneled & Sworn find that it was the ass't of the plff. The Jury came & gave in their verdict. The plaff being called Suffered a Non suit.

On motion of Ja's Forsyth it was ordered that by the Said court that Letters Testamentary issue to Henry Clark of all & singular the Goods & Chattles Rights & Credits of John Hanna Deceas'd. who took the Oath of an Executor according to act of assembly in that Case made & provided.

Henry Clark returns an inventory of the Goods & Chattels of John Hanna deceased prays an order of sale which was accordingly Granted.

On motion of Jno. Williams Junr it was ordered by the Court that Zachariah Bullock Build a grist mill on his Land on Thicketty Creek & that the same be deemed a publick mill he Complying with the act of assembly in that Case made & provided.

A Deed of sale from Robert McClanachan & Elizabeth his wife to James Patton dated the 7th day of September 1766 for 209 acres proved by Wm. Hagins Evidence thereto. Ordered to be Reg'd.

A Deed of Sale from Charles Anderson & Elizabeth his wife to James Patton dated the 5th day of September 1765 for 170 acres proved by Wm. Hagins Evidence thereto. Ordered to be Reg'd.

A Deed of Sale from Charles Anderson & Elizabeth his wife to James Patton dated the 10th of September 1765 for 100 acres proved by Wm. Hagins Evidence thereto. Ordered to be Reg'd.

<u>October term 1769</u>

A Deed of Sale from John Jordon to Ezekiel Polk dated the 26th day of August 1769 for 56 acres. ack'd in Open Court. Ordered to be Registered.

A Deed of Sale from And'w McNabb & Marg't to Robert McNabb dated the 20th day of Sept'r 1767 for 210 acres acknow'd in Open Court. Ordered to be Registered.

Court Adjourned till tomorrow 9 OClock. Met according to adjournment. Present Thos. Neel, Jno Gordon, Henry Clark, Esq'rs.

On motion of Alex'r Martin a Bill of Sale was Recorded in Open Court from James Farr to Michael Crawford Dated the 5th day of June 1769 for one Gray Horse named Emmy's Gray Proved by Richard Farr Evidence thereto.

Ordered that Jno. Kendrick & James Byars serve as Constables under Henry Clark Esq'r and that they swear in before the said Henry Clark.

Ordered that Henry Smith be summoned to appear at the next Court to shew cause if any he can for his contempt in not Serving in the station of a Constable for Henry Clark Esq'r he being legally summoned.

A Deed of Sale from John Wade to Jno Sadler dated the 27th of October 1767 for ___ acres of Land acknowledged in open court. Ordered to be Registered.

In consequence of an order of July Court appointing Moses Crawford and Sundry Other persons Jurors for laying out a road the nearest and best way from Little Broad River to Kings Mountain it is Ordered by this Court that said jurors be Summoned to appear at Jacob Costners there to take the Necessary steps to qualify them for Executing the said Charge.

Jonas Bedford Came into court & took the Oaths by Law appoin'd for the Qualification of Publick Officers Subscribed the test, took the Oath of a Justice of the Peace & took his seat accordingly.

Ordered by the Court that Wm. Shepherd Serve as Constable for Jonas Bedford Esq'r and that he swear in before said Jonas Bedford.

Ordered by the Court that George Deck serve as Constable in Room of George Rutledge & that he swear in before William Moore Esq'r.

Ordered by the Court that Edward Lacey Serve as Constable in Room of Wm Hanna & that he swear in before John Gordon Esq'r.

Ordered that a new appraisement be had on horses taken on execution in the suit John Williams vs Wm Yancey & James Gordon & John Beard Bail for the Producing of said Effects and that Jonas Bedford Esq'r, Jno Hall and Thomas Campbell be praisers of sd Effects.

October Term. Memorandum. All Lists of Probates for Granting Letters Testamentary or of Admn. returned P'r Mr. Johnston.

October Term, Claims on the County of Tryon for the Year 1769

	£	S	D
To a Charter for the County	20		
Expenses in sending for the same	8		
Interest of 20£ Fifteen months.		1	10
To the Surveyor for running the central line		7	10
To Henry Clark, Esqr. one Venire Ticket		2	15
To Charles McClean one Venire Ticket		2	15
To James Henry one Venire Ticket		2	5
To Jno Robinson one Venire Ticket		2	5
To Sheriff for extra services	10		
To Clerk for extra services	10		
To Charles McClean for 2 courts held at his house	5	-	-
	£71	16	10

It appears by the above Claims that the County of Tryon stands Dr. the sum of seventy one pounds sixteen shillings & ten pence for the year one thousand seven hundred and sixty-nine.

The list of Taxables being brought in & Calculatted it appears that the number of taxable persons in Tryon County amounts to One Thousand Two hundred & Twenty One. It is ordered by the court that a tax of three shillings & two pence proclamation Money be raised and levied by the Sheriff of the said County on each of the said Taxable Persons in this the said County for the 1769 afsd, according to the Act of Assembly lately made & provided and in order to defray the above said contingencies of sd County.

Court adjourned till Court in Course. Thos Neel, Jno Gordon, David Anderson.

North Carolina, Tryon County. /To Witt/ Tryon Inferior Court of Pleas and Quarter Sessions begun and held in Jan'y Term Fourth Tuesday A.D. 1770. Present Thomas Neel, Esqr, Chairman. His Majesty's Commission of the Peace being read, the Silence was proclaimed.

Ordered that Letters Testamentary Issue to George Wilfong and Robert Blackburn of all and Singular the goods & Chattels Rights and Credits of Jacob Wilfong Deceased Who Took the Oaths of an Executor according to act of assembly in that Case mae & provided.

Ordered by the Court that John Fondron serve as Overseer of the Road leading from Leepar's Mill to Charles Town (that part between the main branch of Fishing Creek and Wm Brattons and that he Enter on his Charge accordingly.

Robert Blackburn and George Wilfong return an Inventory of the goods and Chattles of Jacob Wilfong deceas'd prays an order of sale which was accordingly Granted.

Pursuant to an order of October Term it is ordered that Hugh Quinn & sundry others serve as jurors to lay out a road as aforesaid and that they appear before Francis Adams Esq'r the second Tuesday in February next to take the necessary steps to qualify them to act in their said charge.

Francis Adams came into court and took the oath by Law appointed for Qualification of publick officers subscribed the test Took the oath of a Justice & Took his Seat accordingly.

<u>January term 1770</u>

Robert Blackburn came into Court & took the oath by Law appointed for Qualification of publick officers subscribed the test Took the oath of a Justice & Took his Seat accordingly. Justice.

Ordered by the Court that James Erwin serve as Constable under Francis Adams Esqr & that he swear in before said Francis Adams accordingly.

Ordered by the Court that Peter Sumy Serve as Constable under Robert Blackburn & that he Swear in before the said Rob't Blackburn Esq'r accordingly.

A Bond from John Tagert, Henry Clark, John Walker, Francis Ross, John Hardin, Henry Smith, and Matthew Floyd to his Excellency William Tryon for the collecting & Accounting for the public Taxes in Tryon County dated 24th of February 1770 taken and acknowledged in open court.

Ordered that William Goltney an orphan boy of the age of Three years be bound unto John Alexander till he arrives to the age of Twenty One Years & by him to be taught the art and mistery of a weaver and in Other things to Comply w't the act of assembly in that Case made & provided.

George Blanton Came into Court took the oath by Law appointed for Qualification of Public Officers Subscribed the Test took the Oath of a Justice & took his Seat accordingly.

A Deed of Sale from Henry Hiltebrand to Christian Rinehart dated 10th January 1770 for 180 acres of land proved by Daniel Warlock Evidence thereto. Ordered to be Reg'd.

A Deed of Sale from Wm Gaston & Jennet his wife to Rob't Gill for 600 acres dated 15th Jan'y 1770 ack'd in Open Court. Ordered to be Reg'd.

A Deed of Sale from Richard Ward to John Morris for 185 acres dated 3d June in the year of Our Lord 1769 proved by Wm Wray Evidence thereto. Ordered to be Reg'd.

A Deed of Sale from Jno Neave & Eve his wife to Wm Coons for 396 acres Dated the 1st day of October 1768 proved by George Brock Evidence thereto. Ordered to be Reg'd.

A Deed of Sale from Richard Ward and Mary his wife to Wm Stogdon for 251 acres Dated the 10th day of April 1769 proved by Rob't Collinswood Evidence thereto. Ordered to be Reg'd.

A Deed of Sale from John Miller & Jane his wife to Robert Siminton dated 19th day of January 1770 for 100 acres proved by Peter Johnston Evidence thereto. Ordered to be Reg'd.

A Deed of Sale from Thomas Williamson & and Rebeca his wife to Thomas Barton Dated 16th August 1769 for 150 acres proved by Robt Nelson Evidence thereto. Ord'd to be Registered.

A Deed of Sale from Marmaduke Dauraugh & Esabell his wife to Wm. Minter Dated the 29th Day of May 1766 for 200 acres proved by Francis Travers Evidence thereto. Ordered to be Registered.

A Deed of Sale from Henry Jacobs to Michael Rudisil Dated the 4th October 1769 for 496 acres proved by Robert Blackburn Evidence thereto. Ordered to be Reg'd.

January term 1770

A Deed of Sale from Dan'l Warlock & Barbara his wife to Nicholas Warlock for 200 acres Dated the 19th day of August 1769 proved by Wm. Reed Evidence thereto Ord'd to be Reg'd.

A Deed of Sale from Dan'l Warlock & Barbara his wife to Elizabeth Warlock Dated 16th Decem'r 1769 for 400 proved by Wm. Reed Evidence thereto Ordered to be Registered.

A Deed of Sale from Dan'l Warlock & Barbara his wife to Valentine Warlock for 227 acres Dated 16th Decem'r 1769 proved by Wm. Reed Evidence thereto. Ord'd to be Reg'd.

A Deed of Sale from Dan'l Warlock & Barbara his wife Dated 16th December 1769 to David Ramsour for 252 acres proved by Wm. Reed Evidence thereto. Order'd to be Registered.

A Deed of Sale from Dan'l Warlock & Barbara his wife to Philip Warlock Dated 16th Decem'r 1769 for 400 acres proved by Wm. Reed Evidence thereto. Ordered to be Registered.

A Deed of Sale from Dan'l Warlock & Barbara his wife to Barbara Warlock for 200 acres Dated 16th Decem'r 1769 proved by Wm. Reed Evidence thereto. Ordered to be Registered.

A Deed of Sale from Dan'l Warlock & Barbara his wife to Nicholas Warlock for 200 acres Dated 20th Decem'r 1769 proved by Wm. Reed Evidence thereto. Ordered to be Reg'd.

A Deed of Sale from Dan'l Warlock & Barbara his wife to Martin Shooford for 191 acres Dated 16 Decem'r 1769 proved by Wm. Reed Evidence thereto. Ordered to be Reg'd.

A Deed of Sale from Dan'l Warlock & Barbara his wife to Valentine Warlock for 260 acres Dated 16th Decem'r 1769 proved by Wm. Reed Evidence thereto. Ordered to be Reg'd.

A Deed of Sale from Dan'l Warlock & Barbara his wife to Martin Shooford for 50 acres Dated 19th Ag't 1769 proved by Wm. Reed Evidence thereto. Ordered to be Reg'd.

A Deed of Sale from Dan'l Warlock & Barbara his wife to Frederick Wise for 260 acres Dated 19th August 1769 proved by Wm. Reed Evidence thereto. Ordered to be Reg'd.

A Deed of Sale from Dan'l Warlock & Barbara his wife to Henry Hiltebrand for 200 acres Dated 19 August 1769 proved by Wm. Reed Evidence thereto. Ordered to be Reg'd.

A Deed of Sale from John Potts to Christian Rinehart for 260 acres dated 13th October 1769 proved by Wm. Reed Evidence thereto. Ordered to be Registered.

Court adjourned till tomorrow 9 OClock. Met according to adjournment. Present Thomas Neel, John Ritshoupt, Jacob Costner, Esq'rs.

Ordered by the Court that Moses Moore, Wm Wray, James Cook, Alexander McGahey, Robert Proctor, David Huddleston, Aaron Moore, Nathan Proctor, Wm Huddleston, Thomas Welsh, John Morris Jacob Coburn serve as Jurors to lay out a road from Aaron Moore's the Nighest & Best Way to Charlestown (as far as the South Line) and that they meet at John Walkers on the 3d Tuesday in Feb'y there and then to take the necessary steps to qualify them for this their charge.

<u>January term 1770</u>

Phillip Henson returns an inventory of the goods and Chattles Rights & Credits of Nicholas Henson deceased and prays an order of sale which was accordingly Granted.

Brumfield Ridly Came into Court & Took the Oath appointed for Qualific'n of Publick Officers Subscribed the Test, took the oath of an Att'y according to Law.

The Grand Jury Joseph Harden, Foreman

2	Robert Adams	9	Jonathan Robison
3	John Watson	10	Perrigreen Magnis
4	Robert Watson	11	Thomas Collins
5	John Alexander	12	John Beard
6	Benjamin Harden	13	John Wilson
7	Oliver Wallace	14	Jabesh Evans
8	Jacob Gardner	15	Joseph Carrol

Ordered that John Thomason appear at our next Court and give in upon oath that part of the Estate of Nicholas Henson D'd he has in his hands.

William Moore Came into court produced a commission appointing him Coroner of Tryon County and took the Oath by Law app'd for Qualification of Public Officers Subscribed the Test and took the oath of a Coroner &C.

Benja Rainey vs Francis Nevil Wayland. Orr. att.

The Petty Jury

1	Wm. McElmurry	7	Wm. Capshaw
2	James Thompson	8	Edwd Rob'ts
3	James Price	9	Thomas Peny
4	Edward Lacey	10	Andw Patrick
5	Jno. Standford	11	James Beaty
6	Robt Collinwood	12	Jno Hardin

Jury Impenneld and Sworn find for the plff and assess damages to £8 9 1½ & /6 cost.

Jacob Randal vs James Patterson. Case. Same Jury. Jury impanneled & Sworn find for the plff and assess damages 1d and /6d costs.

X'r Coleman vs Richard Farr. Orr Att. Same Jury. Jury impanneled & Sworn find for the plff and assess damages £13 15 6d & /6d costs.

Sam' Coburn vs John Armstrong. Case. Same Jury. Jury impanneled & Sworn find for the plff and assess damages £5 4 6d & /6d costs.

Thomas Neel Came into court & produced his commission appointing him Coll of Tryon Regiment and took the Oath of State.

Wm Gallespy vs Jacob Gardner. Case. Same Jury. Jury impanneled & Sworn find for the plff and assess damages £14 11 11d & /6d costs.

Thomas Polk vs Jno Elder. Case Debt Same Jury. Jury impanneled & Sworn find for the plff and assess damages to £11 4 7d & /6 costs.

January term 1770

Ordered by the Court that Jacob Carpenter & Benjamin Bickerstaff Serve as Constables in the room of Peter Aker and that they swear in before Jacob Costner, Esq'r acc'ly.

Ordered by the Court that a deposition of John Thomas be entered on record Wherein he deposseth that on the 24th or 25th of July he lost a needle work Double pocket book Together with a Three pound bill with these words on the Back from Ja's Armstrong to A. Kuykendall as also one piece of Gold to wit the quarter of a Johannis rec'd of Edw'd McNeal for a Caroline one pair of broken carved silver buckels, one bond or penal note from Jno. Gordon for one hundred pounds proc'm money with C'r for all but about £14, 3 notes due from Tho's Hankins for near £5. One other penal note due from John Gordon for the sum of £13 money payable next Christmas, one Bond of performance of land from Giles Tillet to Wm Wofford & the said Wofford assigned.

Jno. Potts returns an inventory of the goods & Chattles of Jeremiah Potts prays an order of sale which was accordingly granted.

John Tagert came into court & produced a Commission of Sheriff of this County from under the Hand and Seal of His Excellency, Took the Oaths by Law appointed for Qualification of Publick officers, Subscribed the Test, Took the oath of a Sheriff & entered on the duty of his office.

Jno. Knuckles, Wm. Reed & Thomas Clark Came into court and took the Oaths by Law appointed for Qualification of Publick officers, Subs'd the Test, Took the oath of a Sheriff and entered in the duty of this office.

Ordered by the Court that John Witherow serve as Constable in the room of Michael Proctor and that he swear in before John Walker, Esqr.

A Deed of Sale from James Smith to Hugh Cummins dated 4th of August 1769 for 200 acres proved by John Cummins Evidence thereto. Ordered to be Registered.

A Deed of Sale from Jane Erwin, widow to James Patterson dated 2d day of November 1769 for 239 acres proved by Wm Patterson Evidence thereto. Ordered to be Registered.

A Deed of Sale from Major Temple to James Patterson for 150 acres Dated the 22d day of Jan'y proved by Thos Polk Evidence thereto. Ordered to be Registered.

A Deed of Sale from Martin Delinger to Peter Costner dated _____ of _____ for 200 acres proved by Jacob Costner Evidence thereto. Ordered to be Registered.

A Deed of Sale from Jacob Johnston & Susanah his wife to Patrick McDavid for 100 acres dated the 24th day of April 1769 proved by George Lampkin Evidence thereto. Ordered to be Registered.

A Deed of Sale from Moses Wylie to Ab'm Belue dated the 8th day of February 1768 for 150 acres formerly in Meckl'g Co'y, now Tryon, proved by James McElwean Ev'ce thereto. Ordered to be Registered.

A Deed of Sale from Ja's Wyat & Behethelum his wife to John Wyat for 100 acres Dated the 24th day of April 1769 proved by George Lampkin Evidence thereto. Ord'd to be Registered.

January term 1770

A Deed of Sale from John Armstrong & Mary his wife to James Cason for 116 acres dated the 4th day of Novem'r 1769 proved by George Rutledge Evidence thereto. Ordered to be Registered.

Venire men appointed for Salsbury Superior Co't 5 March (viz): Henry Clark, Peter Kuykendal, And'w Haslep, Joseph How, Joseph Carrol, James Murphy.

A Bond of performance from John Cathey & Jane Ervin to James Patterson for tract of land containing two hundred & thirty nine acres on the West side of the So. Fork of Cataba River known by the name of Hugh Erwin's plantation in consideration of sixty pounds proc. money. Proved by Henry Henry evidence thereto. Ordered to be Registered.

Charles McClain, Zchariah Bullock, Thomas Beaty & Ephraim McClean Came into court and took the oaths by Law appointed for Qualification of Publick Officers & Subscribed the Test, Having each of them first produced his Excy's Commission, appointing them Captains of the Tryon Regiment of foot whereof Thos Neel Esq'r is Coll.

A Deed of Sale from Wm. Weyat to John Love dated the 29th day of August 1769 for 100 acres proved by Geo: Lamptkin Evidence thereto. Ordered to be Registered.

A Deed of Sale from Thomas Ray to Cornelius McCarty dated the 16th Day of January 1769 for 100 acres proved by Geo: Lampkin Evidence thereto. Ordered to be Registered.

A Deed of Sale from John Walker to Wm. Barr dated the 14th day of January 1770 for 300 acres ack'd in Open Court. Ordered to be Reg'd.

A Deed of Sale from David Watson to Wm. Watson for 200 acres dated 24th January 1769 ack'd in Open Court. Ordered to be Reg'd.

A Deed of Sale from Geo. Lampkin to Jno. Low Dated the 13th Day of Sept'r 1769 for 100 acres ak'd in Open Court. Ordered to be Registered.

A Deed of Sale from Samuel Wilson to Jacob Hoss Dated the 5th Day of Jan'y 1770 for 400 acres proved by John Dun Evidence thereto. Ordered to be Registered.

A Deed of Sale from John Hoyle to Conrad Kinder Dated the 9th day of Sept'r 1769 for 220 acres proved by Jacob Costner Evidence thereto. Ordered to be Registered.

A Deed of Sale from William Wray to Wm Moore for 272 acres formerly in Mecklenburg now Tryon dated the 25 Day of August 1769 ackn'd in Open C't. Ordered to be Registered.

A Deed of Sale from James Moore to David Leech dated the 4th day of July 1769 for 226 acres proved by John Moore Evidence thereto. Ordered to be Registered.

A Deed of Sale from John Low to Wm Weyat dated the 13th day of Sept'r 1769 for 200 acres proved by George Lampkin Evidence thereto. Ordered to be Registered.

A Deed of Sale from Oliver Walace to John Ellis dated the 28th of October 1770 for 400 acres proved by Sam'l McCulloh Evidence thereto. Ordered to be Registered.

A Deed of Sale from Simon Kuykendal to James Millican for 300 acres dated the 20th day of Septem'r 1769 proved by James Hanna Evidence thereto. Ordered to be Registered.

January term 1770

A Deed of Sale from William Anderson to Jno. Hoyle for 280 acres dated the 2d of Dec'r 1769 proved by Wm. Moore Evidence thereto. Ordered to be Registered.

A Deed of Sale from Hezekiah Pigg & Elizabeth his wife to James Forsyth for 161 acres dated the 20th day of March 1769 proved by George Blanton Evidence thereto. Ordered to be Registered.

A Deed of Sale from William Henry & Esabell his wife to Rob't Abernathy for 300 acres dated the 20th August 1769 proved by George Lampkin Evidence thereto. Ordered to be Registered.

A Deed of Sale from Zachariah Bell to Wm. McAdo dated 23d day of Jan'y 1770 for 150 acres proved by David McAdou Evidence thereto. Ordered to be Registered.

A Deed of Sale from John Morris to William Gilbert for 200 acres dated the 14th day of October 1769 proved by Jno. Walker Evidence thereto. Ordered to be Registered.

Court adjourned till tomorrow at 9 Oclock. Met at accord'g to adjournment. Present Thos Neel, Wm. Moore, Jno Retzhoupt, Es'qrs.

Ordered by the court that George Reese serve as Constable in room of Lewis Limeberger & that he swear in before Jno Retzhoupt, Esqr.

Court adjourned and Orphans Court met. Present Thos Neel, Wm. Moore, Jno Retzhoupt, Es'qrs.

Orphans Court adjourned and Court of Pleas Met. Present Thos Neel, Wm. Moore, Jno Retzhoupt, Es'qrs.

Ordered by the Court that Joseph How serve as Constable in room of Jas. Alcorn and that he swear in before Thomas Neel, Esq'r.

Ordered by the Court that Alexander Robison serve as Constable in room of Wm. Henry & that he swear in before John Robison, Esqr.

A Deed of Sale from Thomas Childers & Uradice his wife to Perregreen Magnis dated 25th of January 1770 for 250 acres Ack'd in Open Court by said Thomas Childers & the Feme being privately Examined by Jonas Bedford Esq'r he Returns that the said Feme Did freely and willingly without any compulsion Sign Seal & Deliver the said deed. Ordered to be Registered.

Thomas Polk vs John Elder. Case.

The Petty Jury

1 Jno Hardin	7 Jonathan Price
2 Dav'd Alex'r	8 James Bridges
3 James Weyat	9 Thomas Price
4 Wm Wray	10 Zachariah Gibbs
5 Nicholas Welsh	11 Jno Byars
6 Robt Gordon	12 John Potts

Jury Impenneld and Sworn find for the plff and assess his damages to £12 0 7 and /6 cost.

January term 1770

A Deed of Sale from Ezekiel Smith to Wm. Twitty Dated 21st day of Octo'r 1769 for ____ acres proved by Jonas Bedford Evidence thereto. Ord'd to be Reg'd.

Court adjourned till tomorrow 8 OClock. Met according to adjournment. Present Wm Moore, Wm. Watson, James McElwean, Esqr's.

On Motion of John Dunn it is ordered that Rebekah Foster an Orphan Girl of the Age of Three years be Bound unto James Henry untill she arrives to the age of Eighteen and to Serve him s'd Henry fifteen y'rs he complying with the act of assembly made in the case of Female Orphans.

John Thomas vs Wm. Morrison. Case.
The Petty Jury

1	John Dellinger	7	John Potts
2	Thomas Price	8	John Price
3	Alex'r Lockart	9	Hance McWhorter
4	Jacob Gardner	10	Thomas Beaty
5	John Fondron	11	John Laughlin
6	Abraham Bogard	12	John Byars

Jury Impenneld and Sworn find for the plff and assess his damages to £1 4 2 and /6 cost.

Wm. Saffold vs Jacob Mitchel. Case. Same Jury. Jury Impenneld and Sworn find for the plff and assess his dam'g to one penny & /6 cost.

Court adjourned for half an hour. Met according to adjournment. Present Thomas Neel, Wm. Watson, Francis Adams.

The King vs Clark & Jones. Indict't.
The Petty Jury

1	John Dellinger	7	John Potts
2	Thomas Price	8	John Laughlin
3	Alex'r Lockart	9	John Byars
4	Jacob Gardner	10	David Porter
5	Jno Fondron	11	Wm. Byars
6	Abr'm Bogard	12	John Moffet

Jury Impenneld and Sworn find the defendant Not Guilty.

The King vs Clark & Jones. Indict't. Same jury. Jury Impenneld and Sworn find the defendant Not Guilty.

Jacob Costner vs Wm. Ray & Wm. Morrison. Case. Same Jury. Jury Impenneled and Sworn find for the plff and assess his damages to £9 0 6 & /6 cost.

Wm. Hogg vs Wm. Quinn. Case. Same Jury. The Plff being Called Suffered a non suit.

On Motion of John Dunn, Robert Allison, Orphan Boy of full age to Choose his Guardian Came into Court & made Choice of Charles McClean & Rob't Adams w'h was agreed to by the Court.

January term 1770

A Deed of Sale from Joseph Carrol & Thomas Carrol to James Logan Dated 10th Novem'r 1769 for three hundred acres proved by Saml Carol Evidence thereto. Ordered to be Reg'd.

A Deed of Lease & Release from John & Mary Potts to Nicholas Clay Dated the 6th & 7th of Jan'y 1769 for 150 acres of land proved by Wm. Reed Evidence thereto. Ord'd to be Reg'd.

A Deed of Lease & Release from John Potts and Mary his wife to Nicholas Clay for 450 acres of land Dated the 6th & 7th of Jan'y 1769 proved by Wm. Reed Evidence thereto. Ord'd to be Registered.

A Deed of Lease and Release from Matthias Beaver & Susana his wife to Frederick Markel for 400 acres of land Dated the 11th & 12th Days of Septem'r 1769 proved by John Tagert Evidence thereto. Ordered to be Reg'd.

A Deed of Mortgage from James Foster to Thomas Adams for Sundry Tracts of Land in Tryon County proved by James Forsyth evid'ce thereto. Ordered to be Reg'd.

A Deed of Sale from Nicholas & Eliz'th Fry to Phillip Fry for 200 acres of Land Dated the 26th December 1769 proved by Wm Reed Evidence thereto. Ordered to be Reg'd.

A Deed of Sale from Thomas Beaty to Wm Beaty for 300 acres Dated the 29th of Feb'y 1769 ack'd in Open Court. Ordered to be Reg'd.

A Deed of Sale from Henry Hiltebrand & Mary to John Waggerlin for 300 acres Dated 15 day of Jan'y 1770 proved by Wm. Reed Evidence thereto. Ordered to be Reg'd.

A Deed of Sale from Nicholas Fry & Elizabeth his wife to John Shufort for 88 acres Dated the 6th March 17-- proved by Wm Reed Evidence thereto. Ordered to be Registered.

A Deed of Sale from Rob't McKee & Margaret to Jno Thompson for 300 acres Dated the 27th of Dec'r 1769 proved by Thomas Neel Evidence thereto. Ord'd to be Reg'd.

A Deed of Sale from John Lusk to Geo Hefner for 10 acres Dated the 27th of Sep'r 1769 proved by Wm. Reed Evidence thereto. Ordered to be Registered.

A Deed of Sale from John Shooford & Clara to Martin Shooford Dated the 6th of March 1769 for 299 acres proved by Wm Reed Evidence thereto. Ordered to be Registered.

Court adjourned till tomorrow 9 OClock. Met according to adjournment. Present Thomas Neel, Wm Watson, Francis Adams, Esq'rs.

Joseph Chubb vs Ulrick Crowder. Debt.
The Petty Jury

1	Charles McClean	7	Henry Wright
2	David Porter	8	Wm Hagerty
3	John Fondron	9	Thomas Neely
4	James Bryson	10	Wm. Smith
5	Wm. Henry	11	James Byars
6	Robert Swan	12	John Bryson

Jury Impenneld and Sworn find for the plff and assess his damages to £7 2 8 3/4. Alex'r Martin att'y for Deft Motion _____ of Judg't. Reasons filed.

Court adjourned till Court in Course. Thos Neel, William Watson, Francis Adams.

North Carolina, Tryon County. To Wit Tryon Inferior Court of Pleas & Quarter Sessions begun and held for Said County the Fourth Tuesday in April AD 1770. Present Thomas Neel, John Gordon, Francis Adams, Rob't Blackburn.

On motion of Alexander Martin, it is Ordered by the court that Letters of Adm'n be Granted to Jane cook, Wife & Relick of Roger Cook dec'd, of all and Singular the Goods & Chattles rights & Credits of the sd Roger Cook Deceased. She having proposed for security Robert Swan and Wm. Henry bound in the sum of two hundred pounds. accepted.

It is Ordered by the Court that Charles McClean have a Licence to Keep Ordinary at his Dwelling house where he now lives in the County of Tryon he complying with the Act of assembly in that Case made & provided. He proposes for security James Campbell & Thomas Black.

On Motion of John Dunn it was Ordered by the Court that James Gordon have Licence to Keep Ordinary at his Dwelling house where he now lives in the Tryon County he Complying with the act of assembly in that Case made & provided. He proposes for security John Dunn & Alexander Martin. accepted.

Ordered by the Court that Edmund Bishop Serve as Constable in the Room of John Brandon & That he Swear in before William Watson Esq'r accordingly.

James Erwin garnishee of Edward Williams came into court & Declared on Oath that he has in his hands £13 4 6 and no more.

The Grand Jury

1 James Campbell, foreman

2 Alex'r Campbell	9 John Foster
3 Jabez Evans	10 Sam'l Simpson
4 David Davies	11 Thomas Black
5 James Thompson	12 William Henry
6 Saml Gray	13 John Manner[?]
7 And'w McNabb	14 John McFaddon
8 James McCord	15 Wm. McElwee

Sworn & Charged.

John Robinson & James McIntire came into Court and took the oaths by law appointed for qualification of publick officers subscribed the test and took the oath of a. Justice of the Peace & took their seats accordingly.

Andw Hampton, Ab'm Kuykendal, Henry Clark, Joseph Green Came into Court & produced His Excellency's Commission appointing each a Captain of the Militia of this Province, took the oaths, subscribed the test and entered on the duty of their offices.

Patrick McDavid & Daniel Shipman came into Court and produced his Excellency's Commission appointing each of them a Lieutenant of the Militia of this Province subscribed the test and entered on the Duty of their office.

April term 1770

Perigreen Magnis & John Brandon came into Court and produced his Excellency's Commission appointing each of them an Ensign in the Militia of this Province subscribed the test and entered on the duty of their office.

A Deed of Sale from David Robinson to William Glover Bishop dated the 3d day of June 1769 for 400 acres of land proved by John Wade Evidence thereto. Ordered to be Registered.

A Deed of Sale from Thomas Morgan to Demsey Winborne dated the 8th of May 1768 for 75 acres proved by James Stalions Evidence thereto. Ordered to be Registered.

A Deed of Sale from Gabriel Brown Junr & Ann his wife to Jacob Brown dated the 27th of March 1770 for 100 acres proved by John Nuckols Evidence thereto. Ordered to be Registered.

A Deed of Sale from Alex'r McIntire to John Lusk dated the 23 day of January 1770 for 200 acres proved by James McIntire Evidence thereto. Ord'd to be Registered.

A Deed of Sale from Alex'r Kilpatrick to Joseph Moore Dated the 30th day of March 1770 for 200 acres of Land proved by John Potts Evidence thereto. Ordered to be Registered.

A Deed of Sale from John Seigle Senr to John Seigle Junr dated the 10th March 1770 for 150 acres proved by Thomas Neal Evidence thereto. Ordered to be Registered.

A Deed of Sale from Frederick Knapper to Frederick Shinker dated the 30 day of December 1769 for 200 acres proved by Leonard Sailer Evidence thereto. Ordered to be Registered.

A Deed of Sale from John Foster to Wm. Young Dated the 29th March 1770 for _____ proved by James McElwean Evidence thereto. Ordered to be Registered.

A Deed of Sale from James Dougherty to John Collins Dated the 9th April 1770 for 200 acres of Land proved by Isaac Collins Evidence thereto. Ord'd to be Reg'd.

A Deed of Sale from George Sights & Susanna his wife to Adam Sights Dated the 27th day of Jan'y 1770 for 200 acres of Land. proved by Paul Wisenant Evidence thereto. Ordered to be Registered.

A Deed of Sale from Robert Abernathy & Sarah his wife to Ulrick Crowder dated the 21st day of Feby 1770 for _____ of Land proved by Leonard Sailer Evidence thereto. Ordered to be Registered.

A Deed of Sale from Frederick Rapper to Daniel Will Dated the 30th day of December 1769 for 200 acres of Land proved by _____ Evidence thereto. Ordered to be Registered.

A Deed of Sale from William Hillhouse to Arch'd Robinson Dated the 22d day of January 1770 for 450 acres of Land proved by Stewart Brown Evidence thereto. Ordered to be Registered.

A Deed of Sale from Peter Kuykendall to John Stallions Dated the 6th day of June 1768 for 470 acres of Land proved by Demsey Winborne Evidence thereto. Ordered to be Registered.

April term 1770

A Deed of Sale from Francis Beaty to George Trout Dated the 30th day of March 1770 for 200 acres proved by George Walls Evidence thereto. Ordered to be Registered.

A Deed of Sale from Francis Adams to George Cox Dated the 23d Day of April 1770 for 50 acres of Land ack'd in open court. Ordered to be Registered.

A Deed of Sale from James Means & Rachel his wife to William Means Dated the 3d of April 1770 for 300 acres proved by James McElwean Evidence thereto. Ordered to be Reg'd.

A Deed of Sale from Richard Ward to Jno McDaniel dated the 28th of August 1769 for 200 acres proved by John Beaman Evidence thereto. Ord'd to be Registered.

A Deed of Sale from George Moore to John Haney dated the 22d of March 1770 for 155 acres proved by Simcock Kannon Evidence thereto. Ord'd to be Registered.

A Deed of Sale from And'w Haslip to John Haslep Dated the 21st Feb'y 1770 for 80 acres of land proved by And'w Hampton Evidence thereto. Ordered to be Registered.

A Deed of Sale from Hezekiah Collins to Isaac Collins dated the 7th day of April 1770 for 200 acres ack'd in open court. Ordered to be Registered.

A Deed of Sale from Tho's Welsh & Ann his wife to John Frederick Douber Dated the 22d of July 1769 for 300 acres of Land proved by John Beeman Evidence thereto. Ordered to be Registered.

A Deed of Sale from Mary Feemster to Samuel Feemster Dated the 12th day of March 1770 for 150 acres of Land proved by Arch'd Robinson Evidence thereto. Ordered to be Registered.

A Deed of Sale from Zach'h Bell to Patrick Robinson dated the 2d of December 1769 for 300 acres of Land proved by Arch'd Robinson Evidence thereto. Ordr'd to be Reg'd.

A Deed of Sale from John Wooling Carpenter to Thomas Costner Dated the 16th day of Jan'y 1770 for 3OO acres of Land proved by Henry Master Evidence thereto. Ordered to be Registered.

Ordered by the Court that Moses Henry do build a water grist & Saw [stricken?] Mill on his land on Crowders Creek and that the same be recorded a public Mill he Complying w't the act of assembly in that Case made & provided & under the same Rules & Restrictions as other publick Mills.

Court adjourned till tomorrow at 9 o'clock. Met according to adjournment. Present Thomas Neel, John Gordon, Henry Clark, David Anderson, Esquires.

After proclamation, the Court proceeded to the election of a Sheriff Accordingly there being ten Majestrates on the Bench to wit Robert Blackburn, Jno Walker, Francis Adams, James McElwean, John Robinson, William Watson, David Anderson, Henry Clark, john Gordon & Thomas Neel Esqrs who did Elected & Choose John Tagert, William Watson & Francis Adams to be high Sheriff. Accordingly, there being ten magistrates on the bench, to be recommended to the Governor for his approbation & appointment of one of them to serve as High Sheriff for Tryon County during the ensuing year. It appears by the

April term 1770

pole that John Tagert rec'd 9 votes, William Watson 8, and Francis Adams 6. Ordered to be recommended accordingly.

A Power of Attorney from John Garner & Mary his wife to James Crawford & James Hair Dated 19th December 1769.

Henry Holman Came into Court & took the oaths appointed by Law appointed for Qualification of Publick Officers Repeated & Subscribed the Test, Took the Oath of a Justice & took his seat accordingly. Sworn as Lieu't Col also.

Robert Blackburn Came into Court and produced his Excellency's Commission appointing him a Captain of the Militia in the Tryon Regiment of Foot whereof Thomas Neel is Col'l and took the Oaths by law appointed for Qualification of publick officers, subscribed the test & entered on the duty of his office.

Ordered by the Court that James Wilson & Alex'r Whitly serve as overseers of the Road leading from Ramsours Mill to Buckinghams & that they Enter on the Duty of his Office..

Peter Watkins vs James Bridges. Trover.

The Petty Jury

1	Henry Smith	7	Sam'l Davidson
2	James Capshaw	8	Zach'h Gibbs
3	John Wilson	9	David Porter
4	Wm Capshaw	10	John Carrol
5	Wm Wilson	11	John Potts
6	James Adams	12	Matt'w Wilson

Jury empanneled & sworn find for the plaintiff 5/ Damages & /6d cost.

Ordered by this Court that Joseph Howe & David Garrison serve as Overseers of the Road leading from Leepars Mill to Lands Ford & that they Enter on their Charge accordingly.

A Deed of Sale from William Adams to Phillip Adams dated the 25th day of October 1769 for 200 acres proved by Henry Clark Evidence thereto. Ordered to be Registered.

A Deed of Lease and Release from William Neely to John Carrol Dated the _____ 1768 for _____ acres of Land proved by John Anderson Evidence thereto. Ordered to be Registered.

A Deed of Sale from Francis Dods & Agnis his wife to Henry Leech dated the 2d of April 1770 for 400 acres proved by David Anderson Evidence thereto. Ordered to be Registered.

A Deed of Sale from Robert Love to Tho's Wade dated the 20th day of July 1768 for 375 acres of Land proved by James Love Evidence thereto. Ordered to be Registered.

Court adjourned till tomorrow 8 OClock. Met according to adjournment. Present Thomas Neel, David Anderson, John Robinson, Esq'rs.

On motion of Alex'r Martin it is ordered by the Court that Joseph Carrol be appointed Guardian to Matt'w, Ann & John Armstrong Orphans of John Armstrong Deceased. He

<u>April term 1770</u>

proposes for security Nathaniel Henderson & John Carrol Junr Bound in the sum of one Thousand Pounds. Accepted.

John Price vs John Fondron. Case

The Petty Jury

1	X'r Coleman	7	Nicholas Broadway
2	Thomas Price	8	Peter Watkins
3	James Capshaw	9	Benj'a Phillips
4	Verder Magbe	10	John Hampton
5	Wm Capshaw	11	Wm. Falls
6	Zach'h Gibbs	12	Thomas Rainy

Jury empanneled & sworn find for the plaintiff and assess his Damages £19 6 6½ & /6 Cost.

Peter Watkins vs James Bridges. Case
The Petty Jury

1	X'r Coleman	7	Nicholas Broadway
2	Thomas Price	8	John Hamet
3	James Capshaw	9	Thomas Barr
4	Verdere Magby	10	John Hampton
5	Wm Capshaw	11	William Falls
6	Zach'h Gibbs	12	John Wilson

Jury finds for the plaintiff if the law be for him and assess to the plaintiff such recovery as the law sets forth for But if the law be against the plaintiff we find the defendant not guilty.

Ordered that Martin Shulis serve as Constable for Henry Holman Esqr. and that he swear in before the said Henry Holman Esq'r accordingly.

Ordered that Robert Collinwood & John Carson serve as Overseers of the road leading from Rob't Collinwoods on little Broad River to Kings Mountain & that they enter on their charge accordingly.

The King vs Phebe Wills.   Trespass

1	Wm Burns	7	John Hardin
2	Rob't Gordon	8	John Jordan
3	Rob't Adams	9	John Venable
4	John Ross	10	Rich'd Venable
5	Robert Ferguson	11	John Barber
6	Hance McWhorter	12	John Wilson

Jury Impannelled & sworn find two of them absent themselves (to wit) Wm Burns & Robt Gordon.

Ordered by the Court that William Burns & Robert Gordon be find 10/ Each for their contempt in absenting themselves being jurors in the tryal between our Sovereign Lord the King and Phebe Wills. Fine remitted.

April term 1770

A Deed of Sale from John McKnitt Alex'r to Sam'l Sharp dated the 27th of May 1768 for 200 acres proved by William Sharp Evidence thereto. Ordered to be Registered.

A Deed of Sale from John Sharp to Daniel McCartney dated the 1st day of December 1769 for 200 acres of Land proved by William Sharp Evidence thereto. Ordered to be Registered.

A Deed of Sale from John Harden to William Johnston for 200 acres of Land dated the 26th of April 1770 ack'd in open court. Ordered to be Registered.

A Deed of Sale from Zacheus Routh to Michael Hoyle for 170 acres of Land dated the 25th of November 1769 proved by Frederick Hambright Evidence thereto. Ordered to be Registered.

A Bill of Sale from William Bryant to Jno Tagert for Sundry neat cattle, 2 horses & 2 mares, 2 feather beds & furniture, 2 large trunks, 2 iron potts and all his other household goods whatsoever proved by Robert Leeper Evidence thereto. Ordered to be Reg'd.

Ordered by the Court that Hugh Quinn, Samuel Richardson, Aaron Burlington, John Wilkie, Thos Harod, James McAfee, Robert Swann, Wm. Minter, George Duland, George Gibson, William Hillis, and John Brandon serve as Jurors to lay out a road from Richardsons Shoals on Second Broad River into Charlestown Trading Road at Wm Hillises and that they meet at Francis Adams Esqr, on Friday the first day of June, there to Qualify.

Court adjourned till tomorrow at 8 oclock. Met according to adjournment. Present Thomas Neel, Francis Adams, William Moore, Henry Holman, John Robison, Esq'rs.

John Case vs David Anderson. T. A. B.

Petty Jurors

1 David Watson		Rich'd Venable	7
2 John Wilson		John Beard	8
3 John Venable		Rob't Armstrong	9
4 James Alison[?]		Rob't Gordon	10
5 Rob't Adams		William Burns	11
6 John Jorden		Hance McWhorter	12

Jury Impannel'd & Sworn find that it was the Plaintiffs Own assault. Judg't that the Pltff take Nothing by his Writ.

James Wilson vs Alexr Lockart. Case.

The Petty Jury

1 David Watson		Rich'd Venable	7
2 John Wilson		John Beard	8
3 John Venable		Rob't Gordon	9
4 James Alison[?]		William Burns	10
5 Rob't Adams		Hance McWhorter	11
6 John Jorden		Saml Craig	12

April term 1770

Jury Impanneled & Sworn find for the Pltff and assess the damages £19 11 /6 Cost.

Wm Capshaw vs James Hughy. Case. Same Jury. Jury Impanneled & Sworn find for the plff & Assess Damages to 4/6 Costs.

Wm Brown vs Thomas Rainy. Case.

The Petty Jury

1	David Watson	Rich'd Venable	7
2	John Wilson	John Beard	8
3	John Venable	Rob't Gordon	9
4	John Watson	William Burns	10
5	Rob't Adams	Hance McWhorter	11
6	John Jorden	Saml Craig	12

Jury Impanneled & Sworn find for the Pltff and assesses the damages £10 6 4 & /6 Costs.

Stephen Jones vs Thomas Price. Case.

The Petty Jury

1	John Laughlin	Rob't Gordon	7
2	Wm Hagerty	And'w Patrick	8
3	Matt'w Porter	John Chattim[?]	9
4	Peter Kuykendal	Jos Duff	10
5	Wm Burns	Wm. Wilson	11
6	John Conner[?]	Abel Beaty	12

Jury Impanneled & Sworn. The Pltff being Called Suffered a Nonsuit.

Stephen Jones vs James Price. Case. Same Jury. Jury Impanneled & Sworn. The Plff being called Suffered a nonsuit.

Benj'a Miller vs Richard Farr. Case. Same Jury. Jury Impanneled & Sworn find for the plff & assess his Damages to £18 16 7 & /6 Costs.

Benj'a Miller vs William Farr. Case. Same Jury. Jury Impanneled & Sworn find for the plff & assess his Damages to £5 17 11 & /6 Costs.

Benja'n Miller vs James Walker. Case. Same Jury. Jury Impanneled & Sworn find for the plff & assess his Damages to £6 7 6 & /6 Costs.

On appeal of Charles McNight it is Ordered by the court that a Re-praisement had on a Certain horse taken on ex'n at the suit of Robt Swann vs Charles McNight and that Joseph Hardin & William Byars free holders & Wm. Watson Esqr. be appointed to Revalue the same according to act of assembly. Ordered that the Sheriff produce the said horse Tomorrow for the appraisers to Value the same as aforesaid.

Ordered by this Court that John Foster do Keep a Ferry at his plantation on Broad River by the mouth of Pacolet and that the same be Deemed a Publick Ferry in Complying with the act of assembly in that case made & provided.

April term 1770

A Deed of Sale from Francis Beaty to James Rolley Dated the 29th of March 1770 for 600 acres Ack'd in Open Court. Ord'd to be Reg'd.

A Deed of Sale from James McKee to Francis Beaty Dated the 1st day of Feb'y 1770 for 200 acres of Land proved by James Beaty Evidence thereto. Ordered to be Registered.

A Deed of Sale from James Tate to Francis Beaty Dated the 10th day of March 1770 for 600 acres of Land proved by James Beaty Evidence thereto. Ordered to be Registered.

A Deed of Sale from Francis Beaty & Jno Beaty to James Tate Dated the 20th day of Feb'y 1770 for 640 acres of Land proved by James Beaty Evidence thereto. Ordered to be Registered.

A Deed of Sale from Francis Beaty to James Beaty Dated the 30th of March 1770 for 318 acres of Land Ack'd in Open Court. Ordered to be Reg'd.

A Deed of Sale from James Beaty to Francis Beaty Dated the 30th March 1770 for 300 acres of Land Ack'd in Open Court. Ordered to be Reg'd.

Daniel Drawdy vs James Bridges. Case.

The Petty Jury

1	Ephraim McClean	Jacob Mony	7
2	David Neisbit	John Conner	8
3	Joseph Carrol	James Hamilton	9
4	James Price	Saml Byars	10
5	James Bryson	James Collins	11
6	James Henry	Saml Carrol	12

Jury Impanneled & Sworn find for the Pltff and assesses his damages to £1 12 6½ & /6 Cost.

James Foster vs Francis McBride. Case. Same Jury. Impanneled & Sworn find for the plff & assess his Damages to £8 17 & /6 Costs.

Thomas Potts vs Hagerty & Alcorn. Case. Same Jury. Jury Impanneled & Sworn find for the plff & assess his Damages to £7 12 9 3/4 & /6 Costs.

John Buchanon vs Robt Ferguson. Case. Same Jury. Jury Impanneled & Sworn find for the plff & assess his Damages to £10 & /6 Costs.

A Deed of Lease & Release from James Gordon & Ann his wife to James Duff Dated the 7th & 17th of June 1769 for 150 acres of Land proved by John Robinson Evidence thereto. Ordered to be Registered.

Court adjourned till Court in Course. Thos Neel, William Watson, John Robinson, Francis Adams.

North Carolina, Tryon County. Tryon Inferior Court of Pleas & Quarter Sessions begun and held the Fourth Tuesday in July AD 1770. Present Henry Holman, David Anderson, John Walker, Esquires.

A Deed of Sale from Jno Armstrong & Mary his wife Dated the 14th Feb'y 1770 for 275 acres of Land proved by Benjamin Armstrong Evidence thereto. Ordered to be Reg'd.

Court adjourned until tomorrow 11 OClock. Met according to adjournment. Present William Moore, Robert Blackburn, Jacob Casner, Esq'rs.

Ordered by the Court that David Wilkins serve as Constable for James McIntire and that he Swear in before the said James McIntire accordingly.

Ordered by the Court that Barbara Fink wife & Relict of Jacob Finck have Letters of Administration of all & singular the Goods and Chattles of the said Deceased She proposes for Security Michael Rudisal & George Fink Bound in the sum of Two hundred Pounds. accepted.

Ordered by the Court that Elijah Turner Serve as Constable for Timoth[y] Riggs Esq'r & that he swear in before the s'd Timothy Riggs Esq'r accordingly.

On petition Ordered that Robert Heaslet being a Poor Very Aged and Infirm man Lame and Disabled in both his arms & being altogether Unable to support himself by his Labour be Recommended to the Gen'l Assembly of this Province as an Object of Charity who ought to be Exempted from the payment of Taxes.

Ordered by the Court that upon Motion being made next Court & it being he appearing to have a right to the same Alexr Killion have Letters of adm'n on the Goods & Chattels of John Gready he complying with the act of assembly in that Case made & provided.

A bond from Jno Tagert, Robt Adams, Saml Rich'dson, Nath'l Clark, Jacob Coburn, Nicholas Welsh, Jno Potts, Hugh Quinn, Jno Wade, George Gibson, Jas Alcorn & James McElwean to his Excellency William Tryon for the True Collection & accounting for the Publick Taxes in the County of Tryon dated 26th July taken & ack'd in open Court.

1 Saml Richardson, Foreman.

2 Nicholas Fisher	9 David Leech
3 Aaron Burlison	10 John Scott
4 John Carnahan	11 George Potts
5 William McElmurry	12 Thomas Janes
6 Thomas Barr	13 Thomas Rainy
7 James Henderson	14 Jno Stanford
8 John Jordon	15 Ridearis Clark
	16 Benj'a Phillips
	17 Nath'l Clark

Sworn & Charged.

Court adjourned for one hour. Met according to adjournment. Present Wm. Moore, Francis Adams, John Gordon, Esq'rs.

On motion of Alexander Martin it was ordered by the Court that David Gordon have a licence to Keep an Ordinary at his now Dwelling House in Tryon he Complying with the

<u>July term 1770</u>

act of assembly in that Case made & provided. He proposes for Security James Gordon and William Watson. accepted.

A Deed of Sale from James Wilson & Unite his wife to Wm Temple Cole for 200 acres of land Dated the 26th day of June 1770 proved by John Fifer Evidence thereto. Let it be Registered.

It is Ordered by the Court that Moses Jennings an orphan boy of the age of Fourteen years be bound unto Thomas Campbell till he arrives to the age of Twenty one years & by him to be Taught the art and Mistery of a Blacksmith and to Teach or Cause to Read Write & Figure according to law and in all other things to comply with the act or assembly in that case made & provided.

A Deed of Lease & Release from Benj'a Rainy to And'w Cally Dated the 3 & Second of Jan'y 1768 for 330 acres of Land proved by Rob't Robinson Evidence thereto. Ord'd to be Registered.

A Deed of Sale from John Ramsey & Agnis his wife to Rich'd Jones Dated the 20th July 1770 for 308 acres of Land proved by Abel Beaty Evidence thereto. Ord'd to be Reg'd.

A Deed of Sale from Thomas Rainy to Sam'l Rainy Dated 6th October 1768 for _____ of Land proved by Benjamin Phillips Evidence thereto. Ord'd to be Reg'd.

A Deed of Sale from John Alex'r & Eliz'h his wife to George Louts Dated 4th of June 1770 for 400 acres of Land proved by Robert Blackburn Evidence thereto. Ord'd to be Reg'd.

A Deed of Sale from John Stanly to Boston Best Dated 7th of Sep'r 1769 for 177 acres of Land proved by Jno Low Evidence thereto. Ord'd to be Reg'd.

A Deed of Sale from William Yancey to Benj'a Turner Dated 18th of Feb'y 1770 for 100 acres of Land Ack'd in Open Court. Ord'd to be Reg'd.

A Deed of Sale from Thomas Rainy & Ann his wife to Rich'd Sadler Dated 7th of Nov'm for 177 acres of Land proved by David Leech Evidence thereto. Ord'd to be Reg'd.

A Deed of Sale from George Hafner & Ann his wife to George Loots Dated 9 of May 1770 for 400 acres of Land proved by Rob't Blackburn Evidence thereto. Ord'd to be Reg'd.

A Deed of Sale from Michael Rudisel & Catharina his wife to Jacob Baker Dated 9 of May 1770 for 400 acres of Land proved by Rob't Blackburn Evidence thereto. Ord'd to be Reg'd.

A Deed of Sale from David Leech & Prudence his wife to Rich'd Sadler Dated 25th of July 1770 for 100 acres of Land proved by Thomas Rainey Evidence thereto. Ordered to be Reg'd.

A Deed of Sale from Phillip Hinson to Ab'm Clemons Dated 14th of April 1770 for 100 acres of Land proved by Jonas Bedford Evidence thereto. Ordered to be Reg'd.

A Deed of Sale from Hance McWhorter to John Barber for 243 acres of Land Dated 25th of July 1770 Ack'd in Open Court. Ord'd to be Reg'd.

<u>July term 1770</u>

A Deed of Gift from Thomas Dickson to Benj'a Dickson dated 25th of July 1770 for 220 acres of Land. Ack'd in Open Court. Ord'd to be Reg'd.

A Deed of Sale from Wm. Glenn & Jennet his wife dated 5th Sep'r 1769 for 200 acres of Land Patrick McDavid Evidence thereto. Ordered to be Reg'd.

A Deed of Sale from Eleanor McWhorter to Thomas Draper Dated 12 of May 1770 for 150 acres of Land. Proved by Zach'a Gibbs Evidence thereto. Ord'd to be Reg'd.

A Deed of Sale from James Logan to George Gills Dated the 24th of April 1770 for 100 acres of Land. Ack'd in Open Court. Ordered to be Reg'd.

A Deed of Sale from Giles Connel to Zach'h Gibbs Dated the 23 of Decem'r 1768 for 300 acres of Land. Proved by Wm. Nevel Evidence thereto. Ordered to be Reg'd.

A Deed of Sale from John McFaddon to John Turner Dated the ___ of _____ 1770 for 300 acres of Land. Proved by Robert McMinn Evidence thereto. Ordered to be Reg'd.

A Deed of Sale from James Bridges to Wm Twitty Dated 2d of July 1770 for 375 acres of Land. Proved by Jonas Bedford Evidence thereto. Ordered to be Reg'd.

A Deed of Sale from James Cozart to George Rutledge Dated 11th of July 1770 for 300 acres of Land. Proved by James Rutledge Evidence thereto. Ordered to be Registered.

A Deed of Sale from Phillip Hinson to Jno Scott Dated 7th of August 1769 for 100 acres of Land proved by Wm. Claghorn Evidence thereto. Ordered to be Reg'd.

A Deed of Sale from Wm. Whittenberg to John Sherider Dated 10th of Feb'y 1770 for 350 acres of Land proved by Joseph Wittenberg Evidence thereto. Ordered to be Reg'd.

A Deed of Sale from James Cozart to James Logan Dated 25th of July 1770 for 200 acres of Land. Ack'd in Open Court. Ord'd to be Registered.

A Deed of Sale from Stephen Jones to John Johnston Dated 5th of July 1770 for 150 acres of Land proved by James Forsyth Evidence thereto. Ord'd to be Reg'd.

A Deed of Sale from John Kimbro to John McMichael Dated 11th of Feb'y 1769 for 200 acres of Land proved by Jno Gordon Evidence thereto. Ord'd to be Reg'd.

A Deed of Sale from James McBee to John Weedingman Dated 20th of July 1770 for 200 acres of Land Proved by Robert Luny Evidence thereto. Ord'd to be Registered.

A Deed of Sale from Alex'r McIntire & Jane his wife to Jno Lusk Dated the 23d of April 1770 for 300 acres of Land proved by George Blanton Evidence thereto. Ordered to be Registered.

A Deed of Sale from Jn'o Stanford & Sarah his wife Dated the 21st of July 1770 for 178 acres of Land ack'd in Open Court. Ord'd to be Reg'd.

A Deed of Sale from Nich's Welsh & Ekiz'th his wife to Frederick Wise Dated the 23 of July 1770 for 190 acres of Land Proved by Margaret Welsh Evidence thereto. Ord'd to be Reg'd.

July term 1770

A Deed of Sale from James Steen to John Steen Dated 20th of July 1769 for 400 acres of Land proved by Robert Loony Evid'e thereto. Ord'd to be Reg'd.

A Deed of Sale from Francis Beaty to Wm. Tate Dated 14th of June 1769 for 318 acres of Land ack'd in Open Court. Ordered to be Registered.

A Deed of Sale from Wm Wray to Lodwick Wray Dated 25th of April 1770 for 300 acres of Land Ack'd in Open Court. Ordered to be Registered.

A Deed of Sale from Edward Hogan to Jno Moore Dated 1st of Decemb'r 1768 for 200 acres of Land proved by Wm. Moore Evidence thereto. Ordered to be Reg'd.

A Deed of Gift from Ezek'l Smith to Esther Burton Dated 23d of July 1770 for Two head of horses & 16 head of Cattle proved by Saml Richardson Evidence thereto and to be Registered.

A Deed of Sale from Wm McAdou to David McAdou Dated the 23d of July 1770 for 149 acres of Land ack'd in Open Court. Ordered to be Registered.

A Deed of Gift from Ezekiel Smith to Sarah Burton for 6 head of horse Creatures & twelve head of Cattle Dated 23d of July 1770 proved by Saml Rich'dson Evidence thereto and to be Registered.

A Deed of Gift from Ezek'l Smith to Wm Bassit Dated 23d of July 1770 for 5 head of horses & 16 head of Cattle proved by Saml Richardson Evidence thereto and to be Registered.

A Deed of Gift from Ezek'l Smith to Mary Burtin for one Negro Woman named Flora & four head of horses & Fourteen of Cattle Dated 23d of July 1770 proved by Saml Richardson Evidence thereto and to be Registered.

A Deed of Sale from Thomas Brandon & Elizabeth his wife for 88 acres of Land Dated the 21st day of July 1770 prov'd by Saml Fulton Evidence thereto. ordered to be Registered.

A Deed of Sale from Alex'r Kilpatrick to Jacob Womack Dated the 10th day of Septem'r 1768 for 300 acres of Land proved by Thos. Stuart Evidence thereto. ordered to be Reg'd.

A Deed of Sale from Curtis Culwell to Saml Davison Dated the 25th day of July 1769 for 200 acres of Land proved by Benjamin Hawes Evidence thereto. ordered to be Registered.

A Deed of Sale from Curtis Culwell to Saml Davison Dated the 3d day of Aug't 1767 for 150 acres of Land proved by George Carson Evidence thereto. ordered to be Registered.

A Deed of Sale from James Bridges to Yerby Dubery Dated the 11th day of Novem'r 1769 for 150 acres proved by Wm. Saffold Evidence thereto. ord'd to be Registered.

A Deed of Sale from John Collins to Hezekiah Collins Dated the 16th day of June 1770 for 150 acres proved by Francis Adams Evidence thereto. Ordered to be Registered.

A Deed of Gift from Stephen Jones to And'w Jones Dated 5th of July for 150 acres of Land proved by James Forsyth Evidence thereto. ord'd to be Registered.

<u>July term 1770</u>

A Deed of Sale from John Barns & Rachel his wife to Barbara Barns Dated the 2d of June 1770 for 81 acres proved by Theophilus Favour Evidence thereto.

A Deed of Sale from Joseph Dolitle to Hezek'h Pigg Dated the 28th of June 1769 for 200 acres of Land proved by George Blanton Evidence thereto ordered to be Registered.

A Deed of Sale from John Fulton to James Dervin Dated the 20th July 1770 for 100 acres of land proved by Robert McCarty Evidence thereto Ordered to be Registered.

A Deed of Gift from Charles Moore to And'w Berry Dated 20 July 1770 for 300 acres of Land proved by Thomas McCulloh Evidence thereto ordered to be Registered.

A Deed of Sale from Wm Twitty to Wm. Saffold Dated the 11th day of Novem'r 1769 for 150 acres proved by Wm. Saffold Evidence thereto ordered to be Registered.

A Deed of Sale from Moses Whitly to Nich's Fisher Dated the 11th of Oct'r 1769 for 200 acres of Land proved by Wm. Yancey Evidence thereto ordered to be Registered.

A Deed of Sale from George Wright to Moses Wright Dated the 14th of July 1770 for 600 acres of Land proved by Wm. Wright Evidence thereto ord'd to be Registered.

A Deed of Sale from William Wright to Moses Wright Dated the 18th May 1770 for 600 acres of Land ack'd in open Court. Ord'd to be Registered.

A Deed of Sale from Hugh Quin to Wm Capshaw Dated the 23d of April 1770 for 300 acres of Land proved by James Capshaw Evidence thereto. ordered to be Reg'd.

A Deed of Sale from And'w McNabb to Jemima Sharp Dated the 10th of Decem'r 1769 for 100 acres of Land proved by John Barber.

The Deposition of James McIntire Relative to Certain Transactions of Jacob Money with Solomon Beson dated the 15 day of June 1770 &C. Taken in Open Court. Ordered to be Registered.

Timothy Riggs Came into court & Took the Oath by Law appointed for Qualification of Public Officers Subscribed the test Took of a Justice & Took his seat accordingly.

Court adjourned until tomorrow 8 OClock. Met according to adjournment. Present Thomas Neel, Wm. Moore, James McElwean, Esq'rs.

Phillip Hinson administrator of the Estate of Nicholas Hinson Deceased Returns an Inventory of the said Estate as well as Debts and Credits on Examination of the Disbursments there appears to be in the adm'rs hands Twenty three pounds fourteen shillings & Six pence ½ penny.

Ordered by the Court that James Brown, Jas. Hamet, John Case, John Portman, Benj'a Thomson, Joseph Kelsey, Jesse Connell, Giles Connell, Joseph Park, John Foster, Thomas Wmson, serve as Jurors to Lay out a road from Julians Mill on Broad River to Joseph Kelsys on Fair Forest & That they appear before James McElwean on the 28th day of August then & there to Qualify themselves for this their Charge.

Jane Cook adm'r of the Estate of Roger Cook Deceased Returns an Inventory of the Estate prays an Order of sale which was accordingly granted.

<u>July term 1770</u>

Thomas Carrel Came into Open Court & proved that the maim that appears in the lower part of his right Ear he received in a Quarrel with one Stephen Jones and not by the sentence or Decree of any Court of Law wherever & This is Certifyed to whom it may Concern.

Stephen Jones vs Richd Farr. Orr Att.

The Petty Jury

1	Hugh Quin	7	William Lusk
2	Wm Neely	8	Joseph Nail
3	Alex'r Wilky	9	John Steen
4	James Cook	10	Rich'd Price
5	Jn'o Hartness	11	Phillip Henson
6	Abel Beaty	12	George Cox

Jury Impanneled & Sworn find for the Pltff & assess his damages to £16 18 6 /6 Cost.

And'w Armor asse vs Saml Coburn. Case. Same Jury. Jury Impanneled & Sworn find for the plff & Assess his Damages to £6 13 4 & /6 Costs.

On appeal of John Price it was Ordered by the Court that a Repraisment be had on Four horse Creatures taken on Ex'n at the suit of said Price vs John Fondren & Wm. Watson Esqr. and Wm. Adair & Wm Bratton be appointed to Revalue the s'd Horses.

On appeal of Alex'r Lockart it was Ordered by the court that a Repraisment be had on a Certain Tract of Land Taken on Execution oat the suit of James Wilson vs said Lockart and that Robt Blackburn, Esqr., Nicholas Clay & Peter Sumy be appointed to Revalue the said Land.

James Alcorn vs James McClenahan. Same Jury. Jury Impanneled & Sworn find for the plff & Assess his Damages to £3 15 & /6 Costs.

John Tagert came into Court & produced his Excy's Commission appointing him Sheriff of the County of Tryon & Took the Oaths by law appointed for Qualification of Publick Officers Subscribed the test took [sic] of a sheriff & Ent'd on the Duty of his office.

John Potts returns an Inventory of the Sale of the Goods & Chattles of Jeremiah Potts Deceased to the amount of £336 10 11 proc'n money.

On motion of Bromfield Redley it is Ordered by the Court that Letters of administration Issue to Robert Loony of all and Singular the Goods & Chattles of Adam Loony deceased he Complying with the act of assembly in this Case made & provided. he proposes for Security John Nuckols & Patrick Moor Bound in the sum of two hundred & Fifty Pounds. accepted.

On Motion of W. Avery, Wm. Temple Coles prayed his Stray Brand Recorded (Viz) those taken up in Lord Granvilles Wastes[?] in Roan County. Granted

John Price vs John Rotton. Case.

July term 1770

The Petty Jury

1	Hugh Quin	7	Wm Nevel
2	Wm Neely	8	Jno Steen
3	Alex'r Wilky	9	Rich'd Price
4	James Cook	10	Phillip Henson
5	John Hartness	11	George Cox
6	Joseph Nail	12	John Potts

Jury Impanneled & Sworn find that the def't did assume & y't he did assume within 3 Years from the day of payment specify'd in the Settlement of the Acc'ts & Assesses the pltt's damages to £13 19 1 /6 Cost.

A Deed of Sale from Wm Twitty to Wm. Wilkins Dated the 22d of March 1769 for 200 acres proved by Patrick Moore Evidence thereto ordered to be Registered.

A Deed of Gift from Robert Wilkins to Alex'r Willkins Dated _____ for one Negro Woman named Dinah proved by Patrick Moor Evidence thereto ordered to be Registered.

A Deed of Sale from Wm Henry to Oliver Wallace for Four Hundred and Eighty Eight acres of Land dated the 26th day of July 1770 Acknowledged in Open Court. Ordered to be Registered.

Court adjourned till tomorrow 8 OClock. Met according to adjournment. Present Thomas Neel, Timothy Riggs, Jonas Bedford, Esq'rs.

On issued appeal of Matthew Troy by Waighstill Avery his attorney it was Ordered by the Court that Henry Clark Esqr., Henry Smith & Wm. McMullen be appointed to Revalue a Waggon Taken by Ex'n at the suit of Mathew Troy vs Matthew Floyd.

On issued appeal of Wm Gillespy it was Ordered by the Court that a Repraisement be had on a Certain Tract of Land taken by Ex'n at the suit of said Gillespy vs Jacob Gardner & that Francis Adams Esqr., Francis Ross & Robert Swann be appointed to Revalue the same Land.

Nicholas Welsh Ex'r of the Estate of John Welsh Deceased Returns an acount the Estate as well as Debts, Credit & uppon Examination of the Disbursements there appears to be in the hands of the Ex'r £38 18 8.

Ordered by the Court that James Young be appointed Overseer of the Road Leading from Armors ford to Charlestown (that part between Widow Shaw & John Gordons) & That he summon all the adjacent Tithables to attend & keep in repair the said Road.

On Motion of James Forsyth it is ordered by the Court that Hugh Quin, John Stanford, John Logan, George Gibson, George Julian, William Yancey, George Blanton, James Forsyth, Nath'l Clark, Joseph Nale, John Smith, John Harkness Serve as Jurors to Lay out a road from Hugh Quins ford on Buffelo the Nearest & best way to Julians Mill from thence to George Gibsons on Bullocks Creek from thence the nearest & best way unto Charlestown Trading Road & that they appear before George Blanton Esqr the 28 day of August then & there to take the Necessary steps to Qualify them for their Charge.

July term 1770

Ordered by the Court that John Patton, Saml Watson, Joseph Hardin, Joseph Carrol, Henry Clark & John Fondling serve as Venire men & that they appear at Salsbury on the Fifth day of September next then & there serve Our Sovereign Lord the King as Grand or Petit Jurors.

Jno Nuckols, Thos Clark, Wm. Reed, and Wm. Yancey Came into Court & took the Oath by Law appointed for Qualification of Publick officers subscribed the test & took the oath of an under Sheriff & took their places accordingly.

John Stair vs Matt'w Floyd. Trover.

The Petty Jury

1	Ephraim McClean	7	Nich's Welsh
2	James Henry	8	Patrick Moore
3	X'r Coleman	9	James Bryson
4	Giles Connel	10	Alex'r Wilky
5	Rich'd Price	11	Zach'h Gibbs
6	David Porter	12	Joseph Nale

Jury Impanneled & Sworn find for the Pltff & assess his damages to £3 Proc'n & /6.

Ordered by the Court that James Alexander adm'r of the Estate of John Armstrong Deceased be summoned to appear at our Next Court to Give an acount upon Oath what pat of the Estate he has in his hands.

Ab'm Bogard vs Rich'd Price. Case.

The Petty Jury

1	Ephraim McClean	7	Pat'k Moore
2	Ja's Henry	8	James Bryson
3	X'r Coleman	9	Alex'r Wilky
4	Giles Connel	10	Zach'h Gibbs
5	David Porter	11	Joseph Nale
6	Nich's Welsh	12	Dan'l McCleary

Jury Impanneled & Sworn find the Def't not Guilty.

Ordered by the Court that Nicholas Fisher have Letters of Administration of all & Singular the Goods & Chattles of John Graydy Deceased he Complying with the act of assembly in that Case made & provided he proposes for security Wm. Yancey, John Stanford, & Joseph Neel bound in the sum of Two hundred pounds. accepted.

George Cox vs Zach'h Gibbs. Case.

The Petty Jury

1	Ephraim McClean	7	Pat'k Moore
2	Ja's Henry	8	James Bryson
3	Benj'a Rice	9	Alex'r Wilky
4	Robert Swann	10	Joseph Nale
5	Rich'd Price	11	Daniel McCleary
6	Nich's Welsh	12	Wm Hagerty

<u>July term 1770</u>

Jury Impanneled & Sworn find the Def't not Guilty.

A Deed of Sale from James Howard to Thos Wade for 250 acres of Land Dated the 16th of May 1770 proved by Jno Nuckoles Evidence thereto. ordered to be Registered.

A Deed of Sale from Rob't Abernathy to Wm Moore Dated the 13th day of July 1770 for 102 acres of Land proved by David Alex'r Evidence thereto. ord'd to be Registered.

A Deed of Sale from Thomas Rainy to Rob't Robison Dated the 15th of November 1769 for 50 acres of Land Ack'd in Open Court. Ord'd to be Registered.

Court adjourned till tomorrow 8 OClock. Met according to adjournment. Present Thomas Neel, Francis Adams, William Watson, Esq'rs.

Moses Alexander vs John Woods. Case.
The Petty Jury

1	Wm. Nevel	7	Wm. Neely
2	Sam'l Wilcox	8	Wm. Gillespy
3	Thomas Rainey	9	Wm. Hagerty
4	John Patton	10	Jno Bryson
5	James Bryson	11	James Moore
6	Rich'd Price	12	Benj'a Rice

Jury Impanneled & Sworn find for the Plff & asses his Damages to £13 6 3/4 & /6 Costs.

Moses Alexander vs John Woods. Case.

The Petty Jury

1	Wm. Nevel	7	Wm. Hagerty
2	Sam'l Wilcox	8	John Bryson
3	Tho's Rainey	9	Robert Burns
4	John Patton	10	Wm. Neely
5	James Bryson	11	Isaac Wilcox
6	Rich'd Price	12	Jas Hamilton

Jury Impanneled & Sworn find for the Plff & asses his Damages to £5 & /6 Costs.

Stephen Jones vs James Farr. Case.

The Petty Jury

1	Wm. Nevel	7	Wm. Hagerty
2	Sam'l Wilcox	8	John Bryson
3	Tho's Rainey	9	Robert Burns
4	John Patton	10	Ludwick Ray
5	James Bryson	11	Isaac Wilcox
6	Wm. Gillespy	12	John Chambers

Jury Impanneled & Sworn find for the Plff & asses his Damages to £10 & /6 Costs.

July term 1770

Ordered by the court that there be a Constable appointed in Every Capt's District in Tryon County to Summon & Make Return to their Respective Magistrates of all & Every the Taxable in their Respective Districts to which they are appointed before October Court.

Ordered by the Court that John Hall Serve as Constable in Capt. Saml Watsons District & The he swear in before Wm. Watson Esqr. accordingly.

Ordered by the Court that Robt Swann be appointed Constable for Capt. McCleans District & The he swear in before Wm. Watson Esqr.

Ordered by the Court that Adam Goudelock Be appointed Constable for Capt. Earls District & The he swear in before James McElwean Esqr.

Ordered by the Court that Verdery Magby be appointed Constable for Capt. Earls District & That he swear in before George Blanton Esqr.

North Carolina, Tryon County to wit. July Court 1770. Present his Majestys Justices. Then were the Ordinary keeper Prices rated as Follows. That is to say.

Lodging in a Good feather Bed & Clean Sheets P'r Night	£ 0	0	4
Breakfast & Supper Each	0	0	8
Every dinner not Less than 2 dishes of Good Meat	0	1	0
Madeira & Port wine P'r Quart	0	3	0
Claret wine P'r Quart	0	4	0
Punch with Loaf Sugar & West India Rum Pr Qu't	0	1	6
Tody with Loaf Sugar & West India Rum P'r Quart	0	1	4
Tody with Loaf Sugar & New Engl'd Rum P'r Quart	0	0	8
Brandy & Whisky Toddy P'r Quart	0	0	4
Beer P'r Quart	0	0	6
Cider P'r Quarter	0	0	6
W. India Rum P'r ½ pint	0	0	10
New England Rum P'r ½ pint	0	0	6
Brandy or Whisky P'r ½ pint	0	0	6
Pasturage for every horse or mare for 24 hours	0	0	4
Stabling for Every night w't hay or fodder for Every Horse or Mare	0	1	0

Court adjourned till Court in Course. Thomas Neel, Wm. Watson, Francis Adams.

North Carolina, Tryon County. Tryon Inferior Court of Pleas and Quarter Sessions Begun and held for Said County The Fourth Tuesday in Oct'r AD 1770. Present Thomas Neel, William Watson, John Gordon, John Robinson, Henry Holman, Esq'rs.

Ordered that Joseph Bradner and James Campbel have Letters Testamentary of all and Singular the Goods and Chattles right and Credits of John McCormack Deceased They complying with the act of assembly in that case made and Provided.

On motion of James Forsyth it is ordered by the Court that William Tate have an order to build a Publick Grist Mill on his land on Cherokee Creek and that the same be Deemed a Publick Mill he complying with the act of assembly in that case made and Provided.

October term 1770

Ordered that William Smith, John Workman, John Anderson, William Neely, Robert Robertson, Alex'r Love, James Miskelly, Hugh Neely, James Armstrong, And'w Love, James McNabb, Robert McClellen Serve as Jurors to Lay out a road from The Temporary Line between So & No Carolina nigh Whites Mill on Fishing Creek from thence to Jas Wallace, thence to the Ridge Road Leading from Kings Mountain to William Brattons at a Noted JS and on s'd Road, W of Capt Alex'r Loves Dwelling and that they appear before John Gordon the 27 day of November then and there to take the Necessary steps to Qualify them for their Charge.

A Deed of Lease and Release from Derick Ramsour to Bostain Cline Jun'r Dated the 26th and 27th days of September 1770 for 200 acres of Land proved by Jacob Ramsour Evidence thereto. Ordered to be Registered.

A Deed of Sale from Robert Collinwood & Elizabeth his wife to Peter Aker Dated the 1st day of Aug't 1770 for 300 acres of Land proved by Benjamin Hardin Evidence thereto. Ordered to be Registered.

A Deed of Sale from Zachariah Bullock to George Cowan Dated the 15th day of March 1770 for 300 acres of Land ack'd in open Court. Ordered to be Registered.

A Deed of Sale from Robert Swan & Martha his wife to Matthew Cowen Dated the 16th day of February 1770 for 200 acres of Land proved by And'w Cowen Evidence thereto. Ordered to be Registered.

A Deed of Sale from Michael Hyel to Joseph Schell Dated the 22d day of September 1770 for 200 acres of Land proved by Peter Carpenter Evidence thereto. Ordered to be Registered.

A Deed of Sale from William Davies & Mary Davis to And'w Cowan Dated the 22d day of October 1770 for 150 acres of Land proved by Matthew Cowan Evidence thereto. Ordered to be Registered.

A Deed of Sale from Israel Peterson to And'w Peterson Dated the 11th day of October 1770 for 250 acres of Land ack'd in open Court. Ordered to be Registered.

A Deed of Sale from John Sartain to Zach'h Bullock Dated the 18th day of October 1770 for 200 acres of Land Proved by James Collins Evidence thereto. Ordered to be Registered.

A Deed of Lease & Release from Derrick Ramsour to Jacob Carpenter for 200 acres of Land Dated the 26th & 27th day of Sept'r 1770 Jacob Ramsour Evidence thereto. Ordered to be Registered.

Court adjourned until tomorrow 9 OClock. Met according to adjournment. Present Thomas Neel, William Watson, Henry Holman, John Robinson, Esq'rs.

The Grand Jury: Alexander Love, foreman

2 Thomas Bratton	10 James McAfee
3 And'w McNabb	11 And'w Hampton
4 Christ'r Carpenter	12 Henry Vernor
5 Solomon Beason	13 Phillip Henson
6 Joseph Nale	14 Newbery Stocton
7 George Julian	15 James Capshaw

October term 1770

8 Benjam'n Harden	16 John Laughlin
9 James Collins	17 Math'w Cowan

Sworn and charged.

Ordered that William Gilbert have a Licence to Keep an Ordinary at his Dwelling house in Tryon County he complying with the act of assembly in that case made and Provided. He proposes for Securitys James Cook & Lodowick Ray. accepted.

Samuel Watson and Margaret Shaw adm'rs of the Estate of Robert Shaw Deceased Returns an Inventory of the said Estate and upon Examination of the Disbursements there appears to be in the hands of the Adm'rs the sum of £100 18 2, /3 of which is y'e Property of y'e Widow the remaining to be Divided among 7 Legatees.

Ordered by the Court that the Road Leading from Robt. Leepars Mill to Jno Gordons Esqr be Take of at the West side of Alisons Creek and that Saml Watson, Robt McDowel, James Young, Jas. Armstrong, James Simrel, John Berry, John Anderson, John Dunkan, John Young, John Hall, Arch'd Barren be appointed Jurors to lay out the s'd road the nearest and best way to the upper Road leading from the Tucasege ford to said Gordon and y't they appear before Wm Watson the 3 Day of December the Qualify themselves for this their Charge.

Ordered by the Court that the Jurors formerly appointed to Lay out a road from Robt Lepars Mill to Landes Ford on the Cataba River do make a second review of s'd Road & Rectify if possible former Disputes.

On Motion of John Dunn it was ordered that Margaret Hanna wife and relick of Wm. Hanna deceased have Letters of Administration of all and singular the Goods and Chattles rights and Credits of the said Deceased. She proposes for securitys John Hardin, Benja Hardin & John McIntire bound in the sum of Two hundred pounds. accepted.

On Motion of John Dunn it was ordered that Margaret Willis wife and relick of Henry Willis deceased have Letters of Administration of all and singular the Goods and Chattles rights and Credits of the said Deceased. She proposes for securitys John Hardin, Benja Hardin & John McIntire bound in the sum of Two hundred pounds. accepted.

On Motion of John Dunn it was ordered that Sarah Shearer wife and relick of Matt'w Shearer deceased have Letters of Administration of all and singular the Goods and Chattles rights and Credits of the said Deceased. She proposes for securitys Lewis Witiner & Christopher Carpenter bound in the sum of One hundred pounds. accepted.

A Deed of Sale from John Fondron to James Hanna Dated the 6th day of Oct'r 1770 for 300 acres of Land proved by John Gordon Evidence thereto. Ordered to be Registered.

A Deed of Sale from James Fanning to Joseph England Dated the 12th day of March 1770 for 300 acres of Land proved by John McMichael Evidence thereto. Ordered to be Registered.

A Deed of Sale from George Rutledge to his son James Rutledge Dated the 22d day of October 1770 for 300 acres of Land proved by Wm. Moore Evidence thereto. Ordered to be Registered.

October term 1770

A Deed of Sale from John Patton to Joseph Smith for 200 acres of land Dated the 25th day of Oc'r 1770 proved by Rich'd Berry Evidence thereto. Ordered to be Registered.

A Deed of Sale from James Young to Peter Kuykendal Dated the 2d day of June 1768 for 150 acres of Land ack'd in open Court. Ordered to be Registered.

A Deed of Sale from Saml Coburn & Marg't his wife to James Coburn Dated the 28th day of Sept 1770 for 400 acres of Land proved by William Moore Evidence thereto. Ordered to be Registered.

A Deed of Sale from John Conner to Hugh Quinn Dated the 8th day of August 1770 for 200 acres of Land proved by Peter Quinn Evidence thereto. Ord'd to be Registered.

A Deed of Sale from Michael Mastin [Master?] & Marg't his wife to Peter Lineberger Dated the ____ day of ___ 1770 for 300 acres of Land proved by Henry Mastin [Master?] Evidence thereto. Ordered to be Registered.

A Deed of Sale from And'w Heslip to John Heslip Dated the 11th day of Sep'r 1770 for 390 acres of Land proved by And'w Hampton Evidence thereto. Ord'd to be Registered.

Court adjourned until tomorrow 8 OClock. Met according to adjournment. Present Thomas Neel, William Moore, Francis Adams, Jonas Bedford, Esq'rs.

Ordered by the Court Margaret Willis wife & relick of Henry Willis deceased have an order of Sale for all and singular the Perishable part of the said Estate and that she Return and Inventory of the said sale to our next Court.

Ordered by the Court that George Parris Serve as Overseer of the Road Leading from Pullams Mill to Joseph Kelsys (that part between said Mill and Buck Creek) and that he Enter on his Charge accordingly.

Ordered by the Court that Edward Roberts Serve as Overseer of the Road Leading from Pullams Mill to Fair Forest (that part between Buck Creek & Boaring Shoals on Pacolet) and that he Enter on his Charge accordingly.

Ordered by the Court that Wm. Wofford Serve as Overseer of the Road Leading from Pullams Mill to Joseph Kelso's (that part between the Boaring Shoals and Woffords Mill on Lawsons Fork) and that he Enter on his Charge accordingly.

Ordered by the Court that James Mays Serve as Overseer of the Road Leading from Pullams Mill to Joseph Kelso's (that part between Woffords Mill and Joseph Kelso's) and that he Enter on his Charge accordingly.

Nicholas Fisher administrator of the Estate of John Grady Deceased Returns an Inventory the s'd Estate Prayed an order of sale which was accordingly granted.

Rich'd Jones vs Phillip Henson. Case.

The Petty Jury

1 Robert Loony	7 Rob't Gordon
2 Wm Lusk	8 James McCord
3 Benj'a Rice	9 Gilbert Watson

October term 1770

4	Sam'l Gray	10	John Hampton
5	John Potts	11	Wm Aken
6	Robert Robertson	12	James Moore

Jury Impanneled & Sworn the Plaintiff being solemnly Called failed to prosecute and Suffered a Non pross.

Charles Purvians[?] vs Richd & Wm. Farr. Case. Same Jury. Jury Impanneled & sworn find for the Plff and assess his Damages to £11 2 8 and /6 Costs.

A Deed of Sale from Jas Woods to Hugh Quinn Dated the 19th of Feb'y 1770 for 400 acres of Land ack'd in open Court. ordered to be Registered.

Rich'd Price vs Ab'm Bogard. Case.

The Petty Jury

1	Robert Loony	7	James McCord
2	Wm Lusk	8	John Lewis
3	Benj'a Rice	9	Gilbert Watson
4	John Potts	10	John Hampton
5	Robert Robertson	11	James Moore
6	Robert Gordon	12	Nicholas Fisher

Jury Impanneled & sworn find for the Plff and assess his Damages to £10 16 and /6 Costs.

Gasper Clute vs George Pariss. Case. Same Jury. Jury Impanneled & sworn find for the Plff and assess his Damages to £-- 1d and /6 Costs.

Nicholas Fisher vs John Conner. Case.

The Petty Jury

1	Robert Loony	7	James McCord
2	Wm Lusk	8	John Lewis
3	Benj'a Rice	9	Gilbert Watson
4	John Potts	10	John Hampton
5	Robert Robinson	11	James Moore
6	Robert Gordon	12	John Davison

Jury Impanneled & Sworn find for the Plff and assess his Damages to £6 9 & /6 Costs.

Francis Beaty vs John Elder. Case. Same Jury. Jury Impanneled & sworn find for the Plff and assess his Damages to £8 12 10 & /6 Costs.

Francis Adams vs Henry Turner. Case. Same Jury. Jury Impanneled & sworn find for the Plff and assess his Damages to £4 3 4 & /6 Costs.

Preston Hampton vs Alex'r Coulter. Case.

The Petty Jury

1	Robert Loony	7	James McCord

October term 1770

2 Wm Lusk	8 John Lewis
3 Benj'a Rice	9 Gilbert Watson
4 John Potts	10 James Moore
5 Robert Roberson	11 John Davason
6 Robert Gordon	12 John Armstrong

Jury Impanneled & Sworn find for the Plff and assess his Damages to £5 & /6 Costs.

A Deed of Sale from Simon Kuykendall to Benjamin Kuykendall Dated y'e 16th day of August 1770 for 285 acres of Land proved by Peter Johnston Evidence thereto. Ordered to be Registered.

A Deed of Sale from Simon Kuykendall to Joseph Kuykendall Dated the 16th of August 1770 for 285 acres of Land proved by Peter Johnston Evidence thereto. Ordered to be Registered.

A Deed of Sale from [John Miller and] Jane his wife to William Williamson Dated the 18th of August 1770 for 200 acres of Land proved by Peter Johnston Evidence thereto. Ordered to be Registered.

A Deed of Sale from John Baum to Jacob Whitner Dated the 17th of Aug't 1764 for 400 acres of Land proved by Joshua Bradley Evidence thereto. Ordered to be Registered.

A Deed of Sale from William Sharp to Thos Sharp for 308 acres ack'd in Open Court. Ordered to be Registered.

A Deed of Sale from James Henderson to James McElroy Dated the 7th of Feb'y 1764 for 200 acres of Land proved by William Wofford Evidence thereto. Ordered to be Registered.

A Deed of Sale from Jacob Widener to David Robinson Dated the 15th of Oct'r 1770 for 400 acres of Land ack'd in Open Court. Ordered to be Registered.

A Deed of Sale from Thomas Lovelady to Marshal Lovelady for 200 acres of Land Dated the 9th of June 1770 proved by Jno Nuckols Evidence thereto. Ordered to be Registered.

A Deed of Sale from Arch'd Robinson & Sarah his wife to Wm. Robinson Dated the 22d day of Jan'y 1770 for 450 acres of Land proved by James Wilson Evidence thereto. Ordered to be Registered.

A Deed of Sale from James Woods to John Wood Dated the 23d day of January 1770 for 400 acres of Land proved by John Walker Jun'r Evidence thereto. Ordered to be Registered.

A Deed of Sale from Peter Howard to John Wade Dated the 22d day of March 1770 for ___ acres of Land proved by Zach'h Bullock Evidence thereto. Ordered to be Registered.

A Deed of Sale from John Sloan to Thomas Henry Dated the 28th day of Feb'y 1770 for 150 acres of Land proved by James Henderson Evidence thereto. Ordered to be Registered.

Court adjourned for half an hour. Met according to adjournment. Present John Robinson, Jonas Bedford, John Retzhoupt, Esq'rs.

October term 1770

Robert Loony administrator of the Estate of Adam Loony Deceased Returns an Inventory of the Estate Prays an Order of Sale which was accordingly granted.

John Tagert Came into open Court Five Justices being Present to witt Thomas Neel, William Moore, William Watson, John Robinson & John Retzhoupt and Produced his account of the County Tax, for the year 1769 in order to Settle the Same which was allowed & approve of by the Court which is as follows viz.

John Tagert To Tryon County Dr. to 1274 Taxables for y'e year 1769

at 3/2 Each	£202	14 4
Total C'r	143	7 8
Ballance Due £ 58	6 8	

Contra C'r by

274 Insolvents and Runaways	£ 43	7 8
by Ezek'l Polk	10	
by Peter Johnston	7 10	
by Jno Robinson	2 5	6
by Jas Henry	2 5	6
by Cha's McClean	2 11	10
by Henry Clark	2 12	10
by a Charter & Interest	22 12	
by Jno Tagert	10	
by Chas McClean	5	
by Francis Ross	8	
by Cash Paid	19 2	4
by Comm'ns @ 8 P'r Cent	8	
Total	£143 7 8	

Laid over to next Court, the Collectors not being Able to make a Settlement as the Law Directs.

Jno Tagert high Sheriff abovesaid came into open Court & made oath that the Number 274 of said Taxables which he the s'd Sheriff Excepted against, he Judges to be absconded out of said County or insolvent and that the above account as it stands stated is Just and true which s'd account so stated and Proved the abovesaid Justices of said Court allow and Judges to be a Just and true Settlement of the said Sheriff with the said County for the year aforesaid.

A Deed of Sale from William Whaly to Wm. Stuart Dated the 1st July 1770 for ___ acres of Land proved by Thomas Neel Evidence thereto. Ordered to be Registered.

A Deed of Sale from Francis Adams to Henry Turner Dated the 26th of July 1770 for 400 acres of Land ack'd in open Court. ord'd to be Registered.

Court adjourned until tomorrow 9 OClock. Met according to adjournment. Present Thomas Neel, Wm Moore, William Watson, Jno Robinson, John Retzhoupt, Esq'rs.

A Deed of Sale from Richard Bullock and Mary his wife to Joseph Neel Dated the 7th day of August 1770 for 150 acres of Land proved by Thomas Neel Evidence thereto. Ordered to be Registered.

October term 1770

Ordered by the Court that George Julian Serve as Overseer of the Road Leading from Quinns ford on Buffelo in to Chas Town Trading Road by Wm. Hillises (that part Between

Quinns ford on Buffelo to Julians upper Mill ford) and that he proceed thereon accordingly.

Thomas Brandon from Julians Mill ford on Kings Creek to George Gibsons ford on Bullocks Creek

William McDow from George Gibsons ford on Bullocks Creek to Hillises ford on Turkey Creek.

John Hillis from the said Hillises ford on Turky Creek into the Charlestown trading Road at the South Carolina Line.

	£	S	D
October Term Claims on the Cou'y of Tryon for the year 1770			
To Robert Leepar one Venire Ticket	1	13	6
To James Moore one Do	1	17	6
To Peter Kuykendall one Do	1	17	6
To Joseph Carrol one Do	1	13	6
To Henry Clark one Do	2	10	6
To Joseph Carrol one Do	2	8	6
To John Fondron one Do	2	9	10
To John Collins 1 Wolf Scalp		7	6
To John Collins 2 Do		7	6
To Anthony Metcalf 3 Panther Scalps	1	2	6
To Wm. Adams 2 Wolf Scalps		15	
To George Trout 1 Wolfe Scalp		7	6
To Ditto 1 Panther Scalp		7	6
To Joseph England 1 Wolfe Scalp		7	6
To John Hardin 5 Wolfe Scalps	1	17	6
To Benj'a Hardin 1 Do		7	6
To Jas Paterson 1 Panther Scalp		7	6
To Thomas Williamson 4 Wolf Scalps	1	10	
To John Morris 1 Wolf Scalp		7	6
To John Linn 2 Panther Scalps		15	
To John Linn 2 Panther Scalps		15	
For Books Prescribed by Law	12	10	
To the Sheriff for Extra Services		10	
To the Clerk for		8	
To Charles McClean for the Courthouse		10	
Rent 4 Courts			
	64	13	4.

It appears by the above Claims that the county of Tryon Stands D'r the Sum of Sixty four Pounds Thirteen & Four Pence Proclamation money for the year one Thousand Seven Hundred and Seventy.

The Lists of Taxables being brought in and Calcullated it appears that the Number of Taxables in the County of Tryon amounts to one Thousand Six hundred and Fourteen. It is ordered by the Court that a Tax of Two Shillings & Eleven pence be Levied of Each and

Every Taxable Person within the said County of Tryon to Discharge the aforesaid Sum and that Laid by act of assembly (To wit 2).

Court adjourned till Court in Course. Thos Neel, William Watson, John Robinson.

Memorandum, A List of Letters of Adm'n & Testamentary Returned by T. P.

North Carolina, Tryon County. Tryon Inferior Court of Pleas and Quarter Sessions Begun and held The fourth Tuesday of January AD 1771. Present Willm Watson, Jno Robinson, John Walker, Timothy Riggs, Esq'rs.

Ord'd by the Court that Thomas Young Serve as Constable in the Room of John Kendrick and that he Swear in before Henry Clark Esq'r accordingly.

Ordered by the Court that James McCormack an orphan boy of the age of Eleven years be bound to John Harris till he arrives to the age of Twenty one and by him to Taught the art Trade or Mistery of a Cooper and to Teach or Cause to be taught the said Jas' McCormack in Reading & Writing agreeable to Law and to Give the said apprentice at his freedom Five pounds proc'n money besides what the Law allows and in all other things to comply with the act of assembly in that case made and provided.

Ordered by the Court that John Guffy Serve as Constable in the Room of John Witherow and that he Swear in before John Walker Esq'r.

Ordered by the Court that Alex'r McCarter Serve as Constable for David Anderson and that he Swear in before the said David Anderson Esq'r accordingly.

Ordered by the Court that Urban Whitenener Serve as Constable in the room of Peter Sumy and that he Swear in before Robert Blackburn Esq'r accordingly.

Ordered by the Court that John Slame[?] Serve as Constable in the room of Martin Shutts and that he Swear in before Henry Holman Esq'r accordingly.

Ordered by the Court that James Milligan Serve as Constable in the room of Geo Reese and that he Swear in before John Retzhoupt Esq'r accordingly.

Ord'd by the court that William Bridges serve as overseer of the Road leading from Stephen Howards mill to Charlestown that part lying between said Mill and Cain Creek and that he enter on his Charge accordingly.

Aaron Moore from Cain Creek to Grassy Branch.

William Willis from Grassy Branch to John Carsons.

Ordered by the Court that John Willson serve as Constable in the Room of Hugh Pess[?] and that he Swear in before Wm. Watson Esq'r accordingly.

Ordered by the Court that Dan'l Worlock, Fred'k Wise, Phillip Wisenant, Moses Moore, Thomas Black, Henry Renolds, John Renolds, George Trout, Michael Hofstatler, Nicholas Wisenant, Solomon Beson & Adam Wisenant serve as Jurors to lay out a road from Dan'l Worlocks Mill the nighest and best way to Gap of Kings Mountain where the waggon Road now Crosses and they appear before Timothy Rigs Esq'r on the Fourth Tuesday in Feb'y then and there to take the Necessary Steps to Qualify them to proceed on this their Charge.

January term 1771

Francis Prince Came into Court & produced his Excellency's Commission appointing Lieut. in the Tryon Reg't of Militia whereof Thos Neel Esq'r is Colonel & Took the oaths of State & Took the Test.

A Deed of Sale from Jno McKnit Alex'r to David Reed Dated the 25 of July 1769 for 100 [acres] of Land proved by Garret Morris Evidence thereto. ordered to be Registered.

A Deed of Lease and Release from Sam'l & Lyddy Kennon to William Lee Dated the 21st of Ap'l 1769 for 240 acres of Land proved by Michael Lee Evidence thereto. Ord'd to be Reg'd.

A Deed of Sale from Jno McKnit Alex'r to Francis Traverse Dated the 25th of July 1769 for 150 acres proved by Garret Morris Evidence thereto. ord'd to be Registered.

A Deed of Sale from Dan'l Plummer & Mary his wife to Rainy Belue Dated the 13th Decem'r 1769 for 200 acres of Land proved by Joseph Breed Evidence thereto. Ordered to be Registered.

A Deed of Sale from John Thompson to Alex'r Campbell Dated 22d Janr'y 1770 for 400 acres of Land Ack'd in Open Court. ordered to be Registered.

A Deed of Sale from Dan'l Plummer & Mary his wife to Joseph Breed Dated 13th Dec'r 1769 for 100 acres of Land proved by Rainey Belue Evidence thereto. Ord'd to be Reg'd.

A Deed of Lease and Release from Joseph White to Matt'w Harper Dated 15th Oc'r 1770 for 640 acres of Land proved by Rob't Harper Evidence thereto. Ord'd to be Reg'd.

A Deed of Sale from Francis Price Senr to Francis Prince Jun'r Dated 21st Day of Jan'ry 1771 for 256 acres of Land proved by Joseph Jones Evidence thereto. Ordered to be Registered.

A Deed of Gift from Geo. Bound to Francis Price & Sarah his wife Dated 21st Day of Jan'ry 1771 for 3 Slaves to witt Hannah, Ben and a mullato named Jane proved by Joseph Jones Evid'ce thereto. Ord'd to be Registered.

A Deed of Quit Claim from Martin Armstrong to Peter Kuykendal of 200 acres of Land dated the 2d day of Jan'y 1771 proved by Timothy Riggs Esq'r Evidence thereto ord'd to be Reg'd.

A Deed of Sale from Rob't Humphries to Ab'm Kuykendal Dated 11th of Oc'r 1770 for 333 acres of Land proved by Timothy Riggs Evidence thereto. Ord'd to be Reg'd.

A Deed of Sale from David Huddleston to Wm Smart Dated 22d of Jan'y 1771 for 240 acres of Land ack'd in open Court. Ord'd to be Reg'd.

A Deed of Sale from Moses McCarter to Wm. Bolding Dated 22d of Decem'r 1770 for 257 acres of Land proved by Alex'r Harper Evidence thereto. Ord'd to be Reg'd.

A Deed of Sale from John Sloan to John Bennett Dated the 9th of June 1770 for 134 acres of Land proved by Dan'l McCarty Evd'e thereto. Ord'd to be Reg'd.

January term 1771

A Deed of Lease & Release from Wm. Wilson & Jane his wife to Nath'l Jefferies Dated the 7th of Aug't 1770 for 600 acres of Land proved by Wm. Steen Evidence thereto. Ord'd to be Reg'd.

A Deed of Lease & Release from Andrew Woods & Martha his wife to Ja's Stafford & Dunn Alex'r Dated the 19th of Sep'r 1770 for 400 acres of Land proved by Garret Wilson Steen Evidence thereto. Ord'd to be Reg'd.

Court adjourned until tomorrow 9 OClock. Met according to adjournment. Present Timothy Riggs, Jonas Bedford, Jacob Cosner, Esq'rs.

Ordered by the Court that Nicholas Shram Serve as Constable in the room of Jacob Carpenter and that he Swear in before Jacob Casner Esq'r accordingly.

Nicholas Fisher Returns an Inventory of the Sale of John Gradeys Estate to the amount of Eighty three pounds & seventeen shillings & four pence ordered to be put on record.

Ordered by the Court that William Marteberry and Thomas Stuart Serve as Constables in the room of Wm. Shepherd and that they Swear in before Jonas Bedford Esq'r.

Ordered by the Court that Verderey Magby Serve as Constable in the room of Adam Goudelock and that he Swear in before Henry Clarke Esq'r.

Ordered by the Court that Jacob Randal Serve as Constable in the room of Ja's Ervin and that he Swear in before Francis Adams Esq'r.

On Motion of Waightstill Avery it was or'd by the Court that George Sizemore have Letters of Administration of all and sing'r the Goods & Chattles rights and Credits of William Shepherd Deceased he complying with the act of assembly in that case made & provided. He proposes for securities John Walker Esq'r and Joseph Green. accepted.

Or'd by the Court that Ezek'l Potts have Letters Testamentary of all and singular the Goods & Chattles rights and Credits of John Potts Deceased he as executor complying with the act of assembly in that case made & provided he having taken the oath of an Executor.

The Grand Jury: Robert Adams, foreman

2 John Howe	
3 John Beard Jun'r	10 Wm. Howe
4 Tho's Clark	11 George Denny
5 Thomas Patton	12 John Venables
6 Peregrine Magnis	13 Wm. Henry
7 Wm. Stephenson	14 Ja's Henry
8 James Moore	15 Hugh Shannon
9 James Collins	16 And'w Cammel
	17 Moses Moore

Sworn and charged.

Ordered by the Court that Paul Wisenant Serve as Constable in the room of George Dack[?] and that he Swear in before Wm. Moore Esq'r.

Ordered by the Court that Hugh Shannon Serve as Constable in the room of Alex'r Robinson and that he Swear in before John Robinson Esq'r accordingly.

January term 1771

Ordered by the Court that John Moore Serve as Constable for Timothy Riggs, Esq'r Alex'r Robinson and that he Swear in before Timothy Riggs.

Sarah Shearer adm'r of the Estate of Matt'w Shearer Deceased Returns an Inventory of the said Estate pray'd an order of Sale which was accordingly Granted.

Margaret Hanna adm'r of the Estate of Wm. Hanna Deceased Returns an Inventory of the Sale of said Estate to the amount of £33 6 10.

Margaret Hanna Returns an Inventory of the other part of said Estate and prays an order of Sale which was accordingly Granted.

Margaret Willis Returns an Account of the Sale of the Estate of Henry Willis Deceased to the amount of £141 6.

Margaret Willis, ad'r of the Estate of Henry Willis Deceased, Returns an Inventory of the remainder of said Estate pray'd an order of Sale which was accordingly Granted.

Ordered by the Court that William Ratchford Serve as Overseer of the road leading from Kings Mountain to Charles Town (that part thereof between Michael Megaritys and James McNabbs) and that he summons the adjacent Tithables upon proper occasion to keep said Road in Repair.

Ordered by the Court that Wm Bratton Serve as Overseer of the road leading from Kings Mountain to Chas Town that part between James McNabbs over to William Adairs Creek and that he enter on his Charge accordingly.

On Motion of James Forsyth it was ordered by the Court that Wm. Tate have a licence to keep a ferry on Broad River below the mouth of Buffelow and that he observe the following Rules to wit for a Wagon & Team 5/ single horse /3 & man the same and on all things Comply w't the Act of assembly in that Case made & provided.

A Bill of Sale from John Swent Sen'r to John Swent Junr for one bay horse, on horse Colt, one brown Cow, one Speckled red and white Cow, one black & white Cow, three Spring Calves, two year old heifers, one year old bull, a plow and Tacklings with all his household Furniture and Personal Estate Dated the 31st of July 1770 proved by Robert Blackburn Evidence thereto.

A Deed of Sale from Jacob Womack to James Capshaw Dated the 17th of Aug't 1770 for 300 acres of Land proved by Wm. Capshaw Evidence thereto. Ord'd to be Registered.

A Deed of Sale from John Clark to Jno Megrue Dated the 9th Day of October 1770 for 200 acres of Land proved by John Potts Evidence thereto. Ord'd to be Registered.

James Campbell and Joseph Bradner Return an Account of Sales of the Estate of John McCormick Deceased to the amount of 124 0 1d.

A Deed of Sale from George Cox to Joseph Green Dated the 7th Day of September 1770 for 50 acres of Land proved by Francis Adams Evidence thereto. Ordered to be Reg'd.

A Deed of Sale from William Sims to John Stanford Dated the 24th Day of October 1770 for 200 acres of Land proved by James Capshaw Evidence thereto. Ord'd to be Registered.

January term 1771

A Deed of Lease & Release from Saml Richardson & Mary his wife to John Stanford Dated the 11th of Aug't 1770 for 157 acres of Land proved by Wm. Capshaw Evidence thereto. Ordered to be Reg'd.

A Deed of Sale from John Fondron to the Representatives of Bethesda Congregation Dated the 22 day of Feb'y 1771 for 10 acres of Land Acknowledged in open Court. Ordered to be Registered.

A Deed of Sale from Jacob Garner to Garret Morris Dated the 22d of July 1769 for 100 acres of Land ack'd in open Court. Ord'd to be Registered.

A Deed of Sale from James Hanna and Jane to Thomas Kelllough Dated the 20 of August 1769 for 300 acres of Land proved by Jno Wallace Evidence thereto. Ord'd to be Reg'd.

A Deed of Sale from Nath'l Jefferies to Dav'd George Dated the 22d day of January 1771 for 600 acres of Land ack'd in open Court. Ord'd to be Reg'd.

A Deed of Sale from George Patterson to James Patterson Dated the 27th day of October 1770 for 325 acres of Land proved in open Court by Wm Garner. Ord'd to be Registered.

A Deed of Sale from Wm. Hanna and Jane to George Sadler Dated the 24th of October 1769 for 100 acres of Land proved by Thos Clark thereto. Ord'd to be Registered.

A Deed of Sale from Hugh Quinn & wife to Geo. Blanton Dated the 8th of August 1770 for 200 acres of land Proved by John Stanford Evidence thereto. ordered to be Reg'd.

A Deed of Sale from Geo. Blanton & Susanna his wife Dated the 12th of Decem'r 1770 for 168 acres of land Proved by Wm. Tate Evidence thereto. ord'd to be Registered.

A Deed of Sale from William Moore to Alexander Gilleland Dated the 2d of October 1769 for 272 acres of Land proved by David Alexander Evidence thereto. Ordered to be Registered.

A Deed of Sale from Christian Money to Joseph Hardin Dated the 22d of January 1770 for 200 acres of Land proved by John Patton Evidence thereto. Ordered to be Registered.

A Deed of Sale from John McElmurry to John Patton Dated the 22d of January 1770 for 200 acres of Land proved by John Potts Evidence thereto. Ord'd to be Reg'd.

A Bill of Sale from Hugh Quinn to John Price Dated the 1st of Aug't 1770 for one negro man named Jack Proved by William Adear Evidence thereto. ord'd to be Registered.

A Deed of Sale from William Watson & Violet to William Adear Dated the 22d of Jan'y 1771 for 260 acres of Land proved by John Price Evidence thereto. Ordered to be Registered.

A Deed of Sale from William Dulany and Mary to Michael Grimdorff Dated the 6th of August 1770 for 640 acres of Land proved by Robert Blackburn Evidence thereto. Ord'd to be Reg'd.

A Deed of Sale from Thomas Welsh and Rachel to Wm. Barrach Dated the 10th day of Decem'r 1770 for 300 acres of Land proved by Robert Blackburn Evidence thereto. Ord'd to be Registered.

January term 1771

A Deed of Sale from William Bratton & Martha to William Adear Dated the 22d day of Jan'y 1771 for 200 acres of Land proved by John Price Evidence thereto. Ord'd to be Registered.

A bill of Sale from Thomas Farrol to William Patton for all and Singular his Goods and Chattles, Houshold Stuf and all other his substance whatsoever dated the 1st day of May AD 1770 acknowledged in Open Court.

On Motion of Alex'r Martin it was Ordered by the court that Joseph Hardin and Robert McAfee have Letters Testamentary for all and Singular the Goods and Chattles rights and Credits of James McAfee Deceased who took the oath of Executors according to act of assembly in that case made and provided.

Ordered that John McCormack an orphan boy of the age of Seventeen years be bound to Alexander Akin till he attains to the age of Twenty one to Learn the art trade or Mistery of a Cordwinder by him to be taught in Reading and Writing according to law and in all things to comply with the act of assembly in that case made and provided.

Ordered that Benjamin Hardin do take into his possession an infant boy found at the house of Adam Overwinder and that he have the same at our next court that so he may be provided for agreeable to Law.

A Deed of Sale from John Moffet to Ab'm McCorcle Dated the 24th day of January 1771 for 200 acres of Land acknowledged in open court. Ordered to be Registered.

A Deed of Sale from William Sharp to John Walker Dated the 24th Jan'ry 1771 for two hundred acres of Land ack'd in Open Court. Ordered to be Registered.

A Deed of Sale from William Glover to John Wallace Dated the 14th of January 1771 for ____ ares of Land proved by Thos Rainy Evidence thereto. Ord'd to be Registered.

A Deed of Sale from William Sharp to Matt'w Harper Dated the 17th January 1771 for 300 acres of Land ack'd in Open Court. Ord'd to be Registered.

A Deed of Sale from Matthew Floyd to Wm Sims Dated the 30 of October 1770 for 400 acres of Land proved by Jos. Nale Evidence thereto. Ordered to be Registered.

A Deed of Sale from William Sims to Thomas Walsh Dated the 24th of January 1771 for 146 acres of Land acknowledged in open Court, Ordered to be Registered.

A Deed of Sale from Henry Vernor to Wm. Vernor for 263 acres of land Dated the 18th day of January proved by Alex'r Gilleland Evidence thereto, Ord'd to be Registered.

A Deed of Sale from George Dicky to John McFaddon Dated the 7th of January 1771 for 300 acres of Land acknowledged in open Court, Ordered to be Registered.

Court adjourned until tomorrow 9 OClock. Met according to adjournment. Present Timothy Riggs, Jonas Bedford, Jacob Cosner, Esq'rs.

Ordered by the Court that Jno Walker Esqr., Nicholas Welsh, William Reed, Patrick McDavid, Hugh Quinn & Jno Fondron serve as Jurors at the Ensuing Term at Salisbury.

January term 1771

Wm Read vs Matt'w Shearer. Orr att.

The Petty Jury

1 Ezek'l Potts	8 Stephen Shelton
2 Wm Grant	9 James Capshaw
3 John Low	10 Benj'a Shaw
4 John Dunn	11 John White
5 Ja's Alex'r	12 Jacob Coburn
6 Rich'd Price	
7 Thomas Harod	

Jury Impanneled & Sworn find for the plff /1 Damages & /6.

Alex'r McCarty vs Thomas Yates. Orr att. Same Jury Impanneled and Sworn find for the Plff and assess his Damages to £2 6 5 and /6 cost.

John Bumgarner vs George Fisher. Orr att. Same Jury Impanneled and Sworn find for the Plff and assess his Damages to £12 0 4 and /6 cost.

James Forsyth vs James Bridges. Orr att. Same Jury Impanneled and Sworn find for the Plff and assess his Damages to £8 10 /3 & six pence cost.

Nath'l Clark vs Rich'd Farr. Orr att. Same Jury James Steen in place of Jacob Coburn Impanneled and Sworn find for the Plff and assess his Damages to £8 5 8 and /6 cost.

Wm. Langhorn vs Alex'r Wilky. T A B [Trespass, Assault and Battery].

Petty Jury

1 Ez'l Potts	7 Rich'd Price
2 Wm Grant	8 Stephen Shelton
3 John Towns	9 Ja's Capshaw
4 John Dunn	10 Benj'a Shaw
5 Ja's Alex'r	11 James Steen
6 Rich'd Price	12 John Woods

Jury Impanneled & Sworn find for the plff and assess his Damages to £ - - 1d & /6 costs.

Richard Price vs Joshua Morgan. Case.

Same Jury Thomas Bullion in place of Richard Price Impanneled & Sworn find for the Plff and assess his Damages to Nine Pounds Ten Shillings Proc. Money & Six pence Costs.

Ordered by the Court that William McAfee be appointed Guardian of his two sons Thomas and James McAfee who proposes for Security James McAfee and Benjamin Hardin Bound in the sum of Forty pounds accepted.

Jno Davis vs James Bridges. Orr att. Same Jury.

Jury Impannelled & Sworn finds for the Plff and assess his Damages to £7 10 & /6 cost.

January term 1771

Rob't Lusk vs Cha's Robinson. Case.

The Petty Jury

1 Ezek'l Potts	7 Thomas Harod
2 Benj'a Hardin	8 Stephen Shelton
3 John Towns	9 Jas Capshaw
4 Wm. Wilson	10 Benjamin Shaw
5 Ja's Alex'r	11 James Steen
6 Richard Price	12 John Woods

Jury Impanneled & Sworn find for the plff & assess his Damages to £16 1 9 & /6 costs.

John Nuckols vs Wm. Joiner. Orr Att. Same Jury. Impannelled & Sworn find for the Plff & assess his Damages to £ - 1d & /6 Costs.

Hugh Montgomery vs Henry Smith. Case. Same Jury. Impannelled & Sworn find for the Plff & assess his Damages to £10 7 9½ & /6 Costs.

John Towns vs Joab Mitchel. Case.

The Petty Jury

1 Ezek'l Potts	7 Thomas Harod
2 Benjamin Hardin	8 Stephen Shelton
3 Wm. Wilson	9 James Capshaw
4 Jacob Coburn	10 Benj'a Shaw
5 Richard Price	11 Ja's Steen
6 John Hardin	12 John Woods

Jury Impanneled & Sworn find for the plff & assess his Damages to £19 9 8 & /6 costs.

Ordered by the Court that Robt Hamet Serve as overseer of the road leading from Pullams Mill to Joseph Kelsos in the room of James Mays.

An Indenture from William Wallace to David Porter of his son Tho's Wallace Dated the 24th January 1771 proved by William Reed Evidence thereto.

A Deed of Sale from William McConnel to Thomas Patton Dated the 7th of February 1769 for 258 acres of land Proved by James Beaty Evidence thereto. Ordered to be Reg'd.

A Deed of Sale from John Cathey to Wm. Falls Dated the 25 of Jan'y 1771 for 150 acres of land Proved by Henry Wright Evidence thereto. Ordered to be Registered.

Court adjourned until tomorrow 9 OClock. Met according to adjournment. Present Timothy Riggs, Jonas Bedford, Jacob Cosner, Esq'rs.

A Deed of Sale from John Person to Thos Clark Dated the 20th of September 1770 for 72 acres of land proved by Thos Janes Evidence thereto. Ordered to be Registered.

January term 1771

James Steen vs Jno Portman. Case.

The Petty Jury

1	Joseph Nale	7	Ja's Capshaw
2	Rich'd Price	8	Ab'm Smith
3	Sam'l Carrol	9	John Moffet
4	Thos Bullion	10	Dan'l Ponder
5	Jn'o Carrol	11	Jno Woods
6	Thomas Harod	12	Stephen Shelton

Jury Impanneled & Sworn find for the plff and assess his Damages to £2 10 & /6 costs.

James Steen vs Isaac Rains. Case. Same Jury Impannelled & sworn find for the Plff & Assess his Damages to £4 5 and /6 Cost.

Matt'w Troy vs Wm. Bridges. Case. Same Jury Impannelled & sworn find for the Plff & Assess his Damages to £- - 1d & /6 Cost.

Moses Alex'r vs John Low. Case. Same Jury Impannelled & sworn find for the Plff & Assess his Damages to £9 9 & /6 Cost.

Jno Woods vs Jno McElroy. Case. Same Jury Impannelled & sworn find for the Plff & Assess his Damages to £6 3 1d & /6 Cost.

Court adjourned till Court in Course. Timothy Riggs, Jacob Costner, Jonas Bedford.

North Carolina, Tryon County. Tryon Inferior Court of Pleas and Quarter Sessions Begun and held The fourth Tuesday of April Anno Dommini 1771. Present Thomas Neel, Henry Clark, Jonas Bedford, Wm Watson, Esq'rs.

Ordered by the Court that Nicholas Welsh Serve as overseer of the road leading from Worlicks Mill to Chas Town that part between said Mill to bever Dam Creek & that he enter on his Charge accordingly.

Peter Aker from Beverdam Creek to the top of Kings Mountain.

On Motion of John Dunn Ordered by the Court that the mill now Building by Robert Gaba[?] on Fishing Creek when Built & then after be Deemed a Publick Mill in this County.

On Motion of John Dunn it was Ordered by the Court the Ferry on Cataba River Kept by Matthew Bigger be Deemed & Known to be a Publick Ferry in said County. Ordered by the Court that the Keeper of the said Ferry may take & Receive from Passengers according to the Following rates vi. for a Waggon & Team four shillings a Cart & Teem Four Shillings a man & horse six pence a Footman four pence Single or Drove horses each four pence, horned or Black Cattle six pence each and that the said Matthew Bigger do Give Due Attendance accordingly to an act of the General Assembly of this Province in that Case made and provided.

On Motion Ordered that Thomas Neel Do have a Ferry on Cataba River below the mouth of Mill Creek and the same be Deemed and Known to be a Publick Ferry in said County. Ordered by the Court that the Keeper of the said Ferry may take & Receive from

April term 1771

Passengers according to the Following rates viz. for a Waggon & Team four shillings a Cart & Teem Four Shillings a man & horse six pence a Footman four pence Single or Drove horses each four pence, horned or Black Cattle six pence each and that the said Thomas Neel do Give Due Attendance accordingly to an act of the General Assembly of this Province in that Case made and provided.

Sarah Shearer Returns an account of Sales of the Estate of Matt'w Shearer Deceas'd to the amount of Seventy Eight pound seventeen shillings ordered to be put on Record.

Ordered by the Court that Nicholas Fry and Peter Iker Serve as Overseers from Derrick Ramsours Mill to Jacob Egners mill and that they Enter on their Charge accordingly.

Ordered by the Court that Frances Watts wife and Relick of George Watts deceased have Letters of Administration of all and Singular the Goods and Chattles Rights and Credits of the said Deceased She proposes for Security Moses Moore and Peregrine Magnis. accepted.

Barbara Link adm'r of the Estate of Jacob Link Deceased Returns an acc't of Sales of the s'd Estate to the amount of £93 17 7 ordered to be put on record.

George David garnishee of Peter Savery came into court and made oath that he hath in his hands of the said Saverys Estate 1 Steer.

Wm Carpenter Came into Court & as Garnishee of Peter Savery made oath that he has in his hands of said Saverys Estate two cows & 20/ Shillings proclamation money & no more. 20/ allowed for wintering the cows.

Absalom Faris garnishee of Peter Savery came into court and made oath that he has in his hands of said Saverys Estate one cow & Fifteen Shillings proc money & no more. Ten shillings allowed for wintering the cows.

Joseph Hardin & Robert McAfee Ex'rs of the Estate of James McAfee Deceased Return an Inventory of the Estate of the said Deceased prayd an order of sale which was accordingly Granted. no order Required.

A Deed of Sale from Jno Lusk, Sarah Lusk and William Barnet to Thomas Warrin Dated the 20th of February 1771 for 186 acres of land Proved by Nicholas Fisher Evidence thereto. Ordered to be Registered.

A Deed of Sale from Francis Guthery to James Pursly Dated the 22d Day of April 1771 for 132 acres of land Proved by Alexander Stephenson Evidence thereto. Ordered to be Registered.

A Deed of Sale from Charles Quail to Thomas Mitchel Dated the 6th day of October 1770 for 250 acres of land Proved by Aaron Lockart Evidence thereto. Ordered to be Registered.

A Deed of Sale from Matthew Porter & Mary his wife Dated the 18th day of Feb'y 1771 for 300 acres of land Proved by David Byars Evidence thereto. Ordered to be Registered.

A Deed of Sale from Joab Mitchel to John Grindal Dated the 1st day of August 1769 for 100 acres of land ack'd in Open Court. Ordered to be Registered.

TRYON COUNTY NC COURT MINUTES 1769-1779

<u>April term 1771</u>

A Deed of Sale from Abraham Hollingsworth to James Hawkins Dated the 6th day of Feb'y 1771 for 145 acres of land Proved by John Hawkins Evidence thereto. Ordered to be Registered.

A Deed of Sale from John Lusk and Sarah his wife to James Wilson Dated the 21st day of March 1771 for 300 acres of land Proved by Jonathan Gilkey Evidence thereto. Ordered to be Registered.

A Deed of Sale from Jacob Garner to Barnett Barns Dated the 16th day of June 1770 for 100 acres of land Proved by Peter Jones Evidence thereto. Ordered to be Registered.

A Deed of Sale from George Michal Wisenant to Christian Carpenter Dated the 11th day of February 1771 for 150 acres of land Proved by Adam Wisenant Evidence thereto. Ordered to be Registered.

A Deed of Mortgage from William Bolding to Moses McCarter Dated the 27th day of March 1771 for a Massuage or Tenement on Susa Boles Branch Proved by Wm. Milbanks Evidence thereto. Ordered to be Registered.

A Deed of Sale from Gabriel Brown Jun'r to Gabriel Brown Sen'r Dated the 21st day of February 1770 for 100 acres of land Proved by Thomas Fletchal Evidence thereto. Ordered to be Registered.

A Deed of Sale from Tho's Ray to George Lamkin Dated the 30th day of Dec'r 1769 for 100 acres of land Proved by Jno Low Evidence thereto. Ordered to be Registered.

A Deed of Sale from Thomas Black & Eliz'th his wife to Robert Collinwood Dated the 20th day of January 1771 for 150 acres of land Proved by Benjamin Hardin Evidence thereto. Ordered to be Registered.

A Deed of Sale from James Mahan to William Hanna Dated the 18th day of December 1769 for 250 acres of land Proved by James Hanna Evidence thereto. Ordered to be Registered.

A Deed of Sale from Stophel Valvod & Mary his wife to George Hefner Dated the 19th day of May 1770 for 155 acres of land Proved by William Bost Evidence thereto. Ordered to be Registered.

A Deed of Sale from James McElwean to Dan'l Bush Dated the 2d of March 1770 for 190 acres of land Proved by X'r Coleman Evidence thereto. Ordered to be Registered.

A Deed of Sale from Valentine Mauny to Michael Fledermiller Dated the 18th of April 1771 for 200 acres of land Proved by Adam Wisenand Evidence thereto. Ordered to be Registered.

A Deed of Sale from William Rynolds to Alexander Reynolds Dated the 15th day of Decem'r 1769 [for] 200 acres of land Proved by John Ritzhopt Evidence thereto. Ordered to be Registered.

A Deed of Sale from Rob't Wilkins & Susannah his wife to George Blanton Dated the 21st day of February 1771 for 300 acres of land Proved by Pennywell Wood Evidence thereto. Ordered to be Registered.

April term 1771

A Deed of Sale from Richard Reynolds to Alexander Reynolds Dated the 18th day of April 1771 for 250 acres of land Proved by Timothy Riggs Evidence thereto.

A Deed of Sale from John Beeman to Peter Aker Dated the 7th day of February 1771 for 35 acres of land Proved by Timothy Riggs Evidence thereto. Ordered to be Registered.

A Deed of Sale from Herman Kobb Dated the 16th Feb'y 1771 for 200 acres of land Proved by James Fowler Evidence thereto. Ordered to be Registered.

Court adjourned until tomorrow 9 OClock. Met according to adjournment. Present Thomas Neel, William Watson, Timothy Riggs, Esquires.

Ordered by the Court that Phillip Fry Serve as Constable in the room of Urban Ashibrener and that He swear in before Henry Holman Esq'r accordingly.

Ordered by the Court that Robert Johnston Serve as Constable in the room of Joseph Howe & that He swear in before Thomas Neel Esq'r accordingly.

On Motion of James Forsyth Ordered by the Court that Adam Burchfield be appointed Guardian of William Hix an Orphan boy of age to make such Choice and that the said Adam Burchfield do take into his possession all and Singular the Goods & Chattels rights & Credits Belonging to the estate of the said Orphan and Exhibit an Acc't of the same into this Court agreeable to Law. He proposes for security Wm. Saffold Sen'r, James Fanning. accepted.

The Grand Jury: X'r Coleman, foreman

2 Elijah Wells
3 Wm. McKown
4 Alex'r Hemphill
5 James McAfee
6 Robert McAfee
7 Thomas Harod
8 John Alexander
9 Lewis Widener

10 Lawrence Kyser
11 Nich's Welsh
12 Rich'd Venable
13 Jno Harkness
14 Wm. Gilbert
15 John Brandon
16 Henry Reynolds
17 Wm. Murphy

Sworn and charged.

After proclamation the court proceeded the Election of a Sheriff accordingly there being Eleven Justices Present on the bench to witt Wm. Watson, Timothy Riggs, Francis Adams, Jonas Bedford, Henry Holman, Jno Ritzhoupt, William Moore, Jacob Casner, Thomas Neel, Henry Clark, and George Blanton, Esqrs., who did Elected & Choose Francis Adams Esqr, Jacob Casner and James Duff to be recommended to his Excellency the Governor for his approbation and appointment of one of them to serve as high Sheriff for the Ensuing year; it appears by the poles that Francis Adams has nine Votes, Jacob Casner eight Votes and James Duff five Votes. Ordered to be Recommended accordingly.

Settlement of the Estate of Joseph Sailer Deceased by the Admrs. as Follows, vizt

Amount of Sales	£ 120 15 10	
Amount of Credits	5 7 8	
Ballance	115 8 2 so that there is yet in the hands of the Admrs. the	

above Sum of One hundred and Fifteen pounds Eight Shillings & Two pence.

<u>April term 1771</u>

A Deed of Lease and Release from Jacob Pennington & Mary his wife to Alex'r Lockart dated the 24 Day of Decem'r 1770 for 300 acres of Land Proved by the oath of Jno Pennington Evidence thereto. Ord'd to be registered.

A Deed of Sale from Alexander Kels to Ja's Karuth Dated the 26th day of October 1770 for 200 acres of Land proved by Owen Murfy Evidence thereto. Ord'd to be registered.

A Deed of Lease and Release from John Davidson & Ruth to Henry Good dated y'e 5th & 6th days of April 1771 for 500 acres of Land Proved by Andrew Love Evidence thereto. Ord'd to be registered.

A Deed of Sale from Sam'l Watson & Elizabeth to Archibald Barron dated the 12th day of Novem'r 1770 for 250 acres of Land ack'd in Open Court. Ordered to be registered.

A Deed of Sale from Derick Ramsour to Nicholas Friday Sen'r Dated the 23d of April 1771 for 300 acres of Land proved by Henry Holman Evidence thereto. Ordered to be registered.

A Deed of Sale from Ja's Armor, Ja's Alcorn & Katharine Alcorn to Wm. Armstrong Dated the 9th day of April 1771 for 400 acres of Land proved by Francis Armstrong Evidence thereto. Ordered to be registered.

A Deed of Sale from Robert Adams to James Adams dated the 24th day of Apr'l 1771 for 300 acres of Land ack'd in Open Court. Ord'd to be registered.

A Deed of Sale from Alex'r Hemphill to Sam'l Hemphill dated the 20th day of April 1771 for 400 acres of Land ack'd in Open Court. Ord'd to be registered.

A Deed of Sale from Wm. Hager and Eliz'th his wife to Jonathan and Love Hodgson dated the 28th Day of April 1770 for 200 acres of Land ack'd in Open Court. Ordered to be registered.

A Deed of Sale from Wm. Hager and Eliz'th his wife to Jonathan and Love Hodgson dated the 28th Day of April 1770 for 100 acres of Land ack'd in Open Court. Ordered to be registered.

A Deed of Sale from John Hall to Jn'o Kimboll dated the ____ day of _____ for 200 acres of Land ack'd in Open Court. Ordered to be registered.

A Deed of Sale from Matt'w Bigger to Joseph How dated the 24th day of April 1771 for 49 acres & 2 rods ack'd in Open Court. Ordered to be registered.

A Deed of Sale from Aaron Biggerstaff & wife Mary to Phillip Kinsyller dated the 5th of Feb'y 1771 for 320 acres of Land proved by Wm. Ramsey Evidence thereto. Ordered to be registered.

A Deed of Sale from William Patterson & Elizabeth to Robert Elder late dated the 21st Day of July 1770 for 92 acres of Land proved by Alexander Patterson Evidence thereto. Ordered to be Registered.

A Deed of Sale from John Baird to Adam Baird dated the 24th day of April 1771 for 300 acres of Land ack'd in Open Court. Ordered to be registered.

April term 1771

A Deed of Sale from David Davies to Joseph Bradner Dated the 24th Day of April 1771 for 66 acres of Land ack'd in Open Court. Ordered to be registered.

A Deed of Lease & Release from John Fleming & and Eliz'th Fleming to John Turner dated the 1st day Feb'y 1770 for 297 acres of Land proved by James McCall Evidence thereto. Ordered to be registered.

A Deed of Sale from Robert Walker to George Rutledge dated the 18th Day of August 1768 for _____ of Land proved by James Rutledge Evidence thereto. Ordered to be Registered.

A Deed of Sale from Erasmus Rupert to David Jenkins Dated the 25 January 1769 for about 50 acres of Land proved by Nicholas Friday Evidence thereto. Ordered to be Registered.

A Deed of Sale from Abraham Clements to Bartlet Henson Dated the 11th day of March 1771 for 100 acres of Land proved by Jno McKinney Evidence thereto. Ordered to be Registered.

A Deed of Sale from Rob't Swann to James Templeton Dated the 22d day of Novem'r 1770 for 240 acres of Land ack'd in Open Court. Ordered to be Registered.

A Deed of Lease and Release from James Wood to Henry Wright Dated the 18 & 19th days of Feb'y 1771 for 250 acres of Land Proved by Alex'r McClean Evidence thereto. Ord'd to be registered.

A Deed of Sale from Wm Patterson & Eliz'th to Robert Elder Dated the 21st of July 1770 for 200 acres of Land proved in by Alex'r Patterson Evidence thereto. Ord'd to be Registered.

Ordered by the Court that James Henry Serve as Overseer of the road Leading from Solomon Beesons to Chas Town that part thereof between the Top of Kings Mountain and Ezekiel Polks and that he Entered on his Charge Accordingly.

Court adjourned until tomorrow 9 OClock. Met according to adjournment. Present Thomas Neel, Henry Clark, James McElwean, Esq'rs.

Ordered by the Court that Robert McWhirter Constable be Fined Ten Shillings for his Contempt in absenting himself from his Duty in Attending on the Grand Jury and taht he be Summond to appear at Next Court to Shew cause if any he can why he should not.

The King vs George Ison.
The Petty Jury

1 John Patton	7 James Clinton
2 James Witherow	8 Garvin Black
3 Joseph Neel	9 James McCord
4 Nath'l Clark	10 Jno Lusk
5 James Wilson	11 James Duff
6 James Coburn	12 Jno Woods

April term 1771

Jury Impanneled and Sworn find the Defendant Guilty in Manner & Form Charged in Bill of Indictment and Fine Forty Shillings prock.

Ordered by the Court that William Watson and Samuel Watson have Letters Testamentary of all and Singular the Goods and Chattles rights & Credits of James Watson Deceased they complying with the Act of Assembly in that Case made and provided.

The King vs John Haslet. Ind't.

The Petty Jury

1 Robert Adams	7 Alex'r Lockart
2 Joseph Park	8 James Witherow
3 George Rutledge	9 Joseph Nale
4 John Venable	10 James Wilson
5 Joseph Clark	11 Gavin Black
6 John Patton	12 John Woods

Jury Impannelled & Sworn find the Defendant Not Guilty in manner and form Charges in the Indictment.

Ordered by the Court that John Miller an orphan boy of the age of Seven months be bound unto Thomas Arrington till he arrives to the age of Twenty one years After the manner of an apprentice & by the said Thomas Arrington to be Taught in Reading and Writing agreeable to law and at the Expiration of the s'd Term to Give the said Orphan a Mare and Saddle of the Value of Ten pounds ten Shillings and in all other things to comply with the act of assembly in that case made and provided.

Ordered by the court that George Ison produce securities for his Good behaviour in the sum of two hundred pounds prock. Otherwise be Committed to Jail.

George Ison bound in the sum of Two hundred pound proc'n money for his Good Behaviour till appearance at next Court. Thomas Harod & James Kelly Each bound in the sum of One hundred pounds Like money for his Behaviour and appearance at Next Court.

Five Justices being Present in Court, a Settlement was made by them Demanded of the high Sheriff of the county Tax for the year one Thousand Seven Hundred and Sixty Nine which settlement the said Sheriff was not able to make agreeable to Law.

A Deed of Sale from Abraham and Elizabeth Womack to James Fleman Dated the 13th day of March 1771 for 100 acres of land Proved by Thomas Beaty Evidence thereto. Ordered to be Registered.

A Deed of Sale from Nicholas Wisanant to Peter Wisenant Dated the 15th day of September 1770 for 400 acres of land Proved by Ezekiel Polk Evidence thereto. Ord'd to be Registered.

A Deed of Sale from John Mitchel & Eliz'th to Matt'w Troy Dated the 11th day of March 1771 for 600 acres of land Proved by John Dunn Evidence thereto. Ordered to be Registered.

Court adjourned until tomorrow 10 OClock. Met according to adjournment. Present Thomas Neel, Wm. Watson, William Moore, Esq'rs.

April term 1771

Ordered that Christopher Coleman, Wm. Marchbanks, Freeholders and Geo. Blanton, Majestrate be summoned to revalue a Tract of Land Ex'd in the suit Rob't Lusk vs Chas Robinson and that they make report of such valuation to our next court.

The King vs George Ison.
The Petty Jury

1 Eph'm McClean	7 Wm McMurry
2 John Smith	8 John Wood
3 David Byars	9 Ezek'l Potts
4 Gavin Black	10 John Lusk
5 Ja's Wilson	11 Rich'd Price
6 Ja's Witherow	12 Thomas Clark

Jury Impanneled and Sworn find the Defendant not Guilty in manner & form Charged in the Bill of Indictment.

Settlement of the Estate of Jeremiah Potts Given in by y'e Executors. Amount of Sales £336 10 11.

Ja's Witherow vs Edward Williams. Orr Att. Same jury to the alteration of David Parks in Room of Jas Witherow. Jury Impaneled & Sworn find for the plff & Assess his Damages to £14 5 6 & /6 Costs.

Jas. Hugh vs David Liles. Orr Att. Same Jury. Jury Impaneled & Sworn find for the plff £17 5 ½ and /6 Costs.

Jno Lusk Came in to Court & Took the Oaths by law appointed for Qualification of a Publick Officers subscribed the Test Took the Oath of a Justice & took his Seat accordingly.

John Brandon vs John Elder. Case. Same Jury. Jury Impaneled and Sworn find for the plff & Assess his Damages £18 15 4 and /6 Costs.

John Cathey vs Ja's McClenahan. Orr Att.
The Petty Jury

1 Thos Beaty	7 James Smith
2 David Byers	8 Sam'l Carrol
3 Ezekiel Potts	9 Rich'd Price
4 Wm Byers	10 John Potts
5 Gavin Black	11 James Wright
6 Wm. McMurry	12 John Carrol

Jury Impanneled and Sworn find for the Plff and assess his Damages to £ 5 19 2 and /6 Cost.

John Wade vs James Bridges. Orr Att. Same jury with the alteration of Joseph Harden in Room of John Price. Jury Impannelled and Sworn find for the plff and assess his Damages to £5 5 11.

Ordered by the Court the Order of Court of the first day of this Term for appointing Publick Ferry on Cataba River below the mouth of Mill Creek be reversed.

Court adjourned till Court in Court. William Watson, John Thomas, Fra's Adams.

North Carolina, Tryon County. Tryon Inferior Court of Pleas and Quarter Sessions Begun and held The fourth Tuesday of July AD 1771. Present Thomas Neel, Wm Watson, John Robison, Esq'rs.

Robert Blackburn one of the Executors of the Last will and Testament of John Summy Deceased Came into Court and Relinquishes his right of administration to Peter Summy.

The above will was proved in Open Court by the Oaths of Robert Blackburn and Thomas Wilson.

On motion of Alex'r Martin Ordered by the Court that Letters Testamentary Issue to Peter Summy of all and Singular the Goods and Chattles rights and Credits of John Summy Deceased he complying with the act of assembly in that case made and provided.

On motion of James Forsyth Ordered by the Court that an Advertisement Subscribed by Robert Wilky forewarning all Persons not to take any Purchase of nor other Contract make with his son Alex'r Wilky for a Negro Slave Named Diana, setting forth that any Pretence of right or title which Can be Shown by the same Alex'r Wilky to said slave is and was Fraudulently Obtained.

Ordered that Robert Davies being a Very Poor Aged and Infirm man Lame and Disabled in One of his hands and being altogether unable to support himself by his Labor be Recommended to the Gen'l Assembly of this Province as an Object of Charity who ought to be Exempted from payment of Taxes.

On motion of James Forsyth ordered that Mary Froneberger, wife and relict of Wm. Froneberger, Deceased, have Letters of administration of all and singular the Goods & Chattles of the said Deceased She complying with the act of assembly in that case made and provided. She proposes for Security Peter Aker and Laurence Kyser Bound in the sum of Five hundred pounds. accepted.

On petition ordered by the court that Wm. Logan a very aged poor and infirm man being altogether unable to support himself by this Labour be recommended to the General Assembly of this province as an Object of Charity who ought to be Exempted from payment of Taxes.

The Grand Jury: John Foster, foreman

2 Nath'l Jefferies	9 Geo. Wisenant
3 John Riggs	10 Laurence Kyser
4 Adam Burchfield	11 Newberry Stocton
5 Rederias Clark	12 Benj'a Hardin
6 Joseph England	13 Jno Stanford
7 David Ramsey	14 Alex'r McIntire
8 Nicholas Friday	15 Jabesh Evans

Sworn and Charged.

A Deed of Sale from Bostain Cline Jun'r to Jacob Carpenter Dated the 6th of June 1771 for 200 acres of Land Proved by Robert Blackburn Evidence thereto. Ord'd to be registered.

<u>July term 1771</u>

A Deed of Sale from Jacob Shatly to Michael Williams Dated the 12th day of July 1771 for 150 acres of Land Proved by Rob't Blackburn Evidence thereto. Ordered to be registered.

A Deed of Lease and Release from Thos Cahoon and Mary his wife to James Wilson Dated the __ day of September 1767 for 250 acres of Land proved by Rob't Blackburn Evidence thereto. Ordered to be Reg'd.

A Deed of Sale from Peter Aker to John Beeman Dated the 7th day of Feb'y 1771 for 250 acres of Land ack'd in Open Court. Ord'd to be registered.

A Deed of Sale from John Love and Martha his wife to Thomas Wade Dated the 22d day of July 1771 for 400 acres of Land proved by James Hamilton Evidence thereto. Ordered to be Reg'd.

A Deed of Sale from Peter Plunk to Jacob Hufstateler Dated the 22d day of July 1771 for 200 acres of Land proved by Laurence Kyzer Evidence thereto. Ordered to be reg'd.

A Deed of Sale from Benjamin Turner to John Neighbours Dated the 26th day of May 1771 for 100 acres of Land proved by Stephen Shelton Evidence thereto.

A Deed of Sale from Thomas Jun'r to Thomas Reynolds Sen'r Dated y'e 5th day of July 1771 for 253 acres of Land proved by John Reynolds Evidence thereto. Ord'd to be Reg'd.

A Deed of Sale from Wm Sims to Christian Money Dated the 23d day of July 1771 for 200 acres of Land proved by Jno Dunn Evidence thereto. Ordered to be registered.

A Deed of Sale from Thomas Reynolds Sen'r to Thomas Reynolds Jun'r to Dated the 5th of July 1771 for 100 acres of Land proved by John Reynolds Evidence thereto. Ordered to be Registered.

Court adjourned until to morrow 8 OClock. Met according to adjournment. Present William Watson, John Robison, John Retzhoupt, Esq'rs.

Ordered by the Court that Rich'd Reynolds Serve as Constable in the Room of John Moore and that he Swear in before Timothy Riggs Esq'r accordingly.

Ordered by the Court that Robert Lowry be appointed Overseer of the road Leading from the Tucasege ford on Cataba River to Charles Town (that part between the south side of the south fork and the South side of Crowders Creek) and that he Enter on his Charge accordingly.

William Watson and Sam'l Watson Executors of y'e Last will and Testament of James Watson Returns an account of Sales of the said Estate to the amount of thirteen pounds Six shillings and Seven pence.

George Davies garnishee of Peter Savery, Deforest and Ward, merchants in company, came into Court and made oath that he has in his hands of their Estate one Three year old Steer and Fifty shillings proc'n money to be paid in Butter and stock.

A Deed of Sale from Will'm Wilson by Adam McCool his Att'o to Joseph Woods Dated 20th day of July 1771 for 300 acres of Land proved by John Watson Evidence thereto. Ordered to be Registered.

July term 1771

A Deed of Sale from James Love to Joseph Robison Dated 1st of March 1771 for 410 acres of Land proved by Archibald Robison Evidence thereto. Ordered to be Registered.

Court adjourned for half an hour. Met according to adjournment. Present Thomas Neel, John Thomas, John Walker, Esq'r.

A Deed of Sale from John Erwin and Mary his wife to Jonathan Patterson Dated 4th day of Feb'y 1771 for 300 acres of Land proved by Robert Erwin Evidence thereto. Ordered to be Registered.

A Deed of Sale from Francis Beaty to Christian Mauny Dated the 8th day of December 1770 for 350 acres of Land proved by David Miller Evidence thereto. Ordered to be Registered.

A Deed of Sale from John Hill and Jane his wife to Thomas Espey Dated 4th day of Feb'y 1771 for 350 acres of Land acknowledged in Open Court. Ordered to be Registered.

A Deed of Sale from Nicholas Friday Sen'r to Michael Quigle Dated the 29th day of June 1771 for 150 acres of Land proved by Nicholas Friday Jun'r Evidence thereto. Ordered to be Registered.

A Deed of Sale from John Wallace & Hana his wife to James Calley Dated the 15th day of November 1770 for 300 acres of Land acknowledged in Open Court. Ordered to be Registered.

A Deed of Sale from Matt'w Floyd and Sarah his wife to Joseph Kobb Dated the 9th day of September 1763 for 200 acres of Land proved by Herman Kolp Evidence thereto. Ordered to be Registered.

A Deed of Sale from John Wade to Abraham Smith Dated the 23d Day of January 1771 for 300 acres of Land proved by Nath'l Clark Evidence thereto. Ordered to be Registered.

A Deed of Sale from Thomas Harod to John Oaks Dated the 16th Day of June 1771 for 275 acres of Land proved by James McIntire Evidence thereto. Ordered to be Registered.

A Deed of Sale from Richard Hixh [Hicks] to John Foster Dated the 29th Day of January 1771 for 200 acres of Land proved by Sam'l Barnet Evidence thereto. Ordered to be Registered.

A Deed of Sale from Jno McKnitt Alexander to Francis Gilmore Dated the 14th day of Feb'y 1771 for 250 acres of Land ack'd in Open Court. Ordered to be Registered.

A Deed of Sale from Hugh Berry to John Berry Dated the Twentieth day of July 1770 for 300 acres of Land proved by Andrew Berry Evidence thereto. Ordered to be Registered.

A Deed of Sale from David Crocket to Wm Patterson Dated the 12th day of March 1771 for 250 acres of Land proved by Alex'r Patterson Evidence thereto. Ordered to be Registered.

A Deed of Sale from Moses Ferguson and Martha his wife to Thomas McMurry Dated the 12th day of February 1771 for 1720 acres of Land proved by Dan'l Shaw Evidence thereto. Ordered to be Registered.

July term 1771

A Deed of Sale from Jno Witherow to John Counts Dated the 18th day of March 1771 for 300 acres of Land proved by Jno Walker Evidence thereto. Ordered to be Registered.

A Deed of Sale from Phillip Clonninger to Adam Clonninger Dated the 22d of July 1771 for 200 acres of Land proved by Michael Rudisel Evidence thereto. Ordered to be Registered.

A Deed of Sale from Peter Johnston to Sam'l Guy Dated the 21 of July 1770 for 148 acres of Land proved by Hugh Bratton Evidence thereto. Ordered to be Registered.

A Deed of Sale from Jno McKnitt Alexander to James Davies Dated the 24th day April 1771 for 166 acres of Land ack'd in Open Court. Ordered to be Registered.

A Deed of Sale from Thomas McMury to George Stanly Dated the 11th of Decem'r 1770 for 185 acres of Land proved by Jno Anderson Evidence thereto. Ordered to be Registered.

A Deed of Sale from Jno Kimbol to John Carson Dated the 23d day of July 1771 for ___ acres of Land proved by Robert Ferguson Evidence thereto. Ordered to be Registered.

A Deed of Sale from Jno McKnitt Alexander to David Thomson Dated the 24th day of July 1771 for 138 acres of Land ack'd in Open Court. Ordered to be Registered.

A Deed of Sale from David McRee to John Carson Dated the 21st of July 1771 for 200 acres of Land proved by Peter Johnston Evidence thereto. Ordered to be Registered.

A Deed of Sale from William Dickson to James Hanna Dated the 20th of Decem 1770 for 540 acres of Land proved by Peter Johnston Evidence thereto. Ordered to be Registered.

A Deed of Sale from James Hanna to Rob't Kellough Dated the 20th day of August 1768 for 146 acres of Land proved by Tho's Killough Evidence thereto. Ordered to be Registered.

A Deed of Sale from Thomas Yates to Will'm Crocket Dated the 6th day of March 1771 for 160 acres of Land proved by Jno Hill Evidence thereto. Ordered to be Registered.

A Deed of Sale from Jacob Garner to Isaiah Parker Dated the 5th day of April 1771 for 100 acres of Land. Ordered to be Registered.

A Deed of Sale from Thomas Yates to David Crocket Dated the 11th day of March 1771 for ___ acres of Land. Ord'd to be Reg'd.

Court adjourned until tomorrow 9 OClock. Met according to adjournment. Present Thomas Neel, John Robison, Wm Watson, Esq'rs.

Ordered by the court that John Tagert, Havis McWhirter, Thomas Campbell, Robert Johnston, Joseph Carrol, and Jo's Hardin serve as venire men and that they attend at Salisbury on the 5th day of September then and there to serve our Sovereign Lord the King as Grand and Petit Jurors during the Ensuing Term.

Edmund Faning vs John Steen. Case.

The Petty Jury

July term 1771

1 Verdry Magby	7 Jacob Julian
2 James McAfee	8 Dan'l McCarty
3 Nath'l Clark	9 John Bennet
4 X'r Coleman	10 Alex'r Hemphill
5 Matt'w Bigger	11 James Alcorn
6 James Adams	12 Elijah Wells

Jury Impanneled and Sworn find for the Plff and assess his Damages to £5 8 and /6 Costs.

James Price vs Thomas Bell. Orr att. Same Jury. Impennelled and sworn find for the plff and assess his Damages to £9 4 and /6 Costs.

Jno McKnitt Alex'r vs David Stanly. Orr att. Same Jury with the alteration of Joseph Clark in room of James Adams. Jury Impenneled and Sworn find for the plff and assess his Damages to £10 4 and /6 Costs.

John Williams vs James Bridges. Orr att. Same Jury. Impennelled and sworn find for the act and Deed of the Defendant.

John Davison vs Rucken Dulen. Case. Same Jury. Jury Impennelled and sworn find for the plff and assess his Damages to £10 12 6 and /6 Costs.

John Williams vs James Bridges. Orr att. Same Jury. Impennelled and sworn find for the act and Deed of the Defendant.

John Williams vs James Bridges. Orr att. Same Jury. Impennelled and sworn find for the act and Deed of the Defendant.

Lewis, Miller & Neely vs Wofford and Corudon[?]. Orr att. Same Jury. Impennelled and sworn find for the plff and assess his Damages to £6 13 & /6 Costs.

Geo Crawford vs Middleton Boshears. T. A. B. Same Jury. Impennelled and sworn find for the plff and assess his Damages to /6 & /6 Costs.

Ordered by the Court that William Watson Majistrate, Robert Gordon, Jacob Garner, Freeholders be appointed to Revalue a Tract of Land taken by execution at Instance of John McKnitt Alex'r of the Estate of Matt'w Floyd.

Settlement of the Estate of Jeremiah Potts Deceased by the Executor.
Amount of Sales	£336 10 11
Amount of Credits	96 13 1
	£239 17 10

it appears by the above accounts that there is in the hands of the Executor Two hundred and Thirty nine pounds Seventeen shillings and ten pence.

A Deed of Sale from Thomas Rainy to Benjamin Phillips Dated 8th of Jan'y 1771 for 194 acres of Land ack'd in open Court. Ordered to be registered.

A Deed of Sale from Peter Johnston to Robert Bratton Dated 25 of July 1771 for 170 acres ack'd in open Court. Ordered to be registered.

A Deed of Sale from Peter Johnston to Robert Palmer Dated 24 Decem'r 1768 ack'd in open Court. Ordered to be registered. for 300 acres of Land.

July term 1771

A Deed of Sale from William Sims to Isaac Edwards Dated 7th of April 1770 for 300 acres of Land proved by Peter Johnston Evidence thereto. Ordered to be Registered.

A Deed of Sale from Marshal Lovelatty to John Lovelatty Dated 23d October 1770 for 200 acres of Land proved by Henry Smith Evidence thereto. Ordered to be Registered.

A Deed of Sale from Sam'l Coburn to Alex'r Eaken Dated 23d day of July 1771 for 150 acres of Land proved by William Reed Evidence thereto. Ordered to be Registered.

A Deed of Sale from William Adams to Tho's Price Dated 23d day of Jan'y 1771 for 122 acres of Land ack'd in open Court. Ordered to be Registered.

A Deed of Sale from John Ramsey, Agness Ramsey, Alex'r Boldridge & wife to Thomas Price Dated the 21 December 1770 for 346 acres of Land proved by Rich'd Barry Evidence thereto. Ordered to be Registered.

A Deed of Sale from Wm Jones to Benjamin Ellis Dated 22d day of July 1771 for 250 acres of Land proved by Peregrine Magnis Evidence thereto. Ordered to be Registered.

A Deed of Sale from John Patton to John Smith Dated 24th July 1771 for 245 acres of Land proved by James Alcorn Evidence thereto. Ordered to be Registered.

A Deed of Sale from James Clark to James Alcorn Dated 20 July 1771 for 250 acres of Land proved by Jno Smith Evidence thereto. Ordered to be Registered.

Court adjourned till tomorrow 8 Oclock. Met according to adjournment. Present William Moore, William Watson, John Robison, Esq'r.

William Carpenter garnishee of Peter Savery Came into Court and made oath that he has in his hands of the said Saverys &Cs Estate two Cows and two Calves and 20/. 20/ allowed by the court for wintering the Cows.

Isaac Edwards vs George Gibson.
Petty Jury

1 John McKinny	7 John Harkness
2 John Woods	8 James Jameson
3 Peter Watkins	9 Barney Hanley
4 Thomas Harod	10 Benj'n Shaw
5 Ab'm Smith	11 Sam'l Adams
6 James Moore	12 Verdry Magby

Jury Impanneled and Sworn find for the Plff and assess his Damages to £4 & /6 Costs.

Isom Lee vs Jno McGurnnigen[?]. Case. Same Jury. Impanneled and Sworn the Plaintiff being Solemnly Called Suffered a Nonsuit.

Richard Henderson vs William Joiner. Orr att. Same Jury. Jury Impanneled and Sworn find for the Plff and assess his Damages to £19 & /6 Costs.

George Harrison vs Robert Barns. Case. Same Jury. Impanneled and Sworn the Plaintiff being Solemnly Called Suffered a Nonsuit.

<u>July term 1771</u>

R'd Henderson vs Alex'r Lockart. Case. Same Jury. Impanneled and Sworn assess the Plaintiffs Damages to Four pounds Ten Shillings proclamation money and six pence Costs.

John Williams vs David Huddleston. Debt. Same Jury. Impanneled and Sworn the Plaintiff being Solemnly Called Suffered a Nonsuit.

James Forsyth vs Simcock Kannon. T. A. B. Same Jury. Impannelled and Sworn find the Defendant Guilty and assess the plaintiffs Damages to 1d and /6 Costs.

A Deed of Lease and Release from John Dickinson & his wife to John Patton Dated the 29th day of August 1769 for 600 acres of Land proved by Samuel Adams Evidence thereto. Ord'd to be Reg'd.

A Deed of Lease and Release from John Dickinson and Martha his wife to John Patton Dated the 31st day of August 1769 for 900 acres of Land proved by Samuel Adams Evidence thereto. Ord'd to be Reg'd.

Court adjourned until tomorrow 8 OClock. Met according to adjournment. Present Thomas Neel, Jno Robison, John Walker, Esq'rs.

Jno Lineberger vs Patrick McDavid.
                    The Petty Jury

1 John Woods	7 Solomon Beson
2 Tho's Harod	8 Rich'd Price
3 Wm Ramsey	9 Nich's Fisher
4 Dan'l McCarty	10 Moses Whitly
5 Nath'l Clark	11 Tho's Clark
6 Verdry Magby	12 Rob't Loony

Jury Impanneled and Sworn and assess the Plffs Damages to £9 14 8 & /6 Costs.

Peregrine Magis vs Savery, Deforest & Ward. Orr att. Same Jury. Jury Impanneled and assess the Damages to £27 8 6 & /6 Costs. Seven pounds Eight & Six pence released.

Henry Dellinger vs Thomas Bullion. Case Same Jury. Impannelled and Sworn find the for the plffs and assess Damages to £11 13 10 3/4.

Hans McWhirter vs Sam'l Davison. Case. Same Jury. Impanneled & Sworn assess the plaintiffs Damages to £17 13 4 & /6 Costs.

James Gordon assig. vs John Duncan. Case. Same Jury. Impanneled & Sworn assess the plffs Damages to £6 15 10 & /6 Costs.

James Gordon vs And'w Countryman. Case. Same Jury. Impanneled & Sworn assess the plffs Damages to £5 8 5 & /6 Costs.

Ordered by the Court that Henry Clark justice, Henry Smith & William McMullin Freeholders heretofore appointed to Revalue the Goods Taken at the Suit Matt'w Troy vs Matt'w Floyd proceed to value said Goods & that they make due return of such proceedings to our next court.

July term 1771

Hugh Stuart vs Robert Ferguson. Case. Same Jury. Jury Impanneled & Sworn assess the Damages to £9 10 & /6 Costs.

Thomas Brandon vs Daniel McCarty Sen. Case. Same Jury with the alteration of Jacob Julian in the Room of Daniel McCarty. Impennelled and sworn find the Defendant did not assums.

A Deed of Sale from David Porter and Jane his wife to Samuel Porter Dated the 18 day of May 1771 for 180 acres of Land Proved by Nicholas Watson Evidence thereto. Ordered to be registered.

Francis Adams Came into Court and produced his Excellencys Commission appointing him high sheriff for the County of Tryon and took the oaths by Law appointed for Qualification of Publick Officers, Subscribed the Test, Took the oath of a Sheriff and Entered on the Duty of his office.

Sam'l Adams Came into Court and took the oaths by Law appointed for Qualification of Publick Officers, Subscribed the Test, Took the oath of a Sheriff and Entered on the Duty of his office.

Nicholas Fisher vs William Ramsay. Trover.

Pettit Jury

1 John Woods	7 Moses Whitlow
2 Thomas Harod	8 Thom's Clark
3 Nath'l Clark	9 Robert Loony
4 Verdry Magby	10 James McClohlin
5 Solom'n Beson	11 Sam'l Carroll
6 Rich'd Price	12 Jacob Julian

Jury Impanneled and Sworn find the Defendant Not Guilty and that the mare is the property of the Defendant.

The King vs Moses Whitlow. Adultery.

The Petty Jury

1 Verdry Magby	7 Sam'l Carol
2 Benjamin Rice	8 Ja's McGlohlin
3 Tho's Harod	9 Jacob Julian
4 Rich'd Price	10 Rob't Loony
5 Solomon Beson	11 Tho's Clark
6 John Logan	12 Wm. Ramsey

Jury Impennelled and Sworn find the Defendant Guilty in Manner and form Charged in the Indictment.

The King vs Jacob Mauny.

The Petty Jury

1 Verdry Magby	7 Jacob Julian

July term 1771

2	Benja Rice	8	Robert Loony
3	Tho's Harod	9	Wm. Ramsey
4	John Logan	10	James Alcorn
5	Sam'l Carol	11	James Adams
6	Ja's McGlohlin	12	David Adams

Jury Impennelled and Sworn find the Deft not Guilty in Manner and form Charged in the Indictment.

Ordered by the Court that John Tagert Late High Sheriff be Cited to appear at our Next Inferior Court of Pleas & Court of Pleas and Quarter Sessions to make a settlement for the Taxes for the year 1770 agreeable to Law.

Ordered by the Court that a summons issue under the hand of the Chairman for one constable in Each Captains District within this County to warn the Tithable persons to appear before their Respective Majestrates there to Give in an account of their Taxable persons in his her or their Family.

Court adjourned till Court in Court. Thos Neel, John Walker, Jacob Costner. Probates remitted.

North Carolina, Tryon County. To witt At an Tryon Inferior Court of Pleas and Quarter Sessions Begun and held for said County on the fourth Tuesday in October AD 1771. Present Thomas Neel, John Robison, Robert Blackburn, Esquires.

On motion of Samuel Spencer ordered by the Court that George Sizemore have Letters of administration of the estate of William Shepherd Deceased he complying with the act of assembly in that case made and provided. He proposes for Securities George Winters & John Morris. accepted. Securities bound in the sum of Three hundred pounds.

John Vovrel Came into Open Court and took the oaths b Law appointed for Qualification of Publick Officers, Subscribed the Test, Took the oath of an attorney.

Mary Froneberger Returns an Inventory of the Estate of Wm. Froneberger, Deceased, prayd an order of sale. Granted.

An account of sales of the Estate of Wm. Froneberger Deceased Returned by the administrator the amount of £416 9 3.

Frances Watts Returns an Inventory of the Estate of George Watts, Deceased, as administrator of the said estate prayed an order of sale which was accordingly Granted.

Robert Lusk Came into Court and took the oaths by Law appointed for Qualification of Publick Officers, Subscribed the Test, Took the oath of a sub Sheriff & Entered on the Duty of his office.

The Grand Jury: John Patton, foreman

2	James Lewis	9	Rob't McDowel
3	John Kerr	10	Sam'l Watson
4	X'r Carpenter	11	George Julian
5	And'w Campbell	12	Rich'd Venable
6	David Gordon	13	Gavin Black

October term 1771

7 James Hanna   14 James Moore
8 John Wilson   15 John Lusk

Sworn and Charged.

On motion of Alexander Martin The Will of William Moore being produced in Open Court was proved by the Oath of David Dicky Subscribing Witness with Joseph Hart & Samuel Gray. William Glaghorn, one of the Executors of the said Last will & Testament, releasing his Right to the said Executorship in Open Court. Ordered that Letters Testamentary Issue to Mary Coulter Being the Relict of the said William Moore appointed Executrix &C by the sd. will of all and singular the Goods & Chattles rights & Credits of the said Deceased she complying with the act of assembly in that case made and provided.

A Deed of Sale from Thomas Elliot & Jane Elliot to Joseph Woods Dated the 10th day of August 1770 for 175 acres of Land Proved by Davis Whelkel Evidence thereto.

Court adjourned for one hour. Met according to adjournment. Pres't Thos Neel, Jno Robison, David Anderson.

On Motion of Alexander Martin it was Ordered by the Court that William Gilbert have a Licence to Keep an Ordinary at his now Dwelling house in the County of Tryon he complying with the act of assembly in that case made and provided. He proposes for Securities George Winters & John Morris. accepted.

A Deed of Sale from Dan'l McCar[t]y to Danl McCarty & John McCarty Dated the 22d day of April 1770 for all his goods & chattles. ack'd in open Court. Ordered to be Registered.

A Deed of Sale from John Colins to David George Dated the 22nd day of June 1771 for 200 acres of Land Proved by John Carrier Evidence thereto. Ordered to be Registered.

A Deed of Sale from David Thompson to Ja's Smith Dated the 11th October 1771 for 138 acres of Land Proved by Onslow Barrett Evid'c thereto.

A Deed of Sale from Thomas Bullion to Zach'a Gibbs dated the 22d Octo'r 1771 for 200 ac's Land Proved by Essex Capshaw Evid. thereto. Ordered to be Registered.

A Deed of Sale from Saml Davison to John Bryson dated the 21st Octo'r 1771 for 300 ac's Land Proved by David Gordon Evid. thereto. Ordered to be Registered.

A Deed of Sale from Hugh Quinn & Marg. his wife to William Kempshaw [Capshaw] to William Kempshaw [Capshaw] dated the 21st July 1771 for 300 ac's Land Proved by Essex Kapshaw [Capshaw]. Ordered to be Registered.

A Deed of Sale from Rob't Adams to And'w Campble dated the 22d Octo'r 1771 for 50 ac's Land Proved by James Campble Evid. thereto. Ordered to be Registered.

A Deed of Sale from Leonard Killion & Margret his wife to Thomas Clemonds dated the first Mar 1771 for 250 ac's Land Proved by David Abbernathy Evidence thereto. Ordered to be Registered.

October term 1771

A Deed of Sale from Ja's Carson & Mary his wife to David Abbernathy dated the 19th July 1771 for 116 ac's Land proved by Saml· Rankin Evidence thereto. Ordered to be Registered.

A Deed of Sale from David Alexander to Sam'l Rankin dated the 19th Jan'y 1768 for 150 ac's Land ack'd in Open Court. Ordered to be Registered.

A Deed of Sale from John Collins & Febee his wife to F. Ross dated the 15th July 1771 for 120 ac's Land Proved by Will'm Milbank Evidence thereto. Ordered to be Registered.

A Deed of Sale from John McCulloch to John Smith dated the 13th May 1771 for 126 ac's Land Proved by Geo. Winters Evidence thereto. Ordered to be Registered.

A Deed of Sale from Laurance Kizar to Joseph Kizar dated the 18th Octo'r 1771 for 250 ac's Land Proved by Laurance Kizar Evid. thereto. Ordered to be Registered.

A Deed of Sale from Ja's Ansley of Roan Co'ty to John Morris of Tryon County dated the 9th Sep'r 1771 for 250 ac's Land Proved by And'w Hampton Evid. thereto. Ordered to be Registered.

A Deed of Sale from Giles Tillet to John Gibbs dated the 15th May 1771 for 640 ac's Land Proved by Zacharias Gibbs Evid. thereto. Ordered to be Registered.

A Deed of Sale from Ja's Millikan to John McNeet Alexander dated the 11th Octo'r 1770 for 150 ac's Land Proved by David Moore Evid. thereto. Ordered to be Registered.

A Deed of Sale from Sam'l Fulton to Ja's Davidson dated the 10th Dec'r 1770 for 319 ac's Land Proved by John Davison Evid. thereto. Ordered to be Registered.

Court adjourned until tomorrow 8 OClock. Met according to adjournment. Present Thomas Neel, John Robison, Timothy Riggs, Esq'rs.

Ordered by the Court that Robert Lowry, Jonathan Gullick & John Harris be appointed to Lay out & alter that part of the road Leading from the Tucasigie ford to South Carolina, between Robert Lowrys & Thos Campbells, and that they Begin at the Corner of Robert Lowrys field thence a Straight course between Joseph Neels & Edward Mellons thence into the old road opposite to Thomas Campbells Spring and that they proceed upon the said service accordingly. Issued.

In Consequence of the aforesaid order of administration William Gilberts by John Dun & Alexander Martin his attorneys & prays a caveat in the Secretarys Office according to act of assembly in that case made and provided against the said George Sizemores having administration pursuant to the above order till the controversy be head & determine by his Excellency the Governor and Council of this province whether Letters of administration ought to issue to the said George Sizemore or to the said Wm. Gilbert, he claiming right tot he same. Caveat Granted.

Rex vs And'w Haslep. Petty Larceny.

The Petty Jury

1 James Alcorn
2 Wm. Kerr

7 Nicholas Fisher
8 Benj'a Kuykendall

October term 1771

3	Saml Carrel	9 Samuel Wilkey
4	Robert Corven	10 John Bennet
5	Davies Wilkel	11 James Pursly
6	William Haggerty	12 John Stanford

Impennelled & Sworn find the Defendant not Guilty in manner & form Charged in the Indictment.

The King vs And'w Haslep. Petty Larceny. Same Jury. Impennelled & Sworn find the Defendant not Guilty in manner & form Charged in the Indictment.

Saml Harris vs Jere'h Routh. Case. att. Same Jury. Impennelled & Sworn find for the plaintiff & Assess Damages to 1d /6 and costs.

John Williams vs James Bridges. Case.

The Petty Jury

1	John McKinny	7 John Weedingman
2	James Pursley	8 John Stanford
3	William Kerr	9 John Price
4	Davies Willky	10 William Lusk
5	Sam'l Carrel	11 Ephraim Wilson
6	Benj'a Kuykendall	12 Nicholas Fisher

Jury Impennelled & Sworn find for the plaintiff and assess Damages to £7 10 & /6 Costs.

Pett. Lafferty vs John Perry. Same Jury with the alteration of James Fanning in place of John McKinny. Impenneled & Sworn find for the plff and assess his Damages to £20 & /6.

Arest of Judg't mentioned by J. Dunn. Verdict Confirmed by Judgment of Court.

A Deed of Sale from John Perry to Moses Alex'r Dated the 18th October 1771 for 200 acres of Land Proved by Sam'l Patton Evidence thereto. Ordered to be Registered.

A Deed of Sale from Robert Russel to David Bruton Dated the 28th of August 1769 for 317 acres of Land Proved by Moses Alex'r Evidence thereto. Ordered to be Registered.

A Deed of Sale from John McEllily to John Penny Dated the 16th of Oct'r 1771 for 200 acres of Land Proved by Sam'l Patton Evidence thereto. Ordered to be Reg'd.

Court adjourned until to morrow 9 OClock. Met according to adjournment. Present Thomas Neel, John Robison, Timothy Riggs, Esq'rs.

The will of David Robison Dated the 8th day of July 1771 being produced in Open Court was admitted to Record being proved by Verdry Magbee one of the Subscribing Evidences.

William Yancy garnishee of John Thomason Came into Court and made Oath that he has in his hands of the said John Thomason Fifty shillings in meat & produce and Twenty Shillings in Money and no more.

Ordered by the court that Thomas Rainy serve as Constable in the Room of Edward Lacey & that he swear in before John Gordon, Esqr. accordingly.

October term 1771

Edmund Fanning vs Thomas Beaty. Case.

Petty Jury

1 John Stanford	7 Thomas Clark
2 Nicholas Fisher	8 Ephraim Wilson
3 James McAfee	9 John Williams
4 William Kerr	10 John Anderson
5 Thomas Bond	11 John Weedingman
6 Sam'l Lacey	12 Sam'l Wilky

Jury Impennelled & Sworn find for the plff & assess Damages to £3 & /6 Costs. Appeal pray'd & Waved.

Ordered by the Court that William Kerr be fined forty Shillings for his Contempt in not attending as a Juror being summond; Fine Remitted.

John Weedingham vs William Marchbank. Case.

The Petty Jury

1 John Stanford	7 Thomas Clark
2 N. Fisher	8 Ephraim Wilson
3 James McAfee	9 John Williams
4 Lowry Glover	10 John Anderson
5 Thomas Bond	11 Sam'l Wilky
6 Samuel Lacey	12 David Crocket

Impennelled & Sworn find for the plff & Assess his Damages to £5 & /6 Costs.

John Moore vs Hez'h Doan. Orr. Att. Same Jury with the Alteration of Sam'l Smith in the room of Sam'l Lacey. Impennelled & Sworn find for the plff £4 3 & /6 Costs.

William Smith vs John Armstrong. Same Jury. John Murphy in the room of John Williams. Impennelled & Sworn find for the plff £20 & /6 Costs.

Ordered that James Gordon be Committed to the Stocks for a Quarter of an hour for his Contempt in Open Court.

James Gordon ordered into Custody for Contempt of the Court and upon hearing it was Determined that he be fined 10/. Ep. to pay Next Court.

A bill of sale from Andrew Haslep to Thos Haslep for one Roan horse Branded AH on the Near Shoulder also one rown mare three years old trots and paces, one Sorrel year old Stone horse now in my possession, as also two likely Cows & Calves and all the wearing apparel of John Haslep my son Deceased as also Forty Bushels of Indian Corn, one Chaff bed, two Sheets, two Blankets, one bed Quilt and one bed Stead, Dated the 25th day of October 1771. Acknowledged in Open Court. Ordered to be registered.

A Deed of Gift from Ezekl Smith to Elizabeth Burton daughter of Elizabeth dated the 25th day of Octo. 1771 for Twenty hear of horned Cattle Branded ES and marked with a Staple Fork in each Ear. Proved by Ezekl Polk Evidence thereto. Ord'd to be Reg'd.

October term 1771

John Tagert Came into Court Five Justices being present to Witt Thomas Neal, John robison, William Moore, James McIntire & Timothy Riggs and produced his account of the County Tax for the year of our Lord One Thousand Seven hundred & Sixty Nine which is as follows to witt.

John Tagert to Tryon County D'r to 427 Taxables @ 3/2 Each £201 14 4.

Contra Cr. by 200 Insolvents & runaways   £31 13 4.
County Claims   170 1
                                            201 14 4

Settled in full.

John Tagert Sheriff aforesaid Came into Open Court the above said Justices being present and produced his account of the County Tax for the year 1770 as follows to witt.

John Tagert to tryon County D'r to 1622 Taxables @ 2/11 £236 10 10.

Contra Cr. by 382 Delinquents, Insolv'ts and runaways £ 55 14 2.

John Wyat to Bostain Best for one hundred acres of Land Dated the 20th August 1771 proved by John Retzhoupt Evidence thereto. Ord'd to be Registered.

Thomas Neel, William Watson & John Robinson, bound to his Excellency the Governor in the sum of £1000 proc. 26 October 1771, for Thomas Neel's performance as Register of the County of Tryon. Wit: W. Avery, Ezekl Polk.

Settlement of the Estate John Grady by the Administrator he having produced his account to the amount of £ 71 2 and the same being approved by the Court there appears that there is in the hands of the Administrator Twelve pounds Fifteen shillings & four pence.

Rex vs William Yancey. Indictment
                    Petty Jury

1 Verdry Magbee   7 Thomas Clark
2 Robert Murphy   8 John Stanford
3 Nat'l Clark   9 Nicholas Fisher
4 Rich'd Price   10 Rederias Clark
5 Rich'd Whitaker   11 John Armour
6 Sam'l Smith   12 Nathan Camp

Jury Impennelled & Sworn find the Defendant Guilty.

William Yancey bound in the sum of Fifty pounds proc'n money to appear at Salisbury at the Next Superior Court to be held for the District of Salisbury James Mcintire & Verdry Magbee bound in Twenty five pounds to be void on condition y't the sd. Wm. Yancey do prosecute his said appeal with effect otherwise pay and satisfy all to costs accruing thereon.

John Lusk bound in the sum of Thirty pounds proc'n money to appear at Salisbury at the Next Superior Court to be held for the District of Salisbury on the 5th day of March next as Evidence.

William Lusk bound as afs'd. Evidence.

<u>October term 1771</u>

Ulrick Crowder vs And'w Hampton. Case. Same Jury. Impennelled & Sworn find for the plff & assess Damages to £10 0 8 & /6 Costs. Motion arrest of Judgment by ?.

A Deed of Sale from Matthew Floyd to John McNitt Alexander Dated the 26th day of October 1771 for one hundred & Seventy acres of Land ack'd in Open Court. ordered to be registered.

1771 October Term Claims on the County of Tryon for the year 1771.

	£	S	D
Joseph Hardin one Venire Ticket	2	2	6
Do 1 Do	15	8	
Robert Johnston 1 Do	17		
Moses Moore 1 Scalp Ticket		7	6
Thomas Hair 1 Scalp Ticket		7	6
Thomas Hair 1 Do		7	6
Charles England 1 Do		7	6
Edward Sizemore 1 Do		7	6
Moses Moore 1 Do		7	6
Thomas Davis 1 Do		7	6
James Alley 1 Do		7	6
Austin Yancey 1 Do		7	6
James Rutlege 1 Do		7	6
Thomas Wilson 1 Do	2	12	6
David Ramsey 1 Do		7	6
Wm. Stocton 1 Do		7	6
Adam Wisenar 1 Do		7	6
Wm Murphy 1 Do		7	6
Joseph Boker 1 Do		7	6
Wm. Murph 1 Do		15	
Isaac Folkinbourough 1 Do		7	6
Daniel Shipman 2 Do		15	
Henry Reynolds 1 Do		7	6
Wm. Dryermond 1 Do		7	6
Jacob Randal 1 Do		7	6
John Fisher 1 Do		7	6
Robert Blackburn 2 Do		15	
George Keyzer 2 Do		15	
Do 1 Do		7	6
Nicholas Welsh 1 Do		7	6
Jacob Heckleman 5 Do	1	17	6
John Bumgarner 5 Do	1	17	6
James Duff 1 Do		7	6
John Patton 1 Venire Ticket	2	11	6
John Tagert 1 Do		17	
To Charles McClain for the courthouse 3 Courts		7	10
To Wm Henry for the Jail		4	
To the Sheriff for services		10	
To the Clerk for services		10	
To the Sheriff for Commissions @8 Pr Cent		10	
Necessary Contingencies		49 16	4
	113	12	

The aforesaid sum of One hundred & thirteen pounds Twelve shillings is the whole of the money due by the County of Tryon for the year 1771 it is therefore Ordered that a Tax of One Shilling and Three pence be Levied of Each Taxable person in the said County of Tryon to Discharge the above said sum.

Court adjourned till Court in Court. Thos Neel, William Watson, John Robinson, Timothy Riggs, Jas. McEntire.

North Carolina, Tryon County. to witt. Tryon Inferior Court of Pleas and Quarter Sessions begun and held for the said County on the fourth Tuesday in January AD 1772. Present the Worshipful John Walker, John Retzhoupt, James McEntire, Esq'rs.

The Will of Joseph Green being produced in Open Court was proved by the oath of Robert McAfee a Subscribing Evidence with Henry Reynolds & Alex'r McEntire of the Ex'rs of the said will. Ordered by the Court that Letters Testamentary Issue to Mary Green Wife & Relict of the said Deceased & James McEntire Esq'r for all and Singular the Goods & Chattles Rights and Credits of the said Deceased Who Took the oath of an Executor they complying with the act of Assembly in that Case made and provided.

Ordered that a Road be Laid out from Wm. Davis on Catheys Creek the nearest and best way to the province Line into the Charles Town market road, and that And'w Hampton, George Winters, Sam'l Richardson, Sam'l McFaddon, George Sizemore, James Cook Sen'r, Will'm Wray, William Gleghorn, Sam'l Gray, John Sutton, Robert Nelson & David Huddleston Sen'r do Serve as Jurors to Lay out the said road and that they appear before John Walker Esquire on the third Tuesday in March next then and there to take the Necessary steps to Qualify them for this their Charge and that the sheriff Summon them thereto accordingly.

A Deed of Sale from Joseph Scott & Mary his wife to Alexander Wells Dated 25 October 1770 for 200 acres proved by James Johnston Evidence thereto. Ordered to be Registered.

A Deed of Sale from George Wilfong to John Moire Dated the 21st day of December 1771 for 200 acres of Land proved by Alex Erwin Johnston Evidence thereto. Ordered to be Registered.

A Deed of Sale from Adam Overwinter to George Wilfong Dated the 21st day of December 1771 for 250 acres of Land ack'd in open Court. Ordered to be Registered.

A Power of attorney from William Joiner to William Saffold Jun'r to sue for Recovery & Receive Sundry negro Slaves viz Matt. a male aged about ten years, Tom a male aged about ten years, & Agge a female aged about six years, Granville a male aged about Seven years, Abram a male aged about four years, Lucy a Female aged about Seventeen years Dated the 1st day of September 1770 proved by James Forsyth Evidence thereto. Ordered to be registered.

A Deed of Sale from James McEntire to Benj'a Ellis Dated the 25 Day Jan'y 1772 for 300 [acres] of Land proved by Rob't McAfee Evidence thereto. Ordered to be Reg'd.

A Deed of Sale from Henry Wetner & Catharine his wife to John Mool Dated the 31st May 1771 for 54 acres proved by Abraham Anthony Evidence thereto. Ordered to be Reg'd.

A Deed of Sale from James Reed of Grenville [Granville] So Carolina to Henry Berkly of Rowan County No Carolina Dated the 15th day Aug't 1771 for 300 acres of Land proved by John Reed Evidence thereto. Ord'd to be Registered.

January term 1772

A Deed of Sale from Benj'a Ellis to Ja's McEntire Dated the 25th Jan'y 1772 for 250 acres of Land proved by Robert McAfee Evidence thereto. Ordered to be Registered.

A Deed of Lease & Release from Sam'l Wilson & Sarah his wife [of] Craven County So Carolina to Jacob Anthony of Tryon Co. No Carolina Dated the 14th November 1771 for 200 acres of Land proved by John Mull Evidence thereto. Ord'd to be Registered.

A Deed of Sale from Nath'l Miller to Joseph Thomson Dated the 3d January 1772 for 200 acres of Land proved by Alex'r McCarter Evidence thereto. Ordered to be Registered.

A Deed of Sale from Joseph Dobson to John Fisher Dated the 15th Oc'r 1771 for 200 acres of Land proved by John Mell Evidence thereto. Ord'd to be Reg'd.

A Deed of Sale from William Dearment & wife to Frederick Wise Dated 17th Oc'r 1771 for 400 acres of Land proved by Francis McBride Evidence thereto. Ord'd to be Reg'd.

A Deed of Sale from John Reed & wife to James Finly Dated 27 January 1772 for 300 acres of Land ack'd in Open Court. Ord'd to be Registered.

A Deed of Sale from Thomas Beaty & wife to James Fleming & John McClure Dated the 6th September 1771 for 400 acres of Land ack'd in Open Court. Ord'd to be Reg'd.

A Deed of Lease & Release from Peter Stutes to Conrad Minger Dated the 27th November 1768 for 400 acres of Land proved by Abraham Anthony Evidence thereto. Ordered to be Registered.

A Deed of Sale from Phillip Adams & Catharine his wife [to] Michael Hefner of Frederick County Maryland Dated the 13th December 1771 for 350 acres of Land proved by Abraham Anthony Evidence thereto. Ordered to be Registered.

A Deed of Sale from Paul Anthony & wife of Rowan County to Christian Churches Dated 20th May 1771 for Ten acres of Land proved by Abraham Anthony Evidence thereto. Ord'd to be Reg'd.

A Deed of Sale from William Joiner Dated the 1st day of September 1771 for one Negro Slave named Matt aged about ten years, one male slave named Tom aged about ten years, one male slave named Granville aged about Seven years, one male slave named Abram aged about four years, one female slave named Lucy aged about Seventeen years and one other female slave named Agga aged about six years, proved by James Forsyth Evidence thereto. Ordered to be registered.

A Deed of Sale from Joanna Umphries to Robert Cherry for 200 acres of Land dated 9th April 1771 proved by Thomas Beaty Evidence thereto. Ord'd to be Reg'd.

A Deed of Sale from James Wright and Wm. Wright to William Byers dated the 6th day of September 1771 for 535 acres of Land proved by Charles McLean Evidence thereto. Ord'd to be registered.

Court adjourned until tomorrow 10 OClock. Met according to adjournment. Present William Moore, John Walker, Rob't Blackburn, Esq'rs.

Ordered by the Court that Jacob Mouny serve as Overseer in the room of Peter Acre and that he Enter on his Charge accordingly.

January term 1772

Ordered by the Court that Wm Bridges Serve as Constable in the Room of John Guffy & that he swear in before John Walker Esq'r accordingly.

Ordered by the Court that Joseph Carrol Sen'r Serve as Constable in the room of Hugh Shannon & that he swear in before John Robison Esq'r accordingly.

On Motion Ordered by the Court that Thomas Neel Do have a Ferry on the Cataba River below the mouth of Mill Creek Opposite to Isaac Price and that the same be Deemed and Known to be a Publick Ferry and that he be allowed the same Rates as allowed in an order of April Term he Complying with the act of assembly in that Case made & provided.

Ordered by the Court that Benjamin Bickerstaff serve as Constable in the room of Nicholas Shram & that he swear in before Jacob Costner Esq'r accordingly.

Ordered by the Court that Sam'l Martin serve as Constable under William Moore and that he swear in before said Wm. Moore Esq'r accordingly.

Ordered by the Court that Frederick Wise and Teter Havenor serve as overseers in the room of Nicholas Welsh.

Ordered by the Court that Wm Dearmont serve as Constable in the room of John Stame and that he swear in before Henry Holman Esq'r accordingly.

On Motion of John Dunn ordered by the Court that Katherine Smith have Letters of Administration on all and Singular the goods & Chattles of Jeremiah Smith Deceased she complying with the act of assembly in that case made & provided. She proposes for Securities James Login & Wm Armstrong bound in the sum of £200. accepted

Ordered that a Road be Laid out from William Tates Ferry to the Charles Town Trading road the nearest and best way and that Robert Loony, Verdry Magbee, Thomas Dermond, William Beats, Henry Beats, Jacob Dermond, William Dermond, George Underwood, Isham Saffold, Joseph Burchfield, Adam Burchfield and James Bridges do Serve as Jurors to Lay out the same and that they be summoned by the Sheriff to appear before George Blanton Esq'r on the fourth Tuesday in March then and there to take the Necessary steps to Qualify them for this their Charge.

A Deed of Sale from John Ison to Wm. Carpenter Dated the 11th July 1771 for 300 acres of Land proved by Benj'a Harden Evidence thereto. Ordered to be Registered.

A Deed of Sale from Aaron Burleson to John McTier Dated the 1st day of September 1771 for 200 acres of Land proved by David Wilkins Evidence thereto. Ordered to be Registered.

A Deed of Sale from George Sides to George Wilfong Dated the 28th January 1772 for 200 acres of Land proved by Jacob Anthony Evidence thereto. Ordered to be Registered.

A Deed of Sale from William Byers to David Porter Dated 28th January 1772 for 277 acres of Land ack'd in Open Court. Ordered to be Registered.

A Deed of Sale from Andrew Hudock to Michael Keller Dated the 17th August 1771 for 150 acres of Land ack'd in Open Court. Ord'd to be Registered.

January term 1772

A Deed of Sale from Peter Whistlehunt to John Smires Dated 13th January 1772 for 400 acres of Land proved by Leonard Sides Evidence thereto. Ordered to be Registered.

A Deed of Sale from John Limeberger & wife to John Con Dated the 24 January 1772 for 200 acres of Land proved by Peter Limeberger Evidence thereto. Ordered to be Registered.

A Deed of Lease & Release from Adam Sights and wife to George Sights Dated 28th January 1772 for 200 acres more or less proved by George Fink Evidence thereto. Ordered to be Registered.

A Deed of Lease & Release from Adam Sights & Susanna his wife [stricken] to George Sights Dated 28 January 1772 for 100 acres proved by George Fink Evidence thereto. Ord'd to be Reg'd.

A Deed of Sale from Thos Haslip to And'w Haslip Dated 30th Oc'r 1771 for 390 acres of Land proved by Wm. Lewing Evidence thereto. Ordered to be Registered.

A Deed of Sale from John Wallace & wife to William Barrow Dated 27 Jan'y 1772 for 200 acres of Land proved by Rob't Bratton Evidence thereto. Ord'd to be Registered.

A Deed of Sale from James Wright & William Wright to William Byers Dated the 6th day Septem'r 1771 for 535 acres of Land proved by Chas McLean Evidence thereto. Ord'd to be Reg'd.

A Deed of Gift from Thomas Reynolds to Henry Reynolds Dated the 27th January 1772 for Two Tracts of Land one containing 253 & the other 200 acres of Land proved by James Dougherty Evidence thereto. Ord'd to be registered.

A Deed of Sale from William Davis & wife to Rob't Dickey Dated the 2d Oct'r 1771 for 150 acres of Land proved by George Dickey Evidence thereto. Ordered to be reg'd.

A Deed of Sale from Alexander Reynolds to Thomas Reynolds Sen'r Dated the 19th Novem'r 1771 for 200 acres of Land proved by Henry Reynolds Evidence thereto. Ord'd to be reg'd.

A Deed of Sale from John Mull to John Meyer Dated 13th January 1772 for 200 acres of Land proved by Jacob Anthony Evidence thereto. Ordered to be Registered.

A Deed of Sale from James Moore & wife to George Sigman Dated the 8th Jan'y 1772 for 288 acres of Land proved by John Fisher Evidence thereto. Ordered to be reg'd.

A Deed of Sale from Edward Dickson to Alex'r Dickson Dated 5th March 1770 for 300 acres of Land proved by Joseph Dickson Evidence thereto. Ordered to be Reg'd.

A Deed of Sale from Alex'r Dickson to Edw'd Dickson Dated the 5th Day Feb'y 1770 for 200 acres of Land proved by Joseph Dickson Evidence thereto. Ord'd to be Reg'd.

A Deed of Sale from Wm Hanna & wife to Wm. Barrenhill Dated the 25th November 1771 for 340 acres of Land proved by Sam'l Adams Evidence thereto. Ord'd to be reg'd.

Court adjourned until tomorrow 8 OClock. Met according to adjournment. Present Robert Blackburn, Jacob Casner, John Retzhoupt, Esq'rs.

January term 1772

On motion of James Forsyth Ordered by the Court that john Stanford be fined five shillings proc'n money for Contempt offered the Court. Remitted.

Frances Wells, Administrator of the Estate of George Wells, deceased, returns an account of sales of the said estate to the amount of £66 17 3 which was Ordered to be put on Record.

The Grand Jury: Joseph Harden, foreman

2 Verdry Magbee	9 Alexander Lockart
3 James Bridges	10 Robert McAfee
4 Wm Capshaw	11 John Stanford
5 John Nuckols	12 John McKinny
6 James McAfee	13 Adolph Reele
7 Christian Money	14 Nicholas Worlick
8 Thomas Beaty	15 Michael Hofstatler
	16 Nicholas Wisenant

Sworn & Charged.

James Litel garnishee of Thomas Bell Came into Court and made Oath agreeable to Law that he hath in his hands Seventeen Coat buttons & two Jacket Buttons the Leggs of a pair of Stockings, a Knee Buckle an old Hunting Shirt & old Breeches and no more. Jane Litel garnishee as aforesaid Came into Court & Declares that She has not any thing in her hands of the said Thomas Bell.

Barbara Sailer, adm'x of the Estate of Jacob Link deceased Comes into Court by Waightstill Avery her Attorney and produces a settlement of the estate sales of said Jacob Link which being Examined & aproved of by the court there appears to be in the hands of the administrator £79 9 which was ordered to be put on record.

A Deed of Sale from Thomas Penny & Sarah his wife to Daniel Price dated 29 Ap'l 1771 for 200 acres of Land proved by Samuel Nisbet Evidence thereto.

A Deed of Sale from Sam'l Brice to Joseph Nisbet Dated the 22d Jan'y 1772 for 200 acres of Land proved by Sam'l Nisbet Evidence thereto.

A Deed of Sale from George Story & wife to Joseph Kelso Dated the 1st January 1772 for 224 acres of Land proved by Sam'l Nisbet Evidence thereto.

Waightstill Avery produced the Petition of Wm. Barrow in open Court for building a Grist mill on his Land on the South Fork of Turkey Creek which said Petition was accordingly Granted he Complying with the act of assembly in that Case made & provided.

Robert Bratton garnishee of Daniel Kerr came into Court and made oath that he hath in hands nothing of the Estate of Daniel Kerr.

The Will of William Litel being produced in Open Court & proved by Abel Beaty a Concurring Witness with Archibald Litel & John Beaty upon which it is ordered that Thomas Litel the Executor appointed in said Will have Letters Testamentary of all & Singular the Goods & Chattels of said Wm. Litel Deceased he complying with the act of assembly in that Case made & provided.

January term 1772

A Deed of Sale from Robert Miller & Rachel his wife to John Ford Esq'r of Craven County So Carolina Dated the 17th Aug't 1771 for 400 acres of Land Proved by John Thomas Evidence thereto.

A Deed of Sale from Peter Johnston to Robert Thomas Dated the 30th January 1772 for 400 acres of Land proved by Sam'l Nisbet Evidence thereto.

On motion of John Dunn Ordered by the Court that William Watson majistrate, John Ellis & James Collins, freeholders, be appointed to Revalue a mare & Cow & Calf the property of John Tagert Taken by Execution at the instance of James Alcorn & that the Sheriff Summon them accordingly.

Ordered by the Court that Nicholas Fisher serve as Constable in the room of David Wilkins & that he swear in before Ja's McEntire Esq'r accordingly.

Ordered by the Court that Henry Bullinger serve as Constable in the room of Phillip Fry and that he swear in before Robert Blackburn Esq'r accordingly.

A Deed of Sale from Alexander McEntire & Jennet McEntire to James Collins Sen'r Dated the 17 Day December 1771 for 200 acres of Land Proved by Rob't McAfee Evidence thereto. Ordered to be Reg'd.

A Deed of Sale from Thomas Welsh to Edw'd Hampton Dated the 23d Day of November 1771 for 200 acres of Land Proved by George Davies Evidence thereto. Ordered to be Registered.

A Deed of Sale from Thomas Wade to Wm Merrel Dated the 28th Oc'r 1771 for 250 acres of Land proved by Jacob Randal Evidence thereto. Ordered to be Registered.

A Deed of Sale from Thomas Wade to Wm Merrel Dated the 28th Oc'r 1771 for 100 acres of Land proved by Jacob Randal Evidence thereto. Ord'd to be Registered.

A Deed of Sale from Joseph Nale to Jo's Smith Dated the 27th Oc'r 1771 for 100 acres of Land proved by Jacob Randal Evidence thereto. Ord'd to be Registered.

A Deed of Sale from David Robinson to James Steen Dated the 5th July 1771 for 250 acres of Land proved by Wm Saffold Evidence thereto. Ordered to be Registered.

A Deed of Sale from Rich'd Reynolds to Henry Landers Dated the 16th Jan'y 1772 for 250 acres of Land proved by Timothy Riggs Evidence thereto. Ord'd to be Registered.

A Deed of Sale from Robert Kerr & Hannah Kerr to John Swan Dated the 28 Jan'y 1772 for 400 acres of Land Proved by William Swan Evidence thereto. Ordered to be Reg'd.

A Deed of Sale from John Stroud to Rosana Redick Dated the 15th August 1771 for 100 acres of Land proved by Sam'l Coburn Evidence thereto. Ordered to be registered.

A Deed of Sale from John Lusk to Jacob Lutes Dated the 29th Jan'y 1772 for 186 acres of Land proved by Rob't Blackburn Evidence thereto. Ordered to be registered.

A Deed of Sale from John Lusk to Rich'd Price Dated the 25th Oc'r 1771 for 600 acres of Land proved by Samuel Adams Evidence thereto. Ord'd to be reg'd.

January term 1772

A Deed of Sale from Samuel Adams to John Price Dated the 3d April 1771 for 300 acres of Land ack'd in Open Court. Ordered to be registered.

A Deed of Sale from Nicholas Welsh to Jacob Yorty Dated the 22d January 1772 for 170 acres of Land proved by Thos Welsh Evidence thereto. Ordered to be registered.

A Deed of Sale from Thomas & Mary Linn to John Oaks Dated the 5th October 1771 for 250 acres of Land proved by Rob't McAfee Evidence thereto. Ordered to be registered.

A Deed of Sale from Derick Ramsour to Christian Rinehart Dated the 17th day of August 1771 for 100 acres of Land ack'd in Open Court. Ordered to be registered.

Court adjourned till Tomorrow 10 OClock. Met according to adjournment. Present Thomas Neel, Jonas Bedford, Jacob Casner, Esq'rs.

Ordered by the Court that Verdry Magbee [Joseph Hardin stricken], John Tagert, Frederick Hambright, Wm Henry, John Alexander [William Armstrong, stricken], be summoned to appear & attend at Salisbury on the 5th March next to serve as Grand & Petty Jurors.

A Deed of Sale from Charles Harrenton to Wm. Johnston Dated the 11th July 1771 for 200 acres of Land proved by Edward Dicus Jun'r Evidence thereto. Ordered to be Reg'd.

A Settlement of the Estate of William Hanna Deceased by the adm'r whereby it appears that the amount of Sales was

the amount of Sales was	£38	8 7
Credits	10	8
Ballance	£28	0 7
Widows Thirds	9	6 9
	£18	13 10

Settlement of the Estate of Henry Willis Deceased by adm'rx

Amount of Sales	£174	1 1
Credits	58	12 5
Clear Estate	£115	9 6
Widows Thirds	37	5 2
	£ 75	1 4

On motion of John Dunn Ordered by the Court that Christian Rinehart have a Licence to keep Ordinary at his house in Tryon County he Complying with the act of assembly in that Case made & provided. He proposes for securitys Robert lusk & John Dunn Esq'r. accepted.

Phillip Henson vs John Thomason.

Petty Jury

1 James Graham		7 Thomas Cole
2 David Wilky		8 Sam'l Bickerstaff
3 Nicholas Broadway		9 James Kelly
4 Wm. Johnston		10 Jonathan Robison
5 James Wilson		11 Valentine Mauny
6 James Bradley		12 Alex'r Thomson

January term 1772

Jury Impenneled & Sworn find for the one penny Damage /6 Costs.

Robert Williams vs Elijah Wells. Case. Same Jury. Impennelled & Sworn. The plff being solemnly Called failed to appear & suffered a Nonsuit.

Nich's Friday vs Jacob Beam. Orr att. Same Jury. Impennelled & Sworn find for the plff £9 & /6 Costs.

Henry Wright assignee of James Wood vs Hugh Quinn. Same Jury with the alteration of Wm. Ramsey in the room of Sam'l Bickerstaff. Jury Impennelled & Sworn find for the plff £10 11 & six pence Costs.

A Deed of Sale from Peregrine Magnis to John Carson Dated the 31st January 1771 for 300 acres of Land proved by William Yancey Evidence thereto. Ordered to be reg'd.

Francis Carlisle vs Charles Robison. Case. Same Jury with the alteration of David Ramsey & John Lusk in the room of James Wilson & Alexander Thomson. Jury Impennelled and Sworn find for the plaintiff £12 19 3 & /6 Costs.

Court adjourned till Tomorrow 10 OClock. Met according to adjournment. Present Thomas Neel, Rob't Blackburn, William Moore, Esq'rs.

A Bond of Performance from Nicholas Claye to Henry Holeman & Robert Blackburn [&] Timothy Riggs, Esqrs, Dated the 6th day of December 1772 in 400 pounds for the due performance of his Duties of a Guardian towards Daniel Kingry, Barbara Kingry, Mary Kingry & Elizabeth Kingry heirs of Abraham Kingry Deceased.

Ordered by the Court that John Ellis serve as Constable in the room of Jacob Randall & that he swear in before George Blanton Esq'r accordingly.

An Instrument of Writing under hand of Joshua Jones whereby he acknowledges that all reports by him made touching Margaret Wilson, wife of James Wilson, were False & Malicious & that he never knew any thing unbecoming of the said Margret Wilson proved by John Conner Evidence thereto. Ordered to be Registered.

Ordered by the Court that George Wilfong & And'w Heddick be appointed Overseers in the room of Peter Acre & Nicholas Fry and that they enter on their Charge accordingly.

Ordered by the Court that Henry Clark majistrate and Christopher Coleman, Adam Goudelock, freeholders, be summoned to Revalue two horse[s] taken by Execution at the Instance of John Brandon against Elder Anderson & Gibbes & that they proceed thereto accordingly.

A Bill of Sale from Jacob Money to Maudlin Coup Dated the 27th December 1771 for Sundry Chattles proved by John Tagert Evidence thereto. Ordered to be registered.

Ordered by the court that Robert Loney Serve as Constable in the room of Verdry Magbee & that he swear in before Henry Clark Esq. accordingly.

A Bill of Sale from William Wray to John Tagert for a Negro Female Slave named Dinah Acknowledged in open Court. Ordered to be registered.

<u>January term 1772</u>

Ordered by the Court that Wm Watson majistrate, Joseph Hardin & John Jordan freeholders, be summoned to Revalue a horse taken at the Instance of William Langham [Langhorn?] vs Alex'r Wilky & John Nuckols & that they be summoned to proceed on the said Valuation accordingly.

Ordered by the Court that Wm Watson majistrate, Joseph Hardin & John Jordan freeholders, be summoned to Revalue a mare taken on Execution on the Judgment John Weedingman vs William Marchbanks & that they be summoned proceed thereon accordingly.

Court adjourned till Court in Court. William Moore, Henry Hollman, Rob't Blackburn, Timothy Riggs.

North Carolina, Tryon County. To witt. Tryon Inferior Court of Pleas & Quarter Sessions Begun and held The fourth Tuesday of April 1772. Present Thomas Neel.

His Majestys Commission of the Peace being Read then Silence was Proclaimed.

Thos Neel, Ezek. Polk, James McIntire, Thos Aspy, Came into Court & took the oath by Law appointed for the qualification of public officers, Subscribed the test, took the oaths of Justices & took their seats accordingly.

The will of George Bounds being produced in open Court wherein it appears that Francis Prince is Sole Executor of the said Will & Testament, It is therefore Ordered that Letters Testamentary Issue to the said Francis Prince of all & Singular the goods & Chattles Rights & Credits of the said deceased, he complying with the act of assembly made & provided.

Ordered by the Court that Letters Testamentary Issue to Francis Robinson wife & relict of David Robinson Deceased of all and Singular the Goods and Chattles Rights & Credits of the said deceased, she complying with the act of assembly made & provided.

Jacob Randall came into Court and took the oaths by Law appointed for the Quallification of publick officers, Subscribed the test, took the oath of a Justice of the Peace & took his seat accordingly.

On motion of Alex'r Martin ordered by the court that Nick's Warlock have Letters of administration of all and singular the Goods & Chattles of the Daniel Warlock Deceased who took the oath of an administrator & proposes Security Henry Hollman & Chris'r Rinehart bound in the sum of one thousand six hundred pounds. accepted.

On motion of James Forsyth Ordered by the Court that a Road be viewed and opened from the Island Cherokee ford on Broad River & from Will'm Tates Ferry on y'e s'd River Leading the nearest and best way into the trading road leading towards Charles Town & that the following persons be appointed to view & lay out the same viz Geo. Blanton Esq'r, Wm Tate, Wm. McCown, Vardry McBee, Zac'r Bullock, John Nichols, Joab Mitchell, Rob't Wilkins, Rob't Lusk, Nath'l Jeffries, Adam Goudlock, Will Marchbanks, Christ'r Coleman, William Wilkins, Rob't Luney & that they meet at Jacob Randals on the last Tuesday in May to take the Necessary steps to Qualify them for their Charge.

Marth Cain having had an Illegitimate Female Child now aged about Three months Came into Court by James Forsyth her att'y and for the maintenance thereof and Security of the Parish proposes Hugh Quinn & and Hillery Guy bound in the sum of Fifty pounds. Accepted.

April term 1772

A Deed of Sale from And'w Cowan to David Porter for 150 acres of land dated [24th] of March 1772 proved by Ezel Polk Evidence thereto. Ordered to be registered.

A Deed of Sale from Barnet Barns to Mathew Porter dated the 1st day of Nov'r 1771 for one hundred acres of land including said Barnes Improvement proved by Hugh Quinn an Evidence thereto. Ordered to be registered.

A Deed of Sale from William Ramsey to J. Krass [Kraps?] dated April 28, 1772 for 300 acres of land proved in Court by David Ramsey an Evidence thereto. Ordered to be registered.

A Deed of Lease & Release Dated 4th of Jan'y 1772 from David Davies & Wife to Henry Hartell proved by Francis Price an Evidence thereto. Ordered to be Registered.

A Deed of Sale Dated 4th of Feb'y 1771 from James Kelly to James McIntire for 200 acres of land ack'd in open Court. Ordered to be Registered.

A Deed of Sale Dated Dec'r 21, 1771 from Hugh Quinn to Geo: Dickson for 157 acres of land ack'd in open Court & ordered to be Registered.

A Deed of Sale Dated April 28, 1772 from Moses Moore to Joseph Laurence for 204 acres of land ack'd in open Court. Ordered to be Registered.

A Deed of Sale Dated the 8 of Nov'r 1771 from Abraham Scott to Charles Williams Jun'r for 256 acres of land proved by James Abernathy an Evid. thereto. Ordered to be Registered.

A Deed of Sale Dated the April the 7th 1772 from James Polley [Palley?] to James White for six hundred acres of land proved in Court by Rob't Blackburn an Evidence thereto. Ordered to be Registered.

A Deed of Sale Dated the 14th of Feb'y 1772 from Will'm Patrick to Joseph Guyton for three hundred acres of land proved by Tho's Neel an Evidence thereto. Ordered to be Registered.

Court adjourned till Tomorrow Eight OClock. Mett according to adjournment. Present Tho's Neel, Jacob Randal, Thomas Espey, Esq'rs.

Will'm Moore, Henry Holman, Rob't Blackburn, Jacob Costner, John Retzhoupt, Timothy Riggs Came into Court & took the oaths by Law appointed for the Qualificaiton of Public Officers, Subscribed the test, took the oaths of Justices & took their Seats accordingly.

Katherine Smith, Adm'rx on the Estate of Jeramia Smith Deceased Returns an Inventory of said Estate Prays an Order of Sale which is accordingly Granted.

In pursuance of an order of october Court last past order'd that Letters of Administration Issue to Geo. Sizemore on the Estate of Wm. Shepherd Deceas'd.

Rec'd from his Excellency the Gov'r a Letter Commanding to the Court of Their Duty of Selecting & Recommending fit & proper persons to Execute the office of Sherriff for this County for the Year Ensuing to which Letter the Court Resolved to pay all due & proper Respect. Ordered that the said Letter be filed among the records of this Court.

April term 1772

On motion of John Dunn ordered by the court that Letters of administration issue to Sarah Pettie wife & relict of Chris[topher] Pettie Deceased of all and singular Goods & Chattles rights & Credits of the said Deceased who took the oath of an admins'rx. Proposes for Security James Martin & Leonard Sailor are bound in the sum of £400. accep'd.

Settlement of the Estate of John Summer Deceased Given in by the Ex'rs

Amount of Sales	£27 16 6
Charges deducted	15 2 5
Balance Due to the Estate	£12 14 1 to the Estate.

Ordered by the Court that Geo: Trout Serve as Constable for Tho's Espey Esq'r & that he swear in before him Accordingly.

Settlement of the Estate of John McCormack Deceased by the Executors

Amount of Sales & Whole Estate	£125 16 7
Charges deducted	36 16 4
Balance Due to the Estate	£ 89 6 3 yet Remaining in the

hands of the Executor.

Ordered by the Court that Jacob Shutley Serve as Constable for Jno Retzhoupt Esq'r & that he swear in before him accordingly.

The Grand Jury: Moses Moore, foreman

2	George Ewing	9	John Lusk
3	Sam'l Rich'dson	10	David Ramsey
4	Jno McGuire	11	Jacob Green
5	George Winter	12	John Morris
6	Leonard Sailer	13	John Neighbours
7	James Martin	14	James Cozart
8	John Mull	15	Tho's Robison
		16	John Logan
		17	N's Welch

Sworn & Charged.

Court adjourned for Half an Hour. Met according to adjournment. Present Robert Blackburn, Henry Holman, Jacob Costner, Esq'rs.

Joseph Harding Came into Court & took the oaths appointed by Law for the Quallification of publick Officers Subscribed the test & took the oath of a Justice & took his Seat accordingly.

James Barnet vs Joseph Barnet. Orr. Att.
Petty Jury

1	John Stanford	7	Alex'r Coyle
2	Richard Randol	8	John Harman
3	Wm Ramsey	9	William Harman
4	John Oakes	10	John Moor
5	John Orr	11	Abra'm Hargis
6	William Withrow	12	George Fleming

Jury Impenneled & Sworn find Damages for the Plaintiff £19 11 4 & /6 Costs.

April term 1772

Barnet Collier vs Josna[?] Perkins. Same Jury. Impannelled & Sworn Assess Damage for the Plantiff £21 12 09. Released to £20 0 0 & /6 Cost.

A Deed of Sale Dated the 27 of Dec'r 1770 from Robert McCasland to James Parry for 200 acres of Land was ack'd in open Court by Rob't McCasland & ordered to be Registered.

A Deed of Mortgage Dated the 15th Day of Feb'y 1772 from Geo Potts to Peter Carpender for 400 acres of Land was ack'd in open Court & ordered to be Registered.

A Deed of Sale dated Oct'r 1, 1770 from Michael Heckleman to James Martain for 600 acres of Land was ack'd in open Court. Ordered to be Registered.

A Deed of Sale dated Feb'y the 1st 1772 from Will Reed to Moses Crawford for 300 acres of Land was proved in Open Court by Timothy Riggs an Evidence thereto. Ordered to be Registered.

A Deed of Sale dated February 27th 1772 from John Howell to Peter Petty Pool for 202 acres of Land was ack'd in Open Court. Ordered to be Registered.

A Deed of Sale dated April the 23rd 1772 from Abra'm Kuykendall to Baptist Scott for 317 acres of Land was proved in Open Court by Will Henry an Evidence thereto. Ordered to be Registered.

A Bond of Performance from Jacob & David Ramsour to Derick Ramsour Dated April 27th 1772 was proved in Open Court by John Dunn an Evidence thereto. Ordered to be Registered.

A Deed of Sale from Jacob & David Ramsour to Derick Ramsour Dated April the 27th 1772 was proved in Open Court by John Dunn an Evidence thereto. Ordered to be Registered.

A Deed of Sale Dated April the 27th 1772 from Derrick Ramsour to Jacob Ramsour was proved in Open Court by John Dunn an Evidence thereto. Ordered to be Registered. The same being for 960 acres of land.

A bill of Sale from Derrick Ramsour to Jacob & David Ramsour Dated April the 27, 1772 for 600 acres of Land was proved in Open Court by John Dunn an Evidence thereto. Ordered to be Registered.

Court adjourned till Tomorrow at 8 OClock. Met according to adjournment. Present Thomas Neel, Jacob Casnear, John Retzhaupt, Esq'rs.

Francis Ross garnishee of David Hay[?] came into Court and made oath that he has in his hands of the said Hay's Estate £2 10 which the Garnishee will answer for when called on.

Settlement of the Estate of Jacob Wilfong Deceased by the Exr's
Am't of Sales	£77 7 -
Charges deducted	24 6 10
Balance Due to the Estate	£53 0 2

Remains in the hands of the Exr's.

April term 1772

Charity Ker Adm'x for the Estate William Kerr Deceas'd Returned an Acc't of Sales of the s'd Estate to the Amt of £71 17 11 which was ord'd to be put of Record.

James Alcorn vs Geo Magoun. Jury in this Suit Impanneled and Sworn vizt.

1	William Wilson	7 Jacob Aker
2	Richard Price	8 Daniel Kingery
3	John Crace	9 Geo. Wisenhaunt
4	Frederick Wise	10 Phillip Kinselar
5	Peter Summy	11 Geo Wilfong
6	Frederick Sponcelor	12 Peter Mull

Assess the Damages to the Plaintiff to Forty[?] Pounds proc'n Money & Six pence Costs. Judgment.

John Dunn Esq'r vs Matthew Floyd. The same Jury. Verdict for one penny Damage and Six pence Cost.

Andrew Campbell vs And'w Pitts. Case. The same Jury. Verdict for one penny Damage and Six pence Cost.

Anthony Hutchins vs Jacob Gardener. Case. The Same Jury. Impannelled & Sworn Find for the plaintiff assess Damages to Five pound Sixteen Shillings & /6 Proc. Money & Six pence Cost.

James Nixton vs Nathl Rice. Trover. The Same Jury. Impannell'd & Sworn. The plaintiff being Solemnly Call'd failing to appear was Nonsuited.

Thomas Price vs Benjamin Thomson. Case. The same Jury. Verdict for one penny Damage and Six pence Cost.

Court adjourned for half an Hour. Met according to adjournment.

After proclamation the Court proceeded to the Election of a Sheriff accordingly there being Ten Justices present viz Thomas Neel, William Moore, Jacob Cosner, Robert Blackburn, John Retzhoupt, Timothy Rigs, Jacob Randal, Joseph Hardin, Ezekiel Polk & Henry Holman Esq'rs who did elected & Choose Francis Adams, William moore & Jacob Cosner to be recommended to his Excellency the Governor for his approbation & appointment of one of them to serve as High Sheriff for the Ensuing year. It appears by the poles that Francis Adams had 10 Votes, William moore 8 Votes & Jacob Cosner 8 Votes. Ordered to be recommended accordingly.

Nicholas Warlock Adm'x on the Estate of Daniel Warlock Deceas'd Returns an Inventory of the said Estate prays an Order of Sale, which is accordingly granted.

A Deed of Sale from John Patton to John Hope Dated the 27th day of April 1772 for 250 acres of Land proved by Joseph Harden Evidence thereto. Ord'd to be Registered.

A Bill of Sale from James Alexander to John Tagert Dated the 18 Day of February 1772 for Sundry Goods & Chattles Proved by Waitsell Avery Evidence thereto. Ord'd to be Registered.

April term 1772

Court adjourned till Tomorrow at 8 OClock. Met according to adjournment. Present Thomas Neel, Henry Holman, Thomas Asby, Esq'rs.

Ord'd by the Court that Samuel Withrow serve as Overseer in the Room of William Bridges & that he enter on his Charge accordingly.

Preston Hampton vs Charles McNight. Case. Jury in this Suit Impannelled & Sworn vizt.

1 John Stanford	7 Richard Price
2 John Graham	8 James Thomson
3 James Bradley	9 Alex'r Lockart
4 George Julian	10 John Lusk
5 Dan'l McCarty	11 Geo Sizemore
6 Henry Rannalds	12 Wm McMurry

The plaintiff being Solemnly Call'd failing suffered a Nonsuit.

Charles Robison vs Nath'l Clark. Same Jury with the alteration of Rob't McAfee in the room of Dan'l McCarty. Jury Impannell'd & Sworn the plaintiff being Solemnly Call'd suffered a Nonsuit.

Preston Goforth vs John Patton. Case. Jury Impannell'd & Sworn & Find that the Defendant Did not assume.

Isaac Atkins vs Quinn, Yancey, & Rich'dson. Case. Jury Impannell'd & Sworn the plaintiff being Solemnly Call'd suffered a Nonsuit.

James Foster vs George Walker. Case. Jury Impannell'd & Sworn assess damages to one penny & Six pence Cost.

John Fondron vs John Wade. Case. Jury Impannelled & Sworn the Plaintiff being Solemnly Call'd & failing to appear Suffered a Nonsuit.

George Julian vs John Walker. Same Jury with the alteration of Samuel Farmer in the room of George Julian & James McAfee in the room of Robert McAfee. Being Elected & Sworn Find the Defend't Guilty and assess the plaintiff damages to Five pounds proc;n money & his cost to Six pence like money.

Thomas Litle Ex'r of the Last Will & Testament of William Litle Deceased Returns an Inventory of the said Estate & Prays an Order of Sale Which is accordingly granted.

Adam C. Jones vs James Alex'r & Wife. Same Jury with the Alteration of Geo Julian in the room of Saml Farmer Impannell'd & Sworn. the Plaintiff being solemnly Call'd Suffered a Nonsuit.

John Dunn vs Rich'd Price. Same Jury with the alteration of Samuel Farmer in the room of Rich'd Price Impannelled & Sworn. Jury finds the Defendant guilty & Assess Damages to Five Pounds proc. money & six pence costs.

A Deed of Sale from John Turner to John Ashworth Dated the 18th day of April 1772 for 300 acres of Land proved by William Yancey Evidence thereto. Ordered to be Registered.

April term 1772

A Deed of Sale from John Brown & Francis McCorkall & Wife to John Work Dated the seventh day of November 1771 for 400 acres of Land proved by James Byars Evidence thereto. Ord'd to be Registered.

A Deed of Sale from Jacob Coburn to Elias Morgin Dated the 14th Day of October 1771 for 200 acres of Land ack'd in Open Court and Ord'd to be Registered.

A Deed of Sale from Jacob Ramsour to David Ramsour for 280 acres of Land Dated the 30th Day of April 1772 proved by John Dunn Evidence thereto. Ord'd to be Registered.

William Yancey vs John Logan.

Petty Jury

1 John Stanford	7 James Thomson
2 John Graham	8 Sam'l Farmer
3 James Bradly	9 John Lusk
4 Geo Julian	10 Geo Sizemore
5 Henry Reynalds	11 W'm McMurry
6 Rich'd Price	12 Alex'r Lockart

Jury Impanneled and Sworn find the Defendent guilty assess to one penny Damages and Six pence Costs.

John Logan vs Wm Yancey. Same Jury. Impanneled & Sworn find the Def't Guilty & assess Damages to £ 0 0 1d &/6 Costs.

Court adjourned till Court in Course. Thos Neel, Henry Hollman, Ezekl. Polk.

North Carolina, Tryon County. To wit. Tryon Inferior Court of Pleas and Quarter Sessions begun & held The fourth Tuesday in July 1772. Present the Worshipful Thomas Neel, Wm. Moore, John Ritzhaupt, Thomas Aspey, Esq'rs.

The last Will and Testament of Robert Abernathy Sen'r was Proved in Court by the Oath of James Abernathy according to Law. Miles Abernathy Sole Executor of the Above Robert Abernathy according to the Tenour of the Above Will Came into Open Court and Took the oath appointed by Law for the faithful Discharge of the trust reposed in him as Executor of said Will. On Motion of James Forsyth Esq'r its Ordered that Letters Testamentary Together with the copy of the Will Annexed do Issue to the said Executor.

A Receipt from John Thomas Esquire to John Gordon for the payment of Two Several Sums of money Due to John Thomas Jun'r on Two Several Bonds Amounting in the whole to Two hundred and Thirty Seven Pounds Five Shillings proclamation money being in full of Two bonds which were Lost or Misslaid by said John Thomas and such loss recorded heretofore in this office was proved by the oath of David Gordon according to Law.

John Walker came Court and took the oaths by Law appointed for the Quallification of publick officers, Subscribed the test, took the oath of a Justice of the Peace & took his seat accordingly.

A Deed of Sale from Thomas Dickson to Hugh Bryson Dated the 1st Day of July 1771 for 300 acres ack'd in Open Court. Ordered to be Reg'd.

July term 1772

On Motion of James Forsyth it was Ordered by the Court that Wm. Wray have Letters of Administration of all and Singular the goods and Chattles rights and Credits of James Kelly Deceas'd who took the Oath of an Administrator and proposes for security John Walker and Alex'r Coulter Bound in the sum of Two hundred and fifty pounds. accepted.

Ordered that the perishable part of said Estate be sold accordingly to act of assembly of this province.

A Deed of Sale from Francis Beaty to Phillip Alston dated the Tenth Day of October 1771 for Six Hundred acres proved by the Oath of George Lampkin a Subscribing Evidence thereto. Ord'd to be Reg'd.

William Twitty garnishee on an Attachment returnable to this Court wherein Jno Elliot appears to be plaintiff vs Charles Robinson Deft came into Court on a Citation & Declares on Oath that he has none of the Effects of the said Cha's Robinson in his hands and thereupon discharged by the Court.

A Deed of Sale from Robert Abernathy Ju'r & Anne his wife to John Alston Dated the 3d Day of October 1771 for 300 acres proved by the Oath of George Lampkin a Subscribing Evidence thereto. Ord'd to be Registered.

A Deed of Sale from Moses Whitley to Francis Shub Dated the 20th Day of May 1772 for 467 acres proved by the Rob't Blackburn Evidence thereto. Ordered to be Registered.

A Deed of Sale from Jacob Seits & Mary his wife to John McElroy Dated the 9th day of October 1771 for 250 acres proved by Wm. Moore Evidence thereto. Ordered to be Reg'd.

A Deed of Sale from Samuel Coburn to John Dozer Dated the 21st day of October 1772 [sic] for 176 acres proved by David Crocket Sen'r Subscribing Evidence thereto. Ordered to be Registered.

A Deed of Sale from John Allen to Peter Arrand Dated the first day of April 1772 for 600 acres proved by Thomas Chadwick Evidence thereto. Ord'd to be Reg'd.

A Deed of Sale from John Wood to Benjamin Vaugh Dated the 25th Day of July 1772 for 150 acres proved by Alex'r Coulter evidence thereto. Ord'd to be Registered.

A Deed of Sale from Robert Patrick to John Patrick Dated the 16th day of July 1770 for 120 acres proved by Tho's Neel Evidence thereto. Ordered to be Registered.

A Deed of Sale from Agnes Nevans & Alex'r McGaughey Dated the 25th day of January 1772 for Land proved by Henry Nevins Evidence thereto. Ord'd to be Reg'd.

A Deed of Sale from Thomas Lovelatty & Wife to Robert McMullen Dated the 20th day of May 1772 for 200 acres proved by Rob't Link Evidence thereto. Ord'd to be Reg'd.

Court adjourned till Tomorrow at 8 OClock. Met according to adjournment. Present Thomas Neel, Jacob Costner, Thomas Espey, Esq'rs.

The Grand Jury: John Moore, foreman

2 Sam'l Richardson
3 Geo Hover

9 William Twitty
10 James McFarlin[?]

July term 1772

4 Thomas Campbell	11 William Ramsey
5 William Wilson	12 Peter Coster
6 Leonard Killion	13 Felty Mooney
7 Phillip Henson	14 Nicholas Wisenant
8 Wm Capshaw	15 Alex'r Coulter
	16 William Armstrong
	17 Nicholas Broadaway

Sworn & Charged.

An Inventory of the Sales of the Estate of William Litle deceased sold & returned by Thomas litle Executor amounting to £42 9 9.

The Estate of William Litle Deceas'd to Thomas Litle Executor D'r.

To Sundry Accompts paid Trouble & expences as P'r acct returned & approved by the Court.

$$\qquad\qquad\qquad\qquad £ 54 \ 4 \ 10\frac{1}{2}$$

By Ballance in Ex'rs hands   97 9 10½
£151 14 0

Contra C'r by Sundry sales returned & Bonds & Accounts   £ 42 9 9
109 5 -
£151 14 9

Ordered by the Court that Ephraim Coops an Orphan Boy of the Age of Fourteen Years be Bound to Thomas Campbell till he attains to the Age of Twenty One years to Learn the Art, Trade or Mystery of a Black Smith by him to be Taught in Reading According to Law and in all things to Comply with the Act of Assembly in that Case made and Provided. Indenture made out & signed by the parties 20th of July 1772.

A Deed of Lease & Release from George Clayton to George Black Dated 14th Day of June 1771 for 460 acres proved by James Withrow Evidence thereto. Ordered to be Registered.

A Deed of Sale from John McEntire & Rachel his Wife and George Wigginton Dated the 11th Day of July 1772 for 100 acres proved by the Evidence thereto. Ord'd to be Reg'd.

A Deed of Sale from James Patterson, Sarah Patterson, Thomas Patterson, and Mary Patterson to John Patterson Dated the Fifth day of March 1772 for 300 acres proved by George Fleming Evidence thereto. Ordered to be Registered.

A Deed of Sale from John Gallespy to Thomas Gallespy Dated the ___ Day of ____ 1772 for 200 acres ack'd in Open Court. Ord'd to be Reg'd.

A Deed of Sale from Peter Stoods to Francis Palmer Dated the 1st Day of July 1772 for 500 acres proved by Christopher Beekman Evidence thereto. Ordered to be Registered.

A Deed of Sale from Thomas Warren to John Lusk Dated the 18th Day of October 1771 for 186 acres proved by Wm Parker Evidence thereto. Ord'd to be Reg'd.

A Deed of Sale from Hugh Beaty to Wm Whiteside Dated the 10th Day of July 1772 for two hundred acres proved by Benjamin Bracket Evidence thereto. Ordered to be Reg'd.

July term 1772

A Deed of Sale from And'w Goforth and Elizabeth his Wife to James Ramsey Dated the 1st Day of April 1772 for 136 acres proved by Thomas Price Evidence thereto. Ordered to be Registered.

A Deed of Sale from Nicholas Fisher & Elisabeth his Wife to Thomas Warren Dated the 5th Day of Oc'r 1771 for 200 acres proved by John Lusk Evidence thereto. Ordered to be Registered.

A Deed of Sale from Robert Armstrong and Agness his Wife to James Patterson Dated the 28th Day of March 1772 for 120 acres proved by James Palley Evidence thereto. Ordered to be Registered.

A Deed of Sale from Abraham Alexander to Nathaniel Henderson Dated the 3d Day of July 1772 for 150 acres proved by Wm Mackelmurry Evidence thereto. Ordered to be Registered.

A Deed of Sale from John Tagert high Sheriff to Francis Adams Dated the 4th Day of July 1771 for one hundred acres proved by Robert Lusk Evidence thereto. Ord'd to be Registered.

A Deed of Sale from John Potts and Mary his Wife to Paul Townsend Dated the 27th Day of July 1772 for 300 acres proved by Arthur Rogers Evidence thereto. Ordered to be Registered.

A Deed of Sale from Lyllius Johnston to James Kelly Dated the 24th Day of January 1772 for 72 acres proved by Jonas Bedford Evidence thereto. Ordered to be Registered.

A Deed of Sale from Alex'r McGaughey & Rachel his Wife to Robert McMurry Dated the second Day of June 1772 for Land Acknowledged in Court. Ordered to be Reg'd.

A Deed of Sale from Reese Price to William Edger Dated the 28th Day of January 1772 for 200 acres proved by Thomas Price Evidence thereto. Ordered to be Registered.

A Deed of Sale from John Hill and Jane Hill to Reese Price Jun'r Dated the 27th Day of December 1770 for 200 acres proved by Thomas Price Evidence thereto. Ordered to be Registered.

A Deed of Sale from John Stanford & Sarah his Wife to Thomas Warren Dated the 5th Day of May 1772 for 200 acres proved by John Logan Evidence thereto. Ordered to be Registered.

Jonas Bedford Came into Court and took the Oath by Law appointed for the Qualification of Publick Officers, subscribed the Test, took the Oath of a Justice of the Peace for the County of Tryon and took his Seat accordingly.

A Deed of Sale from Isaac Hinton & James Bochannon Dated the 27th Day of July 1772 for 50 acres ack'd in Court. Ordered to be Registered.

A Deed of Sale from Hugh Beatey the Tenth Day of July 1772 one hundred acres proved by Benjamin Bracket Evidence thereto. Ord'd to be Reg'd.

Court adjourned for Half an Hour. Met according to adjournment. Present Rob't Blackburn, Jonas Bedford, Thomas Espey, Esq'rs.

July term 1772

James Kelly vs Nath'l Clark. Case for words.

Petit Jury

1 John Stanford
2 Henry Delinger
3 George Freeland
4 Alex'r McEntire
5 Wm Murphy
6 Sam'l Bickerstaff

7 John Williams
8 Jacob Vanzant
9 Christopher Hicks
10 Loudy Wray
11 Jno Johnston
12 Thomas Nickols

Jury Impanneled & Sworn find the Defendent Guilty and Assess his Damages to Twenty pounds Proc'n Money & /6 Costs. Judgment prayed by the Plff's Attorneys. Whereupon the Defend't by his Attorney prays an Appeal.

Court adjourned till to Morrow at 8 Oclock. Met according to adjournment. Present Thomas Neel, Timothy Riggs, James McEntire, Esq'rs.

A Deed of Sale from Thomas Beaty to David Hodson Dated the 15th Day of April 1772 for 400 acres proved by Thomas Beatey Evidence thereto. Ordered to be Registered.

A Deed of Sale from Margaret Willis to William Hannah Dated the 11th Day of February 1772 for sundry goods and Chattles therein mentioned proved by James Bochannon Evidence thereto. Ord'd to be Reg'd.

Ordered by the Court that James McEntire Esq'r be appointed Guardian of William Green according to his Choice in Open Court also of Abraham Green, Isaac Green, Mary Green, Jacob Green, & Joseph Green, orphans under the Age of Fourteen years children of Joseph Green Deceased the Guardian proposes for security Sam'l Richardson, John Stanford, Robert McAfee Bound in the sum of Seventeen hundred pounds proclamation money. Accepted.

A Deed of Sale from Mathias Paterson to Michael Ingle Dated the 25th day of June 1772 for 250 acres acknowledged in Court. Ord'd to be Registered.

A Deed of Sale from John McKinny to Peter Watkins Dated the 29th Day of July 1772 for 100 acres proved by Wm. Capshaw Evidence thereto. Ord'd to be Registered.

The King vs James Wilson.

Petit Jury

1 Hugh Quinn
2 Wm Tate
3 Rob't Looney
4 Thomas Warren
5 Wm Parker
6 John Logan

7 John Neighbours
8 James Vassals
9 John Stanford
10 John Lusk
11 John Mickle Wisehunt
12 Abel Beatey

Jury Impanneled & Sworn find the Def't Not Guilty in manner & form Charged in y'e Indictm't.

July term 1772

The King vs Wm. Yancey. Same Jury with the alteration of John Williams in the room of John Neighbours and Benjamin Hardin in the room of John lusk. Jury Find the Defend't Not Guilty in manner & form Charged in the Indictment.

A Deed of Sale from James Wilson to William Wilson Dated the 30th Day of July 1772 for 200 acres acknowledged in Court. Ord'd to be Registered.

A Deed of Sale from William Reed to Anson Reynolds Dated the 11th Day of February 1772 for 200 acres proved by Jesse Reynolds Evidence thereto. Ord'd to be Reg'd.

A Deed of Sale from Adam Dick to George Dick Dated the 19th Day of June 1772 for 141 acres proved by Mathias Patterson Evidence thereto. Ord'd to be Reg'd.

Met according to adjournment. Present Thomas Neel, William Moore, James McEntire, Esq'rs.

Ordered by the court that [Robert McAfee stricken] Benjamin Harden be appointed Gardian of Rachel, Leah, Jacob, and Frances Watts orphans and minors under the age of Fourteen Years Children of George Watts Deceased. the Guardian proposes for Security William Gilbert and Ja's Bochanon bound in one Hundred pounds proclamation money. Accepted & bound.

Edward Williams ass'ee vs William Read. Same Jury. Jury Impannelled and Sworn Find for the Plaintiff and assess his Damages to £5 19 3 3/4 and/6 Cost.

John Williams vs Robert Williams. Orr att.

1 John Houk	7 Wm Gilbert
2 Merry McGuire	8 Benjamin Harden
3 Frederick Summy	9 Wm Yancey
4 Rob't McAfee	10 Jacob Green
5 Thos Nickols	11 Adam Erchart
6 John Dills	12 Jacob Willis

Jury Impanneled & Sworn and assess to £21 release by plffs attorney to £20. Judgment.

Court adjourned till Tomorrow Morning 9 OClock. Met according to adjournment. Present Thomas Neel, William Moore, Rob't Blackburn, Jacob Costner, Henry Holman, James McEntire, Esq'rs.

Ordered by the Court that Henry Holman, Robt Blackburn, Jacob Ramsour, Timothy Riggs, Wm. Wray and William Twitty be Summoned to appear and attend at Salisbury on the 5th day of September next to Serve as Grand & Petit Jurors.

Robert Collinwood & Elisabeth his wife Admr's of the Estate of Leonard Sephrod [sic, for Sefrit] Came into Open Court having settled s'd Estate and after Deducting all Costs and Demand together with the Widows third it appears that there is £63 17 4 coming due to John Sephred Son and Heir at Law of the said Deceased out of which it appears that there is in Notes & bonds in the hands of Timothy Riggs Esq'r whom the Court has appointed Guardian over said orphan fifty six pounds Nineteen and six pence part of the above £63 17 4 and that the Ballance £6 17 8 Remains in the hands of the above Admr and Becoming due to the said Guardian from the said Administrators.

July term 1772

On motion of John Dunn it is Ordered that Timothy Riggs Esq'r be appointed Guardian of the aforesaid Orphan and Minor of Leonard Sephred Deceased who proposes for Security Benjamin Harden, Richard Reynolds & John Neighbours Bound in the sum of one Hundred & thirteen pounds Nineteen shillings and three pence proc. money. Accepted.

Israel Peters vs John Tagert.

Petit Jury

1 Thomas Warren	7 William Wray
2 William Parker	8 William Henry
3 John Lusk	9 Loudwick Wray
4 John Neighbours	10 Robert Murphy
5 Peter Aker	11 John Oaks
6 Wm. Gilberts	12 John Stanford

Jury Impannelled and Sworn Find the plaintiff has sustained no Damages. On Motion Ordered by the Court that a New Tryal be had in the above suit.

An Inventory of the Estate of Christopher Petty Deceased was Returned This Term by Sarah Petty wife & Relict of the Deceased, and also administratrix of said Estate, which Inventory is filed in this office. Ordered by the Court on motion of mr. Dunn that the personal Estate be sold agreeable to Act of assembly of this Province.

Jacob Green vs Nath'l Hart. Orr att.

Petit Jury

1 Alex'r McEntire	7 Jacob Willis T B
2 Jno Nuckols	8 Benjamin Harden
3 Jno Fondron	9 Jacob Pack
4 Jacob Hofstatler	10 X't Sigman
5 Rob't Burns	11 Abrh'm Wilkins
6 James Bochannon	12 Wm Parker D M

Jury Impannelld and sworn assess the Plaintiffs Damages £14 6 8 and /6 Cost.

Thomas Sumpter vs David Amory. Same Jury. Impannelled and sworn assess the Plaintiffs Damages to £20 and/6 Cost.

John Winbron Sr. & Wife vs Wm. Logan and Wife. Same Jury with the alteration of Sam'l Biggerstaff in the room of Alex'r McEntire, Thos Black in the room of Jacob Willis and David moore in the room of Wm. Parker. Jury Impanneld & Sworn. Plaintiff non suit.

Court adjourned till Tomorrow at 9 OClock. Met according to adjournment. Present Tho's Neel, Rob't Blackburn, Jacob Costner, Esq'rs.

John McKinny vs David Bailey. Att.

1 John Nuckols	7 Frederick Sponcelor
2 Jacob Green	8 Jacob Sponcelor
3 John Sigman	9 John Carpenter
4 Robert Looney	10 John Fondron
5 Wm Wray	11 Wm. Wilson

July term 1772

6 David Moore   12 Adam Ephart

Jury impannelled and sworn assess plff's Damages to one penny & /6 Cost.

Robert Murphy vs Robt Lusk. Case. Same Jury with the alteration of Henry Dellinger in the room of David Moore and Rob't McCashland in the room of Wm Wary. Impannelled & Sworn find that the Deft Did not Assume.

Ordered by the Court that the Summons issue Signed by the Chairman for a Constable in each Captains Dist't in this county to warn the Taxable persons in each company to appear before their respective magistrates to give in upon oath a Just account of their Taxables.

A Deed of Sale from John Parks to William Ray Dated the 31st Day of July 1772 for 275 acres acknowledged in Court. Ord'd to be Reg'd.

A Deed of Sale from Edmund Bishop to John Miller dated the third day of February 277 for 200 acres proved by George Ross Evidence thereto. Ordered to be Registered.

North Carolina, Tryon County. to wit. July Court 1772. Present his Majestys Justices. Then were the Ordinary Keepers Prices Rates.

Lodging in a Good feather Bed & Clean Sheets P'r Night	£ 0	0	4
Breakfast and Supper Each	0	0	8
Every dinner not Less than 2 dishes of Good Meat	0	1	0
Madera & Port wine P'r Quart	0	3	0
Claret wine P'r Quart	0	4	0
Punch with Loaf Sugar & West India Rum Pr Qu't	0	1	6
Tody with Loaf Sugar & West India Rum P'r Quart	0	1	4
Tody with Loaf Sugar & New Engl'd Rum P'r Quart	0	0	8
Brandy & Whisky Toddy P'r Quart	0	0	4
Beer P'r Quart	0	0	6
Cider P'r Quarter	0	0	6
W. India Rum P'r ½ pint	0	0	10
New England Rum P'r ½ pint	0	0	6
Brandy or Whisky P'r ½ pint	0	0	6
Pasturage for every horse or mare for 24 hours	0	0	4
Stabling for Every night w't hay or fodder for Every Horse or Mare	0	1	0

Court adjourned till Court in Course. Thomas Neel, Jacob Costner, Henry Hollman.

North Carolina, Tryon County. To wit. Tryon Inferior Court of Pleas and Quarter Sessions begun & held on the Fourth Tuesday in October Anno Domini 1772. Present the Worshipful Henry Holman, Robert Blackburn, Esq'rs.

Court Adjourned till tomorrow at 10 O'Clock. Present Thomas Neel, Jonas Bedford, John Retzhoupt, Esq'rs.

Andrew Neel Came into Court & produced a Commission under the hand & Seal of Samuel Strudwick Esq'r appointing him Clerk of the pleas for the County of Tryon who took the oath by Law appointed for public officers, subscribed the test, Took the oath of a Clerk & entered on the Duty of his office.

October term 1772

A Deed of Sale from John Kinkaid and [to] William Kinkaid Dated the 17th Day of October 1772 for one hundred & fifty acres proved by David Crockat Evidence thereto. Ordered to be Registered.

Bond from Andrew Neel, William Moore and Thomas Neel to his Excellency the Governor in the sum of £1000 proc. money, 8 October 1772 for the performance of Andrew Neel as public register of the County of Tryon. Wit: Rob't Blackburn.

The Grand Jury: James Cook, foreman

2 James Henderson	9 Samuel Coburn
3 Christian Carpenter	10 Nicholas Shrum
4 Andrew Hoyl	11 James Cook Ju'r
5 Richard Jones	12 Robert McCasland
6 David Ramsey	13 Nicholas Beck
7 Martin Shutts	14 Nicholas Warlock
8 Michael Sailor	15 Sam'l Biggerstaff

A Deed of Sale from Sam'l Young to John Alston Dated the fifth Day October in the Year of Our Lord 1772 for 250 acres proved by Jno Kirkconell Evidence thereto. Ordered to be Registered.

A Deed of Sale from Joseph Davies to Wm Alston Dated the third Day of October 1772 for 93 acres proved by George Lamkin Evidence thereto. Ord'd to be Reg'd.

A Deed of Sale from George Lamkin & Hannah his Wife of the one part to Wm Alston Dated 7th Day of March 1772 for 100 acres acknowledged in Open Court by Geo. Lamkin. Ordered to be Registered.

A Deed of Sale from Andrew McNabb and Margaret his Wife to John Alston Dated the 27th Day of March 1772 for one hundred and thirty acres proved by Jno Alston Evidence thereto. Ord'd to be Reg'd.

A Deed of Sale from Andrew McNabb and Margaret his Wife to John Alston Dated the 27th Day of March 1772 for three hundred acres proved by Jno Alston Evidence thereto. Ord'd to be Registered.

A Deed of Sale from Robert Scott and George Lamkin Dated fourteenth Day of November 1771 for 100 acres proved by William Lamkin Evidence thereto. Ordered to be Registered.

A Deed of Sale from Matthew Armstrong & Benjamin Armstrong to Garrot Will Dated the 6th Day of June 1772 for 313 acres proved by Peter Criter Evidence thereto. Ordered to be Registered.

A Deed of Sale from Benjamin Shaw to John Alexander Dated the 31st Day of August 1772 for four hundred acres proved by Robert Blackburn Evidence thereto. Ordered to be Registered.

A Deed of Sale from James Anderson to Wm Callahan Dated the 30th Day of June 1772 for 200 acres proved by Edward Callahan Evidence thereto. Ord'd to be Reg'd.

A Deed of Sale from George Pee to Edward Callahan Dated the 29th Day of August 1772 for 200 acres proved by Andrew Neel Evidence thereto. Ordered to be Registered.

October term 1772

Court adjourned till Tomorrow at 8 OClock. Met according to adjournment. Present Thomas Neel, John Ritzhaupt, Jonas Bedford, Ezekiel Polk, Thomas Espey, Esq'rs.

Nicholas Warlock administrator of the Estate of Daniel Warlock Deceas'd Returns an additional account of Sales of the Estate of the s'd Daniel Warlock Decas'd to the amount of Eight pound one Shilling which was Ordered to be put of Record.

George Lamkin Came into Court and produced his Excellency Commission appointing him high Sheriff of this County Dated the Twenty fourth day of Septem'r 1772 who took the oath by Law appointed for the Qualification of Publick officers, Subscribed the Test, took the Oath of a Sheriff and Entered on the Duty of his office.

William Lamkin also Came into Court took the oath by Law appointed for the Qualification of Publick officers, Subscribed the Test and took the Oath of a Deputy Sheriff of Tryon County and took his place accordingly.

A Bond from George Lamkin, John Alston, Philip Alston, John Kirkconell, Samuel Coburn, James Abernathy, John Stroud and William Gilbert to Josiah Martin, Esqr., Governor and his Successors in the sum of one thousand pounds Sterling for the True accounting of and paying the publick Taxes for the Year 1772 which bond was acknowledged in open Court.

Miles Abernathy Ex'r of the Last will and Testament of Rob't Abernathy Sen'r returns an Inventory of s'd Estate and prays an order of Sale which was accordingly granted.

A Deed of Sale from John Potts to Nicholas Clay Dated the 20th Day of September 1772 for 100 acres proved by Alexander Erwin Evidence thereto. Ordered to be reg'd.

A Deed of Sale from Nicholas Welch to John Coster Dated the 24th Day of October 1772 for 300 acres proved by Nicholas Warlock Evidence thereto. Let it be Registerd.

A Deed of Sale from Nicholas Warlock & Wife to Lewis Warlock Dated the 29th Day of October 1772 for 200 acres Acknowledged in Open Court by Nicholas Warlock his Wife being privately Examined says she does it with her free Consent. Let it be Registerd.

A Deed of Sale from Abraham Keener and Ula his Wife to James Abernathy Dated the 23d Day of Oc'r 1772 for 280 acres proved by Wm. Moore Evidence thereto the Feme being privately Examined says she signed by her own & Voluntary free Consent. Ordered to be Registerd.

A Deed of Sale from Jacob Coburn to John Stroud Dated the 11th Day of August 1772 for 300 acres proved by John Hill Evidence thereto. Ordered to be registered.

A Deed of Sale from John McEntire to Robert Lee Dated the 20th Day of October 1772 for 200 acres proved by Timothy Riggs Evidence thereto. Ordered to be registered.

A Deed of Sale from George Wigginton & Elizabeth his Wife to Alexander Kyle Dated the 10th Day of October 1772 for one hundred acres acknowledged in Open Court. Ordered to be Registered.

On motion of Alexander Martin Ordered by the Court that Thomas Morris have a License to keep Ordinary at his Dwelling House in Tryon County he Complying with the Act of

<u>October term 1772</u>

Assembly in that case made and provided he proposes for Security William Gilbert and John Kirkconnel. accepted.

Court adjourned for an Our. Met according to adjournment. Present Thomas Neel, John Ritzhaupt, Jonas Bedford, Esq'rs.

Court adjourned till tomorrow at 9 Oclock. Met according to adjournment. Present Thomas Neel, Jonas Bedford, Timothy Riggs, Thomas Espey, Esq'rs.

Andrew Keller of Tryon County, North Carolina, sells or mortgages to Laurence Kizer of same, one plantation on the waters of Long Creek, 200 acres, and one horse branded WK Black Culler and

one mare gray Culler and ten head of cow marked on the nigh ear a crop and the off ear a slit and a half penny & six head of hogs marked in the near eat with a crop and off ear a Slit and half penny and further all my house furniture for £23 s1 proc. money, 5 Oct 1772, on condition that Andrew Keller pay the said Kyzer the sum of £23 s1 proc. money by 1 May next. Andrew keller (X) (Seal), Wit: Thomas Espey, _____ [German signature].

The King vs Mary Hoofstaler.
Petit Jury

1 John McElroy
2 James Cozart
3 George Davis
4 Perry Green Magnis
5 John Carpenter
6 Patrick McDavid
7 Andrew Hampton
8 John Moore
9 Wm Bracket
10 Mattison Hunt
11 Francis Gilmore
12 Alexander Coulter

Jury Impanneled & Sworn find the Defendent Not Guilty in manner and form Charged in the Indictment.

The King vs John Hoofstatler. Same Jury Impannelled and Sworn find the Deft. not guilty in manner & form Charged in the Indictment.

A Deed of Sale from John Nuckols and [to] James Cozart Dated the 7th Day of July 1770 for 300 acres of Land proved by Frederick Hambright Evidence thereto. Ord'd to be Registered.

A Deed of Sale from David Jenkins to James Cozart Dated the 23d Day of March 1772 for 52 acres of Land proved by Frederick Hambright Evidence thereto. Ord'd to be Reg'd.

Ordered by the Court that Henry Hiltebrand be appointed Gaurdin of Loudewick Warlock orphan and minor of Daniel Warlock Deceased and that he take the said Orphan into his Care and have him before the Court at next term so that he may Dealt with agreeable to Law Relative to the Estate of said orphan.

John Nuckols vs James Walker. Case. Same Jury. Impannelled and Sworn plaintiff failing to appear was Nonsuit.

October term 1772

M. Boshears vs M. Lovelatty. Case. Same Jury. Impannelled and Sworn plaintiff failing to appear was Nonsuit.

Ezekial Polk vs Danl Heoy. Orr Att. Jury Impannelled and sworn find for the Plaintiff and assess his Damages to £7 10 5 and /6 Cost.

George Irwin vs William Sims. Debt. Same Jury Impannelled and Sworn find it is the Defendants Act and Deed & find the plaintiff £14:0 and /6 Cost.

Jno McKnitt Alexander vs Richard Gullock. Same Jury Impannelled and Sworn find for the plaintiff and assess his Damages to £7 6 3 and /6 Cost.

Settlement of the Estate of George Watts Deceased by the Administratrix.
Amount of Sales and Cash received	£78 2 3
Charges against the Estate	29 18 4
Remains in the hands of y'e Admx or Guardian	48 4 11

A Deed of Sale from Daniel Shipman to Abel Lee Dated the 5th Day January in the Year 1772 for 100 acres proved by Robert Lee Evidence thereto. Ordered to be Registerd.

A Deed of Sale from John Fifer and Catharine his Wife Dated the 29th Day of October 1772 for four hundred acres of Land proved by Harkles Krunright Evidence thereto. Ord'd to be Reg'd.

A Deed of Sale from John Hoofstatler to Andrew Keller Dated the 21st Day of October 1772 for 200 acres proved by Laurence Kyzer Evidence thereto. Ord'd to be Registered.

A Deed of Sale from Laurence Kyzer to George Michael Wisenaunt Dated the 21st Day of October 1772 for 45 acres proved by Philip Wissenaunt Evidence thereto. Ord'd to be Reg'd.

Court adjourned till Tomorrow at 9 OClock. Met according to adjournment. Present Thomas Neel, Rob't Blackburn, Timothy Riggs, James McEntire, Esq'rs.

Ordered by the Court that Christopher Rinehart be appointed Gaurdian to Barbara Warlock Orphan of Daniel Warlock Deceased. He proposes for Security William Moore and Lewis Whitener Bound in the sum of Two hundred pound proc. money. accepted.

A Deed of Sale from Matthias Barrier & Jno Pope to Philip Henry Grader Dated the 12th Day of Septem'r 1772 for 60 acres proved by Christopher Beekman Evidence thereto. Ord'd to be Registered.

Ordered by the Court that Michael Rudiseal be appointed Guardian to Frederick Link, Jacob, Catherine & John Link Orphans of Jacob Link Deceased he proposes for Security Jacob Costner bound in the sum of One hundred and Fifty pounds. accepted.

George Lamkin, High Sheriff, Came into Court and made a protest against the Goal of this County it not being Sufficient.

1772 October Term Claims on the County of Tryon for the year 1772.

October term 1772

	£	S	D
William Reed 1 Venire Ticket		18	6
Jacob Ramsour 1 Do	2	4	2
Henry Holman 1 Do	2	8	8
Robert Blackburn 1 Do	2	8	8
Frederick Hambright 1 Do	2	5	8
John Alexander 1 Do	2	5	8
Tollover Sutton 2 Scalp Tickets		15	
Jacob Grissemore 1 Do		7	6
Adolph Reep 1 Do		7	6
John Sickman Ju'r 1 Do		7	6
John Johnston 1 Do		7	6
Ephraim McLean 2 Do		15	
William Henry 4 Do	1	10	
Frederick Hambright 1 Do		7	6
William Cogdale 1 Do		7	6
John Gullick 1 Do		7	6
Christopher Carpenter 1 Do		7	6
Peter Blank 1 Do		7	6
Hosea Stout 1 Do		7	6
George Trout 1 Do		7	6
James Patterson 1 Do		7	6
Timothy Riggs 1 Venire Ticket	2	14	8
Jno Bunn 4 Scalp Tickets	1	10	
Jno Scott 6 Do	2	5	
Shadrach Green 1 Do		7	6
Jno Sartain 1 Do		7	6
Moses Whitley 1 Do		7	6
Jno Autry 3 Do	1	2	6
Thos Harrod 4 Do	1	10	
Benjamin Campble 1 Do		7	6
Jas Swafford 1 Do		7	6
William Wilson 1 Do		7	6
Jacob Shipman 1 Do		7	6
Jno Baker 1 Do		7	6
Abel Lee 3 Do	1	2	6
Thomas Polk for Service Done in Running the County Line	6	10	
Thomas Neel for Do	6	10	
One Chain Bearer and marker @ 4/ Each P Day	5	4	
One Pack Horse Man 13 days 5/ P Do	3	5	
Peter Johnston Surveyor for his Services for Do	9	15	
Provisions for three hands 13 Days 1 2/	1	6	
To Christopher Rinehart for the Court house 4 Courts	10		
To the Clerk for Exofficio services	8		
To the Sheriff for Commissions @ 8 Pr Cent	6	-	-
	89	16	

The aforesaid Sum of Eighty Nine pound Sixteen Shillings in the whole of the money Due by the county of Tryon for the Year 1772. It is therefore ordered that a Tax of Two

Shillings and Eight pence be Levied on Each Taxable person in the said County of Tryon to Discharge the above said Sum.

Court adjourned till Court in Course. Thos Neel, Timothy Riggs, Jacob Costner, Thomas Espey. Probates Remitted.

North Carolina, Tryon County. To wit. Tryon Inferior Court of Pleas and Quarter Sessions began and holden the fourth Tuesday in January 1773. Present the Worshipful Thomas Neel, John Ritzhaupt, John Walker, Esq'rs.

A Bill of Sale from Michael Hoofstatler Dated the 22nd Septem'r 1772 for therein Puting into possession of the said Michael Hoofstatler all his Cattle Running in the Range in the said County proved by Joseph Kyzer Evidence thereto.

John Carpenter Came into Open Court and prayed he might [be] admitted to take the Oaths of Naturalization which he was accordingly admitted and subscribed the Test.

Ordered by the court that Aaron Ryley Serve as Overseer of the Road Leading from Wm. Davis to the Charles Town Road in that part between Sam'l Grays and opposite to Samuel Richardson and Sam'l Richardson and Sam'l Gray from opposite the sd. Richardsons House to the province Line.

Uel Lamkin came into Court and took the Oaths by Law appointed for the Qualification of publick Officers, Subscribed the Test and Took the Oath of a Deputy Sheriff and Entered in the Duty of his Office accordingly.

The Court in the absence of Alex'r Martin Esq'r Deputy Attorney for the Crown appointed for this Term Waightstill Avery.

A Deed of Sale from George Michael Wisenhaunt to Nicholas Therter Dated the 6th day of January 1773 for 45 acres acknowledged in Open Court. Ordered to be Regist'd.

A Deed of Sale from George Michael Wisenhaunt & Nancey his Wife to Nicholas Therter Dated the 18th Day of December 1772 for 200 acres acknowledged in Open Court. Ordered to be Registered.

A Deed of Sale from William Willis and Margaret his Wife to William Hanna Dated the 12th Day of Decemb'r 1772 for 250 acres proved by Benjamin Harden Evidence thereto. Ord'd to be Registered.

James Graham of Tryon County, North Carolina, sold to James Millikin of said county, three milch cows one a brindled cow 10 years old marked with a Half Crop in the off Ear and Slit in the Near ear, one Brindled Cow 6 years old with a Half Crop in the near ear & alit in the off Ear, one white Cow with 2 Red Ears 3 years old, also three calves 2 Brindled Bulls & one Brown Heifer Calf Crop't in the Nigh Ear, for £8, dated 25 Oct 1772. James Graham (Seal), Wit: Samuel Johnston, And'w Milligan, William Moore.

A Deed of Sale from David Ramsey to William Ramsey for 160 acres Dated the 1st Day of December 1772 ackn'd in Open Court. Ord'd to be Reg'd.

A Deed of Sale from James Martin & Agness his Wife to Sam'l Andrew for 470 acres Dated the 4th Day of Decem 1772 proved by Wm Barr Evidence thereto. Ord'd to be Reg'd.

January term 1773

A Deed of Sale from John Reed and Martha his Wife to Abraham Womack for 150 acres Dated the 23d Day of October 1772 proved by Thomas Beatey Evidence thereto. Ord'd to be Registered.

A Deed of Sale from Daniel McCarty & Agniss his Wife to Andrew Goforth for 300 acres Dated the 17th Day of Nov'r 1772 proved by John Wells Evidence thereto. Ord'd to be Reg'd.

A Deed of Sale from Samuel Givens to William Flack for 100 acres Dated the 23d Day of August 1768 proved by John Walker Evidence thereto. Ord'd to be Reg'd.

A Deed of Sale from Thomas Reynolds to Andrew Mills for 640 acres Dated the first Day of Septem 1770 proved by Moses Moore Evidence thereto. Ord'd to be Reg'd.

A Deed of Sale from Andrew Hampton & Catharine his Wife for 280 acres Dated the 4th Day of July 1771 proved by James Melkillon Evidence thereto. Ord'd to be Reg'd.

A Deed of Sale from Joseph Davies to Nathan Davis for 93½ acres Dated the 9th Day of February 1771 proved by George Lamkin Evidence thereto. Ord'd to be Reg'd.

A Bill of Sale from Dan'l Devour to Joseph England for 3 Horse Kind & 6 Head of Horned Cattle and an improvement whereon he now lives proved by Danl Singleton Evidence thereto. Ord'd to be Reg'd.

Court Adjourned till tomorrow at 8 Oclock. Met according to Adjournment. Present Thos Neel, John Walker, Ja's McEntire.

Ordered that Jacob Rine serve as Constable in the room of Benjamin Biggerstaff and that he Swear in before Jacob Castner Esq'r accordingly.

The Grand Jury: Robert Ewart, Foreman

1 John Hill	9 James Alley
2 John Hoyl	10 Solomon Beson
3 Thomas Beatey	11 Wm Ramsey
4 John Stanford	12 James Beatey
5 Thomas Campbell	13 Thomas Harrod
6 William Berry	14 Thomas Black
7 Frederick Hambright	
8 Henry Reynolds	

Sworn & Charged.

On motion of John Dunn Esqr. Ordered by the court that Hannah Henry Wife & Relict of Wm. Henry Deceased together with John Robison Esq'r have Letters of Administration for the Estate of the said Wm Henry Security proposed Alex'r Gilleland & David Alexander approved of & bound in the sum of £300 who also took the oaths of Administrators accordingly. On Motion it is ordered that the said Adm'r do sell the perishable goods Belonging to the Above Estate.

A Bill of Sale from James Kelly to Leonard Sailer for a negro wench named Precilla dated 27th of January 1773 was Acknowledged in Open Court by the said James Kelly.

January term 1773

A Deed of Sale from James Wyatt and Bethelem his Wife to Zachariah Spencer for 193 acres Dated the 26th Day of Decem'r 1772 proved by Wm Spencer Evidence thereto. Ord'd to be Reg'd.

James Kelly of this County Came into Open Court of his own free will and accord and in the Presence of said court did acknowledge that in a Quarrel between him and a Certain Leonard Sailor on the Evening of the 26 day of January 1773 he did Bite of the upper part of the Left Ear of him the said Leonard Sailor who prays the Same to be Recorded in the Minutes of this Court.

Thomas Sumpter vs David Amory. Case.
                    Petty Jury

1	Aaron Biggerstaff	7 John Alexander
2	Benjamin Bracket	8 James Wyatt
3	Joseph McDaniel	9 Benjamin Harden
4	Phineas Crayton	10 Michael Hoofstatler
5	Nicholas Welch	11 Valentine Mauny
6	Thomas Welch	12 Jacob Yorty

Jury Impenneled & Sworn find for the 1d and /6 Costs.

Alex'r Irwin vs John Sigman & Wife. Case words. Same Jury Impannelled & Sword find for the plaintiff and Assess his Damages to 20/ and /6 Costs.

A Deed of Sale from Jonathan Newman to Charles McLean for 300 acres Dated the 12th Day of Jan'y 1773 proved by David Alex'r Evidence thereto. Ord'd to be Reg'd.

Ordered by the Court that Christopher Rinehart serve as overseer on the Charles Town Road on that part Between my Lords Line and Indian Creek ford.

Ordered by the Court that Jacob Howe Serve as Overseer of the Road in the Room and place where Frederick Wise formerly served.

According to an Order of Last Term it is Ordered by the Court that Henry Hiltebrand be appointed Guardian of Lewis Warlock orphan & minor of Dan'l Warlock Deceased who proposes for Security Martin Shufort and Henry Holman Bound in the sum of £300 accepted.

Ordered by the Court that Thomas Campbell be fin'd Forty Shillings for his Non attendance as Grand Juror according to Act of Assembly.

Ordered also by the Court that the said Thomas Campbell be fined Three pounds proc. money for his Contempt Committed in the Face of the Court. The Three pounds ____ by the Court.

Ordered by the Court that George Sides serve as Constable in the room of Jacob Shutley & that he Swear in before John Ritzhaupt Esq'r accordingly. It is also Ord'd that Martin Bates[?] also serve & Swear in before john Ritzhaupt.

Ordered by the Court that Richard Venable serve as Constable in John Robisons District & that he Swear in before John Robison Esq'r accordingly.

111

January term 1773

Ordered by the Court that James Kelly serve as Constable in the room of George Trout and that he Swear in before Thomas Espey Esq'r accordingly.

A Deed of Sale from John Bucanon & Ann his wife to John Cooper for 200 acres Dated the 23d Day of January 1772 proved by Thomas Polk Evidence thereto. Ord'd to be Reg'd.

A Deed of Sale from Wm Bassett to James Miller for ___ acres Dated the 21st Day of August 1772 proved by Jonas Bedford Evidence thereto. Ord'd to be Reg'd.

A Deed of Sale from James Logan to John Huggins for 200 acres Dated the 10th Day of January 1770 proved by Robert Caruth Evidence thereto. Ord'd to be Registered.

A Deed of Sale from Ezekiel Smith to William Twitty for ___ acres Dated the 19th Day of August 1772 proved by Jonas Bedford Evidence thereto. Ord'd to be Reg'd.

A Deed of Sale from Thomas Robison to Moses Moore for 300 acres Dated the 27th Day of January 1773 and acknowledged in Open Court. Ord'd to be Reg'd.

A Deed of Sale from William Anderson to John Dellinger [for] 200 acres Dated the 19th Day of January 1773 proved by Alex'r Lockhart Evidence thereto. Ord'd to be Registered.

A Deed of Sale from John McElroy and Mary his Wife for 250 acres Dated the 11th Day of August 1772 proved by Jacob Seits Evidence thereto. Ord'd to be Reg'd.

A Deed of Sale from Preston Goforth to Wm Goforth for 200 acres proved by Wm. Berry Evidence thereto and Dated the 26th Day of January 1773. Ord'd to be Reg'd.

A Deed of Sale from Hugh Quinn to Charles Tice for 200 acres of Land Dated the 22nd Day of Septem'r 1772 proved by James Collins Evidence thereto. Ord'd to be Reg'd.

A Deed of Sale from Alexander McCallister & Margaret his Wife to John Baldridge for 640 acres Dated the 30th Day of May 1765 proved by John Ramsey Evidence thereto. Ord'd to be Reg'd.

Court Adjourned till tomorrow at 7 Oclock. Met according to Adjournment. Present Thomas Neel, Henry Holman, John Ritzhaupt, John Walker, Esq'rs.

Rich'd Gullick vs David Davis. Case.

Petty Jury

1 Nicholas Shram	7 Jacob Sheckley
2 James Adams	8 Benjamin Biggerstaff
3 Francis Gilmore	9 Thomas Harrnton
4 Michael Ingland	10 Anson Reynolds
5 Nicholas Warlock	11 Samuel Johnston
6 Leonard Seratt	12 Jonathan Wilson

Jury Impanneled & Sworn assess y'e plffs Damages to £5 and /6 Costs.

David Nisbet vs Preston Goforth. Case. Same Jury Impannelled & Sworn find for the plaintiff £5 5 8 & /6 Costs.

January term 1773

Thomas Litle vs John Beatey. Case. Same Jury Impannelled & Sworn find for the plaintiff £9 14 6 & /6d Costs.

Thomas Litle vs John Beatey. Case. Same Jury Impannelled & Sworn find for the plaintiff £7 15 and /6 Costs.

Robert Collinwood vs Benjamin Bracket. Case. Same Jury Impannelled & Sworn the plaintiff failing to appear was Nonsuit.

Thomas Beatey vs Joseph Johnston. Case. Same Jury Impannelled & Sworn assess the Plaintiff's Damages to /1d and /6d Costs.

Robert Smith vs John Steen. Case. Same Jury Impannelled & Sworn plff's Damages £10 11 7 & /6 Costs.

Nicholas Warlock Administrator of Daniel Warlock Deceased produced his Settlement of s'd Estate.

Amount of Sales	£1181 17 6
Money found in the house	59 8 -
Money due by Book	51 4 -
The whole Amount	£1292 9 6
Disbursements allow'd	22 2 4
Ballance in the hands of the Administrator	£1269 17 2

A Deed of Sale from Henry Dellinger to Martin Shutts for 300 acres Dated the 24th Day of December 1772 acknowledged in Open Court. Ord'd to be Regist'd.

A Bill of Sale from William Yancey to Christian Carpenter for one Negro Girl named Phebe which was acknowledged in Open Court by the Grantor.

Court Adjourned till tomorrow at 8 Oclock. Met according to Adjournment. Present John Ritzhaupt, Timothy Riggs, Thomas Espey, Esq'rs.

Ordered by the Court that John Wells Sen. Serve as Constable for Charles McLean and that he Swear in before Charles McLean Esq'r accordingly.

A Deed of Sale from John Sharp to John Allison for 300 acres Dated the third Day of October 1771 proved by Wm. Sharp Evidence thereto. Ord'd to be Reg'd.

A Deed of Sale from Robert Henderson to Wm. Sharp for 300 acres of Land Dated the 29th Day of January 1772 proved by Waightstill Avery Evidence thereto. Ord'd to be Reg'd.

A Deed of Sale from Aaron Burlison to Rob't McMinn [for] 100 acres Dated the 1st Day of August 1772 proved by Timothy Riggs Evidence thereto. Ord'd to be Registered.

Ordered by the Court that Solomon Beson Serve as Overseer of the Charlestown Road in that part leading from Buffalo Creek to Kings Mountain.

Ordered by the Court that William Moore, George Ewing, Jacob Costner, Nicholas Friday, John Walker & John Alston Serve as Grand and Petet Jurors at the Next Superior Court for the District of Salisbury & that they be Summoned to appear the fifth day of March next accordingly.

Court Adjourned till Court in Course. Thos Neel, Jonas Bedford, Charles McLean, John Robinson.

North Carolina, Tryon County. To wit. Tryon Inferior Court of Pleas and Quarter Sessions begun and held for s'd County the Fourth Tuesday in April Anno Dom. 1773. Present William Moore.

His Majestys Commission of the Peace being Read then Silence was proclaimed.

William Moore, Charles McLane, James McEntire, Timothy Riggs & Thomas Asby came into open Court and took the oath by Law appointed for the qualification of public officers, repeated and Subscribed the test and took the oath of Justices of the Peace and took their seats accordingly.

John Walker Esq'r came into open Court and produced a Commission from His Excellency Josiah Martin Esq'r Governor &C appointing him Coroner of the County Tryon who took the oaths by Law appointed for the qualification of public officers, repeated and Subscribed the test and took the oath of Coroner accordingly.

James Williams Esq'r came into open Court and produced a Licence from His Excellency Josiah Martin Esq'r Governor &C &C impowering him to plead & practice as an attorney he took the oaths for Qualification & was admitted accordingly.

Andrew Neel came into open Court and produced a Commission appointing him Clerk of the Crown from the Honourable Saml Strudwick Esq'r who took the oaths by Law appointed for the qualification of public officers, repeated and Subscribed the test and took the oath of Clerk of the Crown and entered on the duty of his office accordingly.

An Inventory of Sales of the Estate of William Henry Deceased returned by Hannah Henry and John Robinson Adm'x & Administrator of the said Estate to the Amount of £202 6 2.

The Grand Jury: Frederick Hambright, Foreman

2	David Ramsey	10	James Whiteside
3	Martin Shults	11	Jacob Glance
4	Benj'n Harden	12	George Winters
5	John McKinny	13	Thomas Black
6	Michael Keller	14	Aaron Moore
7	James Alley	15	Rob't McCaland
8	Solomon Beson	16	Peter Carpenter
9	Joseph Laurence	17	William Armstrong
		18	William Yancey

Sworn & Charged.

On Motion of Alexander Martin Esq'r Ordered by the Court that Elie Allexander Wife and Relict of Robert Alexander Deceased have Letters of Administration of all and Singular the Goods and Chattles rights and Credits of the said Rob't Alexander who proposes for Security John Walker and John McKinny Bound in £100.

On Motion of Alexander Martin Esq'r Ordered by the Court that Jane Withrow wife and Relict of Sam'l Withrow Deceased have Letters of Administration of all and Singular the Goods and Chattles right and Credits of the said Samuel Withrow who proposes for Security James Wilson and John Walker Bound in the sum of £600. accepted.

<u>April term 1773</u>

Jane Withrow Aministr'x of the Estate of Saml. Withrow returns an Inventory of the said Estate and prays an order of Sale, which is accordingly Granted.

Ordered by the Court that Richard Reynolds Be appointed Overseer of the Road leading from Warlocks Mill to Kings Mountain in that part between the said Mill and Indian Creek and that he enter on the Duty of his Charge accordingly.

Ordered by the Court that Thomas Black serve as Overseer of the Road leading from Warlocks Mill to Kings Mountain in that part between Indian Creek and Long Creek and that he enter on the Duty of his Charge accordingly.

Ordered by the Court that Michael Hofstatler serve as Overseer of the Road leading from Warlocks Mill to Kings Mountain in that part between Long Creek Kings Mountain and that he enter on the Duty of his Charge accordingly.

Court Adjourned for an Hour & a Half. Met According to Adjournment. Present William Moore, Jas McEntire, Thomas Espey, Esq'rs. Court Adjourned till tomorrow at 8 Oclock. Met according to Adjournment. Present William Moore, Charles McLean, Thomas Espy, Esq'rs.

The last will and Testament of Alexander Wells was produced in Open Court and Proved by the Oath of David Crocket. On motion of John Dunn Esq'r Ordered by the court that Robert Ewart and James Johnston Executors of the said will have Letters Testamentary of all and Singular the goods and chattles of the said Deceas'd who took the Oath of Executors which was accordingly granted.

Alexander Thompson, son to James Thompson and Heir to Alexander Wells Deceased, came into Open Court and Made Choice of Robert Edward and James Johnston Gaurdians who propose for Security Thomas Espy and And'w Haslip Bound in £150. accepted.

An Additional Settlement of the Estate of William Little Deceased returned by Thomas Little Executor of the said Estate.

To John Catheys Acct	£1 5 -
To Jane Litle do	· 11 -
To James Little	8 8
To John Littles widow acct of John	6
To Wm Hagers	4
To James Bell	5 4
	£3 0 0
To trouble & Expences further in attending Court	1 7 6
	£4 7 6
In Executors hands	£93 2 4

On motion of Alexander Martin, Esq'r, ordered that Elizabeth Coyle, wife and relict of Alexander Coyle Deceased have Letters of Administration of all and Singular the goods and Chattles rights and Credits of the said Deceased who proposes Security Thomas Caldwell, Thomas Welch and john McEntire bound in £500. accepted.

Elizabeth Coyle, admx of the Estate of Alexr Coyle Deceased, returns an Inventory of the said Estate and prays an order of Sale which is accordingly Granted.

Court adjourned for 2 hours. Met according to Adjournment. Present Wm Moore, Timothy Riggs, Thos Espy, Charles McLean.

[This marks the end of the first volume. The remainder of the minutes for April term of 1773, as well as for July and October terms of 1773 and January and a portion of April term of 1774 appear to be missing. The second volume begins in the midst of April term of 1774.]

Ordered by the Court that a Road be opened form Jenes plantation on Second Broad River to William Gilberts and that Micajah Proctor & James Cook Sen'r lay out the Same and that the said James Cook be overseer of s'd road.

A Deed of Sale for 200 acres of Land Dated the 24th Day of December 1772 from John Wilkins to Samuel Blackburn proved by Robert Blackburn Evidence thereto. Ordered to be Registered.

A Deed of Sale from Elizabeth Biggerstaff to Benjamin Biggerstaff for 300 acres of Land Dated the second Day of Decem'r 1773 proved by Aaron Biggerstaff Evidence thereto. Ordered to be Registered.

A Deed of Sale from James Cozart to James Bell Dated the 23d Day of Novem'r 1773 for 300 acres of Land proved by Frederick Hambright Evidence thereto. Ord'd to be Registered.

Deed of Sale [from] John Beard to William Beard his Son for 250 acres of Land Dated 26th Day of December 1773 proved by John Kirkconel Evidence thereto. Ordered to be Registered.

Philip Alston to James Johnston Deed of Sale for 200 acres of Land Dated the 24th Day May 1773 proved by Wm. Alston Evidence thereto. Ordered to be Registered.

A Deed of Sale from Philip Alston to James Rutledge for One Hundred acres of Land Dated the 9th Day of April 1773 proved by John Kirkconell Evidence thereto. Ord'd to be Registered.

A Deed of Sale from John Alston to Wm. Alston for 300 acres of land Dated the 8th Day of April 1774 proved by John Kirkconell Evidence thereto. Ord'd to be Registered.

A Deed of Sale from Benj'a Biggerstaff to Peter Marstal for one hundred acres of Land Dated the 20th Day of November 1770 proved by Peter Carpenter Evidence thereto. Ord'd to be Registered.

A Deed of Sale from Philip Alston James Johnston for 400 acres of Land dated the 24th day of May 1773 proved by William Alston Evidence thereto. Ord'd to be Registered.

A Deed of Sale from Saml Biggerstaff, Benj'n Biggerstaff and Mary Biggerstaff to Peter Marstal for 320 acres of Land Dated the 30th Day of November 1773 proved by Peter Carpenter Evidence thereto. Ord'd to be Registered.

Rob't Elder to David Elder Deed of Sale for 200 acres Dated the First of june 1773 proved by Saml Elder Evidence thereto. Ord'd to be Reg'd.

Court Adjourned till tomorrow at 8 Oclock. Met according to Adjournment. Present Wm Moore, James McEntire, Thomas Espey, Charles McLean.

April term 1774

John Ritzhaupt & Joseph Harden came into open Court and took the oath by Law appointed for the qualification of public officers, repeated and Subscribed the test and took the oath of a Justice of the Peace and took their seats accordingly.

Ordered by the Court that William Moore, John Hill, John Alexander of India Creek, Moses Moore, Robt McCaslan, James Beard & Joseph Buffington be Summoned by the

Coronor or Sheriff to appear at the Next Court of Oyer & Terminer to be held at Salisbury on the first day of June next accordingly then & there to serve as Grand & Petit Jurors.

A Deed of Sale from Leonard Killian & Martin Killian his Son for 270 Acres of Land Dated the 21st Day of March 1774 Acknowledged in Open Court. Ordered to be Registered.

A Deed of Sale from Alexander Dickson to Ambrose Foster for 200 Acres of Land Dated the 20th Day of May 1773 proved by Jonathan Gullick Evidence thereto. Ord'd to be Reg'd.

A Deed of Sale from Jonathan Gullick & Elizabeth his wife to John Bryson for 300 Acres of Land Dated the 23rd Day of April 1774 proved by Jas. Patterson Evidence thereto. Ord'd to be Reg'd.

A Deed of Sale from Moses Henry to Hugh Bryson for 150 Acres of Land Dated the thirtieth Day of January 1774 ack'd in open Court. Ord'd to be Reg'd.

A Deed of Sale from Moses Henry to Philip Henry for 100 Acres of Land Dated the 17th Day of February 1774 ack'd in open Court. Ord'd to be Reg'd.

A Deed of Sale from Moses Crawford & Jean his wife to George Seely for 300 Acres of Land Dated the 28th Day of Decem'r 1773 proved by John Orr Evidence thereto. Ord'd to be Reg'd.

A Deed of Sale from Thomas Henry to Christian Rinehart for 300 Acres of Land Dated the 23rd Day of August 1773 proved by Wm Alston Evidence thereto. Ord'd to be Reg'd.

A Deed of Sale from Paul Wisenant & Catherine his Wife to Michael Sites for 200 Acres of Land Dated the 24th Day of March 1773 proved by Jacob Seits Evidence thereto. Ord'd to be Reg'd.

A Deed of Sale from James Hemphill & Susannah Hemphill to Thomas Costner for 302 Acres of Land Dated the 22d Day of July 1773 proved by Peter Sides Evidence thereto. Ord'd to be Reg'd.

A Deed of Sale from William Revan to Thomas Perkins for 100 Acres of Land Dated the 1st Day of October 1762 proved by David Jenkins Evidence thereto. Ordered to be Registered.

A Deed of Sale from Jacob Seits to Garret Will for 38 Acres of Land bearing Date the 24th Day of March 1773 ack'd in Open Court. Ord'd to be Reg'd.

A Deed of Sale from Saml Coburn to Wm Smith for 150 Acres of Land Dated the 26 Day of July 1773 proved in Open Court by George Lamkin Evidence thereto. Ord'd to be Reg'd.

April term 1774

A Deed of Sale from Paul Wisenant & Devol his Wife to Jacob Forney for 75 acres Dated the 23d Day of October 1773 for 200 acres proved by George Lamkin Evidence thereto. Ord'd to be Reg'd.

A Deed of Sale from John Walker and Elizabeth his wife to Jones Williams for 200 Acres of Land bearing Date the 12th Day of Novem'r 1773 ack'd by John Walker in Open Court. Ord'd to be Reg'd.

A Deed of Sale from And'w Robinson & Margaret his wife to Hugh Barry for 150 Acres of Land Dated the 8th Day of October 1773 proved by R'd Barry Esq'r Evidence thereto. Ord'd to be Reg'd.

A Deed of Sale from James Henderson to William Massey for 216 Acres of Land Dated the 24th Day of March 1774 proved by George Lamkin Evidence thereto. Ord'd to be Registered.

A Deed of Sale from Henry Vernor to Jno Dunwoody for 286 Acres of Land Dated the 1st Day of April 1773 proved by Andrew Neel Evidence thereto. Ord'd to be Registered.

A Deed of Sale from Wm Baldridge to Jno Tucker for a Quantity of Land Dated the 1st Day of July 1773 ack'd in Open Court. Ord'd to be Reg'd.

A Deed of Sale from Nicholas Broadway to John McKinny for 170 Acres of Land Dated the 15th Day of May 1773 proved by Jonas Broadaway Evidence thereto. Ord'd to be Reg'd.

John McDaniel to William Fanileft[?] Deed of Sale for 200 acres of Land bearing Date the Twenty Seventh day of July 1772 proved by James Withrow Evidence thereto. Ord'd to be Registered.

A Deed of Sale Alex'r Reynolds & Mary his wife to John Landers for 200 acres of Land Dated the 25th Day of April 1774 [proved by] Middert Hunt Evidence thereto. Ord'd to be Registered.

A Deed of Sale from John Oaks to Jonathan Price for 250 Acres of Land Dated the 23d Day of August 1773 proved by Simon Kuykendall Evidence thereto. Ord'd to be Reg'd.

A Deed of Sale from James Bell to Wm Pattison for 200 Acres of Land Dated the 16th Day of October 1773 proved by Thomas Polk Esq'r Evidence thereto. Ordered to be Registered.

Jno McDowell to Wm Cleghorn Deed for 400 Acres of Land proved by William Gilbert Evidence thereto. Ord'd to be Registered.

A Deed of Sale from Thomas Reynolds & Wife to Henry Landers for 200 acres of Land Dated the 24th Day of April 1774 proved by Mader Hunt Evidence thereto. Ord'd to be Registered.

Wm Gilbert to Robt Proctor Deed of Sale for 93 acres of Land Dated the 10th Day of Septem'r 1773 Ack'd by Wm Gilbert Evidence thereto. Ord'd to be Registered.

A Deed of Sale Wm Gilbert to Robt Proctor for 200 acres of Land Dated the 5th Day of January 1773 ack'd in open Court. Ord'd to be Reg'd.

April term 1774

A Deed of Sale from Ja's Cozart to James Logan for 200 acres of Land Dated the 26th Day of July 1773 proved by Jeremiah Smith Evidence thereto. Ord'd to be Registered.

A Deed of Sale from Ja's Cozart to James Logan for 200 acres of Land Dated the 26th Day of July 1773 proved by Jeremiah Smith Evidence thereto. Ord'd to be Registered.

A Deed of Sale from Sam'l Rankin & Eleanor his Wife to Philip Alston for 150 acres of Land Dated the 26th Day of March 1773 ackn'd in Open Court by said Sam'l Rankin. Ord'd to be Reg'd.

A Deed of Sale from Sam'l Rankin to Philip Alston for 200 acres of Land Dated the 26th Day of January 1773 ackn'd in Open Court. Ord'd to be Registered.

A Deed of Sale from Philip Alston to James Johnston for 150 acres of Land proved by Wm. Alston Evidence thereto. Ord'd to be Registered. bearing Date the 24th Day of May 1773.

A Deed of Sale from John Alston to Wm. Alston for 130 acres of Land Dated the 8th Day of April 1773 proved by Jno. Kirkconell Evidence thereto. Ord'd to be Registered.

A Deed of Sale from John Alston to Wm. Alston for 250 acres of Land Dated the 8th Day of April 1773 proved by Jno. Kirkconell Evidence thereto. Ord'd to be Reg'd.

A Deed of Sale from John Alston to Wm. Alston for 350 acres of Land Dated the 8th Day of April 1773 proved by Jno. Kirkconell Evidence thereto. Ord'd to be Reg'd.

A Deed of Sale from John McKinney to Joel Blackwell for 170 acres of Land Dated the 2d Day of November 1773 ackn'd in Open Court. Ord'd to be Reg'd.

Court adjourned till to morrow at 8 Oclock. Met according to Adjournment. Present Wm. Moore, Timothy Riggs, Joseph Harden, Esq'rs.

Ordered by the Court that Rich'd Singleton, Wm. Going, Wm. Shepherd, Wm. Stockton, Benjn Harden, Christopher Walbert, Wm. Lively, James Buchanan, Moses Moore, Benjn Shaw, Ulrigh Carpenter & Benjn Bracket serve as Jurors to Lay out a Road the nearest and best way from Benjamin Shaws place now Belonging to John Alexander to William Goings or so as to Intersect the old Road Leading to Kings Mountain and that they be summon'd by the Sheriff to appear before Joseph Harden Esq'r on the first Tuesday in July next then & there to take the Necessary steps to Qualify them for this their Charge.

Ordered by the court that James Whiteside serve as Overseer of the Road to be laid out between Benjamin Shaws place & No business and that he enter on the Duty of his charge soon as the same shall be laid out.

Ordered by the court that Wm Going serve as Overseer of the Road leading from Benj'n Shaws place to Kings Mountain in that part between No business & Buffaloe and he enter on his charge accordingly.

Ordered by the court that John Carson serve as Overseer of the Road leading from Benj'n Shaws place to Kings Mountain in that part between Buffaloe & Kings Mountain.

Ordered by the court that Nathaniel Aldrige serve as Constable in the room of Rich'd Venable and that he swear in before Charles McLean Esq'r accordingly.

April term 1774

Ordered by the court that Michael Engle serve as Constable in the room of George Sides and that he swear in before John Ritzhaupt Esq'r accordingly.

Ord'd by the Court that Mary Turner, orphan child of Elijah Turner, be Bound to Michael Widener who Cames into Open Court & Agrees to comply with the Law to give three pound proc. money a Cow & Calf a Bed worth four pounds like money one Ewe & lamb and a Spinning Wheel.

Ord'd by the Court that Sarah Turner, another orphan child of Elijah Turner, be Bound to Tho's Low who Cames into Open Court & Agrees to comply with the Law to give three pound proc. money a Cow & Calf a Bed worth four pounds like money one Ewe & lamb and a Spinning Wheel.

Ordered by the court that Jacob Glance serve as Constable in the room of Jacob Rine and that he swear in before John Ritzhaupt Esq'r accordingly.

On motion of John Dunn Esqr. It was Ordered that Martin Coltman have Letters of Administration for the Estate of the Peter Felker Deceas'd the said Martin Coltman having married the Wife and relict of the said Deceas'd & Security proposed George Miller & Michael Keller bound in £120 accepted. Who took the oath of an Administrator accordingly to Law.

A Deed of Sale from Lemuel Saunders & Martha Saunders to James Freeman for 125 Acres of Land Dated the 2d Day of February 1774 proved [by] Michael Rudisel Evidence thereto. Ord'd to be Registered.

A Deed of Sale from Paul Wisenhunt to John Dellinger for 300 Acres of Land Dated the 28th Day of October 1773 proved by John Dunn Esq'r Evidence thereto. Ord'd to be Registered.

After Proclamation the Court proceeded to the Election of a Sheriff accordingly there being five Justices present William Moore, Timothy Riggs, Thomas Espey, Charles McLean, Joseph Harden who did Elect and choose Jacob Costner, Thomas Espey and Timothy Riggs to be Recommended to his Excellency the Governor for his approbation & of one of them to serve as high Sheriff for the Ensuing year. It appears by the poles that Jacob Costner had 5 votes, Thomas Espey & Timothy Riggs 2 Votes Each. Ordered they be recommended accordingly.

Nicholas Welch Ex'r of the Estate of John Welch produced to their Court Sixteen pounds Virginia Currency & four pounds proclamation money belonging to the s'd Estate which money Proves to be Counterfeit. It is ordered that Nicholas Welch be allowed the said sum his Settlement with the court hereafter which said money was ord'd to be burnt which was done accordingly.

Ordered by the court that Robert Weir serve as Constable and that he swear in before Thomas Espey Esq'r accordingly.

Ordered by the court that James Alley serve as Constable and that he swear in before Thomas Espey Esq'r accordingly.

A Deed of Sale from Henry Hiltebrand to Adam Smith for 300 Acres Dated the 28th Day of April 1774 proved by Jesse Williamson Evidence thereto. Ordered to be Registered.

April term 1774

A Deed of Sale from John McFadin to Robert Taylor for 300 Acres of Land Dated the 29th Day of April 1774 proved by Joseph Buffington Evidence thereto. Ord'd to be Reg'd.

William Yancey & Wm. Tate Came into open Court and agreed that Waightstill Avery, Charles McLain, Esq'r, and Benjn Hardin should arbitrate and Settle a suit in this Court that is undetermined wherein Wm. Yancey is plaintiff & Wm Tate Def't And their Award or majority of them to be a Rule of this Court and leave was accordingly granted.

On motion of Waightstill Avery, Esq'r, it was the opinion of the court that Jno Tagert being in Custody by an arrest made at this Court should be discharged he being legally summond as a witness and protected thereby.

A Deed of Sale from Joseph Clark to Saml French for 200 Acres of Land Dated the 29th Day of April 1774 proved by John French Evidence thereto. Ord'd to be Registered.

A Deed of Sale from John Sloan Ju'r to Adam Carruth for ____ of Land Dated the 1st Day of Novem'r 1773 ack'd in open Court. Ord'd to be Registered.

A Deed of Sale from Peter Costner & Molly his wife to Rob't Johnston [for] 200 Acres of Land Dated the 28th Day of April 1774 proved by George Lamkin Evidence thereto. Ord'd to be Reg'd.

A Deed of Sale from Jacob Carpenter to John Whiteside for 200 Acres of Land Dated the 29th Day of April 1774 proved by John French Evidence thereto. Ord'd to be Registered.

John Caruth to John Whiteside Deed of Sale for ___ Acres of Land Dated the 27th Day of April 1774 ack'd in Open Court. Ord'd to be Reg'd.

A Deed of Sale from James McDaniel and Saml Coburn for ___ Acres of Land Dated the 2d Day of June 1773 proved by John Walker Evidence thereto. Ord'd to be Registered.

Ordered by the Court that Thomas Robison, Alex'r McGaughey, Tho's Welch, Rob't Galtney, Benj'n Biggerstaff, Abh'm Kuykendal, John Ashworth, Dav'd Heddlestone Ju'r, Aaron Biggerstaff, Aaron Deviny, Nathan Proctor & Martin Armstrong Serve as Jurors to lay out a Road from John Walkers near by Second Broad River near by Thomas Welches and from thence the nearest & best way to the province line and Bearing a direct course to Charles Town and that they be sum'd by the Sheriff or Coroner to be and appear before Timothy Riggs Esq'r on the fourth Tuesday in May next then & there to take the necessary steps to qualify them for this their Charge.

Ord'd by the Court that Aaron Moore serve as overseer of the road leading from or to be laid out from John Walkers Esqr to the Province line in that part between John Walkers and where the road Crosses Grog Creek and that Dan'l Shipman Serve as overseer of the said road in that part between Grog Creek and the province line and that he Enter on the duty of his charge accordingly.

A Deed of Sale from Adam Wisenant to George Michael Wisenant for 200 Acres of Land Dated the 6th Day of April A. D. 1774 ack'd in Open Court. Ord'd to be Reg'd.

A Deed of Sale from Adam Wisenant for 200 Acres of Land Dated the 26 Day of April A. D. 1774 ack'd in Open Court. Ord'd to be Reg'd.

April term 1774

A Deed of Sale from Lewis Widener to Valentine Mauney for 100 Acres of Land Dated the 22d Day of April 1774 ack'd in Open Court. Ord'd to be Reg'd.

A Deed of Sale from James Black to Sam'l McMurry for 200 acres of Land Dated the 24th day of April 1772 acknowledged in Open Court. Ord'd to be Registered.

Court adjourned till tomorrow at 8 OClock. Met according to Adjournment. Present Wm. Moore, Timothy Riggs, Charles McLean, Thomas Espey, John Ritzhaupt, Esq'r.

A Deed of Sale from James Andrew to William Robertson for 200 Acres of Land Dated the 6th Day of February 1773 proved by Felix Walker Evidence thereto. Ord'd to be Reg'd.

A Deed of Sale from Alexander McGaughey & Rachel his wife to Sam'l McMurry Sen'r for 200 acres of Land Dated the 24 of October 1772 proved by William Dunn Evidence thereto. Ordered to be Registered.

A Deed of Sale from Michael Engle & Barbara his wife to Lemuel Saunders for 250 acres of Land Dated the 26th of April 1773 proved by John Rudisel Evidence thereto. Ord'd to be Registered.

A Deed of Sale from Wm Wray to William Gilbert 300 acres of Land Dated the 15th of Septem'r 1772 proved by James Cook Evidence thereto. Ord'd to be Registered.

A Deed of Sale from Sam'l Kuykendal to John Taylor for 319 acres of Land Dated the 6th of March 1773 proved by Nathan Davis Evidence thereto. Ord'd to be Registered.

A Deed of Sale from Jacob Coburn to William Henry for 335 Acres of Land Dated the 26th Day of Septem'r 1773 proved by John Walker Evidence thereto. Ordered to be Registered.

A Deed of Sale from Philip Henry Grader, Henry Bullinger, Nicholas Fry, Peter Eigbert, John Shufort, Martin Colter, Frederick Markle, Michael Grindstaff, Wm. Deal & John Deal for 60 Acres of Land Dated the 25 Day of May 1773 ack'd in Open Court. Ord'd to be Registered.

A Deed of Sale from Cornelius McCarty to Thomas Hawkins for 100 Acres of Land Dated the 14th Day of January 1774 proved by George Lamkin Evidence thereto. Ord'd to be Registered.

A Deed of Sale from Thomas Gallespie to Paul Wisenet for 300 acres of Land Dated the 16 Day of April 1773 proved by Jacob Seits Evidence thereto. Ord'd to be Registered.

A Deed of Sale from Sam'l Jack to William Henry for 300 acres of Land Dated the 27th Day of April 1773 ack'd in Open Court. Ord'd to be Registered.

A Deed of Sale from Jacob Forney & Paul Wisenhaunt to Davol Crites for 75 acres of Land Dated the 27th Day of April 1773 proved by George Lamkin Evidence thereto. Ord'd to be Registered.

James Cozart to Peter Carpenter A Deed of Sale for 200 acres of Land Dated the 27th Day of April 1773 proved by Valentine Mauney Evidence thereto. Ordered to be Registered.

April term 1774

A Deed of Sale from Alexander Kyle to Thomas Black for 100 acres Dated the 26th Day of April 1774 ackn'd in Open Court. Ord'd to be Registered.

A Deed of Sale from Jacob Coburn to William Henry for ___ Acres of Land Dated the 26th Day of Septem'r 1773 proved by John Walker Esq'r Evidence thereto. Ord'd to be Registered.

A Deed of Sale from George Poff to George Sights for 400 acres of Land proved by Lemuel Saunders Evidence thereto. Ord'd to be Registered.

A Power of Attorney from James Scott to Sam'l Scott impowering him to dispose of a Tract of land lying on little Catawba in Tryon Count & also authorizing him to sign seal & Deliver a deed of conveyance for the same proved by David Miller Evidence thereto.

John Tagert came into Court five Justices present to wit William Moore, Timothy Riggs, Joseph Harden, Charles McLean, Thomas Espey who produced his accompt of the County Tax according to Act of Assembly for the year one thousand seven hundred and Sixty nine and it appears upon Settlement on oath that he remains Indebted to the Publick for 626 Taxables Supernumeratys included.

John Tagert Sheriff aforesaid came into Court five Justices present viz William Moore, Timothy Riggs, Joseph Harden, Charles McLean, Thomas Espey who produced his accompt of the County Tax on oath according to Act of Assembly and it appears upon Settlement that he remains Indebted to the Publick for 630 Taxables for the year 1770 Supernumerarys Included.

Francis Adams Sheriff came into Court five Justices present to wit William Moore, Timothy Riggs, Joseph Harden, Charles McLean, Thomas Espey and produced his accompt of the County Tax for the year one thousand seven Hundred & Seventy One and is follows to wit

Contra C'r By 1177 Taxables Delinquents & Insolvents & fell into So Carolina a 1/3

	£ 69 16 3
County Claims	30
	£ 99 16 3

Francis Adams to Tryon County D'r

to 1622 Taxables at 1/3	£101 7 6
	99 16 3
Ballance Due	£ 1 11 3

Ordered by the Court that Saml Martin serve as Constable and that he Swear in before Wm. Moore Esq'r accordingly.

Ordered by the Court that Richman Fleming serve as Constable and that he Swear in before Timothy Riggs Esq'r accordingly.

Ordered by the Court that James Wilson serve as Constable and that he Swear in before Joseph Harden Esq'r accordingly.

A Deed of Sale from Hugh Mills to John Boyd for 350 acres of Land Dated the 13th Day of December 1771 proved by William Ramsey Evidence thereto. Ordered to be Registered.

April term 1774

A Deed of Sale from William Alston to Robert Alexander for 178 acres of Land Dated the 22d of March 1774 acknowledged in open Court. Ordered to be Registered.

A Deed of Sale from Moses Moore to John Withrow for 150 acres of Land Dated the 27th of January 1773 proved by James Withrow Evidence thereto. Ordered to be Registered.

A Deed of Sale from Alexander Gilliland to Samuel Rankin for 202 acres of Land Dated the 8th of March 1772 acknowledged in open Court. Ordered to be Registered.

A Deed of Sale from Anson Reynolds to James Mitchel for 200 acres of Land Dated the 29th Day of March 1773 proved by Thomas Alley Evidence thereto. Ord'd to be Registered.

A Deed of Sale from John Alston to William Alston for 271 Acres of land Dated the 9th Day of April 1773 proved by John Kirkconell Evidence thereto. Ordered to be Registered.

A Deed of Sale from Sam'l Coburn & Margaret his wife to Philip Alston for 400 Acres of land Dated the 2d Day of September 1772 proved by George Lamkin Evidence thereto. Ordered to be Registered.

A Deed of Sale from Peter Johnston to James Nickels for 200 Acres of land Dated the 24th Day of October 1772 proved by Samuel Spencer Evidence thereto. Ordered to be Registered.

A Deed of Sale from James Bell to Saml Jack[?] for 300 Acres of land Dated the 27th of April 1774 acknowledged in Open Court. Ordered to be Registered.

A Deed of Sale from James Mitchel to James Logan for 200 Acres of land Dated the 18th Day of May 1773 proved by John Huggins Evidence thereto. Ordered to be Registered.

A Deed of Sale from Philip Alston to James Johnston for 600 Acres of land Dated the 24th Day of April 1773 proved by Wm Alston Evidence thereto. Ord'd to be Registered.

A Deed of Sale from Philip Alston to James Johnston for 225 Acres of land Dated the 24th Day of April 1773 proved by William Alston Evidence thereto. Ord'd to be Registered.

A Deed of Sale from James McCord to Francis Gaskins for 150 Acres of land Dated the sixteenth Day of February 1773 proved by Wm. Alston Evidence thereto. Ordered to be Registered.

A Deed of Sale from John Krass to Jacob Horse for 300 Acres of land Dated the 30th Day of January 1773 proved by [German name] Evidence thereto. Ord'd to be Registered.

A Deed of Sale from James McEntire & Ann his wife to George Wisenhunt for 200 Acres of land proved by William Booth Evidence thereto. Ordered to be Registered.

A Deed of Sale from Michael Platner to Tawalt Huntsucker for 385 Acres of land proved by Peter Echert[?] [German signature] Evidence thereto. Ordered to be Registered & Dated y'e sixteenth Day of February 1773.

A Deed of Sale from Jacob Forney & Devol Crites to Paul Wisenant for 75 acres Dated the 14th of October 1773 proved by Jacob Seits Evidence thereto. Ordered to be Registered.

<u>April term 1774</u>

A Deed of Gift from Alexander Kyle to George & Mary Freeland for 100 acres Dated the 11th April 1774 ackn'd in Open Court. Ordered to be Registered.

A Deed of Sale from Nathl Aldridge & Rosamund his Wife to Robert Miller for 100 acres of Land Dated the 1st Day of January 1774 proved by John Guin Evidence thereto. Ord'd to be Registered.

A Deed of Sale from Garret Wells to Hugh Jenkins for 320 acres of Land Dated the 24th of March 1773 proved by David Jenkins Evidence thereto. Ord'd to be Registered.

A Deed of Sale from William McGaughey to William Dunn for 200 Acres of land Dated the 26th Day of April 1774 acknowledged in Open Court. Ordered to be Registered.

Garret Will to John Will A Deed of Gift for 174 acres of Land Dated the ___ day of ___ 1773 proved by Peter Creutz (Crites) [German name] Evidence thereto. Ord'd to be Registered.

A Deed of Sale from George Fink & Mary his Wife to George Reel for 300 acres of Land Dated the 21st of August 1773 proved by Wm Tankersly Evidence thereto. Ord'd to be Registered.

A Deed of Sale from Thomas Welch & Rachel his Wife to Henry Gross for 150 acres of Land Dated the 10th Day of August 1773 acknowledged in Open Court. Ord'd to be Reg'd.

A Deed of Sale from Valentine Warlock to Christian Gross for 227 acres of Land Dated the 18th Day of February 1774 proved by John Wisenant Evidence thereto. Ordered to be Registered.

A Deed of Sale from Thomas Welch and Rachel his Wife to Henry Gross for 300 acres of Land Dated the 10th Day of August 1773 acknowledged in Open Court. Ord'd to be Registered.

A Deed of Sale from Philip Erehart to Jacob Devold for 243 acres of Land Dated the 11th Day of October 1773 proved by Adam Dick Evidence thereto. Ordered to be Registered.

A Deed of Sale from Philip Cloninger to Christian Like for 200 acres of Land Dated the 19th Day of April 1774 proved by Adam Dick Evidence thereto. Ordered to be Registered.

A Deed of Sale from Sam'l Coburn to William Smith for 200 Acres of land Dated the 26th Day of July 1773 proved by George Lamkin Evidence thereto. Ord'd to be Registered.

A Deed of Sale from Adam Wisenant to Paul Wisenant for 100 Acres of Land Dated the 22d Day of August 1773 ack'd in Open Court. Ord'd to be Registered.

A Deed of Sale from Lewis Weidner & Barbara his Wife to Rudolph Hoozer for 150 Acres of Land Dated the 26th Day of April 1774 acknowledged in Open Court. Ord'd to be Registered.

A Deed of Sale from Lewis Widener to Rudolph Hoozer for 124 Acres of Land Dated the 26 Day of April 1774 ackn'd in Open Court. Ord'd to be Registered.

<u>April term 1774</u>

A Deed of Sale from George Lamkin & Hanah his Wife to Robert Abernathy Jun'r for 200 Acres of Land Dated the ___Day of ____ 1774 acknowledged in Open Court. Ordered to be Registered.

A Deed of Sale from John Bennet to Joseph Jenkins for 200 Acres of Land Dated the 21st Day of June 1771 proved by Frederick Hambright Evidence thereto. Ord'd to be Registered.

A Deed of Sale from Nicholas Welch & Elizabeth his Wife to James Lockhart for ___ acres of Land Dated the 30th Day of March 1774 acknowledged in Open Court. Ordered to be Registered.

Court adjourned till Court in Course. William Moore, Jno Riggs, Charles MCLean, Thomas Espey, Joseph Harden.

North Carolina, Tryon County. To wit. At an Inferior Court of Pleas and Quarter Sessions began, opened, and held for said County the Fourth Tuesday in July Anno Domini 1774. Present the Worshipful John Ritzhaupt, Timothy Riggs, Thomas Espey, Esq'rs.

Ordered by the Court that Margaret Burns orphan Child of Conrad Burns be bound to Nicholas Fry to Serve him till she shall arive to the age of Eighteen years who came into open Court & Agrees to Comply with the Act of Assembly in Such Case Made & provided.

The Last will and Testament of John Oaks was produced in Open court & Proved by the oath of Jonathan Price Evidence thereto.

On motion of John Dunn Esq'r Ordered by the Court that Letters Testamentry issue to James Davison of all and singular the Goods & Chattles rights and Credits of the said John Oaks Deceased who took the Oath of an Executor he complying with the Act of Assembly in such case made & provided.

A Deed of Sale from Christopher Walbat to Patrick Scott for 200 Acres of land Dated the 21st Day of October 1773 Acknowledged in open Court. Ord'd to be Registered.

A Deed of Sale from Nicholas Edington & Wife to John McDowell for 600 Acres of Land Dated the 9th Day of July 1772 proved by Joseph McDowell Evidence thereto. Ord'd to be Registered.

The Grand Jury: Benjamin Harden, Foreman

2 Andrew Hampton	10 Wm Robinson
3 Joseph Richey	11 Benj'n Biggerstaff
4 Robert Alexander	12 Tho's Robison
5 John Reynolds	13 John Stanford
6 Nicholas Friday	14 John Lusk
7 John Scott	15 James Miller
8 Thomas Welch	16 Wm Thomason
9 William Huddlestone	17 Alex'r Kyle

Sworn & Charged.

Court Adjourned for an Hour & a half. Met according to Adjournment. Present John Ritzhaupt, Thomas Aspey, Joseph Harden, Esq'rs.

July term 1774

Elleanor McGaughlin an orphan Child of Patrick McLaughlin aged fourteen years came into Court and chose Thomas Reynolds her Guardian & Master. Ordered by the court that the said Eleanor McGlaughlin be bound to the said Thomas Reynolds untill she shall arive

to the age of Eighteen years he being approved of by the Court and agrees to provide and Deliver to the said Orphan at her freedom a Mare Cow & Spinning wheel and in all things to Comply with the Act of Assembly in Such Case Made & provided.

An Account of Sales of the Estate of Alexander Wills Deceased returned by Robert Ewart & James Johnston Executors of the said Estate to the Amount of £41 15 4½ which was Ordered to be put of Record.

Elie Alexander Adm'x of the Estate of Robert Alexander Deceased returns an Inventory of the said Estate and prays an Order of Sale which is accordingly granted.

Ordered by the Court that James Fowler, Bastard child of Mary Fowler, aged five years and a half be bound to Jesse Reynolds to Learn the Art, Trade or Mistery of Weaver and to serve him until he shall arrive to the age of Twenty one years and the said Jesse Reynolds is to find and provide for the said apprentice at his freedom a Horse, Saddle, and Bridle and in all other things to Comply with the Directions of An Act of Assembly in such Case made & provided.

John Walker Esq'r came into open Court and took the oaths by Law appointed for the qualification of public officers, repeated and Subscribed the test and took the oath of a Justice of the Peace and took his seat accordingly and Also took the Oaths as Col'l of the Tryon Regiment of Militia.

Andrew Neel came into open Court and produced a Commission under the hand & Seal of his Excellency Josiah Martin Esq'r Governor &c &c appointing him Major of the Tryon Regiment of Militia who took the necessary oaths for his Qualification.

Jonas Bedford Esq'r produced in open Court a Commission appointing him Adjutant of the Regiment whereof John Walker Esq'r is Col'l who took the necessary oaths for his Qualification.

Ordered by the Court that John Harvey orphan of Joseph Harvey aged fourteen years & seven months be bound unto William Gilbert to Learn the Art, Trade, or Mystery of a Blacksmith and to serve him untill he shall arrived at the age of Twenty one years and the said William Gilbert is to give the said apprentice at his freedom five pounds proclamation money and also provide & to allow time to provide proper Tools to work with and in all other things to Comply with the Act of Assembly in Such Case Made & provided.

Jane Withrow Adm'x of the Estate of Samuel Withrow Deceased returns an Inventory of the Sales of the s'd Estate to the Amount of £416 18 8 and prays the same may be put of Record.

A Deed of Sale from Jonathan Price & Mary his wife to Rebeckah Kuykendall for 20 acres of Land Dated the 8th Day of December 1773 ack'd in open Court. Ord'd to be Registered.

A Deed of Sale from Ephraim McClean to John McLean for 200 acres of Land Dated the 13th Day of July 1773 proved in open Court by Charles McLean Evidence thereto. Ord'd to be Registered.

July term 1774

A Deed of Sale from John Mullinax & Sarah his wife to James Patterson for 400 acres Dated the 22d Day of July 1773 proved in open Court by John Logan Evidence thereto. Ord'd to be Reg'd.

A Deed of Sale from Andrew Lewis to William Graham for 400 acres Dated the 19th Day of January 1774 proved by John Graham Evidence thereto. Ord'd to be Registered.

A Deed of Sale from Dan'l McCarty to Rich'd Walker for 200 acres of Land Dated the 16 Day of Novem'r 1772 proved by Rich'd Mitchel Evidence thereto. Ord'd to be Reg'd.

A Deed of Sale from Paul Wisenhunt to Michael Sitts [Sills?] for 75 acres Dated the 23d Day of October 1773 proved by Jacob Forney Evidence thereto. Ord'd to be Registered.

A Deed of Sale from John Carrol to Alexander Patterson for 200 acres Dated the 30th Day of May 1774 proved by Wm Patterson Evidence thereto. Ord'd to be Registered.

A Deed of Sale from Stevin Shelton to Samuel Hunter for 150 acres Dated the 25 Day of July 1774 ack'd in Open Court & Ord'd to be Registered.

A Deed of Sale from Francis McCorkle & Sarah his Wife to Peter Linebarger for 200 Acres Dated the 1st Day of August in the year of our Lord 1772 proved by Leonard Sailer Evidence thereto. Ord'd to be Reg'd.

A Deed of Sale from Abraham Scott to John Buchanan for 290 acres of Land Dated the 11th Day of April 1772 proved by James Coburn Evidence thereto. Ord'd to be Reg'd.

A Deed of Sale from Jonas Bedford to Caleb Taylor for 150 acres Dated the 5th Day of April 1773 ack'd in Open Court. Ord'd to be Registered.

A Deed of Sale from John Potts to James Cheek for 600 acres of Land Dated the 5th Day of July 1774 proved by in Open Court John Earle Evidence thereto. Ord'd to be Reg'd.

A Deed of Sale from John Ashley to James Upton for 100 acres of Land Dated the 26th Day of July 1774 ack'd in Open Court. Ord'd to be Reg'd.

A Deed of Sale from Robert Davis to Tho's Davis for 100 acres of Land & All the personal estate of the said Rob't Davis Dated the 24th Day of May 1773 proved by in Open Court James Alley Evidence thereto. Ord'd to be Reg'd.

A Bond from George Sealy to Moses Crawford Dated the 14th day of May 1774 proved by Timothy Riggs Evidence thereto. Ord'd to be Reg'd.

A Deed of Sale from William Sharp to Edward Hogan for 100 acres of Land Dated the 18th Day of Novem'r 1772 proved by David Dickey Evidence thereto. Ord'd to be Reg'd.

A Deed of Sale from Thomas Polk Esq'r to John Beard for 220 acres of Land Dated the 10 Day of June 1774 acknowledged in Open Court. Ord'd to be Registered.

A Deed of Sale from Henry Vernor to Peter Hermon for 100 acres of Land Dated the 20th Day of July 1774 proved by Charles McLean Esq'r Evidence thereto. Ord'd to be Reg'd.

A Deed of Sale from Preston Goforth to Tho's Polk Esq'r for 220 acres of Land Dated the 8th Day of March 1773 proved by John Bigger Evidence thereto. Ord'd to be Registered.

July term 1774

A Deed of Sale from John McLean & Jenney his wife to John Morris for 200 acres Dated the 26 Day of July 1774 proved in open Court by James Miller Evidence thereto. Ord'd to be Reg'd.

A Deed of Sale from David George to Sam'l Hunter for 200 acres of Land Dated the 24th Day of July 1774 proved by And'w Hampton Esq'r Evidence thereto. Ord'd to be Reg'd.

A Deed of Sale from William Johnston & Rebeckah his wife to William Lacefield for 200 acres of Land Dated the 17th Day of March 1773 proved by Edward Dicas Evidence thereto. Ord'd to be Reg'd.

A Deed of Sale from James Capshaw to Richard Tubb for 70 acres of Land Dated the 3d Day of July 1774 proved in open Court by Essex Capshaw Evidence thereto. Ord'd to be Reg'd.

A Deed of Sale from Thomas Pulliam to John Ashley for 200 acres of Land Dated the 26th Day of Septem'r 1772 proved by James McFarlen Evidence thereto. Ord'd to be Registered.

Court adjourned till tomorrow 8 Oclock. Met according to Adjournment. Present John Ritzhaupt, Joseph Harden, Thomas Espey, James McEntire, Esq'rs.

On motion of James Williams Ordered by the court that Jannet Lamkin Wife & Relict of William Lamkin Deceased have Letters of Administration of all & Singular the Goods, Chattles, Rights and Credits of the said deceased who proposes for security William Moore Esq'r bound in the sum of £200. accepted

Jannet Lamkin adm'x as aforesaid returns into Court an Inventory of the said Estate & prays an Order of Sale which was accordingly granted.

A Letter from John Beatey Senr to Archibald Graham which Letter was proved by the Oath of William Graham who Swore that he seen John Beaty sign the said Letter and gave it to him to deliver to the said Archibald Graham which letter he delivered to the said Archibald Graham and the said Archibald Graham delivered said Letter to him the s'd Wm. Graham to be delivered to Thomas Beaty & also swore that he delivered the said Letter to Thos Beaty. Ord'd to be Registered.

James Bryson vs James Walker.

1 Isaiah Stout	7 John Reed
2 Wm Carpenter	8 Wm Wray
3 Wm Capshaw	9 John Hoyl
4 John Bean	10 Henry Martin[?]
5 Alex'r Lockhart	11 George Trout
6 Jas Lemar	12 Thos Caldwell

Jury Impannelled & Sworn the plaintiff in this Suit failing to appear was nonsuit.

Wm. Wofford vs Charles Robinson. Case. Same Jury. Impannelled & Sworn find for the plaintiff and assess his Damage to £6 6 3 and /6d Costs.

Ordered that William Cheatwood an Orphan Child of Maryan Cheatwood be brought into next October court in order to his being bound and that Richard Cheatwood have & keep the said Boy in the mean time.

July term 1774

Jacob Costner Esq'r came into open Court & produced a Commission from under the head & Seal of His Excellency Josiah Martin Esq'r Governor &c &c dated the 3d day of June

1774 appointing him Sheriff of the County of Tryon who took the oaths by Law appointed for the Qualification of public officers, repeated & Subscribed the test & took the oath of a Sheriff and Entered on the Duty of his office.

James Logan came into open Court & took the oaths by Law appointed for the Qualification of public officers, repeated and Subscribed the test and took the oath of a Deputy Sheriff and Entered on the Duty of his office.

North Carolina, Tryon County. Jacob Costner, Jacob Carpenter, Michael Rudisel, Peter Aker, Jacob Haws, Adolph Reep & Peter Castner, bound to Josiah Martin, Governor, in the sum of £1000 sterling, 27 July 1774, for the performance of Jacob Costner in the office of Sheriff. Jacob Costner (Seal), Jacob Zimmerman (Seal), Michel Rudisel (Seal), Peter Aker (X) (Seal), Jacob Hass (Seal), Adolf Riel (Seal), Peter Costner (C) (Seal), Wit: John Dunn, Andw. Neel.

Andrew Neel, William Alston, and James Logan bound to Josiah Martin, Governor, in the sum of £1000 proclamation money, 27 July 1774, for the performance of Andrew Neel in the office of Public Register. Andw Neel (Seal), Wm. Alston (Seal), James Logan (Seal), Wit: Timo Riggs, John Ritzhaupt.

North Carolina, Tryon County. We the Commissioners appointed by Act of Assembly for Laying out, constituting & appointing the place whereon to Erect and Build the court House, Prison and Stocks of Tryon County... are of opinion that the place called the Cross roads on Christopher Mauny Land between the heads of Long Creek, Muddy Creek & Beaverdam Creek in the county aforesaid is the most central and convenient for the purpose aforesaid... dated 26th July 1774. Charles McLean (Seal), William Moore (Seal), John Walker (Seal), John Hill (Seal), Christian Carpenter (Seal).

The Last Will and Testament of John Collins Deceased was produced in open Court and proved by the Oath of Robert McAfee.

Ordered by the Court that Letters Testamentry issue to Phebe Collins wife & relict of said deceased and James Collins of all & singular the Goods, Chattles, Rights and Credits of said Deceased who took the oaths of Ex'rs they complying with the Act of Assembly in that Case made and provided.

William Capshaw and James Lemar absenting themselves from their duty as Petit Jurors It was Ordered by the Court that they be find 5/ Each for their neglect. Fine remitted by the Court.

John Williams vs Michael Crawford. Jury the same as before impannelled & Sworn the plaintiff in this suit failing to appear suffered a Nonsuit.

Richard Henderson vs Thomas Rainey. Same Jury Impannelled & Sworn the plaintiff in this suit failing to appear suffered a Nonsuit.

James Collins vs William Saffold. Same Jury Impannelled & Sworn the plaintiff in this suit failing to appear suffered a Nonsuit.

July term 1774

John Williams vs William Farr. Same jury with the alteration of Wm. Buchanan in the room of William Wray. Same Jury Impannelled & Sworn the plaintiff in this suit failing to appear suffered a Nonsuit.

Wm Saffold vs Francis Williams. Same Jury Impannelled & Sworn find for the plaintiff & assess Damage £ 0 0 1 & /6 Costs.

William Thompson vs Elijah Wells. Case. Same Jury Impannelled & Sworn the plaintiff in this suit failing to appear was Nonsuit.

Court adjourned for an Hour. Met according to Adjournment. Present John Ritzhaupt, James McEntire, Thos Espey, Esq'rs.

Court adjourned till tomorrow 8 Oclock. Met according to Adjournment. Present Timothy Riggs, Joseph Harden, Thomas Espey, James McEntire, Esq'rs.

Wm Gilbert vs George Sizemore. Case.
Petty Jury

1 Wm. Ramsey	7 Philip Cansler
2 Jacob Mooney	8 Moses Moore
3 Lawrence Kyzer	9 Mich'l Hofstatler
4 Sam'l Rankin	10 Nicholas Shram
5 Valentine Mauny	11 Lewis Weidner
6 John Huggins	12 George Resminger

Jury Impanneled & Sworn find the Defendant did Assume and assess the plaintiffs Damages £11 17 6 and /6d Costs.

In consequence of the above Judgment William Gilbert came into open Court and releases & Acquits Edward Sizemore of the above sum recovered against George Sizemore.

Martin Collman adm'r of the Estate of Peter Felker returns an accompt of sales of the said Estate to the amount of £63 10 1 and prays the same may be put of Record.

Jacob Castner Sheriff of this County by John Dunn Esq'r came into open Court and makes it appear to the Court that he has no place of confinement for persons commited to his Charge and it was ordered that he be acquitted from such Escapes as may be Occasioned thereby.

Nicholas Welch Ex'r of the Last Will and Testament of John Welch Deceased came into open Court and made final Settlement of his Doings as Ex'r of the said Deceaseds Estate and thereby it appears the sum of £35 8 7 is due to him over & above what the sales of the said Estate Extended to as appears by accompt stated & settled and filed this Term in this Office. It is therefore Ordered that the Land and plantation on which Margaret Whitley the Late Wife and Relict of John Welch Deceased now lives be sold by the said Nicholas Welch or his Order to pay off the said sum of £ 37 17 7 due to the said Executor & that he return a further account of his proceedings on such sale for the benefit of the said widow and orphans.

A Bill of Sale from Stophal Walbert to Teter Havenor for Sundry Goods & Chattles Dated the 17th Day of January 1773. Ack'd in open Court. Ord'd to be Reg'd.

July term 1774

A Bill of Sale from Jesse Williamson to Teter Havenor for one Gray Horse Eight Years old Branded thus IR and one mare aged fourteen years branded thus CC & 3 Cows & Calves Dated the 15th Day of June 1774 proved by John Alex'r Evidence thereto.

Court adjourned for an Hour. Met according to Adjournment. Present Jno Walker, Timothy Riggs, James McEntire, Thomas Espey, Esq'rs.

King vs Laurence Kyzer. Petty Larceney

1	Samuel Rankin	7	David Ramsey
2	Wm. Ramsey	8	Christoph'r Walbert
3	John Huggins	9	Wm Armstrong
4	Philip Cansler	10	Adolph Reep
5	Moses Moore	11	Nicholas Shram
6	Mich'd Hufstatler	12	Lewis Weidner

Jury Impanneled & Sworn find the Defendant not Guilty in manner & form charged in the Indictment.

Ordered by the Court that a road be Laid out and opened from Thomas Jeans Plantation into the road at Davis's Sholes and that the order for Laying out a Road from William Gilberts to Thomas Jeans Plantation be reversed.

Ordered by the Court that James cook Senr serve as Overseer of the said Road.

Court Adjourned till tomorrow at 8 Oclock. Met according to Adjournment. Present John Ritzhaupt, Joseph Harden, Thomas Espey, Esq'rs.

A Bill of Sale from Henry Wright to Adam Terrance for one Iron Gray Mare four years old about fourteen hands high and one inch with a long Patch in her forehead and her right fore foot with white in side of her hoof Branded WC Dated thus 28th Day of July 1774. proved by Tho's Polk Esq'r Evidence thereto.

Israel Peterson vs John Tagert. Case.
Petty Jury by consent

1	James Cook Sen.	7	Jacob Willis
2	Jeremiah McDaniel	8	Jonas Bedford
3	Thomas Caldwell	9	Jonathan Price
4	Alex'r Coulter	10	Christy Mooney
5	Benj'n Kuykendall	11	John Wilson
6	William Going	12	Joseph McDaniel

Jury Impanneled & Sworn find for the plaintiff and assess his Damage £11 2 8 and /6d Costs. Motion in arrest of Judgment by J. D. reasons to be filed next Court.

Catharine Hoofman vs Teter Havener. Case words.

Petty Jury

1	James Cook	7	Lewis Weidner
2	Thomas Caldwell	8	Wm Gilbert
3	Jonas Bedford	9	Nicholas Shram

July term 1774

4 Jonathan Price	10 Christy Mooney
5 Christy Mooney	11 Michael Rudisel
6 Thomas Black	12 James Kelly

Jury Impanneled and Sworn find the Defendant Guilty and assess the Plaintiffs Damages £20 and /6d Costs. Motion in arrest of Judgment A. M. and W. K.

King vs Wm Cronicle. Trespass. The Same Jury with the Alteration of Jeremiah McDaniel in the room of Jonas Bedford Impannelled & Sworn find the Defendant Not Guilty in manner & form Charged in the Indictment.

Court adjourned till tomorrow 8 Oclock. Met according to Adjournment. Present John Walker, Charles McLean, Timothy Riggs, Esq'rs.

Ordered by the Court that John Dunn Esq'r be find five Shillings proclamation money for his Contempt offered in the face of the Court. fine paid.

Ordered by the court that Merry McGuire and James Taylor be appointed Constables and that they wear in before John Walker Esq'r accordingly.

Ordered by the Court that at the end of this term be adjourned to the House of Christy Mauney or the Cross roads on his Land.

The King vs Teter Havener.

1 James Cook	7 Moses Moore
2 John Carpenter	8 Joseph McDaniel
3 Wm McKinny	9 Jeremiah McDaniel
4 Wm Wray	10 James Graham
5 Wm Chronicle	11 William Armstrong
6 Lewis Weidner	12 Jacob Carpenter

Jury Impanneled & Sworn find the Defend't not Guilty.

The King vs Teter Havener. Same Jury·Impanneled & Sworn find the Def't not Guilty.

The King vs James Kelly Sen'r. Same Jury Impannelled and sworn find the Defendant Guilty on his own Submission.

William Wray Adm'r of the Estate of James Kelly Deceased returns an Account of Sales of the said Estate to the Amount of £59 10 11 and prays the same may be put of Record.

Ordered by the Court that the orphan Children of Martin Shearer Deceased be brought to the next court by William Feares and Martha Fares widow of Martin Shearer in order that the orphans be bound out as the Law directs.

Sam'l Wilson vs John Potts. Same Jury with the Alteration of Christy Mauny in the room of Wm. Chronicle Impannelled & Sworn assess the plaintiffs Damages to £11 1 2 and /6d cost.

Hugh Montgomery vs Abel Beatey. Same Jury Impannelled & Sworn assess the plaintiffs Damage to £16 5 8 and /6d costs.

July term 1774

Andrew Haslep vs Dan'l Devour. Same Jury Impannelled & Sworn assess the plaintiffs Damage to £8 3 9 and /6d costs.

Wm. Gilbert assee vs John Carson. Same Jury Impannelled & Sworn assess the plaintiffs Damage to £14 10 6 and /6d costs.

Talifero & Wyatt & Co vs John Anderson. Same Jury Impannelled & Sworn assess the plaintiffs Damage to £6 11 7 & /6d costs.

John Steen vs Robert Hammet. Same Jury with the alteration of Wm. Chronicle in the room of Wm. Armstrong Impannelled and Sworn find for the plaintiff and assess his Damage to £11 16 3 & /6d costs.

Ordered by the Court that a Warrant issue Signed by John Walker Esq'r directed to each constable in this County commanding them to Summon the Master or mistress of every Family in their Districts to appear before their respective Magistrates and give in upon Oath a just account of the Taxable persons in their respective Familys seting forth the name and sex of each Taxable person in their respective districts.

Ordered by the Court that Richard hicks serve as Constable and that he sear in before Timothy Riggs Esq'r accordingly.

Ordered by the Court that William Willis be appointed overseer of the road leading from John Walkers Esqr to Buffaloe in that part between the Grassy branch and Buffaloe and that he Enter on his charge accordingly.

Ordered by the Court that John Breman serve as overseer of the road leading from John Walkers to Buffaloe in that part between the John Walkers and the Grassy Branch and that he Enter on the Duty of his charge.

Court Adjourned till Court in Course. John Walker, Charles McLean, Thomas Espey.

North Carolina, Tryon County. To wit. At an Inferior Court of Pleas and Quarter Sessions begun and held for said County on the fourth Tuesday in October A. D. 1774. Present John Walker, John Ritzhaupt, Charles McLean, Thomas Espey, Esquires.

The Last Will and Testament of John Harman was produced in open Court and proved by the oath of Adam Wisenant and Thomas Maxwell.

On motion of John Dunn Esq'r it was Ordered that by the Court that Mary Harman wife and Relict of John Harman Deceased together with Anthony Harman have Letters Testamentary of all and Singular the goods and Chattles rights and Credits of the said Deceased they complying with the Act of Assembly in that case made and provided.

A Deed of Sale from Thos Williams Sen'r to Wm. Wilson for 150 acres of Land Dated the 8th day of October 1774 proved by Timothy Riggs Evidence thereto. Ord'd to be Reg'd.

A Deed of Sale from Thomas McKnight to Jas Henderson for 169 acres of Land Dated the 13th day of August 1770 proved John Gillespy Evidence thereto. Ord'd to be Reg'd.

Pursuant to an Order of Court at Last Term it was ordered by the Court that William Cheatwood a Bastard Child of Mary Cheatwood aged three years be bound unto William McKinney to Learn the art Trade or Mystery of a House Carpenter and House Joiner to

October term 1774

Serve him untill he shall arive to the age of Twenty one years and the said Wm. McKinney in all things is to Comply with the act of Assembly in that case made & provided.

A Deed of Sale from Thomas Beatey & Margaret His wife to David Ribison for 200 acres of Land Dated the 19th day of August A D 1774 proved ack'd in Open Court. Ord'd to be Registered.

A Deed of Sale from Lewis Lineberry & Barbara his Wife to Robert Abernathy for 100 of Land acres dated the 15th Day of August. Ack'd in Open Court. Ord'd to be Registered.

A Deed of Sale from George Freeland to Joseph Gladdin for 100 acres of Land Dated 18 Day of October 1774 ack'd in Open Court. Ordered to be Registered.

A Deed of Sale from John McEntire to Moses Whitley for 300 acres of Land Dated 12th Day of August proved by William McKinney Evidence thereto. Ord'd to be Reg'd.

A Deed of Sale from Philip Erehart & Catherine his Wife to Robert Abernathy for 100 acres of Land Dated the 27th Day of December 1773 prov'd by John Abernathy Evidence thereto. Ord'd to be Reg'd.

A Deed of Sale from Philip Erehart & Catherine his Wife to Robert Abernathy for 100 acres of Land Dated the 27th Day of December 1773 prov'd by John Abernathy Evidence thereto. Ord'd to be Reg'd.

A Deed of Sale from William Wilson to Thomas Wilson for 200 acres of Land Dated the 8th Day of August 1774 proved by John Sorral Evidence thereto. Ord'd to be Registered.

Court adjourned till to morrow at 8 Oclock. Met according to Adjournment. Present John Walker, William Moore, John Ritzhaupt, Esq'rs.

On motion of William Kennon Esq'r it was ordered that Christian Mauney have a licence to keep an Ordinary at his now dwelling house in Tryon County he complying with the Act of Assembly in that case made & provided. He proposes for security Jacob Mooney Jun'r, Tho's Castner, and Peter Plunk bound for 30 pounds. accepted.

The Grand Jury William Armstrong, Foreman.

2 Thos Arington	9 Thomas Beatey
3 Nathan Proctor	10 Jacob Forney
4 Martin Armstrong	11 James Henderson
5 William Dunn	12 Fred'k Hambright
6 George Winters	13 Peter Castner
7 William Gilbert	14 Michael Keller
8 Peter Plank	15 George Hoves
	16 Lewis Lineberger

Sworn & Charged.

Ordered by the Court that George Sizemore Admr of the Estate of Wm Shepherd deceased be cited by the Sheriff to appear at next court & make final settlement of his doings respecting the said Estate.

October term 1774

Court adjourned for one hour. Met according to adjournment. Present William Moore, Charles McLean, Thomas Espey.

Ordered by the Court that Margaret Crease be appointed guardian to William Hanna an orphan child of William Hanna deceas'd according to his choice in open court who proposes for security John Walker Esq., Wm. Carpenter & Isaac Hinton Bound in Forty pounds. accepted.

Ordered by the Court that Wm Feares be appointed guardian to Nancy & Mary Shearer orphan children of Matthew Shearer Deceased agreeable to their choice in open court. He proposes for security Jacob Mooney Ju'r & Simeon Kuykendal bound in the sum of £100. accepted

A Deed of Sale from Francis Beatey to George Leonard Sealer for 200 acres of Land dated the 2d Day of March 1773 proved by Wallace Beatey Evidence thereto. Ord'd to be Registered.

A Deed of Sale from James Cozart to Joseph Wootenburg for 52 acres of Land dated the 20 Day of Decemb'r 1773 proved by Frederick Hambright Evidence thereto. Ord'd to be Reg'd.

A Deed of Sale from Patrick McDavid to John Moore for 100 acres Dated the 23d Day of February 1773 proved by Wm Moore Evidence thereto. Ord'd to be Reg'd.

A Deed of Sale from Andrew Hoyl to James Wyatt Ju'r for 200 acres of Land Dated the 26 Day of October 1774 acknowledged in Open Court. Ord'd to be Reg'd.

A Deed of Sale from Lewis Weidner to Jacob Forney for 300 acres of Land dated the 21st Day of January 1774 proved by Valentine Mauney Evidence thereto. Ord'd to be Reg'd.

A Deed of Sale from Lewis Weidner to Jacob Forney 200 acres of Land Dated the 21st day of February 1774 proved by Valentine Mauney Evidence thereto. Ord'd to be Reg'd.

A Deed of Sale from Daniel McCleary to Micajah Proctor for ___ acres of Land Dated the 26 Day of October 1774 ack'd in Open Court. Ord'd to be Reg'd.

A Bill of Sale from Sarah Robinson to Abel Beatey for one Negro wench named Pender, two pied cows, one red cow, one brindle stear two years old, one yearling heifer, one black cow, four calves some marked and some unmarked, Dated the 7th Day of Septem'r 1774 proved by Wm. Drew Evidence thereto.

A Deed of Sale from George Lamkin Sheriff to Moses Moore for 200 acres Dated the 22d Day of May 1773 proved by Saml Spencer Esq'r Evidence thereto. Ord'd to be Registered.

Moses moore and Wife to William Going a Deed of Sale for 200 acres of Land Dated the 24th Day of October 1774 proved by Saml Spencer Evidence thereto. Ord'd to be Registered.

A Deed of Sale from Thomas Beaty, Hugh Beaty, and Robt. Armstrong to John Bradley for 280 acres Dated the 5th Day of Oc'r 1774 proved by Wallace Beaty Evidence thereto. Ord'd to be Registered.

October term 1774

A Deed of Sale from Lewis Lineberger to Wm Elder and Sam'l Elder for 200 acres of Land Dated the 15th Day of October 1774 proved by Jacob Seits Evidence thereto. Ord'd to be Registered.

A Deed of Sale from Wm Green & Ja's McAfee to Jonas Bedford for 200 acres Dated the 27th Day of August 1774 proved by James McEntire Evidence thereto. Ord'd to be Registered.

A Deed of Sale from James Carruth to John Sloan for 100 acres Dated the 18th Day of August 1774 proved by John Carruth Evidence thereto. Ord'd to be Regist'd.

A Deed of Sale from James Cozart to Joseph Wootenberg for 300 acres Dated the 20th Day of Decem'r 1773 proved by Frederick Hambright Evidence thereto. Ord'd to be Registered.

A Deed of Sale from William Carpenter to Benjamin Kuykendal for 300 acres of Land Dated the 22d Day of October 1774 proved by Joseph Harden Esq'r Evidence thereto. Ord'd to be Reg'd.

A Deed of Sale from Patrick McDavid to John Moore for 700 acres of Land dated the 16th Day of January 1773 proved by Wm. Moore Evidence thereto. Ord'd to be Registered.

A Deed of Sale from Dan'l Shipman to Thomas Reynolds for 200 acres of Land Dated the 12 Day of Septem'r 1773 proved by Sam'l Gray Evidence thereto. Ord'd to be Reg'd.

A Deed of Sale from Wm Sharp to Hugh Cummins for 125 acres of Land dated the 3d Day of July 1773 ackn'd in Open Court. Ord'd to be Reg'd.

A Deed of Sale from Wm Sharp to John Cummins for 125 acres of Land Dated the 3d Day of July 1773. Ack'd in Open Court. Ord'd to be Reg'd.

A Deed of Sale from James Blyth to George Potts for 200 acres of Land Dated 16th Day of July 1773 prov'd by Wm Sharp, Esq'r Evidence thereto. Ord'd to be Registered.

A Deed of Sale from John Harris and Jean his wife to Isaac Holland for 136 acres of Land Dated the 31st Day of August 1772 proved by Jonathan Gullick Evidence thereto. Ord'd to be Reg'd.

A Deed of Sale from John Harris to William Harris for 200 acres of Land Dated the 20th Day of October 1774 proved by Jonathan Gullick Evidence thereto. Ord'd to be Registered.

A Deed of Sale from James Harris to John Harris for 223 acres of Land Dated the 16th Day of February 1774 proved by Jonathan Gullick Evidence thereto. Ord'd to be Reg'd.

A Deed of Sale from Peter Aker Sen'r to Peter Carpenter for 250 acres of Land Dated the 22d Day of August 1773 proved by Valentine Mauney Evidence thereto. Ord'd to be Reg'd.

A Deed of Sale from James Patterson & Sarah his wife to John West for 400 acres of Land Dated the 14 Day of October 1774 ack'd in open court. Ord'd to be Registered.

A Deed of Sale from Zach'h Bullock to Christopher Rinehart for 102 acres of Land Dated the 9th Day of August 1774 ackn'd in Open Court. Ord'd to be Reg'd.

October term 1774

A Deed of Sale from Moses Alexander to Wm. Cleghorn for 100 acres of Land Dated the 2d Day of January 1769 proved by John McKnitt Alexander Evidence thereto. Ord'd to be Reg'd.

A Power of Attorney from George Shieb to Henry Holman Dated the 13th day of Septem'r 1773 proved by Anthony Holman Evidence thereto. Ord'd to be Registered.

A Deed of Sale from John Martin to Thomas Price for 200 acres of Land Dated the 16th Day of June 1774 proved by David Alexander Evidence thereto. Ord'd to be Registered.

A Deed of Sale from Ulrigh Carpenter to Peter Seits for 200 acres of Land Dated the 7th Day of Septem'r 1774 ackn'd in Open Court. Ord'd to be Registered.

John McKnitt Alexander to Wm Edgar Deed for 520 acres Dated the 29th Day of August 1774 proved by John Robison Evidence thereto. Ord'd to be Reg'd.

Court adjourned till tomorrow at 8 oclock. Met according to adjournment. Present John Ritzhaupt, John Walker, Joseph Harden, Esq'rs.

Ordered by the Court that Thomas Espey Esq'r have a licence to keep an Ordinary at his dwelling house in Tryon County he complying with the Act of Assembly in that case made & provided. He proposes for security James Coburn and John Hill Bound in the sum of thirty pounds. accepted

Pursuant to an order of Court at Last Term James Kerr Esq'r High Sheriff of Rowan County made return of the said order to this court for in these word, viz Pursuant to the within order I have sold the land of John Welch at Ninety pounds proclamation money at Publick sale to Nicholas Welch being the highest bidder. James Kerr Sheriff. Ordered by the Court that the said order and return thereon be Registered.

Alex'r Coulter & Wife Ex'rs of Wm. Moore Deceased vs James Buchanan.

1 Benj'n Harden	7 Leonard Sailor
2 Perregreen Magnes	8 Solomon Bason
3 Wm Whiteside	9 Nicholas Warlock
4 Simeon Kuykendall	10 Jacob Hofstatler
5 Moses Whitley	11 Laurence Kyzer
6 Valentine Mauney	12 Joseph McDaniel

Jury impannelled and sworn. Verdict for the Defendants: Verd't set aside by the Court. New tryal granted.

Ordered by the Court that William Moore, John Walker, James McEntire, Rpbert McCaslan & John Alexander, John McKinney, Thomas Beatey & Jacob Forney be summoned by the Sheriff to be and appear at the Court of Oyer and Terminer to be held at Salisbury the first day of December next then and there to serve our Sovereign Lord the King as Grand & Petit Jurors.

John Robinson came into the open court and took the oath by Law appointed for the Qualification of publick officers, repeated and subscribed the test, & took the oath of a Magistrate for said County and took his seat accordingly.

October term 1774

James Miller came into the open court and took the oath by Law appointed for the Qualification of publick officers, repeated and subscribed the test, & took the oath of a Deputy Sheriff and entered on the duty of his office.

Thos Nickols vs Rob't Murphy. Case.

1	Benj'n Harden	7	Joseph McDaniel
2	Joseph Kyzer	8	Jacob Hofstatler
3	James Bucanan	9	Rob't Gwaltney
4	Simeon Kuykendall	10	Wm Davis
5	Wm Whiteside	11	John Beeman
6	Nicholas Warlock	12	John Scott

Jury Impannelled & sworn assess the pltfs damages to 1 penny & 6/ costs.

Hugh Quinn vs Patrick McGee. Words. Same Jury assess the plffs Damage to 1d & /6d Cost.

Thos Maxwell vs Joshua Barnett. Case. Same jury Impannelled & Sworn assess the pltfs damages to 1d and /6d costs.

Hugh Montgomery vs John Potts. Case. Same Jury Impannelled & sworn assess the plffs damages to £ - 17 6 & costs.

A Deed of Sale from Henry Holman to Anthony Holman for 225 acres of Land Dated the 26th Day September 1773 proved by Henry Holman Esq'r Evidence thereto. Ord'd to be Reg'd.

A Deed of Sale from Ja's Cook Jun'r to James Cook Sen'r for 150 acres of Land dated the 3d Day of March 1774 proved by Wm. Henry Evidence thereto. Ord'd to be Registered.

A Deed of Sale from Wm Wray to Wm. Green for 275 acres of Land Dated 2d March 177- ack'd in Open Court. Ordered to be Registered.

A Deed of Gift from John Beard and Frances his wife to James Beard for 150 acres Dated the 25 Day of July 1774 proved by And'w Neel Evidence thereto. Ord'd to be Registered.

A Deed of Sale from Wm Barnet to Wm. Thompson for 250 acres of Land Dated the 10th Day of June 1774 proved by John Stanford Evidence thereto. Ord'd to be Registered.

A Deed of Sale from Thomas Warren to John Stanford for 200 acres of Land Dated the 19th day of May 1773 proved by Abraham Hargess Evidence thereto. Ord'd to be Reg'd.

A Deed of Sale from Abraham Erehart to George Moosgenung for 140 acres of Land Dated the 3d Day of February 1774 proved by Henry Martin[?] Evidence thereto. Ord'd to be Registered.

A Deed of Sale from Jno Stanford to Abrah'm Hargess for 200[?] acres of Land Dated the 25 Day of July 1774 proved by Wm Capshaw Evidence thereto. Ord'd to be Reg'd.

A Deed of Sale from Preston Hampton to John Potter for 100 acres of Land Dated the 4th Day of June 1772 proved by Wm Capshaw Evidence thereto. Ord'd to be Reg'd.

October term 1774

A Deed of Sale from John McEntire to Ja's Dougherty for 200 acres of Land Dated the 25 Day of July 1774 ack'd in Open Court. Ord'd to be Registered.

A Deed of Sale from Wm Crocket to William King for 160 acres of Land Dated the 22d Day of July 1774 proved by David Abernathy Evidence thereto. Ord'd to be Reg'd.

A Deed of Sale from Sam'l Withrow & Jane his wife to Robert Rankin for 300 acres of Land Dated the 4th Septem'r 1772 proved by Alexander McGaughy Evidence thereto. Ord'd to be Regd.

A Deed of Sale from Jno Deviney & Mary his wife to Ja's Dowdle for 100 acres of Land Dated the 25 Day of July 1772 proved by Alexander McGaughey Evidence thereto. Ordered to be Registered.

A Deed of Sale from Elias Morgan to John Battle for 200 acres of Land Dated the 2d Day of July 1774 proved by Uel Lamkin Evidence thereto. Ord'd to be Registered.

A Deed of Sale from Philip Alston to James Johnson for 200 acres of Land Dated the 21st Day of May 1773 proved by James Coburn Evidence thereto. Ord'd to be Registered.

A Deed of Sale from John McKnitt Alexander to John Black for 300 of Land acres Dated the 29th Day of July 1771 proved by John Scott Evidence thereto. Ord'd to be Registered.

A Deed of Sale from Joshua Hightower to George Harris for 200 acres of Land Dated the 20th Day of Decem'r 1772 proved by John Mcentire Evidence thereto. Ord'd to be Registered.

A Deed of Sale from Moses Moore to John Harman for 350 acres of Land dated the 27th day of July 1771 ackn'd in Open Court. Ord'd to be Registered.

A Deed of Sale from John Stroud & Martha his wife to John Hill for 100 acres of Land Dated the 29th day of Septem'r 1772 proved by James Coburn Evidence thereto. Ordered to be Registered.

A Deed of Sale from Moses McCarley to John Deveney for 200 acres of Land Dated the 22d Day of Decem'r 1772 proved by Alex'r McGaughy Evidence thereto. Ord'd to be Reg'd.

A Deed of Sale from John Moffet to David Thomson for 100 acres of Land Dated the 22d Day of February 1774 proved by Jno Gamble Evidence thereto. Ord'd to be Registered.

A Deed of Sale from John Stanford to George Tub for 195 acres of Land Dated the 21st Day of July 1774 proved by Abh'm Hargess Evidence thereto. Ord'd to be Registered.

A Deed of Sale from John Hightower to John McEntire for 400 acres of Land Dated the 20th Day of Decem'r 1772 proved by Sam'l Wilkins Evidence thereto. Ordered to be Registered.

A Deed of Sale from Dav'd Huddleston to Moses Moore for 350 acres of Land Dated the 27th April 1774 proved by Jno Walker Esq'r Evidence thereto. Ordered to be Registered.

A Deed of Sale from Jacob Mooney to Adam Whiteside for 200 acres of Land dated the ___ of ____ 1774 acknowledged in Open Court. Ord'd to be Registered.

<u>October term 1774</u>

A Deed of Sale from Alex'r Dickson to Peter Quinn for 200 acres of Land Dated the 7th April 1773 proved by Rob't McAfee Evidence thereto. Ord'd to be Registered.

A Deed of Sale from Sam'l Coburn to George Lamkin for 168 acres of Land Dated the 18th Day of Septem'r 1773 proved by James Coburn Evidence thereto. Ord'd to be Registered.

A Deed of Sale from James Collins to Wm. Suiter for 100 acres of Land Dated the 23d Day of July 1774 proved by Rob't McAfee Evidence thereto. Ord'd to be Registered.

A Deed of Sale from James Kelly to James Murphy for ___ acres dated the ___ day of ____ 1773 proved by Wm. Murphy Evidence thereto. Ord'd to be Registered.

A Deed of Sale from James Kelly to Jacob Collins for 100 acres of Land Dated 3d Day of July 1774 proved by Robert McAfee Evidence thereto. Ordered to be Registered.

A Deed of Sale from John Philip File to John Shuford for 100 acres of Land Dated the 15th August 1773 prov'd by Rob't Blackburn Esq'r Evidence thereto. Ord'd to be Reg'd.

A Deed of Sale from George Black to Robert Porter for 150 acres Dated the 1st Day of Decem'r 1773 proved by Alexander McGaughy Evidence thereto. Ord'd to be Registered.

A Deed of Sale from John Cunes to John Scott for 3OO acres of Land Dated the 6th Day of February 1772 proved by Alex'r McGaughy Evidence thereto. Ord'd to be Registered.

A Deed of Sale from Perry Green Magnes to Wm Magnis for ___ acres of Land Dated the 26th Day of April 1774 ack'd in Open Court. Ord'd to be Registered.

A Deed of Mortgage from Christopher Walbert to Matthias Bower for a waggon, harness and four horses ack'd in Open Court. Ord'd to be Registered.

A Deed of Sale from Thomas Harrod to John Harrod to John Wade [sic] for 300 acres of Land Dated the 5th Day of July 1772 proved by John Lusk Evidence thereto. Ord'd to be Registered.

Ordered that Thomas Harrod serve as Constable and that he swear in before Ja's McEntire Esq'r accordingly.

A Deed of Sale from William Gardner to George Christopher Neshiner for 300 acres of Land Dated the 26 Day of October 1774 ack'd in open Court. Ord'd to be Reg'd.

A Deed of Sale from Henry Landers to Abel Beatey for 250 acres of Land Dated the 27th Day of October 1774 ack'd in open Court. Ord'd to be Reg'd.

A Deed of Sale from James Logan to Peter Summy Senr for 200 acres of Land Dated the 7th Day of Septem'r 1774 ack'd in Open Court. Ord'd to be Reg'd.

A Deed of Sale from Henry Wright & Alice his wife to Nath'l Ewing for 250 acres of Land Dated the 25 Day of June 1773 proved by Moses Winsly Evidence thereto. Ord'd to be Registered.

Court adjourned till tomorrow morning at 8 oclock.   Met According to adjournment. Present John Robinson, Charles McLean, Joseph Harden, Thomas Espey, Esquires.

October term 1774

Court adjourned for half an hour. Met according to adjournment. Present Timothy Riggs, Joseph Harden, Tho's Espey, Esq'rs.

Ja's Hanna vs Joab Mitchell.

1	James Adams	7	John McKinney
2	Wm Cronicle	8	Euel Lamkin
3	Philip Wisenant	9	Nicholas Welch
4	Andrew Hoyl	10	Wm Ramsey
5	John Beeman	11	Joseph England
6	Solomon Bason	12	Benj'n Hyde

Jury Impannelled & Sworn find for the plaintiff and assess his Damage to £17 7 & /6 costs.

John McGuire & Wife vs John Sorrells & Wife. words. Same Jury Impannelled and sworn the plff failing to appear suffered a Nonsuit.

William Gilbert vs John Dobbs. Case. Same jury Impannelled and sworn assess the plaintiffs Damages to 1d and /6d costs.

Jane Lamkin Administratrix of the Estate of Wm Lamkin Deceased returns into Court an Inventory of Sales of the said estate to the amount of £29 9 9 proc money and prays the same may be put of record.

Robert Looney vs James Coles. Orr att.

1	James Adams	7	Nicholas Welch
2	Philip Wisenant	8	Wm Ramsey
3	Andrew Hoyle	9	Joseph England
4	John Beeman	10	Benj'n Hyde
5	Solomon Beason	11	Ja's Kelly Ju'r
6	Euel Lamkin	12	Alex'r Coulter

Jury Impannelled and sworn assess the plaintiffs Damage to £ 18 9 and /6d Costs.

Ordered by the Court that Alexander Moore have Licence to keep Ordinary at his fathers House in Tryon County he complying with the Act of Assembly in that case made and provided. He proposes for security Charles McLean and Wm. Moore Bound in the sum of thirty pounds. accepted

John McGaughy by his next friend vs William Gilbert. Assault.

1	James Adams	7	Joseph England
2	Philip Wisenant	8	Benj'n Hyde
3	Andrew Hoyle	9	William Whiteside
4	John Beeman	10	David Miller
5	Solomon Bason	11	Wm Cathey
6	William Ramsey	12	Loudwick Wray

Jury Impannelled and Sworn find the Defendant Guilty and asses the Plaintiffs Damage to £10 proc. money and /6d Costs. Motion in arrest of Judgment.

October term 1774

Ordered by the court that William Ramsey a juror sworn on the Tryal of the suit John McGaughey by his next friend versus William Gilbert be fined Twenty shillings proc money for absenting himself from his fellows during the trial. Fine remitted.

George Lamkin late High Sheriff came into open court there being five Justices present to wit John Robinson, Charles McLean, Timothy Riggs, joseph Harden and Thomas Espey, Esquires and produced his Account of the County Tax for the year of Our Lord A. D. 1772 and is as follows, to wit

C'r by 73 Insolvents and	
Runaways @ 2/8	£ 9 14 8
By Vouchers produced on	
Settlement	91 4 -
	£100 18 4

George Lamkin to Tryon County D'r	
To 1782 Taxables @ 2/8	£104 5 4
To 17 Supermumerary	
Taxables @ 2/8	2 5 4
	£106 10 8
	100 18 4
Balance due the County is	5 12 4

John Robinson, Charles McLean, Timo Riggs, Thomas Espey, Joseph Harden.

Court adjourned till tomorrow at 8 oClock. Met according to adjournment.
Present Wm. Moore, John Walker, John Ritzhaupt, joseph Harden, John Robinson, Charles McLean, Esq'rs.

October Term 1774 Claims on the County of Tryon for the Year 1774

John Robinson 1 venire ticket	1 10 8
William Spencer 1 scalp ticket	7 6
John Hill one venire ticket	1 10 8
William Moore 1 venire ticket	1 10 8
Wm Moore one venire ticket	1 10 8
Wm Moore one scalp ticket	7 6
Jeremiah Gage 1 scalp ticket	7 6
Zachariah Spencer 5 scalp tickets	1 7 6
George Trout 1 scalp ticket	7 6
John Trout 1 scalp ticket	7 6
Jacob Costner 1 venire ticket	19
Thomas Clark 5 scalp tickets	1 7
David Gage 5 scalp tickets	1 7 6
George Kyzer 4 scalp tickets	1 10
Joseph Richey 2 scalp tickets	15
John Reynolds 3 Wolf Scalp tickets	1 2 6
John Reynolds one scalp ticket	7 6
John Withrow six wolf scalp tickets	2 5
Thomas Alley one scalp ticket	7 6
James Cook Senr 1 scalp ticket	7 6
John McKinney 1 scalp ticket	7 6
John McKinney 1 ditto	7 6

October term 1774

Perregreen Magness 2 ditto	15		
James Cook Sen 1 ditto	7	6	
Alexander Autrey 2 do	15		
Charles England 1 do	7	6	
Joseph Harden 1 Venire Ticket	15		
Wm Murphy 1 scalp Tickets	15		
Michael Proctor 1 Wolf Scalp tickets	15		
George Lamkin for Extra Services done as Sheriff	8	-	-
John Walker for ditto as Coroner	2	10	
William Moore for ditto	2	10	
Andrew Neel for Extra Services done by Ezekiel Polk in the year 1772 & Allowed by the Court to Andrew Neel	9		
Andrew Neel for extra services as clerk in the year 1773 & 1774	12	2	-
Total	£60	5	4

The aforesaid sum of sixty pounds five shillings and four pence is the amount of the money due by the County of Tryon for the year one thousand seven hundred and seventy four. It is therefore ordered that a poll tax of one shilling and six pence be levied on each taxable person in the said county of Tryon to discharge the aforesaid sum.

Ordered by the Court that Steven Shelton be appointed Overseer of the road leading from John Walkers to the Province Line on that part between Grog Creek & the Province line.

A Deed of Sale from Thomas McKnight to Ja's Henderson for 119 acres Dated 21st Decem'r 1772 proved by John Gallespie Evidence thereto. Ord'd to be Reg'd.

Ordered by the Court that William Wray have licence to keep am Ordinary at his now dwelling house in Tryon County he complying with the Act of Assembly in that Case made and provided. He proposes for security John Walker and Charles McLean Esquires bound in the sum of thirty pounds. accepted.

Court adjourned till Court in Course. William Moore, John Retzhaupt, John Robinson, Thomas Espey, Charles McLean, John Walker, Timo Riggs, and Joseph Harden. Probates Remitted.

North Carolina, Tryon County. To wit. At an Inferior Court of Pleas and Quarter Sessions begun opened and held for said County of Tryon at the court house of said County on the fourth Tuesday of January A. D. 1775. Present the Worshipful William Moore, John Walker, Thomas Espey, Esquires.

Ordered by the Court that Robert McMinn be appointed Overseer of the Road leading from Col. Walkers to the province line in that part between the head of Grog Creek and Sandy Run and that he enter on the Duty of his charge accordingly.

A Deed of Sale from Daniel Jarratt to Samuel Jarret 250 acres of Land Dated the first Day of Septem'r 1774 proved by Martin Lookinglass Evidence thereto. Ordered to be Registered.

January term 1775

A Deed of Sale from Daniel Jarrett to Jacob Waitsel for 250 acres of Land Dated the first Day of Septem 1774 proved by Martin Lookinglass Evidence thereto. Ordered to be Registered.

A Deed of Sale from James Moore to Tho's Townsen for 200 acres of Land Dated the 24th Day of Decem'r 1774 proved by Christopher Hix Evidence thereto. Ord'd to be Reg'd.

The Grand Jury Moses Moore, Foreman.

2 Christopher Carpenter
3 Michael Hofstatler
4 Nicholas Wisenant
5 Thomas Castner
6 Jacob Hofstatler
7 Thomas Black
8 Valentine Mauney

9 Henry Landess
10 Laurence Kyzer
11 Benjamin Harden
12 William Yancey
13 John Scott
14 John Morris
15 Thomas Welch
16 Robert Porter
17 George Tubbs

Sworn and Charged.

A Deed of Sale from Samuel Barnet to William Stevenson for 100 acres of Land Dated the 5th Day of December 1774 acknowledged in open Court. Ordered to be Registered.

A Deed of Sale from Thomas Haslep to Joseph Jack for 150 acres of Land Dated the 11th Day of January 1775 acknowledged in open Court. Ordered to be Registered.

A Deed of Sale from James Kelly and Marey his wife Jacob Mooney for 200 acres of Land Dated the 7th Day of Septem'r 1774 proved by Simeon Kuykendall Evidence thereto. Ordered to be Registered.

A Bill of Sale from Henry Johnston to Joseph Scott for two Gelding thirteen head of Black cattle and about fifteen head of hogs with all the working Tools, beds & Household furniture belonging to the said Henry Johnston Dated the 5 Day of Septem'r 1774 proved by Ja's Johnston Evidence thereto. Ord'd to be Registered.

A Deed of Sale from Henry Johnston and Katherine his wife to Joseph Scott for 260 acres of Land [Dated] the 2d Day of Septem'r 1774 proved by James Johnston Evidence thereto. Ord'd to be Registered.

A Deed of Sale from Nicholas Wisenant to Christopher Carpenter for 300 acres of Land Dated the 24th Day of January 1775 acknowledged in open Court. Ordered to be Registered.

A Deed of Sale from Daniel Jarrett and Katherine his wife to Martin Lookinglass for 250 acres of Land Dated the 1st Day of Septem'r 1774 proved by Samuel Jarrett Evidence thereto. Ord'd to be Reg'd.

Court adjourned till tomorrow morning at 8 OClock. Met according to adjournment. Present William Moore, John Ritzhaupt, John Robison, Charles McLean, Esquires.

Ordered by the Court that Samuel Dunaway Serve as Constable and that he Swear in before John Ritzhaupt Esquire accordingly.

January term 1775

Ordered that James Patterson have licence to keep Ordinary at his now Dwelling in Tryon County he complying with the Act of Assembly in that case made and provided. He proposes for Securitys William Patterson & James Johnston Bound in the sum of Thirty pounds proc. money. accepted.

A Deed of Sale from Andrew Hampton to Hugh Jenkins for 600 acres of Land Dated the 6th day of July 1772 proved by David Jenkins Evidence thereto.

Ordered by the Court that Christopher Carpenter have Licence to keep Ordinary at his now Dwelling House in Tryon County he complying with the Act of Assembly in that case made and provided. He proposes for Securitys William Moore & John Dunn Esq'rs. accepted.

The Administrators of John Harmon deceas'd Brought into Court an Account of Sales of the said Estate the amount One Hundred & Twelve pound four shillings; and also their account of Disbursements for Debts paid on behalf of said Estate amounting to Seven pound nineteen shillings and two pence by which it appears that there remains in their hands the sum of One Hundred & Four pound four shillings and nine pence including the widows Dower and Six childrens shares; as P acc't stated Settled and Filed in this office.

Ordered by the Court that John Dellinger have Licence to keep Ordinary at his now Dwelling House in Tryon County he complying with the Act of Assembly in that case made and provided. He proposes for Securitys Peter Costner and Jacob Costner Bound in the sum of Thirty pounds. accepted.

Ordered by the Court that James Milliken Serve as Constable in the room of Saml Martin and that he Swear in before Wm. Moore Esq'r accordingly.

Court adjourned for one hour. Met according to Adjournment. Present William Moore, John Ritzhaupt, Charles McLean, Esq'rs.

Ordered by the Court that Wm. Thomason & John McKinney lay out a Road from George Winters mill by the Island Ford on Main Broad River thence the nearest and best way to the So Carolina line.

Ordered by the Court that Joseph Clark be appointed Overseer of the above Road.

A Deed of Sale from John Walker Esq'r to James Patterson for 300 acres of Land Dated the 25 Day of January A D 1775 ackn'd in open Court. Ord'd to be Registered.

A Power of Attorney from Thos Henry to Francis Armstrong Dated the 20th Day of January 1773 proved in Open Court by Ja's Graham Evidence thereto. Ord'd to be Reg'd.

A Deed of Sale from Francis McCorkle & Sarah his wife for 250 acres of Land Dated the 17 Day of January 1775 proved by Archibald Fleming Evidence thereto. Ordered to be Registered.

A Deed of Sale from Archibald Fleming & Agnes his wife to James Fleming for 200 acres of Land Dated the 20th Day of July 1773 proved by George Moorgenunk Evidence thereto. Ord'd to be Reg'd.

January term 1775

A Deed of Sale from Wm. Cleghorn to James Henderson for 300 acres of Land Dated the 20th Day of January 1767 proved by Alex'r Coulter Evidence thereto. Ordered to be Registered.

A Deed of Sale from Francis Beatey to Robert Armstrong for 300 acres of Land Dated the 20th Day of July 1773 proved by Wallace Beatey Evidence thereto. Ord'd to be Registered.

An Instrument of Writing signed by Simeon Kuykendal & confirming a Conveyance formerly made by his Uncle Joseph Harden to Robert Armstrong for 200 acres of Land that formerly belonged to his father John Kuykendal Deceased acknowledged in Open Court and Recorded in the Clerks Office. Ord'd to be Reg'd.

A Deed of Sale from John Falls and Martha his wife to Henry McWhirter for 300 acres of Land Dated the 10th Day of October 1774 proved by Wm Wray Evidence thereto. Ordered to be Registered.

A Deed of Sale from John Sloan and Jean his wife to John Sartain for 200 acres of Land Dated the 2d Day of Novem'r 1774 proved by Ja's [Henderson] Evidence thereto. Ord'd to be Registered.

A Deed of Sale from William Mackey to William Patterson for 239 acres of Land Dated the 25 Day of February 1771 proved by Wallace Beatey Evidence thereto. Ordered to be Registered.

A Deed of Sale from Thomas Campbell to Samuel Loftin for 200 acres of Land Dated the 20th Day of October 1774 acknowledged in Open Court. Ordered to be Registered.

A Deed of Sale from James McEntire & Ann his wife to William Booth for 250 acres of Land Dated the _____ 1773 proved by Moses Whitley Evidence thereto. Ordered to be Registered.

A Deed of Sale from Hugh Beatey to Tho's Townsen for 234 acres of Land Dated the 14th Day of Septem'r 1774 proved by Joel Blackwell Evidence thereto. Ordered to be Registered.

A Deed of Sale from Andrew Goforth & Richard Gullock for 300 acres of Land Dated the 8th Day of June 1774 proved by Preston Goforth Evidence thereto. Ordered to be Registered.

A Deed of Sale from George Moosgenung to Adam Deck for 140 acres of Land Dated the 20th Day of Jan'y 1775 proved by Adam Deck Evidence thereto. Ord'd to be Reg'd.

Court adjourned till tomorrow at 9 Oclock. Met according to Adjournment. Present William Moore, John Ritzhaupt, John Robinson, Esq'rs.

Ordered by the Court that John Harris be appointed overseer of the Road Leading from the Tuccasege Ford to the Province line in that part Between the So fork ford and the Province line and that he Enter on his Charge accordingly.

Ordered by the Court that David Heddlestone Ju'r and Nathan Proctor be appointed Constables for John Walker Esq'r and that they swear in before him accordingly.

William Reed vs Edward Williams. Orr att.

January term 1775

Petty Jury

1	John Hoyle	7	Samuel McFaddon
2	Wm. Kinkaid	8	Wm Ramsey
3	Wm Crocket	9	Thomas Robinson
4	David Crocket	10	William Henry
5	Alex'r Coulter	11	David Ramsey
6	David Biggerstaff	12	Ambrose Foster

Jury Impanneled and Sworn assess the Plaintiffs Damages to 1d Damage and /6d Costs.

Robt Murphy vs John Huggins. Same Jury. Impannelled and Sworn the plff in this suit failing to appear was Nonsuit.

William Nisbett assee &C vs Jacob Mooney. Same Jury. Impannelled and sworn find for the Plaintiff and assess his Damage to £6 18 6 and /6 Cost. Arrest motioned by J. D.

Alex'r Coulter & Wife Exr's of Wm. Moore vs James Buchanan. Case. Same Jury with the alteration of Samuel Gray in the room of Alexander Coulter Impannelled and Sworn find that the Defendant shall pay back the £5 that he had for making the Waggon & s'd Defendant shall have his work back again to do with the same as he pleases & Coulter to have the Irons of s'd Waggon & s'd Buchanan is to pay one penny Damage. Arrest motioned by J. D.

A Deed of Sale from David Byars to Michael McElwrath for 300 acres of Land Dated the 3d Day of Septem'r 1774 proved by Joseph Byars Evidence thereto. Ord'd to be Reg'd.

A Deed of Sale from Robert Evins to John Mattox for 75 acres Dated the 8th of Decem'r 1774 proved by Thomas Robison Evidence thereto. Ord'd to be Reg'd.

A Deed of Sale from James Byars & Margaret his wife to Michael McElwrath for 300 acres Dated the 3d Day of Septem'r 1774 proved by Joseph Byars Evidence thereto. Ord'd to be Reg'd.

A Deed of Sale from Benjamin Hyde to Rebekah Gilkie for 300 acres of Land Dated the 19th Day of Decem'r 1774 proved by Wm Nevans Evidence thereto. Ord'd to be Registered.

A Deed of Sale from Wm Hyde & Jean his wife to Joseph Thomson for 200 acres of Land Dated the 19th Day of Decem'r 1774 proved by John Gilky Evidence thereto. Ord'd to be Reg'd.

A Deed of Sale from John Carson to John Withrow for 570 acres of Land Dated the 23d Day of Decem'r 1774 prov'd by Wm Nevans Evidence thereto. Ord'd to be Reg'd.

Ordered by the Court that Nathaniel Henderson be appointed Constable in the room of Nath'l Aldrige and that he swear in before John Robinson Esquire accordingly.

Ordered by the Court that Elizabeth Flinn orphan Child of Michael Flinn aged fifteen Years and a half be bound unto George Davis (who she made choice of as master) until she shall arive at the age of Eighteen years and the Said George Davis is in all things to comply with the Act of Assembly in that case made and provided.

January term 1775

Court adjourned till tomorrow morning at 9 Oclock. Met according to Adjournment. Present Wm Moore, John Ritzhaupt, Joseph Harden, Esq'rs.

The King vs Thos Espey. Extortion.

1 John Hoyle	7 Wm Going
2 Wm. Kinkaid	8 Joseph Richey
3 Wm Crocket	9 Christopher Walbert
4 Dav'd Crocket	10 David Ramsey
5 Sam'l Gray	11 John Gallespie
6 Ambrose Foster	12 Adolph Reep

Jury Impanneled and Sworn find the Def't not Guilty.

The King vs And'w Hoyle. Extortion.

1 John Hoyle	7 John Gallespie
2 Wm Crocket	8 Adolph Reep
3 Dav'd Crocket	9 Philip Cancelor
4 Ambrose Foster	10 Aaron Biggerstaff
5 Joseph Richey	11 Wm Kinkaid
6 Christopher Walbert	12 Peter Seits

Jury Impanneled and Sworn. Noli Prosequi.

The King vs Robert Miller. Trespass. Jury Impannelled & Sworn find the Defendant not guilty.

The Kings vs Simeon Kuykendal. Ass't. Same Jury with the alteration of Wm. King in the room of William Kinkaid impannelled and sworn find the Defendant not guilty.

Settlement of the Estate of Wm. Henry Deceased by the administrator.

Amount of Sales	£202 6 2
Charges Deducted	28 14 4
Ballance due the Estate yet	£172 11 10
Remaining in the hands of the administrator.	

Settlement of the Estate of William Lamkin Deceased by the administrator.

Amount of Sales	£29 9 9
Charges Deducted	17 7 8
Ballance due the Estate yet	£12 2 1
yet remaining in the hands of the administrator.	

Court adjourned till tomorrow at 8 oClock. Met according to Adjournment. Present Wm Moore, John Ritzhaupt, Joseph Harden, Esq'rs.

Ordered by the Court that James Adear be appointed overseer of a Road leading from Col'l Walkers past Wm Gilberts to the Waggon Ford below the mouth of Green River and that he enter on the Duty of his charge accordingly.

January term 1775

Ordered by the Court that Solomon Bason be appointed Constable in the room of John Wells & that he swear in before Charles McLean Esq. accordingly.

Court adjourned till Court in Course. William Moore, John Ritzhaupt, Joseph Hardin, Thomas Espey.

North Carolina, Tryon County. To wit. At an Inferior Court of Pleas and Quarter Sessions begun opened and held for said County of Tryon at the Court House of said County on the fourth Tuesday of April Anno Domini 1775. Present the Worshipful William Moore, John Ritzhaupt, John Robison, Esquires.

Ordered by the Court that Rachel Goforth wife and Relict of Preston Goforth Deceased together with Alexander Lewis have Letters of Administration of all and Singular the Goods and Chattles Debts and Credits of the said Deceased who proposes for Securitys John Moore and William Wray bound in £100. accepted.

Ordered by the Court that Henry Dellinger have licence to keep Ordinary at his now dwelling House in tryon County he complying with the act of Assembly in the Case made & provided. He proposes for Securitys John Ritzhaupt & Nicholas Friday.

Alice Alexander Administratrix of the Estate of Robert Alexander Deceased returns an account of Sales of the said Estate amounting to £97 4 2 and prays the same may be put of Record.

A Deed of Sale from William Goforth to John Baird Junior for 200 acres of Land Dated the 11th Day of March 1775 proved by Andrew Neel Evidence thereto. Ordered to be Registered.

A Deed of Sale from William Tankersly to Jacob Masters for 250 acres of Land Dated the 25 Day of March 1775 proved by Mathias Devold Evidence thereto. Ordered to be Registered.

Court adjourned till to morrow morning at 8 Oclock. Met according to Adjournment. Present William Moore, John Ritzhaupt, John Robinson, Charles McLean, Esq'rs.

Ordered that Jacob Ramsour be appointed Overseer of the Road leading from Indian Creek by Ramsours mill to Rowan County line and that he enter on the Duty of his charge accordingly.

Ordered by the Court that Andrew Milliken be appointed Constable in the room of James Milliken and that he swear in before Wm. Moore Esquire accordingly.

The Grand Jury Richard Venable, Foreman.

2 Nicholas Friday	9 William Thomason
3 James Coburn	10 Thomas Dills
4 Nicholas Shram	11 John Beeman
5 Christian Rinehart	12 Jonas Bedford
6 Jacob Ramsour	13 Jacob Carpenter
7 John Moore Sen'r	14 John Moore Ju'r
8 Alexander Coyl	15 Nicholas Welch

Sworn & Charged.

April term 1775

Ordered that Wm Alston, John Moore, Joseph Jenkins, Robert Armstrong, Peter Castner, Joseph Davis, John Wells, Jacob Mooney Ju'r, Zachariah Spencer, Fred'k Hambright, Michael Hoyle, Laurence Kyzer, Michael Hofstatler, Robert Alexander and Wm. Massey be appointed a Jury to lay out a Road the nearest and best way from Tryon Court House to the Tuccaseege ford and that they be Summoned by the Sheriff to be and appear before William Moore or John Ritzhaupt on the first Day of May next to take the necessary steps to qualify them for this their Charge.

Ordered by the Court that Essix Capshaw be appointed Overseer of the Road leading rom Pullams mill to the province line in that part between said Mill and Broad River and that Jeremiah McDaniel serve as overseer from Broad River to the Charles Town Waggon Road.

Ordered by the Court that Rawleys Mathews an orphan child aged thirteen years and three months be bound unto Samuel Dunaway until he shall arive to the age of Twenty one years and the said Samuel Dunaway is to teach or cause to be taught the art Trade or Mystery of a Cordwainer and is to give the said Orphan at his freedom one Horse and saddle of the value of Ten pounds and in all other things to comply with the Act of Assembly in that case made and provided.

Court adjourned for an hour. Met according to adjournment. Present Wm Moore, Charles McLean, John Robinson, Esq'rs.

Ordered by the Court that Robert Gilkey together with Jannet Gilkey late wife and Relict of James Finley Deceased have Letters of administration of all and Singular the Goods and Chattles Debts and Credits of the said Deceased who took the oaths by Law appointed for administrators and proposes for Securitys Abel Beaty and Andrew Haslep Bound in £120. accepted.

Ord'd by the Court that Henry Reynolds be appointed Constable in the Room of James Alley & that he Swear in before Thos Espey Esq'r accordingly.

Settlement of the Estate of James Watson Deceased returned by William Watson Executor
amounting to   £59 4 6
Charges against the Estate   19 10 10
Amount in the Executor's hands   £39 15 6
which is to be Divided as followeth Vizt
To his son Wm Watson £ 10 0 0
To his Daughter Susannah 8 7½
To his Daughter Alice 150 acres of Land not valued
To his daughter [not named] 8 7½
To his Grandson Jas Walker 10 0 0
There Remains £18 18 3 which is to be devided between the above named William & Alice.

Court adjourned till to morrow morning at 8 Oclock. Met according to Adjournment. Present William Moore, John Robison, Charles McLean, Esq'rs.

[The following entry marked through:] Jannet Lamkin Administratrix of the Estate of William Lamkin Deceased produced in open Court as vouchers two Notes of hand against the said Estate amounting to £14 which was Examined and approved by the court by which it appears that the admx has paid away all the Estate in her hands & £1 17 11 as by accompt stated settled & Filed in this office.

April term 1775

Wm Martin vs Robert Abernathy. Debt.

Petty Jury

1 James Cook	7 Wm Whitesides
2 William Willis	8 Joel Blackwell
3 Ja's Bucanon	9 Rob't Taylor
4 Abel Beatey	10 Essex Capshaw
5 Jacob Willis	11 Edward Callahan
6 Joseph Clark	12 Francis Gilmore

Jury Impanneled and Sworn assess the Plaintiffs Damage to 1d Damage and /6d Costs.

Verdry Magby vs Robt Looney. Case. Same Jury Impannelled and Sworn. Nonsuit.

John Elliott vs Charles Robison. Orr att. Same Jury Impannelled & Sworn assess the Plffs Damage to £6 2 & /6 Costs.

Anthony Preston vs James Miller. Same Jury Impannelled & Sworn the Plff failing to appear was Nonsuit.

Elizabeth Mayhue vs Wm. Jones. Trover & Conversion. Same Jury with the alteration of Richard Reynolds in the Room of Francis Gilmore Plaintiff failing to appear as Nonsuit.

Thos Jones vs William Cathey. Same Jury with the alteration of Francis Gilmore in the Room of Abel Beatey plff failing to appear was Nonsuit.

William Armstrong vs James Espey & Thomas Espey. Case.

Petty Jury

1 James Cook	7 Joel Blackwell
2 Francis Gilmore	8 Robert Taylor
3 Andrew Haslep	9 Edward Callahan
4 William Willis	10 George Davis
5 Aaron Moore	11 Thomas Colwell
6 James Bucanan	12 John McFaddon

Jury Impanneled and Sworn find for the Plaintiff and assess his Damage to £16 14 5 Damage and /6 Costs. arrest motioned by J. Dunn.

John McFaddon Ju vs Nathan Camp. Case. Same Jury with the alteration of David Miler and Valentine Mauney in the room of John McFaddon and Robert Taylor Impannelled & Sworn assess the plaintiffs Damage to £20 0 0 and /6 Cost.

Jacob Boone vs Philip Goodbread.

Petty Jury

1 James Cook	7 Edward Callahan
2 Francis Gilmore	8 George Davis
3 Andrew Haslep	9 Tho's Colwell
4 William Willis	10 David Miller

April term 1775

5 James Bucanan   11 Valentine Muney
6 Joel Blackwell   12 Robert Taylor

Jury Impanneled and Sworn find assess the Plaintiffs Damage to £7 16 & /6d Costs.

Thomas Espey assee &c vs Thomas Campbell. Same Jury Impannelled and Sworn assess the plffs Damage to £5 7 8 & /6 cost.

Nicholas Warlock adm'r &c. vs David Alexander & Wm. Irwin. Case. Same Jury Impannelled and sworn assess the plaintiffs Damage to £17 4 4 and /6 Cost.

William Patterson assee &c vs Thomas Campbell. Same Jury Impannelled and Sworn assess the plffs Damage to £10 4 2 & /6 cost.

Ordered by the Court that William Moore, Frederick Hambright, James McEntire, Moses Moore, John McKinney, William Gilbert, Abraham Kuykendall and James Johnston be summoned by the Sheriff to be and appear before the Judge of the Court of Oyer and Terminer at the next court to be held for the District of Salisbury at Salisbury on the first Day of June next then and there to serve our Sovereign Lord the King as rand and Petit Jurors.

Ordered by the Court that Michael Rudisel, David Jenkins, John Waggoner, Jacob Forney, George Heager, Robert Gilkey, Leonard Sailor, John Dellinger, Nicholas Friday, Henry Dellinger, Christian Carpenter, and Jacob Carpenter be appointed a Jury to lay out a Road from Beateys old Waggon Ford on Catawba River the nearest and best way to Henry Dellingers to Dellingers Creek and that they be summoned by the Sheriff to be & appear [before] some one of his Majestys Justices of the peace for said County then & there to take the necessary steps to qualify them for this their charge.

Ordered by the Court that David Jenkins be appointed overseer of the said Road in that part between Beateys ford and Jenkins's Creek and that George Sides be appointed overseer of said Road in that part between Jenkins's Creek and Dellingers Creek and that he enter on his charge accordingly.

Timothy Riggs Esquire being appointed Guardian to John Saffold who proposed for Securitys Benjamin Harden, Richard Reynolds and John Neighbours who now come into open Court and pray to be discharged from the said suretyship said Timothy Riggs proposes for new Securitys Jonas Bedford and William Whitesides bound in £126. accepted.

A Deed of Sale from John Lusk and Sarah his wife to Andrew Haslep for 200 acres of Land Dated the 28th Day of January 1774 proved by Thomas Haslep Evidence thereto. Ord'd to be Reg'd.

A Deed of Sale from John Beard Sen'r to Edward Callahan for 140 acres of Land Dated the 20th Day of April 1775 proved by Andrew Neel Evidence thereto. Ord'd to be Registered.

A Deed of Sale from Robert Johnston to Frederick Neister for 50 acres Dated the 13th February 1775 proved by Michael Rudisel Evidence thereto. Ord'd to be Registered.

A Deed of Sale from James Daugherty to James Miller for 250 acres Dated the first Day of February 1775 proved by Alexander Coulter Evidence thereto. Ord'd to be Reg'd.

<u>April term 1775</u>

A Deed of Sale from Abel Lee to Thomas Welch for 100 acres of Land Dated the 18th April 1775 prov'd by Wm Reynolds Evidence thereto. Ord'd to be Reg'd.

A Deed of Sale from Edward Hogan to Thomas Haslep for 50 acres of Land Dated the 13th of February 1775 proved by John McFaddon Evidence thereto. Ord'd to be Reg'd.

Court adjourned till to morrow morning at 8 Oclock. Met according to Adjournment. Present John Robison, Cha's McLean, Joseph Harden, Timothy Riggs, Esq'rs.

The King vs James Miller. ass. Petit Jury Impannelled and sworn.

1 James Cook	7 John Webb
2 Aaron Moore	8 Thomas Baker
3 Benj'n Harden	9 Jacob Willis
4 Wm Davison	10 Francis Gilmore
5 Wm Willis	11 Rob't Taylor
6 James Bucanan	12 Alex'r Coulter

find the Defendant Guilty.

The King vs Patrick Lyon.

Petty Jury

1 Wm Patterson	7 Thos Welch
2 Wm Gilbert	8 Edward Callahan
3 John Morris	9 Joseph Baker
4 Valentine Mauney	10 John Bryson
5 Thomas Campbell	11 Adolph Reep
6 Perry Green Magness	12 Tho's Reynolds

Impannelled and Sworn find the Defendant not Guilty.

The King vs Patrick Lyon. Petty Larceny. Petit Jury. Same as above Impannelled and sworn find the Prisoner Guilty in manner and form as Charged in the Bill of Indictment.

Court adjourned for Ten Minutes. Met according to Adjournment. Present John Robinson, Timothy Riggs, Joseph Harden, Esquires.

The Kings vs Ebenezar Newton. Ass't. Petty Jury

1 James Cook	7 John Webb
2 Aaron Moore	8 Thomas Baker
3 Benjamin Harden	9 Jacob Willis
4 William Davison	10 Francis Gilmore
5 William Willis	11 Robert Taylor
6 James Bucanan	12 Alex'r Coulter

Jury Impannelled and sworn find the Defendant not Guilty.

Peter Sides assee &c vs John Logan & Jas McAfee. Same Jury with the alteration of Essex Capshaw in the room of Aaron Moore, Thos Welch in the room of Francis Gilmore, and Saml Moore in the room of Samuel Moore. Impannelled and Sworn find for the plaintiff and assess his Damage to £8 8 8 and /6d cost.

April term 1775

After Proclamation the Court proceeded to the Election of a Sheriff accordingly there being six Justices present viz William moore, john Robison, Charles McLean, Timothy Riggs, Joseph Harden & Thomas Espey who did elect and choose Jacob Castner, joseph Harden and Charles McLean to be Recommended to his Excellency the Governor for his approbation & appointment of one of them to serve as high sheriff the Ensuing year. It appears by the Polls that Jacob Castner had six votes, Joseph Harden three and Charles McLean two votes. Ordered that they be Recommended accordingly.

A Deed of Sale from James Alley to Thomas Alley and James Alley Ju'r for 200 acres of Land also sundry Horse Creatures, Cattle & Hogs and Houshold furniture Dated the 29th of March A D 1775 prov'd in open Court by Francis Oyles Evidence thereto. Ord'd to be Reg'd.

A Deed of Sale from William Graham unto John Alturn[?] for 200 acres Dated the 8th Day of April 1775 acknowledged in Open Court and Recorded in the Clerks Office. Ord'd to be Reg'd.

A Deed of Sale from John Tagert to Wm Graham for 200 acres of Land Dated the 8th Day of November 1774 acknowledged in Open Court. Ord'd to be Reg'd.

A Deed of Sale from [John] Lame and Mary his wife for 100 acres of Land Dated the 17th April 1773 proved by Christian Rinehart Evidence thereto. Ord'd to be Reg'd.

A Deed of Sale from Thomas Beaty, Hugh Beaty & Rob't Armstrong to William Fearis for 240 acres of Land Dated the 20th day of april 1775 proved to be Executed by Hugh Beaty and Rob't Armstrong for Tho's Beaty by Wm Morrison Evidence thereto. Ord'd to be Registered.

A Deed of Sale from Peter Smith & Elizabeth his wife to Rob't Ramsey for 300 acres of Land Dated the 24th of March 1775 prov'd by David Ramsey. Ord'd to be Registered.

A Deed of Sale from Nicholas Leeper to Jonas Bedford for ___ acres of Land Dated the 5th of Decem'r 1773 prov'd by And'w Neel Evidence thereto. Ord'd to be Registered.

A Deed of Sale from Samuel Sharp to Wm Mills for 200 acres of Land Dated the 15th of August 1774 proved by Walter Sharp Evidence thereto. Ord'd to be Registered.

A Deed of Sale from Walter Sharp to William Mills for 300 acres of Land Dated the 26 Day of April 1775 ack'd in open Court. Ord'd to be Registered.

A Deed of Sale from Wm. Alston to Thomas Hunt for 93½ acres of Land dated the third Day of Decem'r 1773 prov'd by Saml Kuykendall Evidence thereto. Ord'd to be Registered.

A Deed of Sale from Moses Moore to Benjamin Moore for 400 acres of Land ack'd in open Court and Recorded in the Clerks Office. Dated the 18th Day of June 1775. Ord'd to be Reg'd.

A Deed of Sale from Hugh Shannon to James Shannon for 200 acres of Land Dated the 11th Day of March 1775 prov'd in open Court. Ord'd to be Reg'd.

A Deed of Sale from James Scott & Mary Scott to Robert Shannon for 200 acres of Land Dated the 5th Day of February 1775 proved by John Craig Evidence thereto. Ord'd to be Reg'd.

<u>April term 1775</u>

A Deed of Sale from John Moore to William Moore for 296 acres of Land Dated the 25 Day of April 1775 prov'd by Wm Cronicle Evidence thereto. Ord'd to be Reg'd.

A Deed of Sale from Christopher Walbert to Thomas Robison for 200 acres of Land Dated the 27 Day April 1775 ack'd in open Court. Ord'd to be Registered.

A Deed of Sale from John Moore to Zachariah Spencer for 50 acres of Land Dated the 14 Day of Novem'r 1774 prov'd by Wm Moore Evidence thereto. Ord'd to be Reg'd.

Court adjourned till to morrow morning at 8 Oclock. Met according to Adjournment. Present William Moore, Charles McLean, Tho's Espey, Esq'rs.

Thomas Wray being Committed to the Gaol of this county on Suspicion of being a runaway servant and it appearing that no person has any such right to him Ordered that he be Released upon giving Security for his good Behaviour accordingly John Morris and Joseph McDaniel came into open court and acknowledged themselves to owe to our Sovereign Lord the King the sum of Twenty pounds proc. money to be void upon condition that he Thos Wray be of good Behaviour for the term of Five years.

Jannet Lamkin Adm'x of the Estate of Wm Lamkin Deceased produced a voucher for having paid £12 2 1 by which it appears that the said Adm'x has paid away all the Estate in her hands as appears by account stated settled and filed in this office.

Ordered by the court Christopher Mauney be appointed overseer of the Road Leading form the Tuccaseege ford to Tryon Court House in that part between the Court House and opposite to Peter Laboon and Peter Laboon in that part between his house and the south fork and Samuel Martin from the fork to the Tuccaseege Ford.

Ord'd by the Court that Thomas Welch serve as Constable in the Room of Richman Fleming and that he Swear in before Timothy Riggs Esq'r accordingly.

Ord'd by the Court that John Wells Serve as Constable and that he Swear in before Cha's McLean Esq accordingly.

Court adjourned till Court in Course. William Moore, Thomas Espey, Charles McLean.

North Carolina, Tryon County. To wit. At an Inferior Court of Pleas and Quarter Sessions begun Opened and held for the said County of Tryon at the Court House of said County on the fourth Tuesday of July Anno Dom. 1775. Present the Worshipful John Ritzhaupt.

Court adjourned till to morrow morning at 8 Oclock. Met according to Adjournment. Present John Ritzhaupt Esqr. His Majestys Commission of the peace being read Silence was proclaimed.

James McEntire, Timothy Riggs, William Gilbert and William Graham came into open court and took the oaths by Law appointed for the Qualification of Publick officers repeated & subscribed the Test and took the oaths of Justices of the peace accordingly.

Rachel Goforth and Alexander Lewis Administrators of the Estate of Preston Goforth return into Court and inventory of the said Estate and pray an order of Sale which was accordingly granted.

July term 1775

Robert Gilkey and Jean Gilkey Administrators of the Estate of James Finley Deceased return into Court an Inventory of the said Estate & pray an Order of Sale which was accordingly granted.

A Deed of Sale from Peter Kuykendall to Wm. Webb for 300 acres Dated the 20th day of July 1775 proved in open Court by Robert McMinn Evidence thereto. Ordered to be Registered.

A Deed of Sale from John Reed and Martha his wife to Sam'l Hunter for 200 acres Dated the 24th Day of October 1774 proved by Mathew Armstrong Evidence thereto. Ordered to be Registered.

A Deed of Sale from Samuel Coburn to Babtist Scott for 80 acres of Land Dated the 20 Day of September 1773 proved by George Lamkin Evidence thereto. Ord'd to be Registered.

A Deed of Sale from William Cleghorn to Henry Hays for 300 acres of Land Dated the first Day of February 1775 proved by Andrew Hampton Evidence thereto. Ord'd to be Registered.

A Deed of Sale from Boston Best & Catherine his wife to George Cathey for 100 acres Dated the 4 Day of February 1775 proved by George Cathey [sic] Evidence thereto. Ordered to be Registered.

Court adjourned till tomorrow morning at 8 Oclock. Met according to adjournment. Present Timothy Riggs, Ja's Graham, Wm. Gilbert, Esq'rs.

Joseph Harden came into open Court and took the oaths by Law appointed for the Qualification of Publick officers repeated and subscribed the test & took the oath of a Justice of the peace & took his seat accordingly.

The Grand Jury Benjamin Harden, Foreman.

2 John McKinney	10 Alex'r Gilliland
3 John McClare	11 Ja's Martin
4 Ja's Collins	12 Aaron Moore
5 Tho's Welch	13 George Paris
6 Andrew Hampton	14 Rob't Porter
7 James Bucanan	15 John Logan
8 David George	16 Wm Davis
9 George Ewing	

Sworn & Charged.

The Last Will and Testament of Wm Cleghorn Deceased was produced in open Court and proved by the oath of David Dickey Evidence thereto. On motion of William Kennan Esq'r Ordered by the court that Letters Testamentary Issue to Lettice Cleghorn wife & Relict of the s'd Deceased of all & singular the goods & chattles Rights & Credits of said Deceased she complying with the act of Assembly in that case made & provided.

A Deed of Sale from Henry Wright to John Kirkconell for 900 acres of Land Dated the 22d Day of March 1775 proved by And'w Neel Evidence thereto. Or'd to be Registered.

July term 1775

A Bill of Sale from Henry Wright to John Kirkconell for Sundry Goods Dated the 29 Day of October 1774 proved by Andrew Neel Evidence thereto. Or'd to be Registered.

The Last Will and Testament of Sam'l Gray Dated the 22d Day of April 1775 was produced in open Court and proved by the oath of John McClure Evidence thereto. Ord'd to be put of Record.

The Nuncupative Will of Wm Twitty 1775 was proved in open Court by the oath of Thomas Johnston Evidence thereto Ordered to be put of Record. On motion of Alex'r Martin Esq ordered by the Court Letters of Administration issue to Susanna Twitty Wife & Relict of the said Deceased of all & singular the Goods & Chattles of the said Deceased she complying with the Act of Assembly in that case made & provided. Securitys proposed And'w Hampton, John Walker, John Morris £4000. accepted.

Ordered by the Court that William Feares be appointed Guardian to Sarah Shearer & Hugh Shearer orphans, Children of Matthew Shearer Deceased. He proposes for Securitys George Trout & James Collins bound in £100. accepted.

The King vs Jno Brown Skrimshire.

Petty Jury

1	Joseph Jenkins	7	Benj'a Hyde
2	Adolph Reep	8	Ja's Withrow
3	Dav'd Ramsey	9	Michael McElwrath
4	Lawrence Kyzer	10	Peter Carpenter
5	Wm Thomson	11	Miles Abernathy
6	Rob't Gwaltney	12	Jonathan O'Neal

Jury Impannelled and Sworn find the Defendant not Guilty.

Joseph Fraser vs Wm. Nickols. Case. Same Jury Impannelled & Sworn find for the Plaintiff & Assess his Damage to £7 15 9 & /6 Cost.

Wm Gilbert vs George Farr. Case. Same Jury Impannelled and Sworn find for the Plaintiff & Assess his Damage to £8 0 11 & /6 Cost.

The King vs Robert Wier. Trespass. Same Jury Impannelled & Sworn find the Defendant Guilty. arrest motioned by W. R.

Ordered by the Court that Elias Morgan be appointed overseer of the Road Leading from Col. Walkers to Buffalo in that part Between the Grassy branch and Buffaloe and that he Enter on the Duty of his Charge accordingly.

Ordered by the Court that John Lecquer an orphan child of John Leqere aged Twelve years be bound unto John Sloan until he shall arrive at the age of Twenty on years and the said John Sloan is to teach the said apprentice the art, Trade or Mystery of a Weaver & in all things to Comply with the act of Assembly in that case made & provided.

The order for the Tuccaseege Road Renewed and James Henderson & Ja's Logan appointed Jurors in the room of Frederick Hambright & William Massey.

<u>July term 1775</u>

A Deed of Sale from Robert Rankin to Andrew Newberry for ___ acres of Land Dated the 27 day of July 1775 ack'd in open Court. Ord'd to be Registered.

A Deed of Sale from Philip Henson Sen to John McFaddon Ju'r for 200 acres of Land Dated the 11th day of February 1775 proved by Sam'l McFaddon Evidence thereto. Ord'd to be Registered.

A Deed of Sale from Joseph England to Jacob Hofstatler for 300 acres of Land Dated the 27 day of July 1775 ackn'd in open Court. Ordered to be Registered.

A Deed of Sale from James Cozart to John Graham for 300 acres of Land Dated the 9 day of May 1775 proved by William Graham Evidence thereto. Ord'd to be Reg'd.

A Deed of Sale from Wm. Cleghorn to John Huddleston for 97 acres Dated the 8 day of Decem'r 1772 proved in open Court by John McClure Evidence thereto. Ord'd to be Registered.

A Deed of Sale from Wm. Cleghorn to John Scott for 100 acres of Land Dated the 13th day of June 1774 proved in open Court by David Dickey Evidence thereto. Ordered to be Registered.

A Deed of Sale from Sam'l Walker & Mary his wife to Wm. Pickrell for 100 acres of Land Dated the 19 day of July 1775 proved by Sam'l McFaddon Evidence thereto. Ord'd to be Registered.

A Deed of Sale from Bartlet Henson to Jacob Clements for 100 acres of Land Dated the 14 day of April 1775 proved by Thomas Dill Evidence thereto. Ord'd to be Registered.

A Deed of Sale from John Fleming to John McClure for 200 acres dated 10 day of June 1775 proved by James Scott Evidence thereto. Ord'd to be Registered.

A Deed of Sale from Ephraim McLean & Elizabeth his wife to David Nisbet for 420 acres Dated the 30 day of December 1773 proved by John Barber Evidence thereto. Ord'd to be Registered.

A Deed of Sale from Christopher Carpenter to John Carpenter for 300 acres dated the 27 Day of July 1775 ackn'd in open Court. Ord'd to be Registered.

A Deed of Sale from Thomas Beatey, Hugh Beatey & Robert Armstrong to Benjamin Cochran for 140 acres of Land dated the 24 July 1775 proved in open Court by Joseph Byars. Ord'd to be Registered.

A Deed of Dan'l McCarty to James Henderson for 300 acres of Land Dated the 20 day of Septem'r 1774 proved by William Gilmore Evidence thereto. Ord to be Registered.

A Deed of Sale from Wm Glen & Jannet his wife to James Henderson for 200 acres of Land Dated the 27th Day of March 1774 prov'd by Wm. Gilmore Evidence thereto. Ord'd to be Registered.

A Bond of Performance from William Twitty to Saml Walker Dated the 18 Day of March 1774 proved by William Pickrell Evidence thereto. Ord'd to be Registered.

<u>July term 1775</u>

A Deed of Sale from Loudewick Wray to Wm. Gilbert for 300 acres of Land Dated the 10 Day of Septem 1773 ackn'd in open Court. Ord'd to be Registered.

A Deed of Sale from Thomas Welch to John Landis for 250 acres of Land dated the 27th day of July 1775 ackn'd in open Court. Ord'd to be Registered.

A Deed of Trust from George Black to Jane Withrow for 153 acres Dated the 25 Day of January 1775 proved by John Walker & Adley Osborn Evidences thereto. Ord'd to be registered.

A Deed of Sale from James Capshaw to John Cummins for 40 acres of Land Dated the 5 Day of March 1774 proved by Essex Capshaw Evidence thereto. Ord'd to be Registered.

A Deed of Sale from Jacob Costner Sheriff to Maurice Roberts for 300 acres of Land Dated the 26 Day of July 1775 proved by Alex'r Martin Esq'r Evidence thereto. Ord'd to be Reg'd.

A Deed of Mortgage from Patrick Miller to James Milcum for 400 acres of Land Dated the 25 Day of May 1775 proved by Wm McCracken Evidence thereto. Ord'd to be Registered.

A Deed of Sale from John McFaddon to John Dennard for 200 acres of Land Dated the 16 February 1775 proved by Saml McFaddon Evidence thereto. Ord'd to be Registered.

Settlement of the Estate of William Henry Deceased by the Administrators

Amount of the Estate	£218 10 2
Charges against the Estate	29 14 4
Clear Estate	188 15 10
Widows thirds	62 18 7 ¼
Nine Childrens Share	125 17 2
Each Childs Share	13 19 8 ¼

Court adjourned till tomorrow morning at 8 Oclock. Met according to adjournment. Present Joseph Harden, Timothy Riggs, Wm. Gilbert, Wm. Graham, Esq'rs.

Ordered by the Court that Ralph Fleming be appointed Constable and that he Swear in before Wm. Gilbert Esq'r accordingly.

Ordered by the Court that Warrants issue under the hand of Timothy Riggs to the Constables of the Several Districts in this county directing them to summon the Taxable persons to return upon Oath to the Magistrates therein named a true account of their Taxables.

Ord'd by the Court that the order for laying out a Road from Beateys ford to Henry Dellingers be renewed.

Ord'd that Arthur Taylor be appointed overseer of the Road leading from Col. Walkers to the Waggon ford below the mouth of Green River in that part between Col. Walkers and James Adears & that he Enter on the Duty of his Charge accordingly and James Adear serve as overseer between his House & the Waggon Ford below the mouth [of] Green River.

July term 1775

David Jenkins came into Open Court and took the Oaths by Law appointed for the Qualification of Publick officers, repeated & subscribed the Test and took the oath of a Justice of the peace & took his seat accordingly.

Ordered by the Court that George Parish, Saml French, James Capshaw, Wm. Capshaw, Jas Upton, John McClure, James Miller, John Scott, Alex'r Coulter, John McLean, John McFaddon, & Joshua Taylor be appointed Jurors to lay out a Road from Uptons Mill to William Gilberts and that they be summoned by the Sheriff to be & appear before one of his Majestys Justices of the Peace to take the necessary steps to qualify them for this their charge.

Court adjourned till Court in Course. Joseph Hardin, William Graham, W. Gilbert, David Jenkins.

North Carolina, Tryon County. To wit. At an Inferior Court of Pleas and Quarter Sessions begun and held for the said County of Tryon at the Court House of said County on the fourth Tuesday of October Anno Dom. 1775. Present the Worshipful William Gilbert.

Court adjourned till to morrow morning at 8 Oclock. Met according to adjournment. Present James McEntire, William Graham, David Jenkins, Esq'rs.

Susanna Twitty Adm'x of the Estate of Wm Twitty Deceased returns into open Court an Inventory of the s'd Estate & prays the same may be put of Record which was accordingly Granted.

Lettice Cleghorn Ex'x of the Estate of Wm. Cleghorn Deceased returns into open Court an Inventory of the s'd Estate & prays the same may be put of Record.

The Last Will and Testament of William Heager Deceased was Produced in Open Court and proved by the oath of James Little which was ordered to be put of Record.

A Deed of Sale from Peter Costner to Andrew Costner for 300 acres of Land Dated the 2d Day of May 1775 proved in open Court by Peter Sides Evidence thereto. Ordered to be Registered.

A Deed of Sale from Jonathan Gullick to John Glen for 150 acres of Land Dated the 25 Day of October 1775 acknowledged in open Court. Ordered to be Registered.

A Deed of Sale from Peter Summy and Margaret his wife to Patrick Miller for 400 acres of Land Dated the 30 Day of January 1775 proved in open Court by Peter Summy Jun'r Evidence thereto. Ord'd to be Registered.

A Deed of Sale from Patrick Miller & Mary his wife to James Milum[?] for 400 acres of Land Dated the 19th Day of Septem'r 1775 proved in open Court by Andrew Miller Evidence thereto. Ordered to be Registered.

A Deed of Sale from Nathaniel Henderson to James McReynolds for 200 acres of Land Dated the 18 Day of June 1774 proved in open Court by Jonathan Gullick Evidence thereto. Ord'd to be Registered.

A Deed of Sale from Jonathan Potts to John Waterson for 200 acres of Land Dated the 23d Day of October 1775 proved in open Court by Wm. Graham Esq Evidence thereto. Ord'd to be Registered.

October term 1775

A Deed of Sale from James Alley Sen'r to Valentine Warlock for 200 acres of Land Dated the 19 Day of July 1775 proved in open Court by James Alley Ju'r Evidence thereto. Ord'd to be Registered.

A Deed of Sale from Jacob Shatley to Michael Williams for 100 acres of Land Dated the 28 Day of August 1774 proved in Open Court by George Lamkin Evidence thereto. Ord'd to be Registered.

A Deed of Sale from Patrick McDavid to Andrew Hampton for 278 acres of Land Dated the 8 Day of October 1775 proved in Open Court by Adam Hampton Evidence thereto. Ord'd to be Registered.

A Deed of Sale from Andrew Hampton to John Wells for 278 acres of Land Dated the 24th Day of October 1775 acknowledged in Open Court. Ord'd to be Reg'd.

An Instrument of Writing from Hezekiah Balch to Jonathan Gullick giving him liberty to convey a certain tract of Land in Tryon County to John Glen proved in open court by Jno Glen. Ord'd to be Registered.

A Deed of Sale from Robert Lee to John McEntire for 200 acres Dated the 4th Day of May 1775 proved in open Court by Timothy Riggs Esq'r Evidence thereto. Ord'd to be Registered.

A Deed of Sale from Steven Langford to Saml Wilson for 200 acres of Land Dated the 6th Day of October 1775 ack'd in open Court. Ord'd to be Registered.

A Deed of Sale from Wm Cleghorn to David McBride for ___ acres Dated the 6 Day of August 1774 proved in open Court by John Scott Evidence thereto. Ord'd to be Registered.

Court adjourned till tomorrow 8 Oclock. Met according to adjournment. Present Timothy Riggs, Wm Graham, David Jenkins, Esq'r.

Ordered by the Court that William Patrick take into his possession the Orphan Children of Hugh Wallace Deceased to be under his Care till next Court to be then Dealt with agreeable to Law.

Ord'd that Arch'd McCallister be taken into Close Custody till he give Security for Delivering the orphan Children of Hugh Wallace Deceased to William Patrick.

Ordered by the Court that William Davison serve as overseer of the Road in the room of William Going and that he enter on the Duty of his Charge accordingly.

Court adjourned for an Hour. Met according to adjournment. Present William Gilbert, David Jenkins, William Graham, Esq'rs.

Ordered by the Court that William Gilbert, Charles McLean, James johnston ,Moses Moore, Perry Green Mackess [Magness], Abraham Kuykendal and John Potts be summoned by the Coroner to be and appear before his Majestys Judge of the Court of Oyer &c. at the next Court to be held for the District of Salisbury at the Town of Salisbury on the first Day of December next then & there to serve our Sovereign Lord the King as Grand & Petit Jurors.

October term 1775

A Deed of Sale from John Beard Sen. to John Beard Jun'r for 220 acres of Land Dated the 3d Day of October 1775 proved in Open Court by Andrew Neel Evidence thereto. Ordered to be Registered.

A Deed of Sale from Daniel McCarty & John McCarty to Lewis Limeberger for 480 acres of Land Dated the __ Day of ___ 1775 proved by Sam'l Johnston as to Daniel McCarty and ackn'd in open Court by John McCartney [sic]. Ord'd to be Registered.

A Deed of Sale from John Dellinger to William Tankersley for 300 acres of Land Dated the 15th Day of August 1775 proved in Open Court by Henry Dellinger Evidence thereto. Ord'd to be Reg'd.

Court adjourned till tomorrow morning at 8 Oclock. Met according to adjournment. Present Timothy Riggs, David Jenkins, William Gilbert, Wm Graham, Esquires.

Ordered by the Court that Jacob Forney Ju be appointed Constable in the room of Michael Ingle & that he Swear in before David Jenkins Esq'r accordingly.

The Jury appointed to Law out a Road from Wm. Gilberts to Uptons Mill being Summond by the Sheriff to lay out the Same Disagree. Ordered by the Court that John Earle, James Miller, Joshua Taylor, Caleb Taylor, John McFaddin, John McLean, John McClure, Alexander Coulter, James McFaddon Junr. & James Cheek be a Jury to lay out a Road from Wm. Gilberts the nearest & Best way to James Cheeks on the South Carolina line so as to Cross at Twittys Ford on Broad River & that they be summoned to be and appear before some one of his Majestys Justices of the peace to take the necessary steps to Qualify them for this their Charge.

October Term 1774 Claims on the County of Tryon for the Year 1774

	£	S	D
James Adams 1 Scalp ticket		10	
Uel Lamkin 1 Wolf Scalp		10	
Jacob Forney 1 Venire ticket	1	10	8
Abraham Keener 1 Wolf Scalp		10	
Robert McCasland 1 Venire ticket	1	10	8
Benjamin Hardin 2 Wolf scalps	1	0	0
William Gilbert 1 Venire ticket	2	6	
Frederick Hambright 1 Venire ticket	1	10	8
James McEntire 1 Venire ticket		18	8
Thomas Harrod 2 Wolf Scalps	1		
James McAfee 4 Wolf Scalps	2		
William Parker 4 Wolf scalps	2		
Alexander McEntire 1 Wolf scalp		10	
James McEntire 4 wolf scalps	2	0	
To Andrew Neel Clerk of			
the Clerk for Ex officio Services		10	
To Jacob Costner Sheriff for			
exofficio Services		10	
To Jacob Costner for Gaol Lock		12	
To Jacob Costner for Committment			
& Victualing prisoners	1	14	4
	£39	17	6

October term 1775

The foregoing Sum of Thirty Nine pounds Seventeen shillings and Six pence is the whole of the Money Due for Contingencies for the year One thousand seven hundred & Seventh five. It was ordered by the Court that a poll Tax of Nine pence be levied of Each Taxable person in the County of Tryon for Discharging the aforesaid sum of 2/ agreeable to act of Assembly for Building a Court house prison & Stocks in Tryon County the former Tax list for that purpose being found to be insufficient. Court adjourned till Court in Course. Timo Riggs, Wm. Gilbert, David Jenkins.

North Carolina, Tryon County. To wit. At an Inferior Court of Pleas and Quarter Sessions begun and held for the said County of Tryon at the Court House of said County on the fourth Tuesday of January A D 1776. Present the Worshipful Timothy Riggs, William Graham, Esquires.

Court adjourned till tomorrow morning at 8 Oclock. Met according to adjournment. Present Timothy Riggs, Wm. Gilbert, Joseph Harden, Esquires.

The Last Will and Testament of James Gordon Dated the 23d Day of Novem'r 1774 was produced in open Court and proved by the Oath of Nathan Mendinall Evidence thereto.

Ordered by the Court that Letters Testamentary Issues to Anne Gordon and Henry Gordon Executors of the said Will of all and Singular the Goods and Chattles Debts and Credits of the said Deceased they complying with the act of assembly in that case made & provided who took the oath by Law required for Executors.

Ordered by the Court that Wm Chronicle Serve as Constable in the room of Andrew Milliken and that he Swear in before David Jenkins Esq. accordingly.

Court adjourned for an Hour. Met according to adjournment. Present Timothy Riggs, Joseph Harden, William Gilbert, Esq'rs.

The Last Will and Testament of Owen Murphy Dated the 6th Day of Decem'r 1775 was produced in open Court and proved by the Oaths of Richard Lansdell, Alexander Coyl and Henry Williams Evidences thereto.

Ordered by the Court that Letters Testamentary Issue of James Murphy (the Widow & Relict having Relinquished her Right of Executorship under her hand and seal to him) of all and Singular the Goods and Chattles Rights and Credits of the said Deceased he complying with the Act of Assembly in that case made and provided.

Agreeable to an order of Court at Last Term the orphan Children of Hugh Wallace Deceas'd was produced before this Court. It was ordered that the said Children be under the Care of their Mother and step Father till sufficient Reasons be shewn the Court to the Contrary.

A Deed of Sale from George Michael Wisenant to Adam Wisenant for 300 acres of Land Dated the 22d Day of Novem'r 1775 ackn'd in open Court. Ord'd to be Registered.

A Deed of Sale from George Michael Wisenant to Adam Wisenant for 200 acres of Land Dated the 22d Day of Novem'r 1775 ackn'd in open Court. Ord'd to be Registered.

A Deed of Sale from Thomas Hightower to George Morgan for one Hundred & Sixty acres Dated the 21st Day of June 1775 proved in open Court by Joshua Hightower Evidence thereto. Ord'd to be Registered.

January term 1776

A Deed of Sale from Andrew Haslep and Thomas Haslep to Joseph Hightower for 390 acres Dated the 8th Septem'r 1772 proved by George Lamkin Esq Evidence thereto. Ord'd to be Reg'd.

A Deed of Sale from John Freeman to James Freeman for 390 acres Dated the 2d Day of Novem'r 1775 proved by George Lamkin Esq. Evidence thereto. Ord'd to be Reg'd.

A Deed of Sale from Joseph Hightower to John Freeman for 390 acres Dated the 15th Day of October 1775 proved in Open Court by Ja's Freeman Evidence thereto. Ord'd to be Reg'd.

Court adjourned till to morrow 8 Oclock. Met according to adjournment. Present Timothy Riggs, Joseph Harden, William Gilbert, Esq'rs.

A Deed of Sale from Moses Moore to John Walker Esq for 400 acres of Land Dated the 4th Day of Decem'r 1775 proved by Robert Porter Evidence thereto. Ord'd to be Registered.

A Bill of Sale from George Sizemore to William Gilbert for one Negro man Dated the 26 Day of August 1775 proved by David George Evidence thereto. Ord'd to be Registered.

A Deed of Sale from Jesse Finn to John Alexander for 200 acres of Land Dated the 22d Day of Decem'r 1775 ack'd in open Court. Ord'd to be Registered.

Ord'd by the court that Aaron Moore [James Cook Senr marked through] serve as Constable in the room of Dav'd Heddleston & that he swear in before Wm. Gilbert Esq. accordingly. Timo Riggs, Joseph Harden, W. Gilbert.

North Carolina, Tryon County. To wit. At an Inferior Court of Pleas and Quarter Sessions begun and held for the said County of Tryon at the Court House of said County on the fourth Tuesday of April A. D. 1776. Present the Worshipful James McEntire.

Court adjourned till tomorrow morning at Eight Oclock. Met according to adjournment. Present William Gilbert, Esq'r.

There not being the Number of justices present by Law required to proceed in publick Business the Court was adjourned till Court in Course. Wm. Gilbert.

[The following entries dated the fourth Tuesday of January AD 1778 are found before the entries for July term 1777. The date should probably be January 1777, as the deed books indicated that those deeds were recorded at January Court 1777.]

State of North Carolina, Tryon County. The Fourth Tuesday of January A. D. 1778. Pursuant to an Ordinance of the State aforesaid bearing date the 23d day of December One Thousand seven Hundred and Seventy Six for holding County Courts and Quarters Sessions. The Commission of the Peace under the hand & Seal of his Excellency Richard Caswell Esquire Governor &c of the State aforesaid appointed joseph Harden, John Robinson, William Graham, George Lamkin, William Yancey, John McKinney, Jonathan Hampton, Frederick Hambright, James McAfee, Valentine Mauney, Robert johnston, George Black and William Nevill Esq'rs Justices assigned to keep the peace for the County of Tryon aforesaid &c Was Read in open Court as also a Commission of Dedimus Protestatum [sic] impowering the said justices to administer all Oaths appointed for the

January term 1777

Qualification of all Publick officers as also such other Oaths as are appointed by Act of Assembly or Ordinance of the State aforesaid.

Agreeable to the above Commission William Graham, George Lamkin, William Yancey, John McKinney, Jonathan Hampton, Frederick Hambright, James McAfee, George Black & William Nevill Came into open Court and took the Oaths appointed by Law for the Qualification of Publick Officers also the Oath of Justices of the Peace for the County of Tryon aforesaid.

A Deed of Sale from John Baxter to Alexander Mickey [Mackey] for 300 acres of Land dated the 14th Day of October 1775 proved in open Court by the oath of Samuel McFaddon Evidence thereto. Ord'd to be Registered.

A Deed of Sale from John Baxter to John McLean for 640 acres of Land Dated the 14th Day of October 1775 proved in open Court by the oath of Samuel McFaddon Evidence thereto. Ordered to be Registered.

Court 'till to morrow morning at 9 Oclock. Met according to adjournment. Present William Graham, George Lamkin, Fred'k Hambright, Jonathan Hampton, Wm Nevill, Wm Yancey, James McAfee, George Black, John McKinney, Esq'rs.

Ordered by the Court that Jane Scott late Jane Leeper widow of James Leeper Deceased and Nicholas Leeper admrs of the said James Leeper be Cited to appear at the Next Court to give an account of their administration and what Estate they have in their hands belonging to the orphan children of the said deceased. Ordered also that the said administrators be cited to bring to the next Court Mary Leeper, James Leeper and Elizabeth Leeper orphans Children of the s'd James Leeper deceased that they may choose Guardians according to Law.

A Deed of Sale from John McFaddon Jun'r & Ruth McFaddon his wife to John McFaddon Sen'r for 200 acres of Land Dated the 25 day of April 1774 proved by Jonathan Hampton Evidence thereto. Ord'd to be Reg'd.

North Carolina, Tryon County. To wit. At a County Court and Sessions of the peace begun and held for said County on the fourth Tuesday of July A. D. 1777. Present the Worshipful Jonathan Hampton.

The State commission of the peace being Read Silence was proclaimed.

Alexander Gilliland, Robert Alexander, John Sloan, John Moore & Jonathan Gullick came into Open Court and took the Oath to be taken for the Qualification of Publick officers and also the oath appointed to be taken by Justices of the peace and took their Seats accordingly.

Jonathan Hampton also took the Oath appointed to be taken for the Qualification of publick officers and also the oath appointed to be taken by Justices of the peace & took his seat accordingly.

Court adjourned till tomorrow morning 8 Oclock. Met according to adjournment. Present Jonathan Hampton, Alex'r Gilliland, Rob't Alexander, John Sloan, John Moore, Jonathan Gullick, Esq'rs.

TRYON COUNTY NC COURT MINUTES 1769-1779

July term 1777

John McKinney, James McAfee, James Johnston & James Logan came into open Court took the oath appointed for the Qualification of Publick officers and also the oath appointed to be taken by Justices of the peace and took their seats accordingly.

After proclamation the Court proceeded to the Election of a Clerk there being ten Justices present (being those who qualified during the first two days of Court) to wit John McKinney, James McAfee, James Johnston, Alexander Gilliland, John Moore, James Logan, Jonathan Gullick, Robert Alexander and John Sloan, who did elect and Choose Andrew Neel to be Clerk of the County Court & Sessions of the Peace for the County of Tryon.

Pursuant to the said Election Andrew Neel came into open Court and took the oaths by Law appointed for the Qualification of Publick officers and also the oath appointed to be taken by Clerks of the county Court & Session of the peace and entered on the Duty of his office accordingly.

The Court proceeded to the Election of a Register there being ten Justices present to wit John McKinney, James McAfee, James Johnston, Alexander Gilliland, John Moore, James Logan, Jonathan Gulllick, Robert Alexander and John Sloan, who did elect and Choose Jonathan Hampton Esq'r Register of the County of Tryon.

The Court proceeded to the Election of a Sheriff there being ten Justices present to wit John McKinney, James McAfee, James Johnston, Alexander Gilliland, John Moore, James Logan, Jonathan Gulllick, Robert Alexander and John Sloan, who did elect and Choose James Holland to be Sheriff of the County of Tryon for the ensuing Year.

Bond of Andrew Neel dated 23 July 1777 in the sum of £1000 proclamation money with Charles McLean and John Barber securities for his performance as Clerk of the County Court. Wit: John Brown Skrimshire, Jno Wilson, Jas. White.

Bond of James Holland dated 23 July 1777 in the sum of £1000 proclamation money with James Patterson, Ambrose Foster, Thomas Campbell & James Baird securities for his performance as Sheriff of Tryon County. Wit: Geo. Alexander, John Brown Skrimshire, Andw Neel.

The Last Will & Testament of John McFadin dated the 12th Day of March 1776 was produced in open Court and proved by the Oath of David Dickey Evidence thereto. Ordered to be put of Record.

A Deed of Sale from Laurence Kyzer to Peter Sites for 150 acres of Land Dated the 3d day of February 1777 proved in open Court by Christian Carpenter Evidence thereto. Ordered to be Registered.

A Deed of Sale from James Henderson to William Alston for 162 acres of Land Dated the 2d day of March 1774 proved by Andrew Neel Evidence thereto. Ordered to be Registered.

A Deed of Sale from Alexander Hamphill & Mary his wife to Benjamin Armstrong for 250 acres of Land Dated the 7th Day of October 1774 proved by John Kinkaid Evidence thereto. Ordered to be Registered.

A Deed of Sale from William King to Robert Knox for 160 acres of Land Dated 7th Day October 1775 proved by James Johnston Esqr Evidence thereto. Ord'd to be Registered.

July term 1777

A Deed of Sale from John Scott, Lettice Scott & Sarah McKendrick for 302 acres of Land Dated the 26th Day of June 1777 proved by George Lamkin Evidence thereto. Ord'd to be Reg'd.

A Commission for taking the private Examination of Lettice Scott wife of John Scott touching her Executing a Deed to Wm. Alston for 302 acres of land with her Examination Certified by Geo Lamkin and Fred'k Hambright Esq'r. Ord'd to be Registered.

A Deed of Sale from John Scott to Wm. Alston for 200 acres of Land Dated the 11th Day of March 1777 proved by George Lamkin Evidence thereto. Ordered to be Registered.

A Deed of Sale from Alexander Kiles to Robert Weeir for 300 acres of Land Dated the 4th Day of February 1777 proved by William Magness Evidence thereto. Ordered to be Registered.

A Deed of Sale from Henry Master to John Kinkaid for 200 acres of Land Dated the 15th February 1777 proved by Benjamin Armstrong Evidence thereto. Ord'd to be Reg'd.

A Deed of Sale from Martin Phifer to James Millican for 200 acres of Land Dated the 17th Jan'y 1777 proved by Dav'd Dickey Evidence thereto. Ord'd to be Registered.

A Deed of Sale from Thomas Thompson to Robert Patton for 250 acres of Land Dated 8th October 1776 proved by Robert Alexander Evidence thereto. Ord'd to be Registered.

A Deed of Sale from Hugh Shannon to Robert Shannon for 200 acres of Land Dated the 7th Day of July 1777 acknowledged in open Court. Ord'd to be Registered.

A Deed of Sale from Thomas Welch & Nancy his wife to Robert Ferguson for 250 acres of Land Dated the 13th Day of March 1777 ack'd in open Court. Ord'd to be Reg'd.

A Deed of Sale from Nathaniel Henderson and Elizabeth his wife to James Patterson for 450 acres of Land Dated the 1st Day of January 1776 proved by Ja's Holland Evidence thereto. Ord'd to be Registered.

A Deed of Sale from Nathaniel Henderson and Elizabeth his wife to James Patterson for 160 acres of Land Dated the 1st Day of January 1776 proved by Ja's Holland Evidence thereto. Ord'd to be Registered.

A Deed of Sale from Nathaniel Henderson and Elizabeth his wife to James Patterson for 150 acres of Land Dated the 1st Day of January 1776 proved by Ja's Holland Evidence thereto. Ord'd to be Registered.

A Bill of Sale from Martin Greider & Henry Greider to Nicholas Clay & Peter Statler for Sundry Goods & Chattles Dated the 16th Day of July 1776 proved by Jacob Horty Evidence thereto. Ord'd to be Registered.

A Deed of Sale from William Alston to William Sterrett for 300 acres of Land Dated the 5th Day of July 1777 proved by John Brown Skrimshire Evidence thereto. Ord'd to be Regist'd.

A Deed of Sale from William Alston to William Sterrit for 271 acres of Land Dated the 5th Day of July 1777 proved by John Brown Skrimshire Evidence thereto. Ord'd to be Reg'd.

July term 1777

A Deed of Sale from William Alston to William Sterrett for 300 acres of Land Dated the 5th Day of July 1777 proved by John Brown Skrimshire Evidence thereto. Ord'd to be Registered.

A Deed of Sale from William Alston to William Sterrett for 250 acres of Land Dated the 5th Day of July 1777 proved by John Brown Skrimshire Evidence thereto. Ord'd to be Registered.

A Deed of Sale from William Alston to William Sterrett for 300 acres of Land Dated the 5th Day of July 1777 proved by John Brown Skrimshire Evidence thereto. Ord'd to be Registered.

A Deed of Sale from William Alston to Robert Alexander for 204 acres of Land Dated the 10th Day of March 1776 proved by George Lamkin Evidence thereto. Ord'd to be Regist'd.

Court adjourned till tomorrow morning at 8 Oclock. Met according to adjournment. Present Jonathan Hampton, James Johnston, John Sloan, Esq'rs.

James Holland came into Open Court & took the Oath appointed to be taken for the Qualification of publick officers and also the oath appointed to be taken by Sheriffs and entered on the Duty of his office accordingly.

The Last Will and Testament of Christian Aker Dated the 25th Day of June 1776 was produced in Open Court and proved by the oath of Barbara Aker one of the Subscribing witnesses thereto.

Ordered by the Court that Letters Testamentary issue to Peter Aker, Christian Carpenter & John Aker Executors of the last will & Testament of Christian Aker Deceased for all & singular the Goods Chattles Rights & Credits of the said Deceased they complying with the act of Assembly in that case made & provided.

A Deed of Sale from Samuel Rankin to Robert Park for 202 acres of Land Dated the 30th Day of Novem'r 1775 proved in open court by Alexander Gilliland Evidence thereto. Ord'd to be Reg'd.

A Deed of Sale from John Goforth to George Patterson for 300 acres of Land Dated the 22d Day of July 1777 proved by Andrew Neel Evidence thereto. Ord'd to be Regist'd.

A Deed of Sale from William Gilbert to Isaac Cooper for 200 acres of Land Dated the 1st Day of June 1777 acknowledged in open Court. Ord'd to be Registered.

A Deed of Sale from William Gilbert to Isaac Cooper for 200 acres of Land Dated the first Day of June 1777 ackn'd in open Court. Ord'd to be Registered.

A Deed of Sale from John McFadin to James McFaddin for 200 acres of Land Dated the 25 Day of May 1777 proved by James Miller Evidence thereto. Ord'd to be Registered.

Ordered by the court that James Adear serve as Overseer of the road leading from the mouth of Green River by Coll. Walkers to the South line in that part between the Ford on Broad River below the mouth of Green River and his own House, and William Henry on that part of said Road between James Adears and Coll. Walkers and Thomas Welch from Coll. Walkers to the Grassy Branch, George Harris from the Grassy Branch to the muddy

July term 1777

fork of Buffaloe and Solomon Beson from that till the South line and that they enter on the Duty of their charge accordingly.

Ordered by the Court that Alexander Coulter serve as Overseer of the Road leading from James Adears to White Oak Fort Crossing Broad River at Twittys Ford & that he enter on the duty of his Charge accordingly.

John Moore Esquire & Lawrence Kyzer came into open Court and acknowledged themselves indebted to the State the sum of Twenty five pounds proc money each to be void on condition that William moore make his personal appearance at the next County Court to do & receive what shall be then & there enjoined him by the said court and in the mean time to keep the peace toward James Graham.

Ordered by the Court that Christian Carpenter, Laurence Kyzer, Adolph Reep, Jacob Ramsour and John Aker be appointed Commissioners to lay out and mark a Road from Burke county line by Ramsours Mill from that the nearest and best way to Tryon Court house and that they be Summoned by the Sheriff to appear before some Justice of the peace in Order to Qualify for this their Charge.

Ordered by the Court that John Alexander serve as Overseer of the Road to be laid out from Burke county line by Ramsours Mill to Tryon Court House and that he warn in the persons liable to work on the Roads between the Road to be laid out and the long Shole on the one side and as far as the old Road leading from Thomas Blacks to Warlocks mill on the other side, including Capt. Carpenters District and that he enter on the duty of his Charge.

Ordered by the Court that William Moore, Abraham Scott, Ebenezer Newton, John Moore, Zac'h Spencer, Frederick Hambright, Michael Hoyl, Thomas Casner, Jacob Mooney, Peter Laboon, Michael Hofstatler and John Hoyl be a Jury to lay out and mark a Road the nearest & Best way from Tryon Court House to the Tuccasiege Ford and that they be Summoned by the Sheriff to appear before some Magistrate to Qualify for this their Charge.

Ordered by the Court that William Starrett serve as Overseer of the Road to be laid out from Tryon Court House to the Tuccasiege Ford in that part between the South Fork and the Tuccasiege Ford and that Zachariah Spencer from the South fork till Capt. Hambrights or opposite thereto, and Fred'k Hambright from that till Tryon Court House and that they enter on the duty of their Charge.

Ordered by the Court that John Stroud and Michael Engle Serve as Constables and that they Swear in before James Johnston Esq'r accordingly.

Ordered by the Court that Giles Williams & William Dunn serve as Constables and that they Swear in before Jonathan Hampton Esq'r accordingly.

Ordered by the Court that Christopher Walbert serve as Constable in Capt. Singletons District and that he Swear in before Jonathan Gullick Esq'r accordingly.

Ordered by the Court that James McFarlin serve as Constable in Capt. Nevils District and that he Swear in before Jonathan Hampton Esq'r accordingly.

Ordered by the Court that James McReynolds serve as Constable in Capt. Nevils District and that he Swear in before Jonathan Gullick Esq'r accordingly.

July term 1777

Ordered by the Court that Richard Hix serve as Constable & that he Swear in before John McKinney Esq'r accordingly.

Ordered by the Court that David Gage serve as Constable in Capt. Kuykendalls District and that he Swear in before James McAfee Esq'r accordingly.

Ordered by the Court that John Magness serve as Constable and that he Swear in before John Sloan Esq'r accordingly.

Ordered by the Court that Isaac Rice serve as Constable and that he Swear in before James McAfee Esq'r accordingly.

Ordered by the Court that Steven Senter Rice serve as Constable and that he Swear in before Robert Alexander Esq'r accordingly.

Ordered by the Court that John Brown Skrimshire serve as Constable and that he Swear in before John Moore Esq'r accordingly.

Ordered by the Court that Robert Park serve as Constable and that he Swear in before Alexander Gilliland Esq'r accordingly.

Ordered by the Court that Teter Havener and John Reynolds serve as Constables in Capt Carpenters District & that they Swear in before John Sloan Esq'r accordingly.

Ordered by the Court that James Johnston be appointed to receive from every Inhabitant in Captain Forneys District a just and true account of his or her Estate on Oath within one Month after the sitting of the Court at this Term and Deliver the same immediately to the persons appointed to value the property in said District together with an Account of his own Estate upon Oath.

Robert Alexander Esqr to take an account of the property in his District, Alexander Gilliland Esq'r for his won District, John Moore Esq'r for Capt Carpenters District, John Sloan Esq'r for Capt Greens District, James McAfee for Capt Kuykendals District, John McKinney for his own & Capt Nevils District, Jonathan Hampton Esq'r for Capt McFaddons & Capt. Porters District, Jonathan Gullick for Capt. Singletons District, who are each of them to take a just and true account on oath of the Taxable property in their Several Districts agreeable to act of Assembly.

Ordered by the court that the following persons names for the Several Districts be appointed to value on oath the property of each Individual as near as may be in the said District and make return of the same to the next County Court agreeable to act of Assembly.

For Captain Barbers District, Charles McLean, John Barber & John Robinson.

For Captain Alexanders District William Moore, Robert Armstrong, & Ebenezar Newton.

For Captain Forneys District Robert Ewart, James Little & Jacob Forney Senr.

For Captain Nevils District Wm Nevil, John Scott and James Capshaw.

For Captain McKinneys District John McKinney, Thomas Townsend & Joseph Clark.

July term 1777

For Captain Kuykendalls District Abraham Kuykendall, Wm. Johnston & Saml Blackburn.

For Captain McFaddons District Andrew Hampton, Wm. Gilbert & John Bradley.

For Captain Porters Company John Walker, Thos Robison & George Black.

For Captain Singletons District Joseph Harden, Richard Singleton & Wm. Davison.

For Captain Greens Company William Green, James McEntire & John Waterson.

For Captain Carpenters District Valentine Mauney, Adolph Reep & Nicholas Friday.

For Captain Logans District Frederick Hambright, Jacob Casner & John Huggins.

Court adjourned till tomorrow morning at 6 Oclock. Met according to adjournment. Present James Johnston, Jonathan Hampton, Alexander Gilliland, Jonathan Gullick, Esquires.

Ordered by the Court that Andrew Hampton and James Beard be Summoned by the Sheriff to be and appear before the Judges of the court of Oyer and Terminer at the next Court to be held for the District of Salisbury at the Town of Salisbury on the Second Day of September next then & there to serve the State as Grand Jurors.

Ordered by the Court that David Abernathy and Jacob Ramsour be Summoned by the Sheriff to be and appear before the Judges of the court of Oyer and Terminer at the next Court to be held for the District of Salisbury at the Town of Salisbury on the Second Day of September next then & there to serve the State as Petit Jurors.

Court Adjourned till Court in Course. Jonathan Hampton, James Johnston, Jonathan Gullick, Alex'r Gilliland.

North Carolina, Tryon County. To wit. At a County Court and Sessions of the peace begun and held for the County aforesaid on the fourth Tuesday of October Anno Dom. 1777. Present the Worshipful John Moore.

Court adjourned till to morrow morning 10 Oclock. Wednesday Morning Court Met according to adjournment. Present John Moore, James Logan, Jonathan Gullick, Esquires.

Susanna Graham late Susanna Twitty widow of William Twitty Deceased returns into Court an Additional Inventory of the said Deceaseds Estate which was Ordered to be put of Record.

Christian Carpenter, Peter Aker and John Aker Executors of the Last will and Testament of Christian Aker Deceased returns into Court an account of Sales and Credits of the said Deceaseds Estate amounting to One Thousand and Twenty eight Pounds three shillings and nine pence which was Ordered to be put of Record.

A Deed of Sale from James Henderson and Violet his Wife to John McCord for 200 acres of Land Dated the 1st Day of Septem'r 1777 proved by John Moore Esq'r Evidence thereto. Ord'd to be Registered.

A Deed of Sale from John Moore to Zachariah Spencer for 57 acres of Land Dated the 26 Day of September 1777 acknowledged in open court. Ordered to be Registered.

October term 1777

A Deed of Sale from Thomas Morris to George Williams for 200 acres of Land Dated the 20th Day of October 1777 proved by Adam Hampton Evidence thereto. Ordered to be Registered.

A Deed of Sale from Christian Carpenter to Christian Carpenter Ju'r for 300 acres of Land Dated the 22d Day of October 1777 ack'd in open court. Ord'd to be Registered.

A Deed of Sale from Christian Carpenter to John Carpenter for 30 acres of Land Dated the 22d Day of October 1777 acknowledged in open court. Ord'd to be Registered.

Court adjourned till tomorrow morning 8 Oclock. Met according to adjournment. Present John Moore, James Logan, Jonathan Gullick, Esquires.

Ordered by the court that James Patterson serve as Overseer of the Road leading from the Tuccasiege Ford crossing at Armstrongs Ford and so on to the South line, and that he enter on the duty of his charge.

Ordered by the court that Michael Hoyl serve as Overseer of the Road leading from the Tuccasiege Ford to the Court House in that part between where Zechariah Spencer left off working and the Court House and that he enter on the duty of his charge accordingly.

Ordered that Letter of Administration issue to John Beard son of William Beard Deceased of all and singular the Goods and Chattles of the said Deceased who proposed for Securitys Frederick Hambright and Robert Porter bound in £500. accepted.

Jacob Watts an orphan child of George Watts Deceased came into Court and made choice of James Taylor as his Guardian when it was Ordered by the Court that s'd James Taylor be appointed Guardian to Elea & Frances Watts orphan Children of the s'd deceased securities proposed Thos Welch & Sam'l Blackburn Bound in £100. accepted.

William Graham Came into Open Court and expressed his Willingness to deliver up to the Court such Records as were made and what papers came into his hands during the time he was Clerk, when he shall be thereto required by this Court.

Ordered by the Court that James Patterson be appointed to Collect the Taxes Assessed on the inhabitants in Capt. Barbers District.

Martha Butler an orphan child of Jonathan Hogan Butler Deceased came into Court and made choice of John Harris for her Guardian, who proposes for Securities Moses Moore & Thomas Black, Bound in the sum of £100. accepted.

Ordered by the Court that Letters of Administration issue to Joseph Gregory of all and Singular the Goods and Chattles rights and Credits of the John Sartain Deceased, he proposes for Securities John McEntire and John Lusk Bound in £250. accepted.

Ordered by the Court that Robert Goltney serve as Overseer of the Market Road leading from Coll. Walkers to Charles Town in that part between Coll. Walkers & the head of Grog Creek & Thomas Welch of Sandy Run from thence to the South line & that they enter on the Duty of their charge accordingly.

A Deed of Sale from Peregrine Mackness to John Sites for 200 acres of Land Dated the 30th Day of October 1777 acknowledged in open Court. Ordered to be Registered.

October term 1777

A Deed of Sale from David Thompson to William Tubb for 240 acres of Land Dated the 1st Day of March 1777 proved by John Lusk Evidence thereto. Ord'd to be Registered.

A Deed of Sale from John Morris to John Potts for 200 acres of Land Dated the 30th day of August 1777 proved in Open Court by James Miller Evidence thereto. Ord'd to be Registered.

Court adjourned till [to]morrow morning 8 Oclock. Met according to adjournment. Present James Johnston, James Logan, Jonathan Gullick, Esq'rs.

Ordered by the Court that Samuel Blackburn be appointed to collect and gather the Taxes assessed on the Inhabitants in Capt. Kuykendalls District.

Ordered by the Court that John Walker be appointed to collect and gather the Taxes assessed on the Inhabitants in Capt. Porters District.

The Returns of Taxable property with the valuation thereon together with the number of persons liable to pay a poll Tax was produced in Court by the Assessors for the following Districts to wit Capt. Forneys, Capt. Logans, Capt. Barbers, Capt Greens, Capt. Kuykendalls, Capt. Porters, and Capt. McFaddons District, by which it appears that the valuation of Taxable property in the said Districts amounts to One hundred and fifty five thousand Nine hundred and sixty four pounds.

Ordered by the Court that John Hoyle be appointed to collect and gather the Taxes assessed on the Inhabitants in Capt. Logans District.

Ordered by the Court that John Hill be appointed to collect and gather the Taxes assessed on the Inhabitants in Capt. Forneys District.

Ordered by the Court that George Lamkin be appointed to collect and gather the Taxes assessed on the Inhabitants in Capt. Alexanders District.

Ordered by the Court that James McEntire be appointed to collect and gather the Taxes assessed on the Inhabitants in Capt. Greens District.

A Deed of Sale from George Lamkin to William Alston for 136 acres of Land Dated the 1st Day of July 1776 acknowledged in open Court. Ord'd to be Registered.

A Deed of Sale from George Lamkin to Peter Lamkin Matthews for 200 acres of Land Dated the 29th October 1777 ackn'd in open Court. Ordered to be Registered.

Ordered by the Court that Ebenezer Newton serve as Constable in the Room of Steven Center and that he Swear in before Robert Alexander Esquire accordingly.

Ordered that Steven Center Constable be Fined Ni Sci in the sum of £20 for misdemeanours in office and that he be Cited to be and appear before the next Court to shew Cause if any he can why said Fine should not be made absolute.

Ordered by the Court that William Graham be notified by the Sheriff to deliver up at next Court such Records as were made and what papers came into his hands during the time he was Clerk of this Court.

Ordered by the Court that Michael McElwrath be appointed to collect and gather the Taxes assessed on the Inhabitants in Capt. McFaddins District.

Court Adjourned till Court in Course. John Moore, Rob't Alexander, Jonathan Gullick.

North Carolina, Tryon County. To wit. At a County Court of Pleas and Quarter Sessions begun and held for the County of Tryon on the third Monday of January A. D. 1778. Present the Worshipful Robert Alexander.

James Logan, Jonathan Gullick and Jonas Bedford came into Court and took the oaths for the Qualification of public officers and also the oath of Justices of the peace and Justices of the County Court of pleas and Quarter Sessions and took their Seats on the Bench. took the oaths for the Qualification of publick officers and also the oath of a Justice of the peace and Justice of the County Court of pleas and Quarter Sessions Robert Alexander also and took his Seat accordingly.

Andrew Neel Clerk of this Court agreeable to Act of Assembly took the oaths for the Qualification of public officers and also the oath of a Clerk of the County Court of pleas and Quarter Sessions and entered on the Duty of his office.

Ordered that Thomas Price be Summond to attend at this Court to shew his reasons for detaining the Estate of James Price Deceas'd in his hands, which Jesse Finn Claims a right to as Legatee of the said James Price.

Court Adjourned til tomorrow morning at 8 Oclock. Tuesday Morning Court Met according to Adjournment. Present Robert Alexander, James Logan, Jonathan Gullick, Jonas Bedford, Esq'rs.

The last Will and Testament of William Wilson Deceased was produced in open Court and proved by the Oath of James Webb one of the Subscribing Witnesses thereto.

Ordered that Letters Testamentary issue to Joseph Camp and George Blanton Executors of the last Will and Testament of Wm Wilson Deceas'd of all & singular the Goods & chattles Rights & Credits of said Deceased who took the oath appointed to be taken by executors.

James Johnston, Alexander Gilliland, Jonathan Hampton, John Sloan, John moore and James McAfee came into court and took the Oaths appointed for the qualification of Public Officers and the Oath of Justices of the Peace and Justices of the County Court of pleas and Quarter sessions and took their seats accordingly.

After proclamation the Court proceeded to the Election of a Register and made choice of Jonathan Hampton Esq'r as Register for this County.

The Court proceeded to the Election of a proper person to receive Entries of Claims for Lands when James Logan Esquire duly Elected to that office.

The Court proceeded to the Election of a person properly qualified to be Surveyor of Lands in this County when Jonathan Gullick Esq'r duly Elected to that office.

The Court proceeded to the Election of two persons properly qualified to act as Coroners in this County when Jonathan Gullick & James White were duly Elected to that office.

The Court proceeded to the election of a Ranger when Robert Alexander was duly Elected to that office.

January term 1778

John Walker Esq'r came into Court and made a resignation of his appointment as one of the Coroners of this County.

The last Will and Testament of William Whiteside Deceased Dated the 24th Day of October 1777 was produced in open Court and proved by the Oath of James Whiteside one of the Subscribing Witnesses thereto. Ord'd to be put of Record.

State of North Carolina, Tryon County. Samuel Johnston being sworn on the holy Gospel of God Deposeth and Saith that William Massey delivered to him a Bond the contents was for James bell to Sign a Deed for the Conveyance of a certain Tract of Land to William Massey and on his return from Georgia this Deponent lost the said Bond and further saith not. Samuel Johnston. Sworn to before me this 20th Day of Jan'y 1778. Jas Logan.

A Deed of Sale from Jonas Bedford to John Morgan for ___ acres of Land Dated the 16th Day of October 1777 proved by James Miller Evidence thereto. Ord'd to be Registered.

A Deed of Sale from John Moore to William Hamilton for 50 acres of Land Dated the 19th Day of January 1778 ack'd in open Court. Ord'd to be Registered.

A Deed of Sale from John Moore to William Hamilton for 100 acres of Land Dated the 19th Day of January 1778 ack'd in open Court. Ord'd to be Registered.

A Deed of Sale from John Low to Edward Wyatt for 100 acres of Land Dated the 28th Day of Novem'r 1777 proved by Frederick Hambright Evidence thereto. Ord'd to be Registered.

A Deed of Sale from John Neighbours and Sarah Neighbours to George Blanton for 100 acres of Land Dated the 20 Day of Jan'y 1775 proved by Joseph Camp Evidence thereto. Ord'd to be Registered.

A Deed of Sale from William Yancey to Moses Bridges for 50 acres of Land Dated the Seventeenth Day of January 1778 ack'd in open Court. Ordered to be Registered.

A Bill of Sale from Thomas Bullion to John Henry for a certain bay mare therein mentioned Dated the 27 Day of July 1777. Ord'd to be Registered.

A Deed of Sale from John Harris to James Miller for 200 acres of Land Dated the 22d Day of January 1778 ackn'd in open Court. Ord'd to be Reg'd.

A Deed of Sale from George Rutledge to William Cleghorn for 400 acres of Land Dated the 16th Day of February 1766 proved by John Moore Evidence thereto. Ord'd to be Reg'd.

A Deed of Sale from George Trout and Mary Trout to Deborah Beatey, Francis Beatey and James Beatey for 200 acres of Land Dated the 15 January 1778 proved by James Palley Evidence thereto. Ord'd to be Registered.

A Deed of Sale from Charles Federick Frelich and his wife to Paul Staut for 250 acres of Land Dated the 20th Day of Ja'y 1778 proved by John Brown Skrimshire Evidence thereto. Ord'd to be Registered.

January term 1778

A Deed of Sale from George Rutledge to John Walker for 154 acres of Land Dated the 28 Day of October 1777 proved by James Henderson Evidence thereto. Ord'd to be Registered.

A Deed of Sale from James Byars to Alexander Coulter for 300 acres of Land Dated the 26 July 1774 acknowledged in open Court. Ord'd to be Registered.

A Deed of Sale from Arthur Taylor to Wm. Gilbert for 300 acres of Land Dated the 21st Day of January 1778 ackn'd in open Court. Ord'd to be Registered.

A Deed of Sale from Wm Baldrige and John Baldrige 640 acres of Land Dated the 11th August 1776 proved by Robert Ewart Evidence thereto. Ord'd to be Registered.

A Deed of Sale from Archibald McDowell to George Russell for 150 acres of Land Dated the 9th January 1778 proved by Thomas Whiteside Evidence thereto. Ord'd to be Registered.

A Deed of Sale from John Low to James Wyat for 100 acres of Land Dated the 28th Nov'r 1777 prov'd by Fred'k Hambright Evidence thereto. Ord'd to be Reg'd.

A Deed of Sale from Joseph Camp & wife to Joseph Boren for 270 acres of Land Dated the 26 Nov'r 1777 ackn'd in open Court. Ord'd to be Registered.

A Deed of Sale from Benj'n Cochran to John Henderson for 140 acres of Land Dated the 29 Day of April 1776 proved by John Hill Evidence thereto. Ord'd to be Reg'd.

A Deed of Sale from James Collins to Hezekiah Collins for 200 acres of Land Dated the 23d July 1777 proved by George Barkley Evidence thereto. Ord'd to be Reg'd.

A Deed of Sale from Archibald Fleming to John Fleming for 300 acres of Land Dated the 7th Day of June 1775 prov'd by Hugh Killpatrick Evidence thereto. Ord'd to be Registered.

A Deed of Sale from Wm Starret & Wife to John Bucannan [for] 157 acres Dated 8th Septem'r 1777 proved by George Lamkin Evidence thereto. Ord'd to be Reg'd.

A Deed of Sale from Fred'k Hambright to John Low for 300 acres of Land Dated the 28 Nov'r 1777 prov'd by George Lamkin Evidence thereto. Ord'd to be Reg'd.

A Deed of Sale from Thomas Harrod to Thomas Bridges for 640 acres of Land Dated the 20th Day of February 1777 prov'd by James McEntire Ju'r Evidence thereto. Ord'd to be Registered.

A Deed of Sale from George Lamkin to George West for 98 acres of Land Dated the 20th Day of January 1778 acknowledged in open Court. Ord'd to be Registered.

A Deed of Sale from William Waddell & Jane Waddell for 200 acres of Land Dated the 1st Day of Novem'r 1777 prov'd by Peter Aker Evidence thereto. Ord'd to be Reg'd.

A Deed of Sale from Benj'n Shaw to Jacob Simerle for 300 acres Dated the 1st February 1777 acknowledged in open Court. Ord'd to be Registered.

A Deed of Sale from Nathan Davis to Wm. Smith for 150 acres of Land Dated 26 June 1777 proved by John Ashley Evidence thereto. Ord'd to be Reg'd.

<u>January term 1778</u>

A Deed of Sale from Wm Yancey to Alex'r Davison for 150 acres Dated the 4th Dec'r 1777 ack'd in open Court. Ord'd to be Reg'd.

A Deed of Sale from William Alston to John McFarland for 200 acres Dated the 11th Dec'r 1777 prov'd by Robert Alexander evidence thereto. Ord'd to be Reg'd.

A Deed of Sale from Benj'n Ellis to Jacob Vanzant for 300 acres of Land Dated the 8th Day of October 1777 proved by Wm Green Evidence thereto. Ord'd to be Registered.

A Deed of Sale from John Ashly to Katherine Smith for 150 acres of Land Dated the 8th Day of April 1777 prov'd by Jonathan Gullick Evidence thereto. Ord'd to be Reg'd.

A Deed of Sale from [John] Bryson to James Holland for 100 acres of Land Dated the 15th April 1777 proved by Jonathan Gullick Evidence thereto. Ord'd to be Reg'd.

A Deed of Sale from Jeremiah Smith & Katherine Smith to John Ashley for 300 acres of Land Dated the 7th Day of April 1777 proved by Jonathan Gullick Evidence thereto. Ord'd to be Reg'd.

A Deed of Sale from Wm Alston to John McFarland for 302 acres of Land Dated the 11th Dec'r 1777 prov'd by Robert Alexander evidence thereto. Ord'd to be Reg'd.

A Deed of Sale from John Ashley to James Saunders for 150 acres of Land Dated the __ Day of January 1778 ack'd in open Court. Ord'd to be Registered.

A Deed of Sale from Leonard Webb to Wm Cathey for 150 acres of Land Dated the 19th Septem'r 1777 prov'd by James Johnston Alexander evidence thereto. Ord'd to be Reg'd.

A Deed of Sale from Thomas Costner to John Dudrow for 300 acres of Land Dated the 8th Day of July 1776 ack'd in open Court. Ord'd to be Reg'd.

A Deed of Sale from Thomas Bridges to Wm Green for 640 acres of Land Dated the 25 Day of July 1777 prov'd by James McAfee Evidence thereto. Ord'd to be Reg'd.

A Deed of Sale from Jacob Simmerly to John Detrick Beam for 300 acres of Land Dated the 22d August 1777 ack'd in open Court. Ord'd to be Regist'd.

A Deed of Sale from Absalom Waters to Ambrose Cobbs for 200 acres of Land Dated the 2d Day of August 1777 proved by Sam'l Johnston Evidence thereto. Ord'd to be Reg'd.

A Deed of Sale from Thomas Wilson to Thomas Brothers for 200 acres of Land Dated the 4th Day of May 1776 proved by Thomas Harris Evidence thereto. Ord'd to be Registered.

Court adjourned till tomorrow morning at 8 Oclock. Met according to adjournment. Present John Moore, Robert Alexander, Jonas Bedford, Esq'rs.

Court adjourned for half an hour. Met according to adjournment. Present John Moore, Rob't Alexander, Jonas Bedford, Esq'rs.

Ordered by the Court that Peter Best serve as Constable in the room of Ebenezar Newton and that he Swear in before Robert Alexander Esq'r accordingly.

January term 1778

Ord'd by the court that Henry Dellinger be appointed Guardian to Eve Summy orphan child of John Summy Dec'd until next Court when he is to enter into Bond agreeable to Law.

Ordered that George Miller be Sum'd to bring to next Court Elizabeth Summer orphan of John Summy dec'd that she may choose her Guardian and be further dealt with as the Law directs.

Ord'd that Wm. Smith serve as Constable in the room of Isaac Rice and that he Swear in before James McAfee Esq'r.

Joseph Gregory administrator of the estate of John Sartain Dec'd returns into Court an Inventory of the said Estate amounting to £93 16 and prays the same may be put of Record.

Ord'd by the Court that William Wallace an orphan Child of Hugh Wallace Dec'd age ten years be bound unto John Lewis to learn the art Trade or Mistery of a Weaver and the said John Lewis at the Fredom of his said Apprentice is to give him a Loom, three Ruds and three Sett of Harnas & in all other [things] to comply with the act of Assembly in such case made & provided.

The Jury appointed to lay off and mark a Road from Burke county line by Ramsours Mill to this Court House having failed to discharge that Trust, It was ordered that George Kyzer, John Dellinger, and Jacob Carpenter be appointed to lay off and marke the said Road from Burke County line by Ramsours Mill the nearest and best way to this Court House and that they enter upon the duty of their Charge.

Ord'd that John Alexander serve as overseer of said Road.

Ordered that James Miller have Letters of Administration on the Estate of John Johnston Dec'd Securities proposed William Henry and Alexander Coulter accepted and bound in the sum of three hundred Pounds.

The State vs Wm. Hagerty. Principle bound in £50. Abel Beatey & Saml Wilson in 25 Each to be void on Condition that the s'd Wm. Hagarty keep the peace towards Peter Sites and other the subjects of this State for the Term of Six months.

The State vs Casper Club. Recogn. Principle bound in £20. Valentine Crites in 10. to the peace towards George Rees. Recognizance Discont'd.

The State vs Steven Senter. Misdemeanours in office as Constable. The Prosecutor failing to appear and prosecute that Defendant was discharged.

Ord'd that James Taylor Guardian of the orphan Children of George Watts dec'd be Summon'd to be and appear at next Court to give in further securities as to his Guardianship of said orphans.

The Tax lists of Capt. Rob't Alexanders, Capt. Rich'd Singletons, Capt. John McKinneys, Capt. Carpenters, and Capt. Nevills was returned at this Term by which it appears that the Taxable Property in said Districts amounts to One Hundred & Eight thousand four hundred & forty four pounds.

<u>January term 1778</u>

Benj'n Harden produced in Court an account of the expences he incurred in doeing his duty when Guardian to the orphan children of George Watts dec'd amounting to £6 1 By which it appears that there is due from him to said Children or the present Guardian £26 1 7 which acc't is Filed in this Office.

Court adjourned till tomorrow morning 8 Oclock. Thursday Morning Court Met according to adjournment. Present John Moore, Robert Alexander, James Logan, James Johnston, Jonathan Gullick, Esq'rs.

Ordered that Henry Dellinger be appointed overseer of the Road leading from Tryon Court House to Beateys Ford (in that part between his house and Forneys Creek) and Jacob Forney Ju'r from thence to Beateys Ford, and that they enter on their duty accordingly.

Ordered that Andrew Hampton and James Baird be appointed Grand Jurors to be and appear before the Justices of the State at the next Court to be held for the District of Salisbury at the Town of Salisbury on the 5th day of March next then & there to serve the State as Grand Jurors.

Ord'd that Jacob Ramsour and David Abernathy be appointed Grand Jurors to be & appear before the Justices of the State at the next Court to be held for the District of Salisbury at the Town of Salisbury on the 5th day of March next then and there to serve the State as Petit Jurors.

Ordered that the following persons be Summoned by the Sheriff to attend at the next Court to be held for this county then & there serve as Grand & Petit Jurors.

1	James Henderson	16	Peter Casner
2	Robert Abernathy	17	Jacob Casner
3	Hugh Barry	18	William Chronicle Ju'r
4	Nicholas Leeper	19	Nicholas Friday
5	Matthew Leeper	20	George Patterson
6	John Taylor	21	Solomon Bason
7	William Patterson	22	Wm Magnes
8	William Barry	23	James Sloan
9	Isaac Holland	24	Jacob Vanzant
10	Alex'r Robinson	25	Thomas Espey
11	Adam Baird	26	James Rutledge
12	Moses Moore	27	James Coburn
13	Henry Reynolds	28	Rich'd Jones
14	David Ramsey	29	John Kinkaid
15	Jacob Carpenter	30	William Massey

The State vs John Fondren. Principal bound in £250. John McKinney in 250 to be void on Condition that the said John Fondren make his personal appearance at the next Court to be held for this County and in the mean time to be of good behaviour toward this State.

Ord'd by the Court that Richard Hix be appointed to Collect and gather the Taxes assessed on the Inhabitants in Capt. McKinneys District.

Ord'd that George Paris be appointed assessor in Capt. Nevils District in the room of James Capshaw who has refused to Serve.

January term 1778

Ord'd that Saml Dunaway serve as Constable in Capt. Logans District and that he swear in before James Logan Esq.

Ord'd that Rob't Carruth serve as Constable in Capt. Greens District and that he Swear in before John Sloan Esq.

Ordered that Robert Carruth be appointed to Collect and gather the Taxes assessed on the Inhabitants in Capt. Greens District.

Ordered that an order of Court of this Term appointed jurors to lay out & mark a Road from Burk County line by Ramsours mill to the Court House be Rescinded.

Ord'd that Robert Lee have Letters of Administration on the Estate of Abel Lee Deceased who proposes for Securities John Lusk & John McEntire bound in the sum of £400 accepted.

Ord'd that Wm Nevil be appointed to Collect and gather the Taxes assessed on the Inhabitants in his District and make return of the Same to the next Court.

Ord'd that Adolph Reep be appointed to Collect and gather the Taxes assessed on the Inhabitants in Capt. Carpenters Company.

James Logan Esqr. came into Court & took the oath necessary for the Qualification of an Entry taker of Lands in this County.

Jonathan Gullick Esq. came into Court took the oath necessary for the qualification of a Surveyor of Lands in this county.

Court adjourned till Court in Course. James Johnston, Jas. Logan, John Sloan, Robt Alexander, Jon'h Gullick, Jonathan Hampton.

State of North Carolina, Tryon County. to wit, At a Court of Pleas and Quarter Sessions begun and held for the County of Tryon on Monday the twentieth day of April Anno Dom. 1778. Present the Worshipful John Moore, Robert Alexander, James Logan, Esq'rs.

James Miller Adm'r of the Estate of John Johnston Dec'd returns into Court an Inventory of Sales of the said deceased amounting to £111 16 10 which Inventory was filed in this office.

Ordered that Letters of Administration issue to George Paris on the Estate of Jacob Swank, Dec'd. He proposes for Security James Miller, Junr. Bound in £ 100. accepted.

Ordered that George Paris be appointed to Collect and gather the Taxes assessed on the inhabitants of Capt Nevil's District for the year 1777 in the room of Capt. Nevil.

Court adjourned till tomorrow morning 8 oClock. Tuesday Morning. Court Met according to Adjournment. Present John Moore, Robert Alexander, James Logan.

Ordered that David Miller serve as Overseer of the road leading from Gilbert Town by Twittys ford to the South line on that part between said town & Twittys Ford. And George Paris from Twittys ford to Pullams Mill, and Benjn Vaughn to the said line.

April term 1778

Jonathan Potts and Jean Potts, orphan children of Jeremiah Potts Dec'd came into Court being of lawful age to choose their Guardians, made choice of Thomas Spriggs as their Guardian accordingly, who entered into Bond with & Security in the Sum of Five Hundred Pounds for the faithful discharge of the said trust.

Ordered that Ezek'l Potts pay & deliver into the hands of the s'd Guardian all such sums of money becoming due the s'd orphans whether by Rent of Land or otherwise.

John Walker and Davis Whitesides came into Court and took the oaths appointed for the qualification of publick officers and the oath of Justices of the Peace and took their seats on the bench accordingly.

Ordered that Nathan Proctor serve as Overseer of the Road leading from the mouth of Green River by Col. Walkers to the said line in that part between James Adears and Col. Walkers.

Alexander Gilliland and Jonathan Gullick Esq'rs came into Court and took their seats on the bench.

Elizabeth Summy orphan child of John Summy Dec'd came into Court being of lawful age to choose her Guardian and accordingly made choice of George Miller who entered into Bond & Security in the Sum of Fifty pounds.

Ord'd that George Miller Bring Eave Summy orphan Child of John Summy Dec'd to this Court to be bound out according to law.

Ordered that Thomas Whiteside serve as Overseer of the Road leading from the fork of first Little Broad River to Kings Mountain in that part between Lankfords and No business. Wm. Going from thence to Hardens Mill and Saml Wallace from thence to Carsons and that they enter on the duty of their charge accordingly.

John McKinney and James White came into Court and took the oaths by Law appointed for the qualification of publick officers and the oath of Justices of the Peace and took their seats on the Bench accordingly.

Wm. Berry a Juror summoned to attend at this Court for reasons shewn the Court had leave of absence.

Joseph Camp and George Blanton Ex'r of the Estate of Wm. Wilson deceased returned into Court an Inventory which was filed in this office.

Ord'd that Jacob Rine serve as Overseer of the Road leading from Tryon Court House to Beatey Ford in that part between Henry Dellingers and Forneys Creek, as the road now Stands and that he enter on the Duty of his Charge.

James Coburn being appointed a Juror to serve at this Court made it appear to the Court that he had not been legally Summoned, was therefore Dismist.

Wm. Chronicle being appointed a Juror to serve at this term, It appearing to the Court that he was not a Freeholder, was Dismist.

Grand Jury: James Henderson, Foreman

April term 1778

John Taylor	George Patterson
Alex'r Robison	William Magnes
Dav'd Ramsey	Jacob Vanzant
Peter Costner	Thomas Espey
James Rutledge	James Sloan
Jacob Costner	Richard Jones

Sworn and charged.   Ordered that Robert Parks Constable wait on this Grand Jury.

A Deed of Sale from Sam'l Gray to Wm Gray for 300 acres dated the 22d Day of February 1774 proved by Wm. Gray Evidence thereto. Ord'd to be Registered.

A Deed of Sale from John Moore to Isaac West for 200 acres Dated 11th Day of April 1778 ack'd in open Court. Ord'd to be Reg'd.

A Deed of Sale from John Moore to William West for 200 acres of Land Dated the 11th April 1778 ack'd in Open Court. Ord'd to be Registered.

A Deed of Sale from Robert McCombes to Moses Williams for 240 acres dated the ___ Day of ____ 1778 proved by Miles Abernathy Evidence thereto. Ord'd to be Reg'd.

A Deed of Sale from John Stroud to Miles Abernathy for 257 acres of Land Dated the 21st April 1778 proved by George Lamkin Evidence thereto. Ord'd to be Reg'd.

A Deed of Sale from James Coburn & Mary his wife to Miles Abernathy for 400 acres Dated the 25th Day of October 1776. Ackn'd in Open Court. Ord'd to be Reg'd.

A Deed of Sale from John Tagert to James Rice for 200 acres Dated the 25 July 1771 proved by Thomas Neel Evidence thereto. Ord'd to be Reg'd.

A Deed of Sale from Joseph Richey to Sam'l Wallis for 200 acres dated the 14th Day of Oct'r 1777. Ord'd to be Registered.

A Deed of Sale from James Rice to Violet Tagert for 200 acres Dated the 25 Day of Novem'r 1777. Prov'd by John Robison Evidence thereto. Ord'd to be Reg'd.

A Deed of Sale from Martin Fifer to John Fulweider for 450 acres of Land Dated the 26 Day of March 1778 proved by Jacob Ramsour Evidence thereto. Ord'd to be Registered.

A Deed of Sale from Lewis Lineberger & wife to Robert Boyd for 480 acres of Land Dated the 21 April 1778 prov'd by Thos McGill Evidence thereto. Ord'd to be Reg'd.

A Deed of Sale from Wm. Adams to Hugh Gordon for 159 acres of Land Dated the 16 Day of March 1778 ack'd in Open Court. Ord'd to be Reg'd.

A Deed of Sale from Michael Houlthouzer to George Reel for 200 acres of Land Dated the 13th Aug't 1777 prov'd by Adlai Osborn Esq'r Evidence thereto. Ord'd to be Reg'd.

A Deed of Sale from James Patterson to And'w Floyd for 150 acres of Land Dated the 11th Day of April 1778 proved by Jonathan Gullick Evidence thereto. Ord'd to be Reg'd.

A Deed of Sale from John Alexander to Benj'n Shaw for ___ acres of Land dated the 25 Day of Sept'r 1777. ack'd in Open Court. Ord'd to be Reg'd.

<u>April term 1778</u>

A Deed of Sale from George Lamkin to Sam'l Rankin for 300 acres of Land Dated the 12th Day of Jan'y 1775 prov'd by Rob't Alexander Esq'r Evidence thereto. Ord'd to be Reg'd.

A Deed of Sale from Peter Aker to Sam'l Gordon for 250 acres of Land Dated the 22d Day of April 1778. Ack'd in Open Court. Ord'd to be Registered.

A Deed of Sale from Stephen Langford to Davis Whiteside for 100 acres of Land Dated the 7th Day of Nov'r 1777 prov'd by Dan'l Singleton Evidence thereto. Ord'd to be Reg'd.

A Deed of Sale from Martin Fifer to John Fulenwider for 371 acres of Land dated the 6 Day of March 1778 prov'd by Jacob Ramsour Evidence thereto. Ord'd to be Reg'd.

A Deed of Sale from Wm Sharp to George Paris for 200 acres of Land dated the 20th Day of May 1773 prov'd by Wm. Gray Evidence thereto. Ord'd to be Reg'd.

A Deed of Sale from Valentine Mauny to Peter Carpenter for 700 acres of Land Dated the 2d Day of May 1777 ack'd in Open Court. Ord'd to be Reg'd.

Court adjourned till tomorrow morning at 8 o'clock. Wednesday Morning. Court met according to adjournment. Present John Moore, Rob't Alexander, James Logan, Jonathan Gullick, Esq'rs.

Ord'd that Francis Holland a base born Child aged three years and three months the parents not known, be bound unto John Stroud until he shall attain the age of Twenty one years to Learn the Art and Mystery of a cordwainer & the said John Stroud is to give y'e s'd apprentice at his Freedom one suit of clothes one Sett of tools necessary to the s'd Trade, and in all other things to comply with the act of Assembly in that case be made & provided.

James Johnston, Alexander Gilliland and James White, Esq'rs, came into Court and took their Seats on the Bench.

Moses Winsley vs Tho's Campbell.

Petty Jury

Nicholas Friday	Anthony Harman
Wm. Going	Philip Cancelor
Michael Hofstatler	Jno Hofstatler
Uel Lamkin	John Dellinger
Fred'k Rhodes	Alex'r Coulter
Lawrence Kyzer	David Miller

Jury Impannelled and sworn assess the plaintiffs Damage to £7 8 and /6d Costs.

John Hufstatler vs Robt Weir & James Kelly. Case. Same Jury with the alteration of Michael McElwrath and John Aker in the room of Michael Hofstatler. Jury impannelled and sworn find for the plaintiff and assess his Damages to £14 10 8 and Six pence costs.

John Hendrix vs Sam'l Hunter. A. B. Jury the same as in the suit of Moses Winsley vs Thos Campbell. Jury impannelled and sworn assess the plffs Damages to one penny & Six pence costs.

April term 1778

Alexander Coulter vs James Buckanan. Case.

Petty Jury

Nicholas Friday	Anthony Harman
Wm Going	Philip Cancelor
Mich'l Hofstatler	John Hofstatler
Uel Lamkin	John Dellinger
Fred'k Rhodes	Philip Wisenant
Laurance Kyzer	David Miller

Jury impannelled and sworn assess the plaintiffs Damages to one penny & Six pence Cost.

Saml Biggerstaff vs Wm. Harris. Orr Att. Same Jury Impannelled and assess the Plaintiffs Damage to £12 and Six pence cost.

Benjamin Harden late Guardian to the children of George Watts Dec'd to wit Rachel, Leah, Jacob, and Frances minors produced in Court a Settlement of the Shares of s'd Deceaseds estate becoming due to the s'd minors, to wit: a ballance of £22 9 which was approved of by the Court. Ordered that the said ballance be lodged with Andrew Neel Clerk of this Court and to be by him delivered to James Taylor the present Guardian when applied for.

Ord'd that Eve Summy aged Nine years and four months be bound to Peter Summy to serve until she shall attain the age of 18 years and the said Peter Summy is to teach or cause her to be taught to Spin & sew and all business necessary for a House wife and at her freedom to give her two cows & calves, One feather bed weighing 40 ll. one pair of sheets, one pair of blankets, one Spinning wheel, one iron pot, one neat suit of womens apparel, and in all things to comply with y'e Act of Assembly, in such Case made & provided. Peter Summy is to pay the mother of the said Eve Ten pounds in consequence of her being bound as aforesaid.

Ordered that Rawley Matthews apprenticed with Sam'l Dunaway aged Sixteen years be removed and bound unto Fred'k Rhodes to learn the Art and mystery of a wheelwright as much as respects making Spinning wheels, and the said Fred'k Rhodes is in all things to comply with the Act of Assembly in such Case made & provided.

A Deed of Sale from Sam'l Kuykendall to John West for 60 acres of Land dated the 6th Day of April 1778 ackn'd in open Court. Ord'd to be Registered.

Court adjourned till tomorrow morning at 8 o'clock. Thursday Morning Court Met according to Adjournment. Present James Johnston, John McKinny, Robert Alexander, Jonathan Gullick, James White, Esq'rs.

Robert Lee, Admr of Abel Lee Dec'd returns into Court an Inventory of the s'd Deceaseds estate which was filed in this office.

James Logan Esqr claiming 200 acres of land in Tryon County near the north & south fork of White Oak at a marked pine G P L running upwards for Compliment Joining Sprigs entry. April 14th 1778

April term 1778

James Logan Esqr claiming 200 acres of land in Tryon County about a quarter of a mile above a shoal on the Fork of White Oak where John Cummons[?] lives on running up both sides of said Creek for Compliment. 14 April 1778.

Ordered that the following Justices be appointed to administer the Oath of Allegiance in the following Districts as the law directs; and also to receive an acc't on oath of the Taxable property in their several districts and deliver the same to the assessors of such District within one month after this term.

For Forneys old District James Johnston
For Capt Alexanders Dis't Robert Abernathy Esq'r
For Capt Barbers District   Alexander Gilliland Esq'r
For Capt Logans Dis't James Logan Esq'r
For Capt Carpenters Dis't James White Esq'r
For Capt Greens Dis't   James McAfee Esq'r
For Capt Kuykendals Dis't Wm. Johnston Esq'r
For Capt Singletons Dis't   David Whitesides Esq'r
For Capt McKinneys Dis't John McKinney Esq'r
For Capt Porters Dis't   John Walker Esq'r
For Capt McFadins Dis't   Jonathan Hampton Esq'r
For Capt Nevils Dis't   Jonas Bedford Esq'r

Ordered that the following persons be appointed to assess the Taxable property in the following Districts for the year 1778 to wit:

For Forneys old District Jacob Sides, Rich'd Bell, & Dav'd Cherry.
For Capt Alexanders District Rob't Abernathy J'r, James Rutledge and James Beatey.
For Capt Barbers District James Baird, Alexr Robison, and John Alexander.
For Capt Logans District Fred'k Hambright, John Huggins and Jacob Costner.
For Capt Carpenters Dis't Jacob Ramsour, Christian Carpenter, and Robert Ferguson.
For Capt Greens Dis't Wm. Green, John Watterson and John Lusk.
For Capt Kuykendalls Dis't Abrh'm Kuykendall, Rob't McMinn and James Blackburn.
For Capt Singletons Dis't Rich'd Singleton, Benj'n Harden and Wm. Whiteside.
For Capt McKinneys Dis't Sam'l Richardson, Joseph Clark & Tho's Townsend.
For Capt Porters Dis't Wm Porter, Wm. Smart Senr, Wm. Long.
For Capt McFadins Dis't Andw Hampton, James McFadin & John Bradley
For Capt Nevils Dis't Wm Nevil, Geo Paris & John Scott.

Benj'a Camp appointed Constable in Capt Kuykendals District to swear in before Wm. Johnston, Esq'r.

James McFarlin appointed Constable in Capt Nevils Dis't to swear in before Jonas Bedford Esq'r.

Jane Cook Adm'x of the Estate of Roger Cook dec'd produced in open Court a Settlement of said Estate which was approved by the Court and filed in the office.

Ordered that the Clerk of this Court notify all persons having any suits depending in that they attend at the next term with their witnesses in order to have such suits tried otherwise they'll be dismist.

A Deed of Sale from Andrew Hoyl & wife to Vincent Wyatt for 270 acres of Land dated 28th Day of Jan'y 1777 ack'd in Open Court. Ord'd to be Reg'd.

<u>April term 1778</u>

A Deed of Sale from Malcolm Hamilton to John Porter for 250 acres of Land dated the 1st Day of May 1772 proved by James Johnston Esq'r Evidence thereto.

A Deed of Gift from Hugh Jenkins to Joseph Jenkins for 200 Acres of Land Dated 2d Day Jan'y 1778 ack'd in Open Court. Ord'd to be Reg'd.

A Deed of Sale from Wm. Alston to Rob't Alexander for 50 acres of Land Dated the 4th Day of 1777 proved by Sam'l Rankin Evidence thereto. Ord'd to be Reg'd.

Ord'd that the following Persons be summoned by the Sheriff to be and appear at the next Court to be held for this County then & there to serve as Grand & Petit Jurors, to wit.

1	John Kinkaid	16	Mich'l Hoyl
2	Jacob Forney Sen	17	Peter Plunk
3	Miles Abernathy	18	John Reynolds
4	Nicholas Leeper	19	John Morris
5	Rob't Armstrong	20	Tho's Dill
6	Hugh Barry	21	Peregrine Magnes
7	Joseph Jenkins	22	Dav'd Miller Broad River
8	Zach'h Spencer	23	Sam'l French
9	Abh'm Scott	24	Abel Hill
10	Tho's Beaty	25	Wm Wilson
11	John Reed	26	John Richey
12	James Patterson	27	Hugh Kilpatrick
13	John Patrick	28	Jonathan Harden
14	Ambrose Foster	29	Abel Beatey
15	John Alexander Indian Creek	30	Thos Robison 2'd Bro'd

James Coffee to serve as Constable in Capt Singletons District to swear in before David Whitesides Esq'r accordingly.

A Deed of Sale from James Beatey to John Carruth for 300 acres of Land Dated 19th February 1778 ack'd in Open Court. Ord'd to be Reg'd.

Robert Abernathy, Hugh Barry, Nicholas Leeper, Matthew Leeper, Wm. Patterson, Isaac Holland, Adam Baird, Moses Moore, Henry Reynolds, Jacob Carpenter, Solomon Bason, John Kinkaid, and William Massey being summoned to attend this Court to serve as Grand & Petit Jurors and failing to appear according to summons, It was ordered that they be fined ni sci in the Sum of three pounds proc money each and they to be cited to be & appear at the next Court to be held for this County there to shew cause if any they can why the said fine should not be made absolute.

Court adjourned till tomorrow morning at 6 oclock. Present James Johnston, James Logan, Rob't Alexander, Jonathan Gullick, James White, Esq'rs.

Ord'd that Osborn Hechpeth serve as Constable in Captain Carpenter's District and that he swear in before James White Esq'r.

State of North Carolina, Tryon County. This day came Sarah Petty before me James Johnston one of the Justices of the aforesaid Court and made Oath that the Bond that Arch'd Little assigned to Christopher Petty binding him to make a Title to the tract of land on which Sarah Petty now lives that the said Bond is now lost or so mislaid that she cannot

<u>April term 1778</u>

come at it this time & further saith not Sworn & Signed before me this 27 day of Jan'y 1778. Certified by me, James Johnston.   Sarah (her X mark) Petty

We do hereby certify to all whom it may concern that we do hereby release and discharge Arch'd Little from the penaltys & obligation of a bond bearing date the 21st Day of Decem'r 1771 given by the said Arch'd Little to Christopher Petty binding him the said Arch'd Little to make a Title to a certain tract of Land which the said Little fulfilled. as witness our this 27 day of January 1778. James Pattey, Sarah Pattey (X), Test: James Johnston, Tho. Wheeler.

Fines collected this Term for profane Swearing to the am't of 12/6 was lodged with And'w Neel Clerk of this Court.

James Logan Esq'r Entry Taker certified to the Court that the following are disputed Claims to entries of land in ads with him, to wit:

Moses Henry a claim to 200 acres of Land in Tryon County located as follows, vizt on the waters of Crowders Creek joining his own and David Millers survey. 26th January 1778, No. 13. George Pee set up a claim for the same land the 27th Jan'y.

Andrew Haslep a claim to 200 acres of Land in Tryon County on both sides of Buffaloe Creek joining lands of Sam'l Biggerstaff including a shoal on said Creek. 27 January 1778. No. 23. John Ensley set up a claim for the same Land 21st April.

Andrew Haslep a claim of 200 acres of Land in Tryon County on both sides of Buffaloe Creek joining John Carsons land above said survey on said creek, Jan'y 27th 1778. No. 34. Claim set up for the same land by John Ensley 27th April.

Nathaniel McCarrol a claim to 200 acres in Tryon County on both sides of North Pacolet River above Spriggs's improvement. Jan'y 27th 1778. No.35. A claim set up for the same land by James Miller 11th February.

Nathaniel McCarrol a claim to 200 acres of Land in Tryon County on both sides of North Pacolet River below his other entry on said river, including Spriggs improvement. 28th Jan'y 1778. No. 36. A claim set up for the same land by James Miller 11th February.

Isaac Holland a claim to 100 acres of Land in Tryon County on both sides of Little Catawba Creek joining lands of John Gullick Senr. and his own land. 29 Jan'y 1778. No. 69. A claim set up to the same land by And'w Patrick 4th Feb'y.

Perrigrine Mackness Jun'r a claim to 150 acres of Land in Tryon County on the head of Murphy's branch of Buffaloe and Freeland's branch of said waters Joining land of Glading & Wieirs Entry. Feb'y 9th 1778. No. 67. A claim set up to the same land by Joseph Glading 17th Feb'y.

James Miller a claim of 400 acres of Land in Tryon County on Cove Creek of Broad River on both sides of the said creek joining Philip Goodbreads claim. 11th Feb'y 1778. No. 93. A claim set up for the same land by Philip Goodbread 9th March.

William Huddlestons claim of 100 acres of Land in Tryon County on the waters of Cane Creek of Broad River joining lands of John Withrow and his own land 11th Feb'y 1778. No. 102. A claim set up to the same land by James Huey 17th Feb'y.

April term 1778

Jacob Rine a claim of 150 acres of Land in Tryon County on the waters of big Long Creek joining land of John Hoyl, Vincent Wyatt and his own land. 26 Jan'y 1778. No. 22. A claim set up for the same land by Cornelius McCarty 21st April.

James Miller and Wm. Gilbert a claim of 400 acres of Land in Tryon County being at the lower end of the lower Cove of Green River and running up for compliment. 11th Feb'y 1778. No. 109. A claim set up for the same by the Honorable Sam'l Spencer, Esq'r, 1st April.

William Gilbert and James Miller a claim for 450 acres of Land in Tryon County being at the upper end of their first entry in the lower Cove of Green River 11 Feb'y 1778. No. 110. A claim set up for the same land by the Honorable Sam'l Spencer, Esq'r, 11th April.

Ordered that Col'l Charles McLean, James Baird, Adam Baird, Wm. Patterson, James Patterson, Joseph Neel, Hugh Terrance, John Robinson Senr, Wm. Berry, Alexander Robinson, John Bryson, & John Barber be appointed a Jury to try two of the aforesaid disputed claims to entries of Land one between George Pee and Moses Henry the other between Andrew Patrick and Isaac Holland.

Ordered also that Thomas Espey, Benj'n Ormond, John Carruth, Wallace Beatey, Hugh Beatey, Rob't Weeir, James Daugherty Ju'r, John Watterson, Thomas Pots, Benjn Harden, Jonathan Gregory and Joseph Gregory be appointed a Jury to try a disputed claim to land between Joseph Glading and Peregrine Mackness Ju'r.

Ordered also that Joseph Harden, Benj'n Harden, Uel Lamkin, Sam'l Biggerstaff, Adam Kuykendall, Wm. Murphy, Thos Arington, George Harris, henry Reynolds, John Reynolds, Phinehas Clayton and John Anderson be appointed a Jury to try two disputed claims to land between John Ensley & Andw Hazlep.

Ordered also that Wm. Nevil, John Earle, George Paris, Wm. Mills Ju'r, Wm. Capshaw, James Capshaw, Benj'n Jenkins, John McFadin, Alex'r Coulter, John Scott, Elias McFadin & Andrew Hampton be a Jury to try two disputed claims to land between the Honourable Saml Spencer Esq'r & Wm Gilbert & James Miler and two between James Miller and Nath'l McCarrol.

Ord'd that Wm. Grant, John Potts, Jones Williams, George Williams, Jno Morris, Mich'l McElwrath, John Bradly, Benj'n Hyder, Alex'r McDonnald, Lodowick Wray, Dav'd George & Wm Morgan be a Jury to try a disputed claim to lands between Philip Goodbread and James Miller.

Ord'd that Benj'n Biggerstaff, Aaron Moore, Joseph Lawrence, Wm Robison, Alex'r McGaughy, Rob't Porter, Wm. Dunn, Wm. White, Aaron Biggerstaff, Saml McMurry, James Cook Sen & James Cook Ju'r be a Jury to try a disputed claim to lands between ; James Huey and Wm. Huddleston.

Ordered that the Sheriff summon the afores'd juries and having given the several parties ten days previous notice shall go with the s'd juries on the several premises in dispute and the juries being sworn to do equal right between the parties to cause the witnesses on both sides to be examined and the allegations of the parties to be made before the juries and to receive the verdicts of the several juries and to return the same with the pannel to the next Court.

April term 1778

Ordered that Wm. Armstrong Sen, Garret Vanzant Sen, George Lamkin, Hugh Shannon, Saml Dunaway, Wm. Vernor, John Ashley, Jeremiah Smith, Wm. Hamilton, Wm. Massey, James Hillhouse, Wm. Smith Sen. be a Jury to try a disputed claim between Cornelius McCarty and Jacob Rine and they be summoned by the Sheriff for that purpose.

Court adjourned til Court in Course. James Johnston, Robt. Alexander, Jas Logan, John Moore, Jas White.

State of North Carolina, Tryon County. At a Court of Pleas and Quarter Sessions begun and held for the County of Tryon on Monday the Twentieth Day of July A D 1778. Before the Worshipful Robert Alexander, John McKinney, Jonathan Hampton, David Whitesides, Esq'rs.

Joseph Harden came into open Court and took the oath appointed for the qualification of public officers and also the oath of a Justice of the Peace and Justice of the County Court of pleas and quarter Sessions and took his seat on the bench.

Court adjourned till tomorrow morning at 8 oclock. Met according to adjournment. Present John Walker, Joseph Harden, Rob't Alexander, Wm. Johnson.

Ordered that Letters of administration issue to Francis Ross on all & singular the goods & chattles rights and credits of John Hartness Dec'd. He proposes for Securitys John Walker & Abraham Scott Bound in the sum of £400.

Thomas Espey, George Black, William Gilbert, George Paris and Abraham Kuykendal came into open Court and took the oath appointed for the qualification of public officers and the Oath of Justices of the Peace and Justices of the County Court of Pleas & Quarter Sessions and took their seats on the bench.

Grand Jury. Thomas Beatey Foreman

1	John Kinkaid	9	James Patterson
3	Jacob Forney	10	Peregrine Magnes
4	Robert Armstrong	11	John Patrick
5	Nicholas Leeper	12	Ambrose Foster
6	Hugh Barry	13	John Morris
7	Zach'h Spencer	14	John Alexander
8	John Reed	15	Dav'd Miller
		16	Abel Beatey

Sworn and charged.

Joseph Moore came into open court and being of lawful age to Choose his guardian made choice of Alexander Coulter who entered into Bond & Security in the Sum of Five hundred pounds.

Ordered that Letters of Administration issue to Thomas Potts on all & singular the good chattles rights & Credits of George Potts dec'd who gave bond and Security in the sum of five hundred pounds.

Ord'd that George Winters, Nathan Proctor, Thos Robison, John Moris, James Linn, James Reynolds, Aaron Deviney, Wm. Henry, James McFaden, David Miller, Mich'l McElwrath, James Miller and Rob't Rankin be a Jury to lay out and mark a Road the nearest & best way from James Adams to Thomas Welches and that they be sum'd by the Sheriff to

<u>July term 1778</u>

appear before some one Justice and to qualify them for this their charge. Thomas Welch overseer of said road.

Robert Gilkey and Jane Gilkey admr's of James Finlay Dec'd return into Court an Inventory of the aforesaid dec'ds Estate amounting to £45 14 2,

Court adjourned till tomorrow morning at 8 oclock. Wednesday Morning Court Met according to Adjournment. Present John Walker, Wm. Gilbert, Jonathan Hampton, Alex'r Gilleland, Esq'rs

The Exr's of Wm Steel vs Wm. Wray.

Petty Jury

1 George Ewing	7 Tho's Black
2 James Beatey	8 George Taylor
3 Matthew Leeper	9 Tho's Casner
4 Joseph Jenkins	10 Steven Langford
5 Mich'l McElwrath	11 John Anderson
6 James Cook	12 John Anderson

Jury Impanneled & Sworn assess plaintiffs Damages to £14 18 9 & /6 Costs.

Moses Whitley vs Wm. Lusk & John McEntire. Same Jury with the alteration of Tho's Maxwell in the room of George Taylor. Assess plaintiffs Damages to £17 15 & /6d costs.

John Walker vs Richman Flement. Same Jury impanelled and sworn assess the Plaintiffs Damages to /1d and /6d costs

Thomas Espey vs George Trout. Same jury impanelled and sworn assess the plantiffs damages to 1d &/6d costs.

John Trout vs James Kelly. Same jury impannelled and sworn assess the plaintiffs damages to /1d & /6d costs.

Hugh Montgomery vs Wm Falls. Same jury impannelled & sworn assess the plaintiffs damages to /1d & /6d costs.

Wm Gilbert vs John Chisom. Same jury impannelled & sworn assess the plaintiffs damages to £7 12 2 & /6d costs.

Sam'l McCombs vs John Beeman. Same jury impannelled & sworn assess the plaintiffs damages to £21 11 6 & /6d costs.

Hugh Megary vs Wm Patton. Same jury impannelled & sworn assess the plaintiffs damages to 1d & /6d costs.

Sam'l Hunter vs John Morris. Same jury impannelled & sworn assess the plaintiffs damages to 1d & /6d costs.

William Gilbert vs Geo. Sizemore, Geo. Winters & Jno Morris. Sci fa. Same Jury Impannelled and Sworn the Defendants did make a Bail Bond and were Bail. Judgment.

July term 1778

Wm Silbey vs Robert Wiere. Same jury impannelled & sworn assess the plaintiffs damages to £18 15 and /6 costs.

Collectors of the Tax for the following Districts

John Camp for Capt Kuykendals District
George Parish Esq'r for Capt. Nevils District
John Walker Esq'r for Capt Porters District
William Gilbert for Capt McFadins District
John McKinney Esq'r for his own District
James Rutledge for Capt Alexanders District
Fred'k Hambright for Capt Logans District
James Sloan for Capt Greens District

The Court proceeded to the Election of a Sheriff there being twenty justices present to wit John Walker, Joseph Harden, James Johnston, Robert Alexander, Alexr Gilliland, John Sloan, Jonathan Hampton, John Moore, Geo. Black, David Whitesides, James White, Jonas Bedford, William Gilbert, Geo. Paris, James Logan, Thos Espey, James McAfee, John McKinney, Wm. Johnston & Abh'm Kuykendal who did elect James Miller Sheriff for this County for the ensuing year who took the oath appointed for qualification of public officers, entered in Bond and Security agreeable to law.

Constables appointed
Henry Dowlin to Swear in before George Paris Esq'r.
John Gilkey to swear in before John Walker Esq'r.
Wm Withrow to swear in before Geo. Black Esq'r.
George Taylor to swear in before Jonas Bedford Esq'r.
Jonathan Price to swear m before Joseph Harden Esq'r.
John Alexander to swear in before Alex'r Gilliland
Wm Berry to swear in before Jonth'n Gullick, Esq'r.

John Robinson and John Earle came into open Court and took Oath appointed for the qualification of public officers and the oath of Justices of the Peace & Justices of the county Court of pleas & quarter Sessions & took their seats accordingly.

Court adjourned till tomorrow morning at 8 oclock. Thursday Morning. Met according to adjournment. Present William Gilbert, Rob't Alexander, Davis Whitesides, Geo. Black, Esq'r.

William Gilbert vs James Bridges

Petty Jury

And'w Patrick	George Ewing
Tho's Campbell	James Cook Ju'r
Joseph McDaniel	Christopher Walbert
Alex'r Coulter	Jonathan Price
David Abernathy	Peregrine Magnes
Wm Henry	James Wells

Jury impanelled & sworn assess the plaintiffs damage to £9 17 7 & /6 costs.

Robert Cobb vs George Taylor.

<u>July term 1778</u>

Petty Jury

And'w Patrick	Christopher Walbert
Tho's Campbell	Jonathan Price
Alex'r Coulter	Joseph Barnet
Dav'd Abernathy	Timothy Riggs
Geo Ewing	Peregrine Magnes
James Cook	Benj'a Harden

Jury impannelled & sworn find for the plff & assess Damage to £7 16 1O & /6d costs.

John Harvey being heretofore bound unto William Gilbert to learn the art trade or mystery of a Black Smith but the s'd John Harvey being a person extremely disorderly and disobedient, it was ordered by the Court that the said Wm Gilbert and the said apprentice be released from their covenant to each other.

Deeds proved or acknowledged in open Court and ordered to be Registered.

Moses Ferguson & Martha to John McMichael 300 acres Dated 10th October 1777 prov'd by Wm McMichael.

William Henry to James Henry 64 acres dated 23d July ack'd.

William Henry to James Henry 335 acres dated 23d July ack'd.

Thomas Beaty, Hugh Beatey & Robt Armstrong to Wallace Beaty 160 acres Dated 23d July 1778 ack'd.

Thomas Beatey to Hugh Beatey 320 acres Dated the 21st July 1778 ack'd.

Thomas Beatey & Robert Armstrong to Hugh Beaty 160 acres 23d July 1778 ack'd.

Thomas Beaty, Hugh Beatey & Robert to Joseph Dickson 300 acres Dated 20th April 1775 ack'd.

Nathaniel Aldrige to John McFarland 150 acres dated 23 July 1778 ack'd.

John McMichael to James White 300 acres dated 21st July 1778 proved by Alex'r Gilleland.

John McDowell to Arthur Patterson 600 acres dated 26 Jan'y 1778 proved by Geo. Patterson.

James Wyat Ju'r to James Wyatt Sen 100 acres dated 23 July 1778 proved by Geo. Lamkin.

John Dellinger & wife to John Phingers 300 acres Dated 17th July 1778 ack'd.

William Alston to John Beele 184 acres Dated 10 March 1777.

John McFadin to William Lusk 100 acres dated 19th April 1778 ack'd.

Wm Smith to John Moore Mortgage on 379[?] acres Dated 28th April 1775 proved by Jacob Carpenter.

July term 1778

John Moore to Alex'r Moore 299 acres Dated the 18 July 1778 ack'd.

John Alexander to Stevin Langford 100 acres Dated the 25th Septem'r 1777 proved by Thos Pearson.

Benj'n Shaw to Steven Langford 400 acres Dated the 25 Sept'r 1777 prov'd by Thos Pearson.

John Dellinger & Wife to John Fingers 100 acres Dated 7th July 1778 ack'd.

William Massey to George Lamkin 200 acres Dated 21st july 1778 ack'd.

Francis Gascoin to John Beele 150 acres dated 8th March 1775 prov'd by Geo Lamkin.

John McLean to John Morris 640 acres Dated 3d June 1778 proved by David Miller.

Jonas Bedford to David Miller 40 acres Dated 21st July 1778 ack'd.

Peter Sites to Adam Neel 20 acres Dated 22d April 1778 ack'd.

Wm Adams to Hugh Gordon 115 acres Dated 13th March 1778 proved by Alexr Gilleland Esq.

George Potts to James Huggins 300 acres Dated the 15th Septem 1777 prov'd by John Sloan.

John Walker to Wm. Gilbert Deed 300 acres Dated 28th March 1778 ack'd.

William Kinkaid to John Kinkaid 250 acres Dated 2d Feb 1778 proved by Jas Johnston Esq'r.

Steven Lyon to David Blaylock 150 acres Dated 21st July 1777 ack'd.

Thos Anderson & Wife to Thos Anderson Ju'r 100 acres Dated 2d Decem'r 1776 proved by Steven Lyon.

Robert Elder to Saml Elder ninety two acres Dated 20th June 1773 proved by David Elder.

George Henry Berger & Lucas Beard to George Reel 200 acres Dated 4th June 1778 proved by Jacob Master.

Wm. Smith Jun'r to Danl Gray 150 acres Dated 11 July 1778 proved by George Lamkin.

John McFain to Wm. Hall 50 acres Dated 14th July 1777 ack'd.

Arch'd McDowell to John McFadin 200 acres dated 24 August 1777 proved by Wm. Gray.

John Graham to Wm Graham 300 acres dated 20 Oc'r 1775 proved by Jacob Mooney Jun'r.

James Murphy to John Weeir 200 acres dated 5 Nov'r 1776 ack'd.

Divald Crites & wife to Jacob Forney 275 acres dated 275 acres Dated 2 Feb'y 1777 prov'd by John Beele.

July term 1778

Thos McKnight to Thomas Henry 195 acres dated 1st August 1772 proved by Thomas Beatey.

Miles Abernathy & wife to Arthur Benson 200 acres Dated 25th Jan'y 1777 ack'd.

John McLean to Thomas Wherry 320 acres dated 5 July 1778 prov'd by Dav'd Miller.

Arch'd McDowell to Elias McFadin 200 acres dated 27 April 1778 prov'd by Mich'l McElwrath.

James Wyatt to George Horton 100 acres dated 29th Dec'r 1777 prov'd by Ja's Withers.

Arch'd McDowell to Mich'l McElwrath 300 acres Dated 27th April 1778 proved by Elias McFadin.

Elias McFadin to Sam'l McFadin 100 acres dated 14 July 1778 ack'd.

Tho's Hunt to Robert Alexander 93 acres dated 7 July 1778 proved by Ja's Holland.

George Morgan Senr to Edward Camp 160 acres dated 19th Dec 1777 prov'd by Robert Childress.

Andrew Miller and wife to And'w Neel 200 acres Dated 11th March 1778 proved by Ja's Holland.

Andrew Miller and wife to And'w Neel 100 acres dated 11th March 1778 prov'd by Ja's Holland.

Boston Best to David Jenkins 177 acres of Land Dated 14th July 1774 prov'd by Fred'k Hambright.

William Patterson to John Beeker 250 acres dated 9th January 1777 prov'd by Jacob Seits.

Henry Hays to John Flack 300 acres dated 22d Day of June 1778 proved by Jonathan Hampton.

Valentine Mauney to John McEntire _____ acres Dated 22nd Aug 1777 ack'd.

Christian Carpenter to Joseph Goods 300 acres dated 22nd July 1778 ack'd.

Richard Barry to John McKnitt Alexander Deed for 640 acres Dated 20th Aug't 1778 prov'd by Tho's Beatey.

John Whitesides to Joseph McDannald 250 acres dated 5th August 1777 proved by John Earle.

Fred'k Hambright to Thomas Morris 20 acres Dated 23d July 1778 ack'd.

Court adjourned till tomorrow morning at 8 o'clock. Friday Morning. Met according to adjournment. Present John Robinson, James White, Jonathan Gullick, Thomas Espey, Esq'rs.

July term 1778

George Parris Admr of the Estate of Jacob Swank returned into Court an Inventory of the Sales & credits of said dec'ed amounting to £65 18.

Court adjourned for half an hour to meet at Christian Maunys. Met according to Adjournment. Present John Robison, Joseph Harden, Wm. Gilbert, Tho's Espey, John Sloan, Esq'rs.

William Gilbert Esq'r appointed assessor in Capt McFadins District in the Room of John Bradley Dec'd for the year 1778.

Henry Reynolds Ju. appointed Constable in the room of Osborn Hechpeth to swear in before James White Esq'r.

James Espey appointed Constable to swear in before Tho's Espy Eq'r.

Ord'd that Jonas Bedford, Timothy Riggs, John Hill and John Sloan be appointed Jurors to attend next Salisbury Superior Court on the 15 September next and that they be summoned by the Sheriff to attend accordingly.

Jurors appointed to attend the next Court to be held for this County to wit:

James Polley	Jacob Mauney
Adam Neel	Peter Aker Sen
Benj'n Ormand	Arthur Patterson
John Beard Ju	Wallis Beatey
William Patterson	Robert Ferguson
Isaac Holland	Jonathan Potts
James McEntire	Jacob Carpenter
John Lusk	Thomas Black
Solomon Beson	Henry Reynolds
Hugh Killpatrick	Moses Moore
John Scott	John Oats
Alex'r Coulter	William Morrison
Thomas Townsend	Saml Barnet
Elias Alexander	James Patterson C. Creek
John Richardson	John Smith

Ordered that John Beal be appointed to Collect the Taxes assessed on the inhabitants in Capt. Reeds District for the year 1778.

The valuation of Taxable property in the County of Tryon for the year 1777 amounts to

£264 408 @ ½[?] Pr Pound is	£550	17
Collectors Commission @ 6 Pr Ct.	33	1
	£517	16
County Treasurers Commission	10	7
	£507	9

Ordered that the several orders of last Court for trying disputed claims of land be reissued as there has been nothing Done as appears by the Sheriffs Returns.

The Clerk of this Court to forbear Issuing Tax Lists for Capt. Kuykendalls, Capt. McKinneys, Capt. Nevils & Capt. Singletons District as it appears to the Court the property in said Districts has not been valued agreeable to Law.

July term 1778

Ordered that the Poll Tax of two shillings laid for the public buildings of this County in October Court 1775 be laid aside; and that a Tax of one Shilling and six Pence be levied on each on each hundred pound taxable property and on equivalent tax on all poll taxables for the purpose aforesaid. And six pence on each hundred pound on all taxable property and six pence on each poll taxable in this County to defray the contingent charges of the County.

Court adjourned till Court in Course. Thos Espey, John Sloan, James White.

State of North Carolina, Tryon County. At a Court of Pleas and Quarter Sessions begun and held for the County of Tryon on Monday the 19th Day of October A D 1778. Before the Worshipful William Gilbert.

Court adjourned till tomorrow morning at 9 Oclock. Tuesday Morning Court Met according to adjournment. Present Wm Gilbert, Thomas Espey, James White, Geo. Black, Wm. Johnston, Esq'rs.

Ord'd that John Wood orphan of Benj'n Wood aged Fourteen years and Six months be bound unto John Wood his Grand Father to learn the Art Trade or Mystery of a Weaver the said John Wood is to Teach or cause the said apprentice to Read, Write and Figure and in all other things to comply with the Act of Assembly in that case made & provided.

Ord'd that Mary Ann Casner an orphan aged Five years be bound unto John Wood till she arrive at the age of Eighteen Years and the said John Wood is to cause the said orphan to be Taught Housewifery such as Spinning & Sewing and in all other things to comply with the Act of Assembly in that case made & provided.

The Last Will and Testament of Girard Will was produced in open Court and proved by the oath of Michael Cloninger one of the Subscribing witnesses thereto.

Ord'd that Letters Testamentary John will Adam Cloninger and Jacob Sides Ex'rs of the said Will on the Estate of the said Dec'd when John Will and Adam Cloninger qualified as Executors.

Upon the Petition of Charles Tice for leave to build a Grist mil on his own Land at the Sholes of first little Broad River, It was ordered that he had leave accordingly and that the same when built be deemed and known to be a Public Mill he complying with the act of assembly in that case made & provided.

Spruce McCoy Esq'r produced in open Court a licence under the hands & Seals of Honorable Saml Ashe and Saml Spencer to practise as an attorney at law in the several county courts of this state and was admitted accordingly.

Ord'd that Spruce McCoy Esqr be appointed Attorney in behalf of this State for this County pro temporary.

Grand Jury. Moses Moore Foreman.

2	James Polly	9	Robert Ferguson
3	Adam Neel	10	Jonathan Potts
4	Isaac Holland	11	Solomon Bason
5	John Lusk	12	Thomas Black
6	Elias Alexander	13	Henry Reynolds

October term 1778

7 John Richardson	14 Wm Morrison
8 Wallace Beatey	15 Jacob Mauney

Sworn & Charged.

Ord'd that John Camp constable wait on this Grand Jury.

Uel Lamkin came into open Court and took the oath appointed for qualification of public officers and that oath of a Deputy Sheriff & entered on the Duty of that office.

The Last Will & Testament of John Bradley was produced in open Court and proved by Jonathan Hampton Esq one of the Subscribing witnesses thereto.

Ord'd that Letters Testamentary issue to Mary Bradly Relict of the s'd dec'd Ex'x and Rich'd Ledbetter Ex'r of said Will on said Decds Estate pursuant to which Mary Bradley qualified as Executrix.

The Last Will and Testamentary of John Beatey Dec'd was produced in open Court and proved by the oath of John Reed one of the Subscribing witnesses thereto.

Ord'd that Letters Testamentary issue to Thomas Beatey Ex'r on the said Deceased Estate who qualified as an Executor.

Rawley Matthews being bound an Apprentice to Fred'k Rhodes in April Term last & having since left his said Masters Service and entered as a Soldier in the Service of the Continent, It was ord'd that the said Fred'k Rhodes and Rawley Matthews be release from their Covenant to each other.

Court adjourned till tomorrow morning at 8 o'clock. Wednesday Morning Court Met according to adjournment. Present Thomas Espey, James McAfee, George Black, Esq'rs.

William Yancey came into open Court and took the oath appointed for qualification of public officers and the Oath of a Justice of the peace and Justices of the County Court of Pleas and Quarter Sessions & took his seat accordingly.

Ord'd that David Miller warn the Inhabitants within six miles on the west side and within five miles on the east side to work on the road where he is overseer.

Ord'd that John McFarland be appointed overseer of the Roads leading from the Court House to the Tuccasiege Ford in that part between the South fork and the Tuccasiege Ford and that he enter on the Duty of his charge accordingly.

Joseph Harden, Wm. Gilbert and James White Esq. came into court and took their Seats on the Bench.

Saml Biggerstaff vs John McFadin Ju.

Petty Jury

James Cook	Wm Eaves
James Patterson	Benj'n Johnston
James Conn	John Huggins
John Jackson Moore	Jonathan Harden
Thos Harrod	Joseph Kyzer

October term 1778

Alexander Patterson   Moses Whitley

Jury Impannelled and sworn find for the plaintiff and assess his Damage to £9 3 4 &/6d Costs.

Zachariah Bullock vs James Adams.

                                        Petty Jury

James Cook	Benj'n Johnston
James Patterson	John Huggins
James Conn	Jonathan Harden
John Jackson Moore	Wm Eaves
Thos Harrod	Joseph Kyzer
Alexander Patterson	Sam'l Biggerstaff

Jury Impannelled and sworn find that the Def't did not assume.

Ord'd that George Taylor, Jesse Nevill, constable, be fined Ten shillings each for not attending Court agreeable to Summons. Geo Taylors Fine Remitted.

Alexander Lewis one of the administrators of the Estate of Preston Goforth produced in open Court a Settlement of the said Deceaseds estate which was filed in the office.

Thomas Potts adm'r of the Estate of George Potts Dec'd returned into open [court] an Inventory of the said Decds Estate and prays an order of sale which was accordingly granted.

Deeds &C Proved or Acknowledged in open Court and ordered to be Registered.

Arch'd White & Mary his wife to Wm. Dunn 250 acres Dated the 11th October 1777. ack'd.

John Custer & Elizabeth his wife to Christian Aker 300 acres of Land Dated the 2d Sept'r 1778. acknowledged.

George Davis to George Patterson 200 acres of Land Dated 21st October 1778 ackn'd.

John Custer & Elizabeth Custer to Christian Aker 300 acres of Land Dated the 2d Sept'r 1778. ack'd.

William Henry to Saml Bell 200 acres of Land Dated the 21st of October 1778. ack'd.

James Sloan to Jacob Connell 200 acres Dated 21st Day of October 1778. ackn'd.

William Edger to George Black 520 acres of Land Dated the 25 October 1777 proved by Adam Edgar.

John Beeman to Saml McMurry 250 acres of Land dated the 30th Day of Decem'r 1776 proved by Henry Callahan.

William Nevins to Archibald White 250 acres of Land dated 29th Day of Novem'r 1774 proved by Archibald White.

October term 1778

George Lamkin to Charles Mattox 80 acres of Land dated 29th Day of August 1777 proved by John Mattox.

Adam Smith to Thomas Warden 300 acres Dated 28th Septem'r 1778. ack'd.

Rebekah Gilkey to John Gilkey 300 acres Dated the 16th Septem'r 1777 proved by Wm. Porter.

Jacob Davold to Garrot Will 243 acres of Land Dated the 21st Day of Nov'r 1776 proved by John Hill.

James Kerr to William Tate 400 acres Dated the 9th March 1773 ack'd.

Tho's Beatey & Margaret his wife Abel Beatey, Matthew Armstrong and Mary Armstrong to James Kerr Dated 9th March 1773 proved by John Reed.

James Kerr to William Tate 400 acres of Land Dated the Ninth Day of March 1773 ackn'd.

Hezekiah Collins to William Graham 300 acres of land Dated the 28th Day of March 1778 proved by William Gates.

Thomas Haslip to Wm Burges 40 acres of Land Dated the 17th Jan'y 1776 proved by Anthony Metcalf.

Tho's Beatey & Margaret his wife Abel Beatey, Matthew Armstrong and Mary Armstrong to James Kerr Dated 9th March 1773 proved by John Reed.

Adam Cloninger to Gerhard Will 200 acres dated the 27th Nov'r 1776 proved by John Will.

Wallace Beatey to Robert Carruth 200 acres of Land Dated the 25 Day of May 1776 ackn'd.

Robert McMinn to Abraham Kuykendall 200 acres of Land dated the 19th Day of October 1778 proved by Wm. Johnston Esq'r.

John McKnitt Alexander to Charles Tice 100 acres of land dated the 1st April 1778. proved by Saml Hendrix.

John Polk and Agnis his wife to Wm. Hannah 400 acres of Land Dated the 19th day of March 1778 proved by Uel Lamkin.

John Cathey to Thomas Robison 621 acres of Land dated the 17th July 1778 proved by Charles Mattox.

John Sloan to George Palmer 200 acres of land Dated the 20th October 1778 ackn'd.

Steven Shelton to Tho's Murrey 100 acres of land Dated 17th Jan'y 1778 proved by John Anderson.

Philip Wisenant to Adam Wisenant and Henry Helterbrand Mortgage on Sundry Articles Dated the 14th February 1778 proved by Thos Pearson.

October term 1778

James Henderson to Wm. Porter 300 acres Dated the 22d Day of Novem'r 1778 ack'd.

Jacob Mooney Ju to William Oates 200 acres of Land Dated 22d Day of October 1778. ack'd.

John Huggins Ju to John Huggins Sen for 100 acres Dated the 28th Day of March 1778 ackn'd.

Andrew Neel to John Kirkconell 60 acres of Land Dated 28th Day of March 1778 ack'd.

Andrew Neel to John Kirkconell 200 acres of Land Dated 28th Day of March 1778 ackn'd.

Andrew Neel to John Kirkconell 400 acres of Land Dated 28th Day of March 1778 acknowledged.

Peter Johnston to John Kirkconell 350 acres Dated 21st October 1778 ack'd.

Peter Johnston to John Kirkconell 250 acres Dated 21st October 1778 acknowledged.

Peter Johnston to John Kirkconell 300 acres Dated 21st October 1778 acknowledged.

Peter Johnston to John Kirkconell 200 acres Dated 21st October 1778 ack'd.

Peter Johnston to John Kirkconell 300 acres Dated 21st October 1778 ackn'd.

Peter Johnston to John Kirkconell 200 acres Dated 21st October 1778 ack'd.

Wm Harris and Anne Harris to John McClure 240 acres of Land Dated the 12 August 1778. proved by Jonathan Gull[ick].

Wm Harris and Anne Harris to John McClure 40 acres of Land Dated the 12 August 1778. proved by Jonathan Gullick Esq'r.

James Rice to William Rice 174 acres of Land Dated the 16th Day of October 1778 proved by Jonathan Gullick Esq'r.

Claims on the County of Tryon for the Year 1775

	£	S	D
Jacob Ramsour 1 Venire Ticket	5	4	8
John Sloan Esq'r 1 Venire Ticket	5	11	11
William Moore 1 Venire Ticket	1	6	8
William Moore 1 Ditto	1	7	8
Timothy Riggs 1 Venire Ticket	6	5	8
James Beard 1 Venire Ticket	5	4	8
Jacob Cosner 1 Venire ticket	2	5	8
Wm Moore 1 Ditto	1	3	6
James Morris 1 wolf Scape & wild Cat	1	5	
James Miller for Extra Services done as Deputy Coroner from July Court 1775 to April 1776	25		
Andrew Neel for Extra Services done as Clerk of the Court from October 1775 to April 1776	25		
James Holland for Extra Services as Sheriff for the year 1777	50		

October term 1778

Andrew Neel for Extra Services as Clerk of the Court from July Court 1777 to July Court 1778	50	
Osborn Hetchpeth for Serving as Constable in July Court 1778	2	
Alexander Denny Wild Cat Scalp Ticket		5
Osborn Hedgpeth for Attendance at Ocr Court 1778	2	
Moses Moore 1 Venire Ticket	1	11 8

Thursday Morning Court Met according to adjournment. Present Joseph Harden, Wm. Gilbert, James McAfee, Esq'rs.

Ord'd that Richard Singleton be appointed to Collect and gather the Taxes assessed on the Inhabitants in his District for the year 1778.

On Motion of Alexander Martin Esquire Ordered by the Court that Letters of Administration issue to Katherine Statler Relict of Peter Statler and Conrad Statler on all and Singular the goods and Chattles Rights & Credits of the said Dec'd who Entered into Bond with Joseph Harden & Benjn Harden Securities in the sum of £1200.

Benj'n Wilkins & Wife vs Richard Hogan.
Petty Jury

Alexander Coulter	Wm McGaughey
Valentine Mauney	George Ewing
Wm Vernor	Wm Henry
James Beatey	Jacob Vanzant
Joseph Clark	Hugh Beatey
Wm Moore	Peter Aker

Jury Impannelled and sworn find the Deft Guilty & assess the plffs Damage to £20 and /6 Costs.

William Henry vs Francis Readding.
Petty Jury

Charles McLean	Richard Singleton
Alexander Coulter	George Ewing
David Miller	Wm Whitesides
David Abernathy	Benj'n Harden
Valentine Mauney	Fred'k Hambright
James Beatey	John Dellinger

Jury Impannelled and sworn enquired into the Plaintiffs Damage and do assess the same to £500 and /6 Costs. Motion in Arrest of Judgment Reasons Filed by B. B. ?

Court adjourned till tomorrow morning at 9 oclock. Met According to Adjournment. Present Joseph Harden, Wm Gilbert, Tho's Espey, James Logan, James White, Jonathan Gullick, John Sloan, Esq'rs.

Ord'd that Wm Graham & Susannah his wife admrs of the Estate of Wm. Twitty Dec'd bring to next April Court Wm Twitty, Susanna, Allen, Russel, Polly, Arabella, Bellariah and

October term 1778

Charlotte Twitty orphans of the s'd Wm Twitty that Guardians may be appointed them according to Law.

Saml Rankin assee &c vs Saml Adams.

Petty Jury

George Ewing	Lawrence Kyzer
James Henders[on]	Boston Best
Fred'k Hambright	John Gallespey
Wm Henry	David Abernathy
Wm Patrick	James Patterson
Michl Hofstatler	James Beatey

Jury Impannelled Sworn assess the plff Damage to £14 11 7 and /6 Cost.

The State vs Wm. Going.

Petty Jury

George Ewing	Lawrence Kyzer
James Henderson	Boston Best
Saml Biggerstaff	John Gallespey
Dav'd Miller	Dav'd Abernathy
Wm Patrick	James Patterson
Michael Hofstatler	James Beatey

Jury Impannelled and Sworn Find the Defendant Guilty in Manner & Form as Charged in the Bill of Indictment. Motion in Arrest of Judgment.

The Taxable Estate of John Chittam was Valued in open Court to £701 16 when it was ord'd that the former valuation be set aside and that the s'd John Chittam pay only £6 13 3 for his Taxes instead of his former assessment.

The Taxable Estate of Joseph Beatey was Valued in open Court to £142 18 when it was ord'd that the former valuation be set aside and that the s'd Joseph Beatey pay only £ 1 7 3 for his Taxes instead of the former Sum.

Court adjourned till tomorrow morning at 8 oclock. Saturday Morning Court Met According to Adjournment. Present Wm Gilbert, Tho's Espey, John Sloan, Jonathan Gullick, James White, Esq'rs.

Ord'd that Thomas Espey Esq'r be appointed Collector of the Tax for Capt Dellingers District for the year 1778.

Ord'd that the following persons be appointed to serve as Jurors at the next Court to be held for this County to wit

Christian Carpenter	John Hutson
John Beard Jr.	Christian Rinehart
John Wilson	Adolph Reep
Adam Beard	Valentine Warlock
Arthur Patterson	Peter Carpenter
John Carruth	John Alexander Indian Creek
Peter Quinn	Thos Townsend

October term 1778

John Stanford	Thos Dills
Robert McMinn	Robert Ewart
Wm Webb	Alexander Baldrige
Wm Huddleton	James Chitwood
John Guffey	Moses Whitley
James Cook Ju	Benj'n Harden
John Morris	Fred'k Hambright
John Scott	
Joseph Jenkins	

Ord'd that Wm Armstrong Serve as overseer of the Road leading from the Court House to the Tuccasiege Ford in that part between the Court House and the Long Mountain.

Ord'd that Mich'l Hofstatler serve as overseer of the Road leading from Moses Moores to the So line in that part between Beaver Dam Creek and the So line and that he warn in all the Inhabitants on the East side of the Road below the Tuccasiege Road within 5 Miles and those on the West side as far as the Muddy Fork of Buffaloe and between the two Market Roads to work thereon and that he enter on the duty of his charge accordingly.

Ord'd that Jonathan Potts serve as overseer of the Road leading from Col Walkers to the So line between the Muddy Fork of Buffaloe and the So line and that he warn in all the Inhabitants within five Miles on the west side of the said Road to work on the same.

Ord'd that Aaron Moore serve as overseer of the Road leading from Wm Bridgets to King Mountain in that part between Wm Bridgets and Cane Creek and he enter on the duty of his charge accordingly by obliging the Inhabitants on the No side of Second Broad River to work on the said Road & keep the same in repair.

Patrick Morris was Find Seven Shillings and Six pence which was paid into the hands of John Sloan Esqr.

Ord'd that James Cook serve as Overseer of the Road leading from George Blacks to Wm. Gilberts and that he oblige the Inhabitants on the So side of Second Broad River & Catheys Creek as low as Mr. Gilberts to work on the same and that he enter on the duty of his charge.

Ord'd that George Sailor serve as Constable in the room of James Espey & that he Swear in before Thos Espey Esqr.

Ord'd that John Sloan Esq'r be appointed Trustee for the County of Tryon for the Ensuing Year.

Rates of Liquors to be taken by Ordinary keepers and others in Tryon County.

Whiskey pr half pint	£ - 3
Wiskey Pr Quart	8
Norward French or any other kind	
except West Indian Rum Pr Pint	3
Ditto Pr Quart	8
West India Rum pr ½ pint	6
West India Rum Pr Quart	16
Beer Pr Quart	2
Cyder Pr Quart	2

October term 1778

Mathaglin   2

Court adjourned till Court in Course. John Robinson, Thos Espey ,John Sloan, Jas White, Jonathan Gullick, Wm. Gilbert.

Tryon County. Tryals of Disputed Claims to Land October Court 1778.

George Pee vs Moses Henry. Claim to 200 acres of Land 2 Courts. Ex'd and returned. J. Miller. Verdict that George Pee is to have the said disputed Land. Copy made out. Costs paid. 1. 16 for Shff.

Cornelius McCarty vs Jacob Rine. Claim to 150 acres, 2 Courts. Ex'd. R. Allison. Verdict that Cornelius McCarty is to have the said Land in Dispute that is to say so on Hills & Rhines Lands westerly between Roads & John Hoyle for Compliment. Fifa vs Rine for Costs. Copy made out.

Andrew Patrick vs Isaac Holland. Claim to 100 acres 2 Courts. Ex'd. J.M. Andrew Patrick is to have 250 acres of Land on little Catawba Creek joining Robt Finleys & Joseph Carrles land. The Lines run by Wm. Sims 1771. Copy made out.

James Miller vs Nath'l McCarroll. 200 acres, 2 courts. Nothing done. to Issue to Wm. Nevil Esq. Verdict Filed. Ord'd that y'e warrant issue to y'e surveyor. Cost paid.

James Miller vs Nath'l McCarroll. 200 acres, 2 courts. Nothing done. to Issue to Wm. Nevil Esq. Verdict Filed. Warrant to issue. Cost paid. Copy made out.

John Ensley vs Andw Haslep. 200 acres 2 Courts. Made up and agreed. Fifa for Costs Issued.

John Ensley vs Andw Haslep. 200 acres 2 Courts. Made up and agreed. Fifa for Costs Issued.

Philip Goodbread vs James Miller. 400 acres 2 Cor. To issue to Jonathan Hampton Esq'r. Issued.

Hon'l Saml Spencer Esqr vs Wm Gilbert & Ja's Miller. 400 acres of land at the lower end of the lower cove of Green River running up for compliment. Wm. Gilbert & James Miller Draw their Entry. Caveat Discont'd by Wm. Gilbert & James Miller withdrawing their Claims. Fees paid by Mr. Gilbert.

Hon'l Saml Spencer Esqr vs Wm Gilbert & Ja's Miller. 450 acres being at the upper end of the first entry in the lower end of Green River. Wm. Gilbert & James Miller Draw their Entry. Caveat Discont'd by Wm. Gilbert & James Miller withdrawing their Claims. Fees paid by Mr. Gilbert.

James Huey vs Wm Huddleston. 100 acres of Land on the Waters of Cane Creek of Broad River joining Lands of John Withrow & his own land. Made up & agreed. Fi fa vs Both for Costs. Issued.

Joseph Gladdin vs Perregrine Magness Ju. 150 acres Land on the Head of Murpheys Branch of Buffaloe and Freelands Branch of s'd waters joining land of Glading & Weers Entry. Cont.d Issued made up Perregreen Magnes pays cost.

Appeals Returns to October Court 1778

John Killian vs James Beard. Claim to 200 acres of land on little Catawba Creek joining lands of Abh'm Alexander, Nathl Henderson, Hugh Barry also joining Duharts Mountain. 26th Jany 1778.

Andw Neel vs Gilbreath Falls. Claim to 325 acres of Land joining Lands of Michl Hofstatler, Andw Keller, Christian Mauny, Christian Carpenter including Wm. Wrays Improvement. 23d April.

John Mattox vs Joseph Beatey. Claim of 100 acres of Land on the So Fork of Catawba River joining Lands of John Chittim, Francis Armstrong & John Mattox. 9 May 1778. Issued. made up & agreed. Costs paid. Copy made out.

Boston Best vs William McKinsey. Claim to 646 acres of Land on the No side of the So Fork of Catawba River including Benjn Taylors improvement. 8 July 1778. Issued. Verd't that Boston Best is to have the said land in Dispute. Copy made out.

Charles Medlock vs Hon Saml Spencer. Claim to 400 acres of Land on both sides of upper Buffaloe Creek of Main Broad River joining Wm Bassetts survey. 8 July 1778. Issued. Abated Mr. Medlocks Caveat not entered in due Time.

Hon. Saml Spencer vs James Miller & Wm. Gilbert. Claim to 400 acres of Land at the lower end of the lower Cove of Green River. Issued. 10 Oct 1779.

Caveats returned to October Court 1778

Hon. Saml Spencer vs James Miller & Wm. Gilbert. Claim to 450 acres of Land at the upper end of the their first entry on Green River in the lower Cove. 21st July 1778. Issued. Oct 1779.

Ambrose Cobb vs Hugh Jenkins. Claim to 400 acres of Land on both sides of Dutchmans Creek on Caney Branch. 21st July 1778. Verdict that Hugh Jenkins is to have the said Disputed land. Issued. Copy made out.

Thomas Simmons Vs Steven Langford. Claim to 200 acres of Land on Marlins reek of First Broad River including Langfords Improvement. 22d July 1778. Issued. paid.

Benjn. Johnston vs Wm. Graham. Claim to 100 acres of Land on Buffaloe Creek on both sides of sd. creek Joining Grahams upper line. 23d July 1778. Made up Graham to get the Land. Issued. Copy made out.

Absalom Gregory vs James Magnes. Claim to 150 acres of Land in Tryon County on little Broad River including the mouth of Long ____ including Gregorys Improvement. 2d August 1778. Verdict filed. Copy made out. Ord'd that the Sheriff summon a Jury on each of the s'd disputed Claims and made a return of the proceedings thereon to the next Court. Issued.

James Stepp vs Aaron Reilly. Claim to 100 acres of Land in Tryon County on both sides of Green River below his other entry and Joining including Ja's Steps Improvement by Aron Reiley the 5 Dec.r 1778 & Jas Step 9th Decr. Ord'd that the Sheriff Summon a Jury to try the said Disputed claim.

October term 1778

Wm. Vernor vs George Palmer. Claim to an Entry of Land on the meadow Branch of little long Creek joining his own land on the No side by Geo Palmer. 1779 & Wm. Vernor. Iss'd to July Cou. nothing Done. Iss'd. to Ocr.

July Court 1778. Appearance of Jurors that failed to Attend last Court agreeable to Summons.

The State vs Nicholas Leeper. Notice. Sum'd. J.H.

The State vs Matthew Leeper. Notice. Sum'd. J.H.

The State vs Adam Baird. Notice. Sum'd. J.H.

The State vs Wm Patterson. Notice. Made Known. Discharged paying the Fees. J.H.

The State vs Henry Reynolds. Notice. Sum'd. J.H. Discharged paying the Costs. Sum'd. Paid A.N.

The State vs Solomon Bason. Notice. Sum'd. J.H.

The State vs Rob't Abernathy. Notice. Sum'd. J.H. Disch'd paying the Costs. Paid.

The State vs Wm Massey. Notice. Sum'd. J.H. Disch'd paying Costs.

The State vs Moses Moore. Notice. Sum'd. J.H. Disch'd paying Costs. Paid A.N.

The State vs Isaac Holland. Notice. Sum'd. J.H. Disch'd paying Costs.

The State vs Hugh Barry. Notice. Sum'd. J.H.

State of North Carolina, Tryon County. to wit, At a County Court of Pleas and Quarter Sessions begun and held for the County of Tryon at the Court House of said County on Monday the Eighteenth day of January A. D. 1779. Present the Worshipful Thomas Espey.

Court adjourned till tomorrow morning 8 oClock. Tuesday Morning. Court Met according to Adjournment. Present John Moore, John McKinney, James White, Abraham Kuykendal, Wm. Nevil.

James Center Sen. came into Court and made ___ he was assessed a Fourfold Tax for not giving the account of his Taxable property in due time, and it appear that he had not an opportunity by reason of ___ . It was ordered that the sd. James ___ giving in when he offered.

Ord'd by the Court that John Aker serve as overseer of the Road leading from Burke county line by Ramsours Mill to Tryon Court House and that he warn in the persons liable to work on the Road between the said Road and the long Shole on the one side and as far as the old Road leading from Thomas Blacks to Warlocks Mill on the other side including that part of Capt. Dellingers District and that he enter on the duty of his Charge.

Ord'd that David Ramsey serve as Constable in Capt. Dellingers District and that he swear in before James White Esqr.

TRYON COUNTY NC COURT MINUTES 1769-1779

January term 1779

Ord'd that Spruce McCoy Esq'r be appointed attorney in behalf of the State for this County for this Term.

Ord'd that And'w Davis an orphan Child of Henry Davis Dec'd aged Thirteen Years be bound unto Jacob ---lins until he shall attain the age of Twenty one years to Learn the art Trade or Mystery of a wheel wright as much as respects making spinning wheels and in every respect to comply with the act of Assembly in that case mae & provided.

Ord'd that Isaac Connors a Mulatto Boy aged Twelve Years be bound unto George Pearis Esqr to serve him after the manner of a servant until he attains the age of Thirty one years and -----.

Whereas it was proved in Open Court by the oath of George Pearis Esq that George Green in a Fight with one Samuel Miller on 22d Day of March 1777 had part of his Ear bit Of. Ordered the Same be Recorded.

Court adjourned till tomorrow morning at 10 oClock. Wednesday Morning Court Met according to Adjournment. Present John Moore, Wm. Nevil, Jonathan Hampton, Esq'rs.

Ord'd that John Milligan pay only Nineteen Shillings for his Tax for the year 1778 instead of the Former assessment.

Ord'd that John McLean pay only Nineteen Shillings for his Tax for the year 1778 instead of the former assessment.

Ord'd that James Cook pay only £5 for his Tax for the year 1778 instead of the former assessment.

Ord'd that Alex'r Moore pay only Nineteen Shillings for his Tax for the year 1778 instead of the former Assessment.

Ord'd that John Lemare pay only Nineteen Shillings for his Tax for the year 1778 instead of the former Assessment.

Grand Jury. Robert Ewart, Foreman.

Alexander Robison	Wm Webb
Fred'k Hambright	Alex'r Mackey
Joseph Jenkins	Anthony Dickey
John Carruth	Valentine Mauney
Benj'n Ormond	Mich'l Hofstatler
James Cook	David Ramsey

Sworn and Charged.

Court adjourned for half an Hour. Met according to Adjournment. Present Thomas Espey, Wm. Nevil, Wm Yancey, Esq'rs.

Ord'd that Wm Parker serve as Constable and that he Swear in before Wm. Yancey Esqr.

Ord'd that Thomas Beatey be appointed Overseer of the road leading from Tryon Court House to Beateys Ford in that part between Forneys Creek and Beateys Ford and that he enter on the duty of his Charge.

552422232431242342334233234243232323342323243232323232323232323232323232323232323

January term 1779

Deeds &c. proved in open Court and Ordered to be Registered.

Thomas Haslep to Edward Hogan 10 Acres of Land Dated the 20th Dec 1775 ack'd.

Thomas Beatey, Hugh Beatey & Robt Armstrong to James Polley 400 Acres dated the 23d day of July 1778 proved by Adam Neel.

James McCombe & Mary his wife to John Beale Dated 22d Day of Dec 1778 for 235 acres proved by Richard Beale.

David Nisbet to John Wilson 416 acres Dated the 19th Septemr 1778 proved by Timothy Riggs Esqr.

John Templeton & Margaret to James Dickey 200 acres Dated the 1st February 1770 prov'd by Hugh Kilpatrick.

Saml Hunter to Eaton Hakings 400 acres Dated the 20th Day of May 1778 prov'd by Thos Harris.

James Miller to Isaac Ledbetter 200 acres the 14 Nov'r 1778 ack'd.

John Walker Esqr. to James Cook 79 acres 19 Oct 1778 ack'd.

Jones Williams to Mary Bradley 100 acres 22d Nov 1778 proved by Jonathan Hampton Esq.

Robert Haslep & Mary his wife to Christopher Horse 370 acres Dated the 27 Day of March 1776 proved by Jacob Horse.

James Swafford to Perregreen Magnes 300 acres Dated the 7th Dec 1778 proved by Uel Lamkin.

William Callahan to William White 200 acres Dated the 31st Jan'y 1779 prov'd by Edward Callahan.

Philip Wisenant to John Harris 300 acres Dated the 21st Jan'y 1779 ack'd.

Christian Carpenter to Isaac White 300 acres of Land Dated the 12th Day of Dec 1778 proved by James White Esq.

James Logan Claim to 100 acres of Land in Tryon County on the middle Branch of Skiluica a Branch of No Pacolet including a Flat of Sapling Land above the Fork of s'd Creek. 12 Dec 1778

Jonathan Gullick & Jas Logan Claim to 100 acres of Land in Tryon County on Vaughns Creek of No Pacolet near 2 miles from the mouth thereof including the upper part of the Shole and that Flat known by the name of Sipsons Camps. Decr 12th 1778.

James Logan Claim to 100 acres of Land in Tryon County on No Pacolet River above Thos Springs Entry on the Little Cane Break. 12th Dec 1778.

James Logan 100 acres in Tryon County on No Pacolet River above his other Entry No. 248 including Hoops Camp. Dec. 12th 1778.

<u>January term 1779</u>

James Logan claim to 200 acres of Land in Tryon County on ____ Creek of 2nd Broad River near 3 qrs of a Mile from ____ thereof on both sides of s;'d Creek including John Turners. 12th Dec 1779. [*sic*]

Court adjourned till tomorrow morning at 10 Oclock. Thursday Morning Court Met according to adjournment. Present John Moore, Thomas Espey, John McKinney, Esq'rs.

Ord'd that John Walker Esq., Thomas Beatey, James Little and Peter Plunk be appointed to serve as Grand & Petit Jurors at the next Superior Court to be held for the District of Salisbury on the 15th day of March next and that the Sheriff Summon them to attend accordingly.

Court adjourned for half an Hour. Met according to Adjournment. Present Thomas Espey, James Logan, Wm. Yancey, Esq'rs.

Ord'd that Thomas Espey Esq. be appointed Coroner for this County.

On Motion Ord'd that Moses Henry have leave to Build a Grist Mill on a Branch of Crowders Creek being his own Land on both sides and that same when built be Deemed and known as a Public Mill he complying with the Act of Assembly in such case made & provided.

Jurors appointed to attend at next Court.

Christian Carpenter	Wm Green
Jacob Mooney Ju	James McAfee [stricken]
John Ashley	Perregreen Magnes Sen
Samuel White [stricken]	Wm Baker
Tho's Townsend	Abraham Kuykendal [stricken]
Tho's Dills	John Cummins
James Beard	Dav'd Miller
Matthew Brown	Sam'l McFadin
Adam Baird	James Withrow
John Hoyle	Wm Long
Zach'h Spencer	Steven Lankford
Rob't McMinn	John Whitesides
Sam'l Blackburn	Moses Whitley
John Richman	Henry Reynolds
John Stanford	Rob't Abernathy
Wm. Capshaw	John McFarlin
	Abraham Scott

Court Adjourned till tomorrow Morning at 10 OClock. Friday Morning Court Met according to Adjournment. Present Thomas Espey, James Logan, James White, Esq'rs.

Ord'd that Jonathan Hampton Esq. and John Wilson be appointed Inspectors to Superintend the Election for Members of the General Assembly to be held at the Court House of this county on the 10th Day of March next.

Thomas Espey Esq. in open Court took the oath for qualification of public officers and the Oath of a Coroner for the County of Tryon.

<u>January term 1779</u>

On motion it was ordered that the Grist Mill belonging to John Oats on Crowders Creek shall be Deemed and known to be a public Mill in the County of Tryon he Complying with the Act of Assembly in that Case made and provided.

On motion Ord'd that the Grist Mill belonging to James Huggins on the little catawba Creek shall be Deemed and known to be a public Mill in the County of Tryon he Complying with the Act of Assembly in that Case made and provided.

Ord'd that Andrew Neel be appointed Trustee for the County of Tryon according to Law.

Ord'd that Geo. Winters, James Adair, John McClure, John Morris, James Linn, Tho's Welch, Aaron Deviney, Wm. Henry, James McFaden, Dav'd Miller, Mich'l McElwrath, George Dickey and Rob't Rankin be a Jury to lay out a Road the nearest & Best way from James Adairs to Thomas Welchs & that they be sum'd by the Sheriff to appear and qualify for this their charge.

Court adjourned til Court in Course. Thomas Espey, Jas Logan, Jas White.

A List of Orders for Letters Testamentary & of administration granted the preceeding Year Returned to the Secretarys Office.

[This volumes continues with the minutes for Lincoln County beginning April term 1779.]

PERSONAL NAME INDEX

Joseph 154
Thomas 154
Wm 210
Balch, Hezekiah 162
Baldridge, John 112
Wm 118
Baldrige, Alexander 204
John 177
Wm 177
Barber 173,174,186
John 7,30,35,38,159,
167,171,189
Barkley, George 177
Barnet, James 92
Joseph 92,193
Samuel 14,69,145,196
William 8,60,139
Barnett, Joshua 139
Barns, Barbara 38
Barnet/t 61,91
John 38
Rachel 38
Robert 72
Baron, Thomas 5
Barr, Thomas 30,34
Wm 9,22,109
Barrach, Wm. 55
Barren, Arch'd 45
Barrenhill, Wm. 85
Barrett, Onslow 76
Barrier, Matthias 107
Barron, Archibald 63
James 4
William 4,5
Barrow, William 85,86
Barry, Hugh 118,180,187,
190,206,207
Richard 72,118,195
William 180
Barton, Thomas 18
Bason, Solomon 138,142,
150,180,187,197,207
Bassett, Wm 112,206
Bassit, Wm 37
Bates, Martin 111
Battle, John 140
Baum, John 48
Baxter, John 166
Beal/e, John 196,209
Richard 209
Beam, Jacob 89
John Detrick 178
Beaman, John 28
Bean, John 129
Beard, Adam 203
Frances 139
James 117,139,172,201,
206,210
John 16,20,31,32,116,

128,139,153,163,173
John Jr. 53,163,196,203
Lucas 194
William 116,173
Beason, Solomon 44,142
Beatey 153,160,180,182
Abel 100,133,136,141,
152,179,187,190,200
Deborah 176
Francis 136,147,176
Hugh 99,147,159,189,
193,202,209
James 110,176,186,187,
191,202,203
John 113,129,198
Joseph 203,206
Margaret 135,200
Thomas 100,110,113,
135,138,159,190,195,
198,200,208,209,210
Wallace 136,147,189,
198,200
Wallis 196
Beats, Henry 84
William 84
Beaty, Abel 3,6,32,35,39,
86,151
Francis 4,28,33,37,47,
69,97
Hugh 98,136,155,193
James 20,33,58
John 33,86
Thomas 22,24,25,65,66,
79,83,86,100,129,136,
155,187,193
Wallace 136,193
Wm 25
Beaver, Matthias 25
Susana 25
Beck, Nicholas 104
Beckham, John 9
Bedford, Jonas 1,14,16,
23,24,35,36,40,46,48,
53,56,58,59,62,88,99,
103,105,106,112,114,
127,128,132,133,137,
150,153,155,175,176,
178,186,192,194,196
Beeker, John 195
Beekman,   Christopher
98,107
Beele, John 193,194
Beeman, John 4,28,62,68,
139,142,150,191,199
Beeson, Solomon 64
Bell, James 115,116,118,
124,176
Rich'd 186
Saml 199

Thomas 71,86
Zachariah 23,28
Belue, Ab'm 21
Rainy/ey 52
Bennet/t, Agnes 2
John 2,52,71,78,126
Benson, Arthur 195
Berger, George Henry
194
Berkly, Henry 82
Berry, Andrew 38,69
Hugh 69
John 45,69
Rich'd 46
William 110,112,182,
189,192
Beson, Solomon 7,14,15,
38,51,73,74,110,113,
114,170,196
Best, Bostain 80
Boston 35,157,195,203,
206
Catherine 157
Peter 178
Bickerstaff, Benjamin
21,84
Sam'l 88,89,100
Biger/Bigger, Catharine 9
John 9,128
Joseph 5,63
Matthew 59,63,71
Biggerstaff, Aaron 63,111,
116,121,149,189
Benjamin 110,112,116,
121,126,189
David 148
Elizabeth 116
Mary 63,116
Saml 102,104,116,185,
188,189,198,199,203
Bishop, Edmund 26,103
Robert 8
William Glover 4,27
Black, Eliz'th 61
Garvin/Gavin 64,65,
66,75
George 98,141,160,165,
166,172,190,192,197,
198,199,204
James 122
John 1,140
Thomas 14,26,51,61,
102,110,114,115,123,
133,145,170,173,191,
196,197,207
Blackburn, James 186
Robert 9,17,18,26,28,
29,34,35,39,51,54,55,
67,68,75,81,83,85,87,

213

89,90,91,92,94,97,99,
101,102,103,104,107,
108,116,141
Samuel 116,172,173,
174,210
Blackwell, Joel 9,119,147,
152,153
Blank, Peter 108
Blanton, George 12,18,23,
36,38,40,43,55,61,
62,66,84,89,90,175,
176,182
Susanna 55
Blaylock, David 194
Blyth, James 137
Bochannon, James 99,
100,102
Bochanon, Ja's 101
Bogard, Abraham 24,
41,47
Boker, Joseph 81
Bolding, William 52,61
Boldridge, Alex'r 72
Boles, Susa 61
Bond, Thomas 79
Boone, Jacob 152
Booth, William 124,147
Boren, Joseph 177
Boshears, M. 107
Middleton 71
Bost, William 61
Bound, George 52,90
Bower, Matthias 141
Boyd, John 123
Robert 183
Bracket, Benjamin 98,99,
111,113,119
Wm 106
Bradly/ey, James 88,95,96
John 136,172,186,189,
196,198
Joshua 48
Mary 198,209
Bradner, Joseph 43,54,64
Brandon, Elizabeth 37
John 1,12,26,27,31,62,
66,89
Thomas 2,37,50,74
Brattin, Thomas 15
Bratton, Hugh 70
Martha 56
Robert 71,85,86
Thomas 44
William 7,13,17,39,44,
54,56
Breed, Joseph 52
Breman, John 133
Brice, Sam'l 86
Bridges, James 7,23,29,30,

33,36,37,57,66,71,78,
84,86,192
Moses 176
Thomas 177,178
William 51,59,84,95
Bridget, Wm 204
Broadway/Broadaway
Jonas 118
Nicholas 30,88,98,118
Brock, George 18
Brothers, Thomas 178
Brown, Ann 27
Gabriel 61
Gabriel Jr. 27,61
Jacob 27
James 38
John 96
Joseph 4
Matthew 210
Stewart 27
Thos 8
Wm 32
Bruton, David 78
Bryant, William 31
Bryson, Hugh 96,117
James 25,33,41,42,129
John 25,42,76,117,154,
178,189
Bucanan/Bucanon/Bucan-
nan/Buchanan/Buchanon/
Buckanan
Ann 112
James 119,138,139,148,
152,153,154,157,185
John 11,33,112,128,177
Wm. 131
Buckingham 29
Buffington, Joseph 117,
121
Bullinger, Henry 87,122
Bullion, Thomas 15,57,59,
73,76,176
Bullock 12,13,40,50
Mary 49
Richard 49
Zachariah 8,9,11,15,22,
44,48,90,137,199
Bumgarner, John 57,81
Bunn, Jno 108
Burchfield, Adam 62,
67,84
Joseph 84
Burges, Wm 200
Burleson/Burleston/Bur
lison
Aaron 12,34,84,113
Burlington, Aaron 31
Burns, Conrad 126
Margaret 126

Robert 42,102
William 30,31,32
Burris, William 7
Burtin, Mary 37
Burton, Elizabeth 79
Esther 37
Sarah 37
Bush, Dan'l 61
Butler, Jonathan Hogan
173
Martha 173
Byars/Byers, David 1,3,13,
60,66,148
James 16,25,96,148,177
John 23,24
Joseph 148,159
Margaret 148
Saml 33
William 24,32,66,83,84,
85
Wy 11
Cahoon, Mary 68
Thos 68
Cain, Marth 90
Caldwell, Eleanor 3
Thomas 115,129,132
Callahan, Edward 104,
152,153,154,209
Henry 199
William 104,209
Calley, James 69
Cally, And'w 35
Cammel, And'w 53
Camp, Benj'a 186
Edward 195
John 192,198
Joseph 175,176,177,182
Nathan 80,152
Campbell/Campble
Alex'r 26,52
Andrew 75,76,94
Benjamin 108
James 4,26,43,54
Thomas 16,35,70,76,77,
98,110,111,147,153,
154,167,184,192,193

Cancelor/Cansler, Philip
131,132,149,184,185
Cannon, Simcock 4
Capshaw (also see Kaps-
haw)
Esix/Essex/Essix
8,13,76,129,151,152,
154,160
James 6,29,30,38,44,54,
57,58,59,129,160,161,
171,180,189
William 6,20,29,30,32,

215

Cook, James 9,19,39,40,
45,82,104,116,122,
132,133,139,143,144,
152,154,165,189,191,
193,198,199,204,208,
209
  James Jr. 104,139,189,
  192,204
  Jane 26,38,186
  Roger 26,38,186
Coons, Wm 18
Cooper, Isaac 169
  John 112
Coops, Ephraim 98
Corudon 71
Corven, Robert 78
Cosner/Cosnar, Jacob
  3,12,53,56,58,94,201
Coster/Costner, Andrew
  161
  Jacob 3,16,19,21,22,24,
  59,75,84,91,92,97,101,
  102,103,107,109,113,
  120,130,143,146,160,
  163,183,186
  John 105
  Molly 121
  Peter 21,98,121,130,
  146,161,183
  Thomas 28,117,178
Cotter, Moses 11
Coulter, Alexander 47,97,
  98,106,132,138,142,
  147,148,153,154,161,
  163,170,177,179,184,
  185,189,190,192,193,
  196,202
  Mary 76
Countryman, And'w 73
Counts, John 70
Coup, Maudlin 89
Cowan/Cowen, And'w
  44,91
  George 44
  Matthew 44,45
Cox, George 28,39,40,
  41,54
Coy/Coyl/Coyle, Alexan-
  der 92,115,150,164
  Elizabeth 115
Cozart, James 36,92,106,
  116,119,122,136,137,
  159
Crace, John 2,14,94,155
Craig, Saml 31,32
Crawford, Geo 71
  James 29
  Jean 117
  Michael 16,130

Moses 16,93,117,128
Crayton, Phineas 111
Crease, Margaret 136
Creutz, Peter 125
Criter, Peter 104
Crites, Davol 122,124
  Divald 194
  Peter 125
  Valentine 179
Crocket, David 69,70,79,
  97,104,149,115,148
  Wm 70,140,148,149
Cromikel, William 8
Cronicle, Wm 133,142,
  156
Crowder 3,7,28,68,188,
  210, 211
  Charity 14
  Ubey 14
  Ulrick 25,27,81
  Welrich/k 7,10
Culp, Henry 5
  Peter 5
Culwell, Curtis 37
Cummins, Hugh 21,137
  John 21,137,160,210
Cummon, John 186
Cunes, John 141
Custer, Elizabeth 199
  John 199
Custion, Hugh 9
Dack, George 53
Daniel, James 6
Daugherty, James 153
  James Jr. 189
Dauraugh, Esabell 18
  Marmaduke 18
David, George 60
Davidson, Ja's 77
  John 63
  Ruth 63
  Sam'l 29
Davis/Davies, And'w 208
  David 26,64,91,112,132
  George 7,68,87,106,148,
  152,199
  Henry 208
  James 10,70
  Jno 57
  Joseph 104,110,151
  Mary 44
  Nathan 110,122,177
  Robert 67,128
  Thomas 81,128
  William 44,82,85,109,
  139,157
Davison, Alex'r 178
  James 126
  John 47,48,71,77

Saml 15,37,73,76
  William 154,162,172
Davold, Jacob 200
Deal, John 122
  Wm. 122
Dearment/Dearmont,
  Wm 83
Deck, Adam 147
  George 16
Deforest 68,73
Dellinger 203,207
  Henry 73,100,103,113,
  150,153,160,163,179,
  180,182
  John 24,112,120,146,
  153,163,179,184,185,
  193,194,202
  Martin 21
Dennard, John 160
Denny, Alexander 202
  George 53
Dermond, Jacob 84
  Thomas 84
  William 84
Derossett, Lewis Henry
  13
Dervin, James 38
Deveney, John 140
Deviney, Aaron 121,190,
  211
  Jno 140
  Mary 140
Devold, Jacob 125
  Mathias 150
Devour, Dan'l 110,133
Dicas, Edward 129
Dick, Adam 101,125
  George 101
Dickey, Anthony 208
  David 128,157,159,167,
  168
  George 85,211
  James 209
  Rob't 85
Dickinson, John 73
  Martha 73
Dickson, Alexander 85,
  117,141
  Benj'a 36
  Edward 85
  Geo 91
  Joseph 85,193
  Thomas 36,96
  William 70
Dicky, David 76
  George 56
Dicus, Edward Jr. 88
Dill/s, John 101

Havener/Havenor/
Heavenor
  Teter 6,84,131,132,133,
  171
Haw(e)s Benjamin 37
  Jacob 130
Hawkins, James 61
  John 61
  Thomas 122
Hay, David 93
Hayell, Andrew 8
Hays, Henry 157,195
Hazlep, Andw 189
Head, John 8
Heager, George 153
  William 161
Heatherly, George 9
Hechpeth, Osborn 187,
  196
Heckleman, Jacob 81
  Michael 93
Heddick, And'w 89
Heddleston/e, David 165
  David Jr. 121,147
Hedgpeth, Osborn 202
Hefner, George 25,61
  Michael 83
Helterbrand, Henry 200
Hemphill, Alex'r 62,63,71
  James 117
  Sam'l 63
  Susannah 117
Henderson, Elizabeth 168
  James 34,48,104,118,
  133,135,144,147,
  158,159,167,172,
  177,180,182,201,203
  John 177
  Nathaniel 30,99,148,
  161,168,206
  Richard 72,73,113,130
  Violet 172
Hendrix, John 184
  Saml 200
Henry, Esabell 23
  Hannah 110,114
  Henry 22
  James 12,14,17,24,33,
  41,49,53,64,193
  John 176
  Moses 28,117,188,189,
  205,210
  Philip 117
  Thomas 48,117,146,195
  William 2,3,4,15,23,25,
  26,40,53,81,88,93,102,
  108,110,114,122,123,
  139,148,149,160,169,

179,190,192,193,199,
202,203,211
Henson, Bartlet 64,159
  Diana 11
  Nicholas 11,14,20
  Phillip 11,14,20,39,40,
  44,46,88,98,159
Heoy, Danl 107
Hermon, Peter 128
Heslip, (see also Haslep)
  And'w 46
  John 46
Hetchpeth, Osborn 202
Hicks, Christopher 100
  Richard 69,133
Higdon, Daniel 8
Hightower, John 140
  Joseph 165
  Joshua 140,164
  Thomas 164
Hill 205
  Abel 187
  Jane 69,99
  John 69,70,99,105,110,
  117,130,138,140,143,
  174,177,196,200
Hillhouse, James 190
  William 27
Hillis/e, John 50
  William 12,31,50
Hiltebrand, Henry 18,
  19,25,106,111,120
  Mary 25
Hinson, Nicholas 38
  Phillip 35,36,38
Hinton, Isaac 99,136
Hix, Christopher 145
  Richard 69,171,180
  William 62
Hodgson, Jonathan 63
  Love 63
Hodson, David 100
Hofstatler, Jacob 102,138,
  139,145,159
  John 184,185
  Michael 51,86,115,131,
  145,151,170,184,185,
  203,204,206,208
Hogan, Edward 37,128,
  154,209
  Richard 202
Hogg, Wm. 24
Holeman, Henry 89
Holland, Francis 184
  Isaac 137,180,187,188,
  189,196,197,205,207
  James 167,168,169,178,
  195,201

Hollingsworth, Abraham
  61
Holman, Anthony 138,
  139
  Henry 1,29,30,31,34,43,
  44,51,62,63,84,90,91,
  92,94,95,96,101,103,
  108,111,112,138,139
Hoofman, Catharine 132
Hoofstaler, Mary 106
Hoofstatler, John 106,107
  Michael 109,111
Hoozer, Rudolph 125
Hope, John 94
Horse, Christopher 209
  Jacob 124,209
Horton, George 195
Horty, Jacob 168
Hoss, Jacob 22
Houk, John 101
Houlthouzer, Michael
  183
Hover, Geo 97
Hoves, George 135
Howard, James 42
  Peter 48
  Stephen 51
How/e, Jacob 111
  Joseph 11,22,23,29,62
  John 53
  Wm. 11,53
Howell, John 93
Hoyl/e, Andrew 104,136,
  142,149,186
  John 22,23,110,129,148,
  149,170,174,189,205,
  210
  Michael 31,151,170,173,
  187
Huddleston/e, David
  19,52,73,82,140
  John 159
  William 19,126,188,189,
  205
Huddleton, Wm 204
Hudock, Andrew 84
Huey, James 188,189,205
Hufstateler, Jacob 68
Hufstatler, John 184
  Mich'd 132
Huggins, James 194
  John 4,112,124,131,132,
  148,172,186,198,199,
  201
  John Jr. 201
Hugh/y, James 32,66
Humphries, Rob't 52
  see also Umphries
Hunt, Mader 118

Mattison 106
Middert 118
Thomas 155,195
Hunter, Samuel 128,129,
157,184,191,209
Huntsucker, Tawalt 124
Hutchins, Anthony 94
Hutson, John 203
Hyde, Benjamin 142,148,
158
Jean 148
Wm 148
Hyder, Benj'n 189
Hyel, Michael 44
Iker, Peter 60
Ingland, (also see Eng-
land) Michael 112
Ingle, Michael 100,163
(see also Engle)
Irwin, (see also Erwin)
Alex'r 111
George 107
Wm. 153
Ison, Edward 7
George 64,65,66
John 84
Jack, Joseph 145
Saml 122,124
Jacobs, Henry 18
Jameson, James 72
Janes, Thomas 34,58
Jarret/Jarratt/Jarrett
Daniel 144,145
Samuel 144,145
Katherine 145
Jarrot, John 8
Jarvin, John 3
Jeans, Thomas 10,132
Jefferies, Nath'l 53,55,67,
90
Jene 116
Jenkins, Benj'n 189
David 64,106,117,125,
146,153,161,162,163,
164,195
Hugh 125,146,187,206
Joseph126,151,158,187,
191,204,208
Jennings, Moses 35
Johnson, James 140
Wm. 190
Johnston 16
Alex Erwin 82
Benjn. 198,199,206
Henry 145
Jacob 21
James 82,115,116,119,
124,127,145,146,153,
162,167,169,170,171,

172,174,175,180,181,
184,185,186,187,188,
190,192,194
John 36,100,108,179,
181
Joseph 113
Katherine 145
Lyllius 99
Peter 9,18,48,49,70,71,
72,87,108,124,201
Rebeckah 129
Robert 11,62,70,81,121,
153,165
Samuel 9,109,112,163,
176,178
Susanah 21
Thomas 8,158
William 31,88,129,172,
186,192,197,200
Joiner, William 58,72,
82,83
Jones 24
Adam C. 95
And'w 37
Joseph 3,52
Joshua 89
Peter 61
Stephen 32,35,36,37,39,
42,46,104,180,183
Thos 152
Wm 72,152
Jordan/Jorden/Jordon,
John 7,16,30,31,32,
34,90
Julian 12,38,40,50
George 12,40,44,50,75,
95,96
Jacob 71,74
Kannon, Simcock 28,73
Kapshaw, (also see Cap-
shaw) Essex 76
Karr, Charity 13
William 13
Karuth, Ja's 63
Keener, Abraham 105,
163
Ula 105
Keller, Andrew 106,107,
206
Michael 84,114,120,135
Kelllough, Thomas 55
Kellough, Rob't 70
Kelly, Ja's Jr. 142
James 65,88,91,97,99,
100,110,111,112,133,
141,145,184,191
Marey 145
Kels, Alexander 63
Kelso, Joseph 46,58,86

Kelsy/Kelsey, Joseph
38,46
Kempshaw, William 76
Kendrick, John 16,51
Kennan, William 157
Kennon, Lyddy 52
Sam'l 52
William 135
Ker, Charity 94
Kerr, Daniel 86
Hannah 87
James 138,200
John 75
Robert 87
William 77,78,79,94
Keruth, Adam 8
Kiles, Alexander 168
Killian/on, Alexr 34
John 206
Leonard 76,98,117
Margret 76
Martin 117
Killough, Tho's 70
Kilpatrick, Alex'r 27,37
Hugh 177,187,196,209
Kimbol/l, Jno 63,70
Kimbro, John 36
Kinder, Conrad 22
King, George 4
William 140,149,167
Kingry, Abraham 89
Barbara 89
Daniel 89,94
Elizabeth 89
Mary 89
Kinkaid, John 104,167,
168,180,187,190,194
William 104,148,149,
194
Kinselar/Kinsyller, Phillip
63,94
Kirkconell, John 104,105,
106,116,119,124,157,
158,201
Knapper, Frederick 27
Knox, Robert 167
Knuckles, John 2,21
Kobb, Herman 62
Joseph 69
Kolp, Herman 69
Kraps, J. 91
Krass, J. 91
John 124
Krunright, Harkles 107
Kuykendal/l 12,171, 174,
196
A. 21
Abraham 4,5,10,26,
52,93,121,153,162,

172,186,190,192,200,
207,210
Adam 189
Benjamin 48,77,78,132,
137
James 6
John 147
Johnathan 6
Joseph 48
Peter 4,5,13,14,22,27,
32,46,50,52,157
Saml 122,155,185
Simeon/Simon 22,48,
118,136,138,139,145,
147,149
Rebeckah 127
Kyle, Alexander 105,123,
125,126
Kyser/Kyzer/Kizar
George 81,143,179
Joseph 77,109,139,198,
199
Laurance 77,106,185
Laurence/Lawrence
62,67,68,107,131,132,
138,145,151,158,167,
170,184,203
Laboon, Peter 156,170
Lacefield, William 129
Lacey, Edward 14,16,
20,78
Joshua 14
Ruben 14
Samuel 79
Lafferty, Patrick 2
Pett. 78
Prudence 2
Lame, John 155
Mary 155
Lamkin/Lampkin, Euel
142
George 14,21,22,23,61,
97,104,105,107,110,
117,118,121,122,124,
125,126,136,141,143,
144,157,162,165,166,
168,169,174,177,183,
184,190,193,194,200
Hannah 104,126
Jane 142
Jannet 129,151,156
Uel 109,140,163,184,
185, 189,198,200,209
William 104,105,129,
142,149,151,156
Land/e 11,29,45
Landers, Henry 87,118,
141
John 118

Landess, Henry 145
Landis, John 160
Langford/Lankford, 182
Stephen/Steven 184,
162,191,194,206,210
Langham, Comford 3
John 3
William 90
Langhorn, William 57,90
Lansdell, Richard 164
Laughlin, John 3,11,24,
32,45
William 14,15
Laurence/Lawrence,
Joseph 91,114,189
Laverty, Patrick 2
Prudence 2
Lawson 46
Leaper, Nicholas 7
Lecquer/Leqere, John
158
Ledbetter, Ephraim 10
Isaac 209
Rich'd 198
Lee, Abel 107,108,154,
181,185
Isom 72
Michael 52
Robert 105,107,162,
181,185
William 52
Leech, David 22,34,35
Henry 29
Prudence 35
Leepar/Leeper/Lepar
17,29
Elizabeth 166
James 166
Jane (Scott) 166
Mary 166
Matthew 180,187,191,
207
Nicholas 155,166,180,
187,190,207
Robert 11,31,45,50
Lemar/e, James 129,130
John 208
Lewing, Wm. 85
Lewis, 71
Alexander 150,156,199
Andrew 128
James 3,14,75
John 47,48,179
Like, Christian 125
Liles, David 66
Limeberger, John 14,85
Lewis 23,163
Peter 14,85
Lindsey, Ezekiel 10

John 10
Linebarger/Lineberger,
Jno 73
Lewis 2,135,137,183
Peter 46,128
Lineberry, Barbara 135
Lewis 135
Link, Barbara 60
Catherine 107
Frederick 107
Jacob 60,86,107
John 107
Rob't 97
Linn, James 190,211
John 50
Mary 88
Thomas 88
Litel/Litle/Little,
Archibald 86,187,188
James 86,115,161,171,
210
Jane 86,115
John 115
Thomas 86,95,98,113,
115
William 86,95,98,115
Lively, Wm. 119
Lockart/Lockhart/Lock-
ard, Aaron 1,2,60
Alexander 7,9,24,31,39,
63,65,73,86,95,96,112,
129
James 126
Loftin, Samuel 147
Logan, James 25,36,84,
112,119,124,130,141,
158,167,172,173,174,
175,180,181,184,185,
186,187,188,190,192,
202,209,210,211
John 40,74,75,92,96,99,
100,128,154,157
Wm. 67,102
Long, Jno 4
Wm 186,210
Lookinglass, Martin
144,145
Looney/Loney/Loony,
(see also Luny)
Adam 39,49
Robert 37,39,46,47,49,
73,74,75,84,89,100,102,
142,152
Loots/Louts, George 35
Love, Alexander 44
Andrew 44,63
James 29,69
John 22,68
Martha 68

Richard 14
Robert 29
Lovelady, Marshal 48
  Thomas 48
Lovelath, Marshall 11
Lovelatty, John 72
  M. 107
  Marshal 72
  Thomas 97
Low, John 22,35,57,59,61,
  176,177
  Tho's 120
Lowry, Robert 68,77
Luny/Luney, Robert
  36,90
Lusk, John 10,25,27,
  36,60,61,64,66,76,80,
  87,89,92,95,96,98,99,
  100,101,102,126,141,
  153,173,174,181,186,
  196,197
  Robert 58,66,75,88,90,
  99,103
  Sarah 60,61,153
  William 39,46,47,48,78,
  191,193
Lutes, Jacob 87
Lyon, Patrick 154
  Steven 194
Mackelmurry, Wm 99
Mackey, Alexander 166,
  208
  William 147
Mackleroy, John 4
Mackness, Peregrine
  173,188
  Peregrine Jr. 189
Magbee/y, Verdry
  30,43,53,71,72,73,74,
  78,80,84,86,88,89,152
Magnis/Magis/Magnes/
  Magness(see also Mack
  ness)
  James 206
  John 171
  Peregrine 53,60,72,73,
  89,187,190,192,193
  Perigreen 20,27
  Perregreen 9,23,138,
  144,205,209,210
  Perregrine Jr. 205
  Perry Green 106,141,
  154,162
  William 141,168,180,
  183
Magoun, Geo 94
Mahan, James 61
Manner, John 26

Marchbanks, William
  7,10,66,79,90
Markel/le, Frederick
  25,122
Marlin 206
Marstal, Peter 116
Marteberry, William 53
Martin, Agness 109
  Alexander 1,6,7,15,16,
  26,29,34,56,67,76,77,
  90,105,109,114,115,
  158,160,202
  Henry 129,139
  James 92,93,109,157
  John 138
  Josiah 105,114,127,130
  Samuel 84,123,146,156
Massey, William 118,151,
  152,158,176,180,187,
  190,194,207
Master/Mastin, Henry
  28,46,168
  Jacob 150,194
  Marg't 46
  Michael 46
Matthews, Peter Lamkin
  174
  Rawley 151,185,198
Mattox, Charles 200
  John 148,200,206
Mauny/ey, Christian
  69,135,196,206
  Christopher 130,156
  Christy 133
  Jacob 74,196,198
  Valentine 61,88,111,
  122,131,136,137,
  138,145,152,154,
  165,172,184,195,202,
  208
Maxwell, James 6
  Thomas 133,139,191
Mayers, John 8
  Sarah 8
Mayhue, Elizabeth 152
Mays, James 46,58
McAdo/u, David 23,37
  Wm. 23,37
McAfee, James 5,31,44,
  56,57,60,62,71,79,86,
  95,137,154,163,165,
  166,167,171,175,178,
  179,186,192,198,202,
  210
  Margaret 5
  Robert 56,60,62,82,83,
  86,87,88,89,95,100,
  101,130,141
  Thomas 57

William 57
McBee (see also Magbee)
  James 36
  Vardry 90
McBride, David 162
  Francis 33,83
McCaland, Rob't 114
McCall, James 64
McCallister, Alexander
  112
  Arch'd 162
  Margaret 112
McCarley, Moses 140
McCarrol/l, Nathaniel
  188,189,205
McCarter, Alex'r 51,83
  Moses 52,61
McCartney, Daniel 31
  John 163
McCarty, Alex'r 57
  Agniss 110
  Cornelius 22,122,189,
  190,205
  Daniel 52,71,73,74,76,
  95,110,128,159,163
  David 8
  John 76,163
  Robert 38
McCashland, Rob't 103
McCaslan/d, Robert
  93,104, 117,138,163
McClain, Charles 12,
  22,81
McClanachan, Elizabeth
  15
  Robert 15
McClare, John 157
McClean 43
  Alex'r 64
  Charles 6,13,17,24,25,
  26,49,50
  Elizabeth 4
  Ephraim 4,22,33,41,66,
  127
McCleary, Daniel 41,136
McClellen, Robert 44
McClenahan, James 39,66
McClohlin, James 74
McClure, John 83,158,
  159,161,163,201,211
McCombe, James 209
  Mary 209
  Robert 183
  Sam'l 191
McConnel, William 58
McCool, Adam 68
McCord, James 26,46,47,
  64,124
  John 172

McCorkle/McCorkall
Ab'm 56
Francis 96,128,146
Sarah 128,146
McCormack, James 51
John 43,54,56,92
McCown, Wm. 90
McCoy, Spruce 197,208
McCracken, Wm 160
McCulloh, John 12,77
Sam'l 22
Thomas 38
William 6
McCurdy, Robert 2
McDaniel, James 121
Jeremiah 132,133,151
John 28,118
Joseph111,132,133,138,
139,156,192
McDavid, Patrick 21,26,
36,56,73,106,136,137,
162
McDonnald,McDannald
Alex'r 189
Joseph 195
McDow, William 50

McDowell/McDowel
Archibald 177,194,195
Eleanor 4
John 118,126,193
Joseph 126
William 4
Robt 45,75
McEllily, John 78
McElmurry, John 55
William 20,34
McElroy, James 48
John 59,97,106,112
Mary 112
McElwean, James 14,21,
24,27,28,34,38,43,61,64
McElwee, Wm. 26
McElwrath, Michael
148,154,158,175,184,
189,190,191,195,211
McEntire, Alexander
82,87,100,102,163
Ann 124,147
James82,83,87,100,101,
107,110,114,115,116,
124,129,131,132,137,
138,141,147,153,156,
161,163,165,172,174,
196
James Jr. 177
Jennet 87

John 98,105,115,135,
140,162,173,181,191,
195
Rachel 98
McFadden/McFaddon
171,172,174,175,192,196
Elias 189,195
James 169,186,190,211
James Jr. 163
John 14,26,36,56,121,
152,154,160,161,163,
166,167,169,189,193,
194
John Jr. 159,166,198
Ruth 166
Samuel 82,148,159,160,
166,195,210
Thomas 8
McFain, John 194
McFarland, John 178,193,
198
McFarlen, James 97,129,
170,186
McFarlin, John 210
McGahey, Alexander 19
McGaughey/McGaughy
Alexander 97,99,121,
122,140,141,189
John 142,143
Rachel 99,122
William 125,202
McGaughlin/McGlohlin
Elleanor 127
Ja's 74,75
McGee, Patrick 139
McGill, Thos 183
McGuire, John 92,142
Merry 101,133
McGurnnigen, Jno 72
McIlwean, James 1,12
McIntire, Alex'r 27,36,67
James 12,26,27,34,38,
69,80,90,91
Jane 36
John 45
McKee, James 33
Margaret 25
Rob't 25
McKendrick, Sarah 168
McKinny/McKinney 196
John 5,12,72,78,86,64,
100,102,114,118,119,
138,142,143,146,153,
157,165,166,167,171,
179,180,182,185,186,
190,192,207
William 133,135
McKinsey, William 206
McKnabb, James 3

McKnight, Charles 6
Jennet 6
Thomas 133,144,195
McKown, Wm 8,9,62
McLain/McLane, Charles
114, 121
McLaughlin, Patrick 127
McLean, Charles 83,85,
111,113,114,115,116,
119,120,122,123,126,
127,128,130,133,136,
141,142,143,144,145,
146,150,151,154,155,
156,162,167,171,189,
202
Elizabeth 159
Ephraim 108,159
Jenney 129
John 127,129,161,163,
166,194,195,208
McMichael, John 36,45,
193
Wm 193
McMinn, Robert 36,113,
144,157,186,200,204,
210

McMullen/in, Robert 97
William 3,40,73
McMurry, Robert 99
Saml 122,189,199
Thomas 69,70
William 3,11,66,95,96
McNabb, Andrew 15,16,
26,38,44,104
James 44,54
Margaret 16,104
Robert 16
McNeal, Archibald 9
Edw'd 21
McNight, Charles 32,95
McRee, David 70
McReynold, James 161,
170
McTier, John 84
McWhirter, Hans 73
Havis 70
Henry 147
Robert 64
McWhorter, Eleanor 36
Hance 24,30,31,32,35
Means, James 28
Rachel 28
William 28
Medlock, Charles 206
Megarity, Michael 13,54
Megary, Hugh 191
Megrue, Jno 54
Melkillon, James 110

70,73,75,76,77,78,80,
82,84,88,89,90,91,93,
94,95,96,97,100,101,
102,103,104,105,106,
107,108,109,110,112,
114,183
Neely 71
  Hugh 44
  Thomas 25
  William 4,29,39,40,
    42,44
Neighbours, John 68,92,
  100,101,102,153,176
  Sarah 176
Neil, Thomas Jr. 1
  (see also Neal/Neel)
Neister, Frederick 153
Nelson, Robert 18,82
Neshiner, George -
  Christopher 141
Nevans/Nevins, Agnes 97
  Henry 97
  William 148,199
Nevil/Nevill/Nevel 170,
  171,179,180,192,196
  Jesse 199
  William 36,40,42,165,
    171,166,181,186,189,
    205, 207,208
Newberry, Andrew 159
Newman, Jonathan 111
Newton, Ebenezar/er 154,
  170,171,174,178
Nichols, John 90
  James 124
  Thomas 100,101,139
  Wm. 158
Nisbet/Niesbet/Nisbett,
  David 33,112,159,209
  Joseph 86
  Samuel 8,86,87
  William 148
Nixton, James 94
Nuckles/Nuckoles
  John 2,9,41,42,48,27,39,
    58,86,90,102,106
O'Neal, Jonathan 158
Oaks, John 69,88,92,102,
  118,126
Oates, William 201
Oats, John 196,211
Ormand/Ormond, Benj'n
  189,196,208
Orr, John 92,117
Osborn, Adlai/Adley
  160,183
Otts, John 5
Overwinder, Adam 56,82
Oyles, Francis 155

Pack, Jacob 102
Palley, James 91,99,176
Palmer, Francis 98
  George 200,207
  Robert 71
Paris/Pariss/Parris/Parish
  (see also Pearis)
  George 46,47,157,161,
    180,181,184,186,189,
    190,192,196
Park/s, David 66
  John 10,103
  Joseph 38,65
  Robert 169,171,183
Parker, Isaiah 70
  William 98,100,102,163,
    208
Parry, James 93
Patrick, Andrew 2,11,15,
  20,32,188,189,192,193,
  205
  John 97,187,190
  Robert 11,97
  Thomas 11
  William 3,91,162,203
Patterson, Alexander
  63,64,69,128,199
  Arthur 193,196,203
  Elizabeth 63,64
  George 12,55,169,180,
    183,193,199
  James 20,21,22,50,55,
    98,99,108,117,128,
    137,146,167,168,173,
    183,187,189,190,196,
    198,199,203
  John 98
  Jonathan 69
  Mary 98
  Mathias 100,101
  Sarah 98,137
  Thomas 98
  William 21,63,64,69,
    128,146,147,153,
    154,180,187,189,
    195,196,207
Pattey, (see also Petty)
  James 188
  Sarah 188
Pattison, Wm 118
Patton, James 15
  John 12,41,42,46,55,64,
    65,72,73,75,81,94,95
  Robert 168
  Sam'l 78
  Thomas 53,58
  William 56,191
Pearis, George 208
  (see also Paris)

Pearson, John 14,15
  Thos 194,200
Pee, George 104,188,189,
  205
Pennington/Peninton
  Benejah 5
  Jacob 63
  Jno 63
  Mary 63
  Micajah 9
  Rachel 9
Penny/Peny, John 78
  Sarah 86
  Thomas 20,86
Perkins, Josna 93
  Thomas 117
Perry, John 78
Person, John 58
Pess, Hugh 51
Peters, Israel 102
Peterson, And'w 44
  Israel 44,132
Petty/Pettie,
  (see also Pattey)
  Christopher 92,102,187,
    188
  Sarah 92,102,187,188
Phifer, Martin 168
Phillips, Benjamin 11,30,
  34,35,71
Phingers, John 193
Pickrell, William 159
Pigg, Elizabeth 23
  Hezekiah 23,38
Pitts, And'w 94
Plank, Peter 135
Platner, Michael 124
Plummer, Dan'l 52
  Mary 52
Plunk, Peter 68,135,187,
  210
Poff, George 123
Polk, Agnis 200
  Ezekiel 1,12,13,16,49,
    64,65,79,80,90,91,94,
    96,105,107,144
  John 200
  Thomas 5,20,21,23,108,
    112,118,128,132
Pollock, Hugh 13
Polly/Polley James 91,
  196,197,209
Ponder, Dan'l 59
Pool, Peter Petty 93
Pope, Jno 107
Porter 171,172,174,192
  David 7,24,25,29,41,58,
    74,84,91
  Jane 74

227

Peter Jr. 161
Sumpter, Thomas 102,111
Sutton, John 82
   Tollover 108
Swafford, James 108,209
Swann, John 87
   Martha 44
   Robert 25,26,31,32,40,
      41,43,44,64
   William 87
Swank, Jacob 181,196
Swent, John 54
   John Jr. 54
Tagert, John 2,3,4,5,13,
   18,21,25,28,29,31,34,
   39,49,70,75,80,81,87,
   88,89,94,99,102,121,
   123,132,155,183
   Violet 183
Talifero 133
Tankersley, William 125,
   150,163
Tate, James 33
   William 37,43,54,55,84,
      90,100,121,200
Taylor, Arthur 160,177
   Benjn 206
   Caleb 128,163
   George 191,192,199
   James 133,173,179,185
   John 122,180,183
   Joshua 161,163
   Robert 121,152,153,154
Temple, Major 21
Templeton, James 6,64
   John 209
   Margaret 209
Terrance, Adam 132
   Hugh 189
Tevonhill, Jno 11
Therter, Nicholas 109
Thomas, John 5,21,24,67,
   69,87,96
   John Jr. 96
   Robert 87
Thomason, John 20,78,88
   William 126,146,150
Thompson, Alexander
   115
   Benjamin 7,9,10
   David 76,174
   James 20,26,115
   John 5,25,52
   Thomas 168
   William 131,139
Thomson, Alexander
   88,89
   Benjamin 38,94
   David 70,140

James 95,96
   Joseph 83,148
   Wm 158
Tice, Charles 112,197,200
Tillet, Giles 21,77
Towns, John 57,58
Townsen/d, Thomas
   145,147,171,186,196,203,
   210
   Paul 99
Travers, Francis 2,18,52
Trout, George 28,50,
   51,92,108,112,129,
   143,158,176,191
   John 143,191
   Mary 176
Troy, Mathew 40,59,65,73
Tryon, William 18,34
Tub/b, George 10,140,145
   Richard 129
   William 174
Tucker, Jno 118
Turner, Benjamin 35,68
   Elijah 34,120
   Henry 47,49
   John 36,64,95,210
   Mary 120
   Sarah 120
Twitty 163,170,181
   Allen 202
   Arabella 202
   Bellariah 202
   Charlotte 203
   Polly 202
   Russel 202
   Susanna (Graham) 172
   Susanna 158,161,202
   William 1,24,36,38,40,
      97,101,112,158,159,
      161,172,202,203
Umphries, Joanna 83
Underwood, George 84
Upton 163
   James 128,161
Valvod, Mary 61
   Stophel 61
Vance, David 5
   Ruth 5
Vanzant, Garret 8,190
   Jacob 100,178,180,183,
      202
Vassals, James 100
Vaugh/n 209
   Benjamin 97,181
Venable, John 4,7,15,30,
   31,32,53,65
   Richard 4,30,31,32,62,
      75,111,119,150

Vernor, Henry 44,56,118,
   128
   Wm 56,190,202,207
Vovrel, John 75

Waddell, Jane 177
   William 177
Wade, John 16,27,34,48,
   66,69,95,141
   Thomas 4,9,14,29,42,68,
      87
Waggerlin, John 25
Waggoner, John 153
Waitsel, Jacob 145
Walbat, Christopher 126
Walbert, Christopher 119,
   132,141,149,156,170,
   192,193
   Stophal 131
Walker 149,169,173,204
   Elizabeth 4,9,118
   Felix 122
   George 95
   James 32,106,129,151
   John 1,3,7,8,9,10,18,19,
      21,22,23,28,34,51,53,
      56,69,70,73,75,82,83,
      84,95,96,97,109,110,
      112,113,114,118,121,
      122,123,127,130,132,
      133,135,136,138,140,
      143,144,146,147,158,
      160,165,172,174,176,
      177,182,186,190,191,
      192,194,209,210
   John Jr. 48
   Mary 159
   Rich'd 128
   Robert 64
   Saml 159
Wallace, Hana 69
   Hugh 162,164,179
   Jas 44
   John 55,56,69,85
   Oliver 14,20,22,40
   Saml 182
   Tho's 58
   William 58,179
Wallis, Sam'l 183
Walls, George 28
Walsh, Thomas 56
Wammack, James 6
Ward 68,73
   Mary 18
   Richard 14,18,28
Warden, Thomas 200
Warlock 115,170,207
   Barbara 19,107
   Daniel 18,19,90,94,105,

[negro], Tom 82,83
[negro], Tonday 6

PLACE NAME INDEX

Heritage Books by Brent H. Holcomb:

Ancestors and Descendants of Charles Humphries (d. 1837)
of Union District, South Carolina, 1677–1984

Bute County, North Carolina, Land Grant Plats and Land Entries

CD: Early Records of Fishing Creek Presbyterian Church,
Chester County, South Carolina, 1799–1859

CD: Kershaw County, South Carolina, Minutes of the County Court, 1791–1799

CD: Marriage and Death Notices from The Charleston [S.C.] Observer, *1827–1845*

CD: South Carolina, Volume 1

CD: Winton (Barnwell) County, South Carolina Minutes of
County Court and Will Book 1, 1785–1791

Chester County, South Carolina, Deed Abstracts,
Volume I: 1785–1799 [1768–1799] Deed Book A-F

Chester County, South Carolina, Will Abstracts: 1787–1838 [1776–1838]

Death and Marriage Notices from the Watchman *and* Observer, *1845–1855*

Early Records of Fishing Creek Presbyterian Church, Chester County,
South Carolina, 1799–1859, with Appendices of the Visitation List of
Rev. John Simpson, 1774–1776 and the Cemetery Roster, 1762–1979
Brent H. Holcomb and Elmer O. Parker

Guide to South Carolina Genealogical Research and Records, Revised

Jackson of North Pacolet: Descendants of Samuel Jackson, Sr.

Kershaw County, South Carolina, Minutes of the County Court, 1791–1799

Laurens County, South Carolina, Minutes of the County Court, 1786–1789

Marriage and Death Notices from Columbia, South Carolina Newspapers,
1838–1860; Including Legal Notices from Burnt Counties

Marriage and Death Notices from Baptist Newspapers of South Carolina, 1835–1865

Marriage and Death Notices from The Charleston Observer, *1827–1845*

Marriage and Death Notices from the
Charleston, South Carolina, Mercury, *1822–1832*

Marriage and Death Notices from the Southern Presbyterian:
Volume I: 1847–1865
Volume II: 1865–1879
Volume III: 1880–1891
Volume IV: 1892–1908

Marriage and Death Notices from the Up-Country of South Carolina
as Taken from Greenville Newspapers, 1826–1863

Memorialized Records of Lexington District, South Carolina, 1814–1825

Newberry County, South Carolina Deed Abstracts,
Volume III: Deed Books E Through H, 1786–1787

Orangeburgh District, South Carolina, Estate Partitions
from the Court of Equity, 1824–1837

Parish Registers of Prince George Winyah Church,
Georgetown, South Carolina, 1815–1936

Petitions for Land from the South Carolina Council Journals
Volume I: 1734/5–1748
Volume II: 1748–1752
Volume III: 1752–1753
Volume IV: 1754–1756
Volume V: 1757–1765

South Carolina Deed Abstracts, 1773–1778, Books F-4 through X-4

South Carolina Deed Abstracts, 1776–1783, Books Y-4 through H-5

South Carolina Deed Abstracts, 1783–1788, Books I-5 through Z-5

South Carolina's Royal Grants,
Volume One: Books 1 through 9, 1731–1761
Volume Two: Books 10 through 17, 1760–1768
Volume Three: Books 18 through 24, 1768–1773
Volume Four: Books 25 through 31, 1772–1775
Volume Five: Books 32 through 37, 1735-1776
Volume Six: Books 38 through 41, 1670–1785
Volume Seven: Books 42, 43 and Other Grants, 1711–1775

South Carolina's State Grants
Volume I: Grant Books 1 through 6, 1784–1790
Volume II: Grant Books 7 through 11, 1785–1786
Volume III: Grant Books 12 through 15, 1786–1787
Volume IV: Grant Books 16 through 20, 1786–1787
Volume V: Grant Books 16 through 20, 1786–1787

Spartanburg County, South Carolina, Will Abstracts 1787–1840

The Bedenbaugh-Betenbaugh Family:
Descendants of Johann Michael Bidenbach
from Germany to South Carolina, 1752

Tryon County, North Carolina, Minutes of the Court of Pleas
and Quarter Sessions, 1769–1779

Union County, South Carolina Deed Abstracts,
Volume II: Deed Books G-K, 1800–1811 [1769–1811]
Volume III: Deed Books L-P, 1811–1820 [1770–1820]
Volume IV: Deed Books, 1820–1828
Volume V: Deed Books T-W, 1828–1835 [1778–1835]

Union County, South Carolina, Will Abstracts, 1787–1849

Winton (Barnwell) County, South Carolina Minutes of
County Court and Will Book 1, 1785–1791

York County, South Carolina, Deed Abstracts:
Volume 1: Deed Books A-E, 1786–1801 [1772–1801]

York County, South Carolina, Will Abstracts, 1787–1862 [1770–1862]

www.ingramcontent.com/pod-product-compliance
Lightning Source LLC
Chambersburg PA
CBHW070404270326
41926CB00014B/2688